Praise for Ager

"*Agent Zigzag* is a true-history thriller, a̶ ... , superbly written. It belongs to my favorite genre: the 'Friday night book'—start it then, because you *will* want to stay with it all weekend."

—Alan Furst

"The best book ever written." —Alex Beam, *Boston Globe*

"Meticulously crafted . . . an enormously fascinating book about an enormously fascinating man." —*Washington Times*

"Chapman's life had more hair's-breadth escapes than you'll find in ten Ian Fleming novels." —*Details*

"A revelation . . . a portrait of a man who double-crossed not only the Nazis, but just about every principle and person he encountered. In doing so, Eddie Chapman made all thriller writers' jobs harder, because this spy tale trumps any fiction." —*Men's Journal*

"This is the most amazing book, full of fascinating and hair-raising true-life adventures . . . and beautifully told. For anyone interested in the Second World War, spying, romance, skullduggery or the hidden chambers of the human mind, it would be impossible to recommend it too highly." —*The Mail on Sunday* (London)

"Speaking as a former MI6 officer, take it from me: there are very few books which give you a genuine picture of what it feels like to be a spy. This is one . . . an enthralling war story."

—*The Daily Express* (London)

"Macintyre tells Chapman's tale in a perfect pitch: with the *Boys' Own* thrills of Rider Haggard, the verve of George MacDonald Fraser and Carl Hiaassen's mordant humor. . . . Hugely entertaining."

—*The Observer* (London)

AGENT ZIGZAG

AGENT ZIGZAG

A TRUE STORY OF NAZI ESPIONAGE, LOVE, AND BETRAYAL

BEN MACINTYRE

THREE RIVERS PRESS
NEW YORK

Published in the United States by Three Rivers Press, an imprint of the
Crown Publishing Group, a division of Random House, Inc., New York.
www.crownpublishing.com

Three Rivers Press and the Tugboat design are registered trademarks
of Random House, Inc.

Originally published in hardcover in the UK as *Agent Zigzag: The True Wartime
Story of Eddie Chapman, Lover, Betrayer, Hero, Spy* by Bloomsbury Publishing PLC,
London, and subsequently in the United States by
Harmony Books, an imprint of the Crown Publishing Group,
a division of Random House, Inc., New York, in 2007.

Library of Congress Cataloging-in-Publication Data
Macintyre, Ben, 1963–
Agent Zigzag : a true story of Nazi espionage, love, and betrayal / Ben Macin-
tyre.—1st ed.
Includes bibliographical references.
1. Chapman, Edward Arnold.   2. World War, 1939–1945—Secret service—
Germany.   3. World War, 1939–1945—Secret service—Great Britain.
4. Spies—Great Britain—Biography.   5. Spies—Germany—Biography.
6. Espionage—Germany—History—20th century.   7. Espionage—
Great Britain—History—20th century.   I. Title.
D810.S8C385 2007
940.54'8641092—dc22   2006101603

ISBN 978-0-307-35341-2

Printed in the United States of America

Design by Leonard Henderson

10 9 8 7 6 5 4 3 2 1

First American Paperback Edition

For Kate

zigzag *n* : a pattern made up of many small corners at an acute angle, tracing a path between two parallel lines; it can be described as both jagged and fairly regular.

It is essential to seek out enemy agents who have come to conduct espionage against you and to bribe them to serve you. Give them instructions and care for them. Thus double agents are recruited and used.

—SUN-TZU, *The Art of War*

War makes thieves and peace hangs them.

—GEORGE HERBERT

AUTHOR'S NOTE

THE TRUE STORY that follows is based on official papers, letters, diaries, newspaper reports, contemporary accounts, and memoirs.

I was first alerted to the existence of the Englishman Eddie Chapman by his obituary in the *Times* of London. Among the lives of the great and good, here was a character who had achieved a certain greatness, but in ways that were far from conventionally good. The obituary was intriguing as much for what it did not say—and could not know—about Chapman's exploits in the Second World War, since those details remained under seal in MI5's secret archives. At that time, it seemed the full story of Eddie Chapman would never be told.

But then, under a new policy of openness, MI5 began the selective release of hitherto classified information that could not embarrass the living or damage national security. The first "Zigzag files" were released to the UK National Archives in 2001. These declassified archives contain more than seventeen hundred pages of documents relating to Chapman's case: transcripts of interrogations, detailed wireless intercepts, reports, descriptions, diagrams, internal memos, minutes, letters, and photographs. The files are extraordinarily detailed, describing not only events and people but also the minutiae of a spy's life, his changing moods and feelings, his hopes, fears, and contradictions. Chapman's diligent case officers set out to paint a complete picture of the man, with a meticulous (sometimes hour-by-hour) account of his actions. I am particularly grateful to MI5 for agreeing to my request to declassify additional files relating to the case, and to Howard Davies of the National Archives for helping to facilitate those supplementary releases.

Eddie Chapman's own memoirs were first published in 1954 under the restrictions of the Official Secrets Act. These, however, are partial, unreliable, and sometimes deliberately misleading; as Chapman's MI5 handlers noted, he had no sense of chronology whatsoever. I have therefore accepted Chapman's version of events only when his account can be corroborated by other sources. All quotations are cited in the endnotes, but for clarity I have standardized spelling and have selectively used reported speech as direct speech. Chapman's story has also emerged from the memories of the living, people touched, directly or indirectly, by the individuals and events described, and I am grateful to the dozens of interviewees in Britain, France, Germany, and Norway—including Betty Chapman—who were willing to talk to me for so many hours, recalling a past now more than half a century old. For obvious reasons, some of those involved in the more clandestine areas of Chapman's life have requested anonymity.

Just weeks before this book was due to go to press, MI5 discovered an entire secret file, overlooked in previous transfers to the public archives, and generously provided me with full access to its contents. That file (which will now become available at the National Archives) gives extraordinary psychological insights into Chapman's character, as seen by his case officers. It is, perhaps, the last missing piece in the Zigzag puzzle.

CONTENTS

AGENT ZIGZAG

Prologue

A GERMAN SPY drops from a black Focke-Wulf reconnaissance plane over Cambridgeshire. His silk parachute opens with a rustle, and for twelve minutes he floats silently down. The stars are out, but the land beneath his feet, swaddled in wartime blackout, is utterly dark. His nose bleeds copiously.

The spy is well equipped. He wears British-issue army landing boots and helmet. In his pocket is a wallet taken from a British soldier killed at Dieppe four months earlier: inside are two identity cards, which are fake, and a letter from his girlfriend, Betty, which is genuine. His pack contains matches impregnated with quinine for "secret writing," a wireless receiver, a military map, £990 in used notes of various denominations, a Colt revolver, an entrenching tool, and some plain-glass spectacles for disguise. Four of his teeth are made from new gold, paid for by Hitler's Third Reich. Beneath his flying overalls he wears a civilian suit that was once of fashionable cut but is now somewhat worn. In the turnup of the right trouser leg has been sewn a small cellophane package containing a single suicide pill of potassium cyanide.

His name is Edward Arnold Chapman. The British police also know him as Edward Edwards, Edward Simpson, and Arnold

Thompson. His German spymasters have given him the code name of Fritz or, affectionately, Fritzchen—"Little Fritz." The British secret services, as yet, have no name for him. That evening the chief constable of Cambridgeshire, after an urgent call from a gentleman in Whitehall, has instructed all his officers to be on the lookout for an individual referred to only as "Agent X."

•   •   •

Eddie Chapman lands in a freshly ploughed field at 2:25 a.m., and immediately falls face-first into the sodden soil. Dazed, he releases his parachute, then climbs out of his blood-spattered flying suit and buries the bundle. He shoves the revolver into a pocket and digs into the pack for a map and a flashlight. The map has gone. He must have dropped it in the dark. On hands and knees, he searches. He curses and sits on the cold earth, in the deep darkness, and wonders where he is, who he is, and whose side he is on.

CHAPTER ONE

The Hotel de la Plage

SPRING CAME EARLY to the island of Jersey in 1939. The sun that poured through the dining-room window of the Hotel de la Plage formed a dazzling halo around the man sitting opposite Betty Farmer with his back to the sea, laughing as he tucked into the six-shilling Sunday Roast Special "with all the trimmings." Betty, eighteen, a farm girl newly escaped from the Shropshire countryside, knew this man was quite unlike any she had met before.

Beyond that, her knowledge of Eddie Chapman was somewhat limited. She knew that he was twenty-four years old, tall and handsome, with a thin mustache—just like Errol Flynn in *The Charge of the Light Brigade*—and deep hazel eyes. His voice was strong but high-pitched with a hint of a Northern accent. He was "bubbly," full of laughter and mischief. She knew he must be rich because he was "in the film business" and drove a Bentley. He wore expensive suits, a gold ring, and a cashmere overcoat with mink collar. Today he wore a natty yellow spotted tie and a sleeveless pullover. They had met at a club in Kensington Church Street, and although at first she had declined his invitation to dance, she soon relented. Eddie had become her first lover, but then he vanished, saying he had urgent business in Scotland. "I shall go," he told her. "But I shall always come back."

Good as his word, Eddie had suddenly reappeared at the door of her lodgings, grinning and breathless. "How would you like to go to

Jersey, then possibly to the south of France?" he asked. Betty had rushed off to pack.

It was a surprise to discover they would be traveling with company. In the front seat of the waiting Bentley sat two men: the driver a huge, ugly brute with a crumpled face; the other small, thin, and dark. The pair did not seem ideal companions for a romantic holiday. The driver gunned the engine and they set off at thrilling speed through the London streets, screeching into the Croydon airport, parking behind the hangar, just in time to catch the Jersey Airways plane.

That evening, they had checked into the seafront hotel. Eddie told the receptionist they were in Jersey to make a film. They had signed the register as Mr. and Mrs. Farmer of Torquay. After dinner, they moved on to West Park Pavilion, a nightclub on the pier, where they danced, played roulette, and drank some more. For Betty, it had been a day of unprecedented glamour and decadence.

War was coming, everyone said so, but the dining room of the Hotel de la Plage was a place of pure peace that sunny Sunday. Beyond the golden beach, the waves flickered among a scatter of tiny islands, as Eddie and Betty ate trifle off plates with smart blue crests. Eddie was halfway through telling another funny story when he froze. A group of men in overcoats and brown hats had entered the restaurant and one was now in urgent conversation with the head-waiter. Before Betty could speak, Eddie stood up, bent down to kiss her once, and then jumped through the window, which was closed. There was a storm of broken glass, tumbling crockery, screaming women, and shouting waiters. Betty Farmer caught a last glimpse of Eddie Chapman sprinting off down the beach with two overcoated men in pursuit.

• • •

There was much that Betty did not know about Eddie Chapman. He was married. Another woman was pregnant with his child. And he was a crook. Not some halfpenny bag snatcher, but a dedicated professional criminal, a "prince of the underworld," in his own estimation.

For Chapman, breaking the law was a vocation. In later years, when some sort of motive for his choice of career seemed to be called for, he claimed that the early death of his mother, in the TB ward of a pauper's hospital, had sent him "off the rails" and turned him against society. Sometimes he blamed the grinding poverty and unemployment in northern England during the Depression for forcing him into a life of crime. But in truth, crime came naturally to him.

Edward Chapman was born in Burnopfield, a tiny village in the Durham coalfields, on November 16, 1914, a few months into the First World War. His father, a marine engineer and too old to fight, had ended up running the Clippership, a dingy pub in Roker, and drinking a large portion of the stock. For Eddie, the eldest of three children, there was no money, not much love, little in the way of guidance, and only a cursory education. He soon developed a talent for misbehavior and a distaste for authority. Intelligent but lazy, insolent and easily bored, the young Chapman skipped school often, preferring to scour the beach for lemonade bottles, redeemable at a penny a piece, and then while away afternoons at the cinema in Sunderland.

At the age of seventeen, after a brief and unsatisfactory stint as an unpaid apprentice at a Sunderland engineering firm, Chapman joined the army, although underage, and enlisted in the Second Battalion of the Coldstream Guards. Early in his training at Caterham, he slipped while playing handball and badly gashed his knee; the resulting scar would provide police with a useful distinguishing feature. The bearskin hat and smart red uniform made the girls gawp and giggle, but he found sentry duty outside the Tower of London tedious, and the city beyond beckoned.

Chapman had worn a guardsman's uniform for nine months when he was granted six days' leave. He told the sergeant major that he was going home. Instead, in the company of an older guardsman, he wandered around Soho and the West End, hungrily eyeing the elegant women draped over the arms of men in sharp suits. In a café in Marble Arch, he noticed a pretty, dark-haired girl, and she spotted him. They danced at Smokey Joe's in Soho. That night he lost his virginity. She persuaded him to stay another night; he stayed for two months, until they had spent all his pay. Chapman may have forgotten about the army, but the army had not forgotten about him. He was sure the dark-haired girl told the police. Chapman was arrested for going absent without leave, placed in the military prison in Aldershot—the "glasshouse"—and made to scrub out bedpans for eighty-four days. Release and a dishonorable discharge brought to an end his first prison sentence, and his last regular job. Chapman took a bus to London with £3 in his pocket, a fraying suit, and a "jail-crop haircut." He headed straight for Soho.

Soho in the 1930s was a notorious den of vice, and spectacular fun. This was the crossroads of London society, where the rich and feckless met the criminal and reckless, a place of seamy, raucous glamour. Chapman found work as a barman, then as a film extra, earning £3 for "three days doing crowd work"; he worked as a masseur, a dancer, and eventually as an amateur boxer and wrestler. He was a fine wrestler, physically strong, and lithe as a cat, with a "wire and whipcord body." This was a world of pimps and racecourse touts, pickpockets and con artists; late nights at Smokey Joe's and early champagne breakfasts at Quaglino's. "I mixed with all types of tricky people," Chapman wrote later. "Racecourse crooks, thieves, prostitutes, and the flotsam of the night-life of a great city." For the young Chapman, life in this seething, seedy enclave was thrilling. But it was also expensive. He acquired a taste for cognac and the gaming tables. Soon he was penniless.

The thievery started in a small way: a forged check here, a snatched suitcase there, a little light burglary. His early crimes were unremarkable, the first faltering steps of an apprentice.

In January 1935, he was caught in the back garden of a house in Mayfair, and fined £10. A month later, he was found guilty of stealing a check and obtaining credit by fraud. This time the court was less lenient, and Chapman was given two months' hard labor in Wormwood Scrubs. A few weeks after his release, he was back inside, this time in Wandsworth Prison on a three-month sentence for trespassing and attempted housebreaking.

Chapman branched out into crimes of a more lurid nature. Early in 1936, he was found guilty of "behaving in a manner likely to offend the public" in Hyde Park. Exactly how he was likely to have offended the public was not specified, but he was almost certainly discovered in flagrante delicto with a prostitute. He was fined £4 and made to pay a fee of 15 shillings 9 pence to the doctor who examined him for venereal disease. Two weeks later, he was charged with fraud after he tried to evade payment of a hotel bill.

One contemporary remembers a young man "with good looks, a quick brain, high spirits and something desperate in him which made him attractive to men and dangerous to women." Desperation may have led him to use the attraction of men for profit, for he once hinted at an early homosexual encounter. Women seemed to find him irresistible. According to one account, he made money by seducing "women on the fringes of society," blackmailing them with compromising photographs taken by an accomplice and then threatening to show them to their husbands. It was even said that having "infected a girl of 18 with VD, he blackmailed her by threatening to tell her parents that she had given it to him."

Chapman was on a predictable downward spiral of petty crime, prostitution, blackmail, and lengthening prison terms—punctuated by episodes of wild extravagance in Soho—when a scientific breakthrough in the criminal world abruptly altered his fortunes.

In the early 1930s, British crooks discovered the high explosive gelignite. At about the same time, during one of his stints inside, Chapman discovered James Wells Hunt—the "best cracksman in London"—a "cool, self-possessed, determined character" who had perfected a technique for taking apart safes by drilling a hole in the lock and inserting a "French letter" stuffed with gelignite and water. Jimmy Hunt and Chapman went into partnership and were soon joined by Antony Latt, alias Darrington, alias "Darry," a nerveless half-Burmese burglar whose father, he claimed, had been a native judge. A young felon named Hugh Anson was recruited to drive their getaway car.

In 1934, the newly formed "Jelly Gang" selected as its first target Isobel's, a chic furrier in Harrogate. Hunt and Darry broke in and stole five minks, two fox-fur capes, and £200 from the safe. Chapman remained in the car, "shivering with fear and unable to help."

The next was a pawnbroker's in Grimsby. While Anson revved the Bentley outside to cover the sound of the explosions, Chapman and Hunt broke into an empty house next door, cut their way through the wall, and then blew open four safes. The proceeds, sold through a fence in the West End, netted £15,000. This was followed by a break-in at the Swiss Cottage Odeon cinema using an iron bar, a hit on Express Dairies, and a smash-and-grab raid on a shop in Oxford Street. Escaping from the latter scene, Anson drove the stolen getaway car into a lamppost. As the gang fled, a crowd of onlookers gathered around the smoking vehicle; one, who happened to be a small-time thief, made the mistake of putting his hand on the hood. When his fingerprints were matched with Scotland Yard records, he was sentenced to four years in prison. The Jelly Gang found this most amusing.

Chapman was no longer a reckless petty pilferer, but a criminal of means, and he spent money as fast as he could steal it, mixing with the underworld aristocracy, the gambling playboys, the roué actors, the alcoholic journalists, the insomniac writers, and the dodgy politicians drawn to the demimonde. He became friendly with Noël Coward, Ivor Novello, Marlene Dietrich, and the young filmmaker Terence Young (who would go on to direct the first James Bond film). Young was a suave figure who prided himself on his elegant clothes, his knowledge of fine wine, and his reputation as a lothario. Perhaps in imitation of his new friend, Chapman also began buying suits in Savile Row and driving a fast car. He kept a table reserved at the Nest in Kingley Street, where he held court, surrounded by bottles and girls. Young remarked: "He was able to talk on almost any subject. Most of us knew that he was a crook, but nevertheless we liked him for his manner and personality."

Young found Chapman intriguing: He made no secret of his trade, yet there was an upright side to his character that the filmmaker found curious. "He is a crook and will always be one," Young observed to a lawyer friend. "But he probably has more principles and honesty of character than either of us." Chapman would steal the money from your pocket, even as he bought you a drink, but he never deserted a friend, nor hurt a soul. In a brutal business, he was a pacifist. "I don't go along with the use of violence," he declared many years later. "I always made more than a good living out of crime without it."

Careless, guiltless, and godless, Chapman reveled in his underworld notoriety. He pasted press clippings describing his crimes into a scrapbook. He was particularly delighted when it was reported that police suspected American gangs were behind the recent spate of safecracking because chewing gum had been found at the crime scenes (the Jelly Gang had merely used chewing gum to stick the gelignite to the safes). By the summer of 1935, they had stolen so much money that Chapman and Darry decided to rent a house in Bridport on the Dorset coast for an extended holiday; but after six weeks they grew bored and "went back to 'work.'" Chapman disguised himself as an inspector from the Metropolitan Water Board, gained access to a house in Edgware Road, smashed a hole through the wall into the shop next door, and extracted the safe. This was carried out of the front door, loaded into the Bentley, and taken to Hunt's garage at 39 St. Luke's Mews, Notting Hill, where the safe door was blown off.

But cash could not confer all the benefits of class, and mixing with authors and actors, Chapman became conscious of his lack of education. He announced that he intended to become a writer, and began reading widely, plundering English literature in search of knowledge and direction. When asked what he did for a living, Chapman would reply, with a wink, that he was a "professional dancer." He danced from club to club, from job to job, from book to book, and from woman to woman. Late in 1935, he announced he was getting married, to Vera Freidberg, an exotic young woman with a Russian mother and a German-Jewish father. From her, Chapman picked up a grounding in the German language. But within a few months, he had moved into a boardinghouse in Shepherd's Bush with another woman, Freda Stevenson, a stage dancer from Southend who was five years his junior. He loved Freda, she was vivacious and sassy; yet when he met Betty Farmer—his "Shropshire Lass"—in the Nite Lite Club, he loved her, too.

The Jelly Gang might mock the dozy coppers studying their

abandoned chewing gum for clues, but Scotland Yard was beginning
to take a keen interest in the activities of Edward Chapman. A "gelignite squad" was formed. In 1938, the *Police Gazette* published Chapman's mug shot, along with those of Hunt and Darry, identifying
them as suspects in a recent spate of cinema safe breaks. Aware that
the police were closing in, early in 1939, the gang loaded several
golf bags packed with gelignite into the trunk of the Bentley and
headed north. Having checked into an expensive hotel, they broke
into the offices of the Edinburgh Cooperative Society and emptied
the safe. As Chapman was climbing out through a skylight, he
smashed a pane of glass. A passing policeman heard it and blew his
whistle. The thieves fled over the back wall and onto a railway line;
one of the gang slipped, breaking an ankle, and was left behind.
The others met up with car and driver and immediately headed
south, but were intercepted by a police car, bell clanging. Chapman
fled over a wall but was caught. The four burglars were thrown into
the Edinburgh prison, but then, for reasons no one can explain,
Chapman was granted fourteen days bail at £150.

When Case Number Seventeen came before the Edinburgh
High Court, it was found that Chapman and his accomplices had absconded. A general bulletin was issued, photographs were distributed, and every police force in Britain was told to be on the lookout
for Eddie Chapman—crook, jailbird, adulterer, blackmailer, safecracker, Soho denizen, and now among Britain's most wanted men.
On February 4, 1939, the gang extracted £476 and 3 shillings from a
co-op store in Bournemouth. Darry had sent a letter to his girlfriend
hinting that the gang was heading for Jersey; police intercepted it
and a warning went out that the suspects might make for the Channel Islands, and then the Continent: "Be prepared for trouble as
one at least of the men might be armed and all are prepared to put
up a fight to resist arrest."

Which is how Eddie Chapman came to be pounding down a Jersey beach leaving in his wake two plainclothes policemen, a dis-
traught young woman, and half a sherry trifle.

CHAPTER TWO

Jersey Gaol

The Jersey Evening Post

Monday, February 13, 1939

STARTLING SCENE AT JERSEY HOTEL

———

POLICE SWOOP AT LUNCH HOUR

———

Two Guests Handcuffed
Thief Gets Away through Window
Alleged Dangerous Gang of Safe Breakers

A letter sent to a girl in Bournemouth led yesterday to the arrest of two members of a gelignite gang wanted for the 'blowing' of a safe at a co-operative store and the theft of £470. A third man got wind of the impending police swoop on the Hotel de la Plage, Havre-le-Pas, and escaped.

Residents at La Plage Hotel were at lunch when Centenier C. G. Grant of St Helier, and six members of the paid police in civilian clothing entered and, before most of the lunchers knew what had happened, two men had been handcuffed and chase was being given to the third man, alleged to be the leader of the gang. One of them, apparently more alert than the others, made his escape by way of the windows of the dining room overlooking the promenade and got clean away.

The third man, for whom active search still continues, is described as:—Edward Chapman, alias Arnold Edward Chapman, Edward Arnold Chapman, Edward Edwards and Thompson, a professional dancer, slim build, six feet in height, fresh complexion, small moustache, dressed in white shirt, yellow spotted tie, blue sleeveless pullover, grey flannels and brown sandals and no socks. He is believed to be a dangerous character. He may, by now, have obtained a jacket or an overcoat from somewhere as he has money in his possession.

The search for Chapman goes on and all ships are being watched. Anyone who may see this man or who may know anything of his whereabouts is requested to inform the Police Station immediately.

Although the police soon abandoned the chase, Chapman continued running for a mile or so up the beach before doubling back, and then cutting across the island. He found a school, empty on a Sunday, and hid inside. That evening, he strolled back into Havre-le-Pas wearing a mackintosh he had found on a peg, the collar turned up. On the edge of town, he checked into a tatty boardinghouse and shaved off his mustache with a soapy penknife. When he came downstairs, the landlady, Mrs. Corfield, demanded cash up front. Chapman gave her what he had in his pocket, and said he would pay the balance in the morning. Without money, he was trapped. He would need to steal some more.

In the darkness, Chapman reemerged and set off toward the West Park Pavilion nightclub, where the gang had spent the previous night. As soon as her lodger was gone, Mrs. Corfield put on her bonnet and headed down to the police station.

Chapman found the pavilion deserted. He broke in through a window in the men's bathroom, discovered the office safe, and carried it to the basement. Turning it upside down, he worked off the bottom with a pickax and a pair of pincers from the boiler room of the building. Inside lay £15, 13 shillings, and 9 pence in silver, several pounds in coppers, and twelve 10-shilling notes. Chapman returned to the boardinghouse, his pockets laden, and went to sleep, resolving to steal or bribe his way onto a boat the next morning.

The Jersey Evening Post

Tuesday, February 14, 1939

ALLEGED SAFE BREAKER
BEFORE COURT

WANTED MAN ARRESTED IN BED
CHARGED WITH BREAKING INTO WEST PARK PAVILION
ACCUSED APPEALS FOR 'GIRL FRIEND'

The island-wide search for the man Chapman, who escaped when police raided the Hotel de la Plage, is at an end. Chapman, through information received by the St Helier Police, was found last night in bed in a lodging house in Sand Street, and admitted his identity to police constables. He also admitted breaking into West Park Pavilion last night.

Chapman gave the police no trouble and made a voluntary statement that he had 'done in' the safe.

This morning Chapman appeared before the magistrate, and after being remanded asked if his girlfriend could be allowed to leave the island. 'I have a girl-friend here,' he said, speaking in a cultured tone, 'and she is in a very embarrassing position. She has been cross-examined by police and watched and I would like to ask if these investigations might cease as she knows nothing of why we are here.'

The Magistrate: 'If she had been wise she would have gone already. We do not want her here. There is nothing against her and she is free to leave the island when she likes.'

The accused was then removed to the cells and his 'girl friend', an attractive blonde with blue eyes and a long page-boy bob, whose name is said to be Betty Farmer, also left the court.

Betty had suffered many indignities in the preceding forty-eight hours: being searched by the manageress at the Hotel de la Plage, being grilled by those horrible detectives, and then having to move to the smaller, cheaper, and far scruffier Royal Yacht Hotel. As Chapman was led from the court in handcuffs, she handed one of his guards a love note to pass to him, written on hotel letterhead. He put it in his pocket, grinned, and waved.

Breaking into the West Park Pavilion nightclub had been an act of astonishing foolishness but also, on the face of it, an immense stroke of luck. Darry and Anson had already been shipped back to the mainland to face multiple charges at the Central Criminal Court in London. Chapman, however, had broken the law in Jersey, with its ancient legal code and traditions of self-government, and would now have to face island justice.

On March 11, 1939, Edward Chapman appeared before the Royal Court of Jersey and pleaded guilty to charges of housebreaking and larceny. The attorney general of Jersey, prosecuting, cited Chapman's extensive criminal record and pointed out that the safebreaking at the nightclub had been "done with deliberation and skill which showed considerable experience and showed he was determined to rely on this sort of conduct for a living." He demanded that this "dangerous criminal who had failed to accept certain chances that had been given to him" receive the maximum sentence of two years' hard labor. The jury agreed.

• • •

Jersey Gaol, Chapman soon discovered, was a "dreary little cage" where the handful of prisoners stuffed mattresses for eight hours a day and slept on planks raised a few feet off the concrete floor. The prison regime was remarkably lax. The governor, Captain Thomas Charles Foster, a retired soldier, regarded prisoners as an inconvenience in an otherwise pleasant life that revolved around visiting his neighbors, sunbathing, and fishing. Foster took a shine to the new inmate when Chapman explained he had been a soldier, and he was soon put to work as the governor's personal batman, weeding the garden and cleaning his house, which backed onto the hospital block.

On the sunny afternoon of July 7, Captain Foster, Mrs. Foster, and their eighteen-year-old son, Andrew, climbed into the family car and headed down the coast to St. Brelade to attend the Jersey Scottish Society's annual summer fete, a highlight of the island's social calendar. Chapman was instructed to clean the governor's kitchen in his absence. Chief Warder Briard had taken the day off, leaving Warder Packer to mind the shop. Packer unlocked the front gate to allow the governor's car through, and Captain Foster, resplendent in his kilt, muttered as he motored off that he should "keep an eye on Chapman."

As the sound of the governor's car faded, Chapman put down his mop and darted upstairs to the empty bedroom of Andrew Foster. From the young man's wardrobe, Chapman extracted a gray pinstriped suit, brown shoes, a brown trilby, and two checked caps made by Leach & Justice of Perth. The suit was a little tight under the arms, but a reasonable fit. He also found a suitcase, into which he packed the governor's spectacles, a jar of sixpences Mrs. Foster had been saving, £13 from the governor's desk drawer, a flashlight, and a poker from the fireplace. Climbing through a skylight, he scrambled over the roof, dropped into the hospital compound, scaled a wall topped with glass, and walked away. Mrs. Hamon, who worked in the laundry, noticed a figure on the roof, but assumed he must be a workman.

An hour later, Warder Packer—who had been busy flirting with the matron's daughter, Miss Lesbird—casually wandered into the governor's kitchen to see how Chapman was progressing with his chores. He did not worry unduly to find the house empty. "At that moment," he recalled, "I still thought Chapman was playing a joke, and was hiding in the prison." He searched the garden and the outhouse; then he summoned the other warders to help search the prison. Then he panicked. It took a full two hours to track down Captain Foster at the Scottish Society fete. The chief constable was unearthed in the golf club, and a posse led by young Andrew Foster was dispatched to watch the airport. Hotels and boardinghouses were scoured, boats were prevented from leaving harbor, and every policeman and volunteer on the island was mobilized for the greatest manhunt in island memory.

Walter Picard, resident of Five Mile Road, was one of the few people on the island unaware that a prisoner had escaped. He had spent the evening under a hedge with a woman who was not Mrs. Walter Picard. After this encounter, Picard and his girlfriend were strolling back to his car in the darkness when they were surprised to see a man in an ill-fitting suit bending over the open hood of the car, apparently attempting to jump-start it.

The man looked startled, but declared: "Do you know who I am? I'm a member of the police." Picard launched himself at the "car thief." His girlfriend screamed. A scuffle ensued; Picard was upended and thrown over a wall, and Chapman vanished into the night. On the passenger seat of his car, the shaken Picard found a brown trilby, a flashlight, and three sticks of gelignite.

Chapman had passed a most eventful day. Barely a mile from the prison, Mr. A. A. Pitcher had obligingly offered him a lift in his car, and driven him to a public telephone box, where he had phoned the airport, only to be told the last plane for the mainland had departed. Pitcher dropped him off at the pier. After a meal at the Milano Café, Chapman had checked into La Pulente Hotel, and ordered a taxi. Telling the Luxicab driver he was "interested in quarries," Chapman took a tour of the island's mines and selected his target. That afternoon, when the workers had left L'Etacq Quarry on the western edge of Jersey, Chapman scaled the gate, found the small, reinforced bunker that served as the explosives storehouse, and prized open the door with a crowbar from the quarry toolshed. He emerged with five pounds of gelignite and two hundred detonators. It was while walking down Five Mile Road with his explosive loot that evening that Chapman spotted Walter Picard's parked car and decided to steal it.

Knowing that the encounter would be reported immediately, Chapman walked on until he came across an empty bungalow belonging to Frank Le Quesne. He broke in, made himself a cup of tea (using enough tea bags "for about fifty people," the owner later complained), and fell asleep.

In the meantime, Walter Picard made an edited report to the police.

> He was driving his car on his way home when he was hailed by a young woman, whom he did not recognise, who asked him for a lift as far as a bungalow on the Five Mile Road. He replied that he would take her as far as his house; he did so but she then persuaded him to drive her further on and some little distance along the road his lights failed for no apparent reason. He stopped the car and his passenger then told him that the bungalow she wished to get to was fairly close and asked him to walk as far with her. After some demur he complied with her requests, but only went half way and then, turning round, saw the lights of his car had come on again. He approached the car and saw a tall man bending over the ignition. The stranger turned round and struck him and then made off.

Even the police found Picard's elaborate story "strange," and what Mrs. Picard made of it can only be imagined.

Early the next morning, a fisherman carrying a large shrimping net could be seen striding purposefully along the Plémont beach. Closer inspection would have revealed that beneath the fishing overalls the man was wearing business attire, and beneath that, a striped bathing suit belonging to Frank Le Quesne. Chapman had calculated that with holidaymakers enjoying the summer sun, a bathing suit might be a good disguise. In his pockets, he carried enough explosives to wage a small war.

Later that morning, Mrs. Gordon Bennet reported that a man more or less fitting the description of the escaped prisoner had visited her tearooms on the cliff overlooking the beach. Centenier Percy Laurie, a volunteer policeman, and Police Constable William Golding were sent to investigate. Both were in plainclothes. Golding decided to explore the beach, while Laurie searched the caves in the cliffside. On the sand, some holidaymakers were playing football, observed, from a short distance, by a tall fisherman with a net. Golding approached the spectator. "Your name is Chapman," he said.

"My name is not Chapman," said the fisherman, backing off. "You are making a great mistake."

"Are you coming quietly?"

"You had better take me," he replied. As Golding seized his arm, Chapman shouted that he was being assaulted, and called on the footballers to come to his aid. Laurie emerged from the caves, and ran to help, several spectators weighed in, and a free-for-all ensued, with the policemen trying to get the handcuffs on Chapman as they, in turn, were attacked by a crowd of seminaked holidaymakers. The fracas ended when Golding managed to land a punch to Chapman's midriff. "This appeared to distress him," said Golding. Chapman's distress also doubtless came from the knowledge that he had eight sticks of gelignite and fifteen detonators in his pockets; a blow in the wrong place would have destroyed him, the policemen, the footballers, and most of Plémont beach.

The Jersey Evening Post

Friday, July 6, 1939

PRISONER'S ESCAPE FROM GAOL

———

DRAMATIC STORY OF ISLAND-WIDE SEARCH

———

ALLEGED ATTACK ON MOTORIST

———

GELIGNITE STOLEN FROM QUARRY STORE

———

Captured After Fight on Beach with Police Constable

After having been at liberty less than 24 hours, a prisoner who escaped from the public prison was recaptured. Every available police officer in the island had been on duty continuously in an island-wide search.

The missing man was Edward Chapman, possessor of several aliases and a record of previous convictions. He was described as a dangerous man and associate of thieves and dangerous characters and an expert in the use of dynamite.

Chapman was arrested at 2 o'clock this afternoon after a stand-up fight with a police constable on the sands at Plémont.

When the prison van arrived a large crowd waited to catch a glimpse of Chapman. He appeared perfectly composed and looked around with interest at the people, a smile flitting across his face.

Later, the constable of St Helier expressed his warm appreciation of all ranks of the police who had assisted in the most thrilling man-hunt which has taken place in Jersey for some years.

Captain Foster, the prison governor, was both enraged and humiliated. The prison board castigated him for his "gross misconduct [in] permitting a prisoner with such deplorable criminal antecedents as Chapman so much unsupervised liberty." Foster took out his anger on the warders, the prisoners, and, above all, on Chapman, who was brought back to the prison and harangued by the governor, who bitterly accused him of inventing a military past to ingratiate himself: "You have never been a soldier as you informed me, you are therefore a liar and you deserve a flogging," he bawled. "Why did you do it?" Chapman thought for a moment, and gave the only honest reply: "One, I don't like prison discipline; and two, since I am sure of more imprisonment on completion of my present sentence in England, I thought I would make one job of the lot."

Back in his cell, Chapman made a bleak calculation. On his release, he would be sent back to the mainland and tried on a string of charges, just like Darry and Anson, who were now in Dartmoor. Depending on what Scotland Yard could prove, Chapman reckoned he would be in one prison or another for the next fourteen years. The Jersey community was close knit and law abiding, and the legal authorities took a dim view of this convict who dared to steal from its prison governor, throw its inhabitants over walls, and provoke pitched battles with its policemen.

On September 6, 1939, Chapman was brought before the Criminal Assizes and sentenced to a further year in prison, to run consecutively with his earlier conviction. The news of his sentencing, somewhat to Chapman's irritation, merited only a single paragraph in the *Evening News,* for by now the people of Jersey had other concerns. Three days earlier, Britain had declared war on Germany.

CHAPTER THREE

Island at War

ALL WARS — BUT this war in particular—tend to be seen in monochrome: good and evil, winner and loser, champion and coward, loyalist and traitor. For most people, the reality of war is not like that, but rather a monotonous gray of discomforts and compromises, with occasional flashes of violent color. War is too messy to produce easy heroes and villains; there are always brave people on the wrong side, and evil men among the victors, and a mass of perfectly ordinary people struggling to survive and understand in between. Away from the battlefields, war forces individuals to make impossible choices in circumstances they did not create, and could never have expected. Most accommodate, some collaborate, and a very few find an internal compass they never knew they had, pointing to the right path.

News of the war barely penetrated the granite walls of Jersey prison. The prison slop, always repulsive, grew ever nastier with rationing. Some of the warders left to join up, and those that remained provided fragmentary, unreliable information. The Nazi blitzkrieg, first the invasion of Denmark and Norway in April 1940, then France, Belgium, Luxembourg, and the Netherlands, did not touch Chapman; his was a world just six feet square. When the Germans entered Paris on June 14, 1940, he was barely midway through his three-year sentence.

Chapman read all two hundred books in the prison library.

Then he reread them. With some aged grammar books, he set about teaching himself French and improving his German. He memorized the poems of Tennyson, and read H. G. Wells's *Outline of History,* a textbook purporting to describe the past but imbued with Wells's philosophy. He was particularly struck by Wells's idea of a "federal world state" in which all nations would work in harmony: "Nationalism as a God must follow the tribal gods to limbo. Our true nationality is mankind," Wells had written. Meanwhile, the evil god of National Socialism marched ever closer.

Chapman read and reread Betty's love note on the Royal Yacht Hotel letterhead. But soon another letter arrived that temporarily extinguished thoughts of Betty. From an address in Southend-on-Sea, Freda Stevenson, the dancer with whom he had been living in Shepherd's Bush, wrote to inform Chapman that he was now the father of a one-year-old girl, born in the Southend municipal hospital in July 1939, whom she had christened Diane Shayne. She enclosed a photograph of mother and child. Freda explained that she was desperately poor, barely surviving on wartime rations, and asked Chapman to send money. Chapman asked for permission to write to her, but Captain Foster refused, out of spite. Freda's unanswered letters became increasingly anguished, then angry. Frustrated at his inability to help Freda or hold his first child and cut off from the rest of humanity in a seabound prison, Chapman sank into a bleak depression.

The Jersey Evening Post

Saturday, June 29, 1940

FIERCE AIR RAIDS ON CHANNEL ISLANDS
HARBOURS BOMBED

HEAVY CASUALTIES IN BOTH ISLANDS

Nine people are known to have been killed and many injured in a bombing and machine gun attack carried out by at least three German aircraft over Jersey last night.

The Harbour was the chief objective and a bomb struck the pier, causing considerable damage to property belonging solely to civilians . . .

Chapman was lying on his plank bed when he heard the first Luftwaffe planes droning ahead. Three days later, the Channel Islands earned the unhappy distinction of becoming the only part of Britain to be occupied by Germany during the Second World War. There was no resistance, for the last defending troops had pulled out. Most of the population opted to remain. Chapman was not offered a choice. Idly, he wondered whether a bomb might hit the prison, offering either death or the chance for escape. The British inhabitants of Jersey were instructed to offer no resistance. The bailiff, Alexander Moncrieff Coutanche, who had presided over Chapman's trial, told them to obey German orders, return home, and fly the white flag of surrender. Hitler had decided Jersey would make an ideal holiday camp, once Germany had won the war.

With German occupation, the Jersey prison service was simply absorbed into the Nazi administration, along with the police. Sealed away behind stone and iron, the prisoners were forgotten. The prison food became more meager than ever, as the free inhabitants of Jersey competed for the few resources allowed them by the German invaders. There were no more letters from Freda. Chapman consoled himself with the thought that as long as the Germans controlled Jersey when he was finally released, they could not send him back to the waiting manacles.

The Germans ran their own courts, parallel to the civil judiciary. In December 1940, a young dishwasher from the Miramar Hotel, named Anthony Charles Faramus, fell foul of both. A Jersey islander with a reputation as a tearaway, twenty-year-old Faramus was sentenced to six months by the Jersey court for obtaining £9 under false pretenses by claiming an allowance for a nonexistent dependent.

The German field court slapped on a further month after Faramus was found to be carrying an anti-German propaganda leaflet.

Chapman regarded Faramus, a furtive, delicate man, with a pencil mustache and darting blue eyes, as a strange but likable fellow. He was a hopeless crook. He blushed easily, and exuded a "sort of dispossessed gentleness," though he possessed a sharp, obscene wit. Tall and slender, he looked as if a puff of wind might carry him off. He had worked as a hairdresser in a salon in St. Helier, before taking a job at the hotel. Chapman and Faramus became cellmates, and firm friends.

On October 15, 1941, a few weeks short of his twenty-sixth birthday, Chapman was finally released. Gaunt and paper-faced, he weighed just 131 pounds. Faramus, released a few months earlier, was waiting for him at the prison gates. Chapman knew nothing of the Nazi invasion of Greece and Yugoslavia, the sinking of the *Bismarck,* or the siege of Leningrad, but the effects of war were visible in the transformation of Jersey. On his last day of freedom, Chapman had wandered a beach thronged with happy, well-fed holidaymakers. Now it was an island ground down by occupation, exhausted and hungry, beset by all the moral confusion that comes from the choice between resistance, acquiescence, or collaboration.

Faramus had rented a small shop on Broad Street in St. Helier, and with a few chairs, some old mirrors, scissors, and razors, he and Chapman opened what they referred to, rather grandly, as a hairdressing salon. Their clientele mainly comprised German officers, since the Channel Islands—Hitler's stepping-stone to Britain—were now a vast, heavily defended barracks, home to the largest infantry regiment in the German army.

Faramus shaved German beards and cut German hair, while Chapman made polite conversation in basic German. One of the few British regulars was a middle-aged former bookmaker from Birmingham by the name of Douglas Stirling. An opportunist of the sort produced by every war, Stirling was a black marketer, buying cigarettes, tea, and alcohol from the Germans, and then selling them at a profit to the local people. The barber's shop was the ideal front for what soon became a thriving trade that combined illegal profiteering with grooming the enemy.

One morning, setting out on his bicycle from the flat he shared with Faramus above the shop, Chapman momentarily forgot that a new German law required everyone to drive on the right and rode straight into a German motorcycle dispatch rider hurtling around a corner. Neither man was hurt, but the German was furious. Chapman was duly summoned to the police station and interrogated by three officers of the Feldgendarmerie, the German military police. One of these, a small man who spoke good English, eyed Chapman unpleasantly and said: "Look, we've reason to believe you've got some German arms. Now, where is the German rifle?"

"I haven't got any German rifles," Chapman replied, bemused.

"Have you any arms?"

"No."

"Now look, we've got our eyes on you, so if you try any trouble, we'll make trouble too. I'm only warning you."

"Thanks for the warning," Chapman replied, and left swiftly.

This was no warning; it was a threat. He was fined 80 reichsmarks for the traffic violation, but, more worryingly, the interview seemed to suggest he had been singled out as a suspected member of the resistance, or even a saboteur. The run-in with the Feldgendarmerie had unsettled him, and set Chapman thinking of another plan to get him off this island prison. He outlined his idea to Faramus and Douglas Stirling. What if they offered to work as spies for the Nazis? If they were accepted, there was surely a chance they might be sent over to mainland Britain, undercover. At the very least, it would break the monotony. Stirling was enthusiastic, saying that he would suggest the ruse to his son. Faramus was more cautious, but agreed the plan was worth a shot.

With hindsight, Chapman admitted that his motives in 1941 were hazy and confused. He later claimed that the offer to spy for Germany was prompted by the simple and sincere desire to escape and to be united with Diane, the child he had never seen: "If I could work a bluff with the Germans, I could probably be sent over to

Britain," he wrote. But Chapman understood his own nature well enough to know that there was more to his decision that this. "It all sounds fine talk, now," he later admitted. "Perhaps it was phony talk even then, and I don't pretend there were no other motives in the plans I began to turn over in my mind. They did not occur to me, either, in one moment, or in one mood." He felt a genuine animus toward the British establishment. Like many justly imprisoned criminals, he saw himself as the victim of cruel discrimination. Moreover, he was impressed by the discipline and general politeness of the Germans in their smart uniforms. Nazi propaganda relentlessly insisted that their forces were invincible, and the occupation permanent. Chapman was hungry, he was bored, and he longed for excitement. In his Soho days, he had mixed with film stars, and he had long imagined himself as the central character in his own drama. He had played the part of a high-rolling gangster. Now he recast himself in the glamorous role of spy. There was little thought, if any, given to whether such a course was right or wrong. That would come later.

Chapman and Faramus composed a letter in carefully wrought German, and sent it to the Kommandatur, the German command post in St. Helier, addressed to General Otto von Stulpnägel, the senior officer in command of the occupation forces in France and the Channel Islands. A few days later, Faramus and Chapman were summoned to the office of a German major, where Chapman blithely explained that he and his friend would like to join the German secret service. He listed his crimes, stressed the outstanding warrants he faced in Britain, emphasized his expertise with explosives, and concluded with a spirited anti-British rant. "His whole theme was revenge," Faramus wrote later. "He said he had no time for the English ruling class, and sought only a chance to get even with them." The major nodded blandly, while a secretary took notes and wrote down the young men's names and addresses. The matter, said the major, would be discussed with "senior officers."

After that, nothing seemed to happen. Over the next few days, Chapman made a point every time a German came into the shop of reciting a "tale of loathing for the society that had hounded him, and his hatred for the English and all their works," in the hope that word would filter back to the German authorities. But the days passed, and still there was no word from the Kommandatur. Clearly, their application had been rejected, or merely ignored, on the long-standing principle that anyone who applies to join an espionage service should be rejected.

Chapman had all but forgotten the plan and was busy hatching a fresh scheme to open up a nightclub serving black-market alcohol when, one damp evening in December, he and Faramus were roused from their beds by a furious hammering at the door and the sound of raised German voices. On the doorstep stood two German officers. Chapman's immediate assumption was that the application to spy for Germany had borne fruit. He could not have been more wrong. These were not members of the German intelligence service, but the Gestapo. Chapman and Faramus were not being recruited, but arrested. They were handcuffed, bundled into a Vauxhall waiting in the drizzle, and driven to the dock. The senior officer, a captain, or *Hauptmann,* brusquely informed the pair that they were now prisoners, and if they attempted to escape they would be shot. From the car, they were marched onto a small landing barge and manacled to an iron bar bolted to the wheelhouse. The boat engine roared and swung out of the port, heading due south, with the coast of France faintly visible through the drizzle. The Gestapo officers sat in the warmth belowdecks, while Chapman and Faramus shivered in the biting rain.

The next few hours passed in a miasmic rush of fear and movement: the port at Saint-Malo in the chill dawn; two hours handcuffed to a bench in the police station, where a gendarme slipped them a baguette and some stale cheese; locked inside a compartment on the train to Paris; and finally, arrival at the Gare du Nord, where a military truck and armed escort awaited them. The German guards would not speak and shrugged off every question. Faramus was white with terror, moaning gently, his head in his hands, as they sped through the broad boulevards of the occupied French capital with their silent Gestapo escort. Finally, the truck passed through a broad gateway with iron gates draped in huge ringlets of barbed wire, and into another prison.

In the weeks before Chapman's arrest, several telephone wires on the island had been cut, the latest in a series of acts of sabotage. The German authorities consulted the Jersey police, some of whom were now active collaborators, and they immediately pointed the finger at Chapman and Faramus, the most notorious of the usual suspects. Chapman reflected ruefully: "The British police told them that if there was any trouble, I was probably in it."

For the young criminal, this was an entirely new experience. He had been arrested for a crime he had not committed.

CHAPTER FOUR

Romainville

THE FORT DE ROMAINVILLE glowers over the eastern suburbs of Paris. A brutal stone giant, by 1941 it had been made into another Nazi vision of hell. Built in the 1830s on a low hill, the hulking bastion was part of the defensive ring constructed around Paris to protect the city from foreign attack, but it also held troops who could be deployed in the event of popular insurrection—a bloated, moated, impregnable monstrosity. For the Nazis, the ancient fort served a similar psychological purpose—as a hostage camp, a place of interrogation, torture, and summary execution, and a visible symbol of intimidation, inescapable in every way. Romainville was "death's waiting room," a prison for civilians—resistance fighters, political prisoners, prominent Jews, Communists and intellectuals, suspected spies, political subversives, and "trouble-makers," as well as those who had simply failed to show sufficient deference to the new rulers of France.

This shifting prison population formed an important element in the brutal arithmetic of Nazi occupation, for in reprisal for each act of resistance, a number of prisoners would be selected from the cells and shot. An attack on German soldiers at the Rex Cinema in Paris, for example, was calculated to be worth the lives of 116 Romainville hostages. The more serious the incident of defiance, the higher the death toll at the hostage depot. Sometimes, hostages were told which specific act had cost them their lives. Mostly, they were not.

Chapman and Faramus, political prisoners and suspected sabo-teurs, were stripped, clad in prison overalls, and then taken before the camp commandant, Kapitän Brüchenbach, a stocky little man with thick glasses and eyes "like two bullet holes in a metal door." Brüchenbach grunted that he had orders from the Gestapo to de-tain them until further notice. The fastidious Faramus noted that the man "stank of drink."

They were then marched to a barracks building surrounded by a twelve-foot barbed-wire fence, and guarded at either end by sentries with searchlights and machine guns. The men were pushed into a room, unheated and lit by a single bulb, containing half a dozen empty bunks, and locked inside. As they lay on rotting straw mat-tresses, the friends discussed their chances of survival. One voiced brittle optimism, the other was sunk in deepest despair.

"How would you like to be shot, Eddie?" asked Faramus.

"I don't think I'd mind so terribly as all that," came the self-deluding reply. "I've had a pretty good life."

The next morning, as they filed into the courtyard, Chapman and Faramus learned from the whispers of their fellow prisoners that sixteen people had been executed that morning, in retaliation for the assassination of a German officer in Nantes by members of the resistance. On the door of each cell was a warning: "*Alles Ver-boten*" (everything is forbidden). This was no exaggeration. The writ-ing and receiving of letters was not permitted. Red Cross and Quaker parcels were intercepted. The beatings were ferocious, and unexplained. Denied contact with the world outside, the inmates measured time by the movements of the guards and the traffic in the distant Paris streets. Rations were strict and unvarying: a pint of watery vegetable soup, four ounces of black bread, and an ounce of rancid margarine or cheese. At first, the two newcomers fished the maggots out of the soup; after a few days, they, like everyone else, sucked it all down.

The male and female inmates were allowed to mix in the fort's giant courtyard, but sexual relations were strictly forbidden, as one of the guards made clear on their first day with an elaborate, multi-lingual charade: "Madame prisonniers. Parler, promenade, ja! Aber

NIX, verboten, fig-fig—Nix!" And then, in case of any lingering confusion on the matter, he added: "NIX. Keine fig-fig!" To Chapman, this sounded like a challenge.

The inmates of Fort Romainville were a peculiar assortment: rich and poor, brave and treacherous, guilty and innocent. Chapman and Faramus were the only Englishmen. There was Paulette, a blond woman who had been arrested for espionage, and Ginette, whose husband had already been executed for spying. Other women were being held as hostages for husbands or fathers who had joined the Free French, or were known to be active in the resistance. There was Kahn, a wealthy German-Jewish banker, along with Michelin—the tire magnate—two Belgian diamond merchants, and a mysterious individual called Leutsch, a German-speaking Swiss journalist who wore horn-rimmed spectacles and claimed to have worked for British intelligence. Among the French prisoners were the former minister of information and a radio journalist named Le François, jailed for refusing to broadcast German propaganda. One woman, a waitress from a café in Montparnasse, was there, she claimed, because she had slapped an SS officer who had fondled her. One old fellow named Weiss, a multilingual eccentric who suffered from hydrophobia, had been arrested for writing an article discussing how a defeated Germany should be partitioned. Many had simply fallen foul of the invaders. Some claimed to have no idea why they were there.

Every inmate had a different story, yet all guarded their words; some declined to reveal their identities beyond a first name. For the prison was also riddled with informers, stool pigeons whose task it was to draw out the truth from spies and agitators, and then expose them. Among the inmates, suspicion fell heavily on a Belgian named Bossuet. He claimed to have been born in Cardiff, and could speak English well, though laced with slang. At first, Chapman had warmed to the Belgian, only to be told that Bossuet was a "professional denouncer," a *mouchard*, who had earned himself the nickname "Black Diamond." It was rumored that his betrayals had sent twenty-two prisoners to their deaths. Most inmates shunned him, and some attacked him when the guards were not looking. Eventually, Bossuet was removed from the prison. This was seen as proof of Bossuet's guilt, but it was part of the regime of neurosis at Romainville that prisoners arrived and were removed without warning or explanation. A middle-aged man called Dreyfus, a Jewish descendant of the other famous victim of anti-Semitism, was briefly held, and then inexplicably released. Immediately, it was assumed that he must have turned traitor. "It wasn't safe to talk to anyone," Chapman reflected. "No one knew who was who. No one would talk."

Yet alongside the corrosive atmosphere of fear and distrust existed an equally powerful urge for intimacy. The ban on sex between prisoners was not just ignored, but violated with abandon. Men and women sought every opportunity: in the washrooms, under the stairs, in the coal store and the darker corners of the courtyard. The barracks rooms had not been designed as cells, and the locks were simple to pick. Elaborate plans were hatched by the inmates to find sexual release. No one ever escaped from Romainville, but here was a way to escape, briefly. Within weeks of arriving in Romainville, Chapman had paired off with the blond Paulette, who was some ten years his senior, while Faramus had begun a sexual relationship with another female inmate named Lucy. Looking back, both men certainly exaggerated the extent of their "conquests." Chapman, more worldly than his partner, seemed to accept the strange merging of sex and fear as the natural order, but Faramus, a sexual ingenue, was insistent that these "were real love affairs, passionate and sincere." In this closed and treacherous society, where death came without warning or explanation, sexual expression was the only remaining liberty.

While Chapman and Faramus were devising complicated trysts with the female prisoners, their offer to spy for Germany, now long forgotten by them, was slowly progressing through the German military bureaucracy. From Jersey, their letter had passed to Berlin, then on to the branch of the German secret service at Hamburg, then back to Jersey again. Chapman was serving two weeks' solitary confinement in the fort dungeons when the letter finally caught up with him, in December 1941. Chapman had been consigned to the *cachots,* the underground cells, after a fight with the hated Bossuet.

Prisoners in solitary received one meal of bread and soup every three days. Chapman's cell was lightless, freezing, and sodden. In an effort to conserve his body heat, he scraped the gravel from the floor and tried to cover himself with it.

Chapman was a week into his sentence in solitary when he was pulled from the dungeon, escorted under guard to Brüchenbach's office, and locked in a back room. Moments later, he was confronted by an SS officer, who carefully locked the door behind him. The visitor was tall and spare, with pale blue eyes and hollow cheeks streaked with broken red veins. He stood looking at Chapman for several moments before he spoke. Then, in perfect English, without a hint of accent, he introduced himself as Oberleutnant Walter Thomas. Without preamble or explanation, he sat down at a desk and began to interrogate Chapman about his past crimes, his experience with explosives, his imprisonment in Jersey, and his proficiency in German. Occasionally, he referred to a file. He seemed to know every detail of Chapman's criminal record, not only the crimes for which he had been sentenced, but those for which he was only suspected. The officer spoke with familiarity of Britain, of Chapman's years in Soho, his arrest in Edinburgh, and his flight to Jersey; as he spoke, he twined the long fingers of his hands or gesticulated. His expression did not change, but he seemed satisfied by Chapman's answers. Chapman reflected later that his interrogator seemed "the scholarly, staid" type. After an hour, the man indicated that the meeting was over, and Chapman was escorted from the office, not back to the punishment dungeon, but to the barracks room.

"What happened?" Faramus asked, astonished by Chapman's early release from solitary.

Chapman swore him to secrecy and then described his encounter with the SS officer. It must mean, he continued, that their offer to work for Germany had provoked a response at last. "All right for you," said Faramus, suddenly fearful. "They're sure to make use of you. But what about me? What am I worth to them?" Chapman tried to reassure the younger man, but both knew Faramus was right. The Nazis might conceivably find use for a fit, wily,

and experienced criminal, with a long record and a convincing reason for hating the British establishment. But what use could the
Third Reich find for a slight, twenty-year-old hairdresser whose sole
crime had been a failed attempt to acquire £9 by deceit?

Further evidence of the Nazis' interest in Chapman surfaced a
few days later, in the form of a military photographer with a Leica
camera, who took dozens of pictures of the prisoner, full face and in
profile, and then departed.

In early January 1942, Chapman was once more summoned to the
commandant's office. This time, his interrogator could not have been
more different from the dead-eyed Oberleutnant Thomas. Arranged
across the commandant's armchair was a vision of female loveliness;
with large brown eyes, long red-painted fingernails, and an expensive black lamb's-wool coat by her side, she looked, to Chapman's
mind, as if she had just stepped off a film set. Chapman was momentarily stunned by the apparition. Standing alongside her was a man
in civilian clothes. Chapman noted his athletic physique and sun-
tanned face; with their elegant apparel and faintly bored expressions, they might have been modeling for a fashion shoot.

The man asked questions in German, which the woman translated into English, with an American accent. There was no attempt
to disguise why they had come. Chapman was peppered with questions about what work he thought he could do for the German secret service, and his motives for offering to do so. They demanded
to know how much he expected to be paid, and what he would be
prepared to do if sent back to Britain undercover. The woman
smoked cigarette after cigarette from a long black holder. "Supposing you didn't feel like coming back to us?" she asked suddenly.

"You'd have to trust me," Chapman replied.

As the woman picked up her coat to leave, Chapman spotted the
label inside: Schiaparelli, the Italian designer. Clearly, he reflected,
Nazi spies—if that is what this couple were—could afford the height
of fashion.

For a few weeks, normal prison routine resumed, broken only by
the ferocious RAF bombardment of the huge Renault factory at
Boulogne-Billancourt, directly across the Seine from Romainville.

The factory was now part of the Nazi munitions machine, making lorries for the German army. On March 3, the RAF launched 235 low-level bombers at the plant, the largest number of aircraft aimed at a single target during the war. From the barracks windows, Chapman and Faramus saw flares, tracers, and flak light up the night, felt the crump of explosive tremble through air, and watched as the city sky turned an evil orange. Chapman could sense his companion's fear. "They'll probably send you to a civilian internee camp," he said. "Or maybe keep you here—if they accept me. Listen Tony, don't worry: leave it to me. Trust me."

The two Englishmen had been in Romainville for almost four months when Chapman was taken to Brüchenbach's office for what would be the last time. Waiting for him was Oberleutnant Thomas, but this time accompanied by a more senior officer, dressed in the uniform of a cavalry *Rittmeister,* the equivalent of a captain. At his throat he wore the Iron Cross. Oberleutnant Thomas introduced him as "Herr Doktor Stephan Graumann." With an almost courtly gesture, Graumann invited Chapman to be seated, and then began to interrogate him in precise, old-fashioned English, in a soft voice with an upper-class British accent. He asked how Chapman had been treated in Romainville. When the Englishman described his time in the *cachots* on Brüchenbach's orders, Graumann sneered and remarked that the commandant was "simply a trained brute."

Graumann had a lofty yet benevolent air, and Chapman found himself warming to the man. Graumann often smiled to himself, as if enjoying a private joke. He would consider Chapman's answers carefully, leaning back in his chair, the index finger of one hand hooked into the side pocket of his uniform, the other stroking his thinning hair. From time to time, he would don thick-rimmed spectacles and peer at the open file in front of him. Chapman decided he must be "a man of understanding and tolerance."

Graumann quizzed Chapman once more about his past: his catalog of crimes, his grasp of German and French, the members of the Jelly Gang and their current whereabouts. Time after time, he returned to the question of whether Chapman was motivated more by hatred of Britain or by the promise of financial gain. Chapman responded that both were factors in his desire to spy for Germany. The interrogation continued for three hours.

Finally, Graumann fixed Chapman with his watery blue eyes and came to the point. If Chapman would agree to be trained in sabotage, wireless telegraphy, and intelligence work and then undertake a mission to Britain, he could promise him a substantial financial reward on his return. Chapman agreed on the spot. He then asked whether Tony Faramus would be coming too. Graumann's reply was blunt. Faramus was "no use" to the German secret service. Graumann picked his words carefully: "In times of war we must be careful, and one of you must remain here." Though his language was opaque, Graumann's meaning was obvious: Faramus would remain behind, as a hostage for Chapman's good behavior.

As they shook hands, Chapman noticed the fat gold ring with five black dots on Graumann's little finger, and remarked to himself on the softness of his hands. These were hands that had never known manual labor. The voice, the hands, the signet ring: clearly, the man must be some sort of aristocrat. If Chapman could avoid getting into any more trouble, Graumann remarked from the doorway, he would be out of Romainville in two weeks.

Chapman returned to his barracks cell elated, but also troubled by the veiled "half-threat" to Faramus. He did not relate the German's words to his cellmate, but the news that Chapman would soon be leaving alone left the younger man in no doubt that his position was perilous. "Supposing you slip up," Faramus pointed out. "Then I'll be the one to get it in the neck. What if once you have set foot in England, you don't want to come back, Eddie? I don't fancy being shot. Besides, I'm too young to die."

Chapman tried to reassure him. "Look here, Tony, let me play this my way. I am gambling with my own life, too, don't forget." The truth of the remark was undeniable: Their fates were now linked. Most Romainville victims never discovered why they had been chosen for death. If Faramus was shot, he would know he had been betrayed by Eddie Chapman. Privately, Faramus reflected that "agreeing to play Eddie's game might cost me my life." Could this "bold bluff" possibly succeed? "Desperately and fearfully," Faramus wrote, "I hoped so, for my sake as well as his."

On April 18, 1942, Chapman was escorted from his cell. "Goodbye and good luck," he said, slapping Faramus on the back and grinning. "Look me up in London after the war!"

"Goodbye and good luck," replied the Jerseyman, as brightly as he could.

Chapman was met in the commandant's office by Oberleutnant Thomas. The few possessions he had brought from Jersey were returned to him, along with his civilian clothes, while Brüchenbach signed the release papers. Chapman walked out of the Romainville gates and was ushered by Thomas into a waiting car. He was free. But as Thomas observed, as they settled into the backseat and the driver headed west, this was freedom of a very particular sort. "You are among friends and we are going to help you," said the German officer, in his clipped, precise English. "So please do not try anything silly like attempting to escape, because I am armed." From now on, Thomas added, when in public, Chapman should speak only German.

At Gare Montparnasse, the duo transferred to a reserved first-class compartment on the train for Nantes. In the dining car, Chapman gorged himself. The ascetic-looking Thomas ate little. Chapman finished his supper for him.

It was evening when the train pulled into Nantes, France's western port where the great Loire flows toward the Atlantic. A burly young man in civilian clothes with an impressively broken nose was waiting on the platform. He introduced himself as "Leo," picked up Oberleutnant Thomas's suitcase and Chapman's bag of belongings, and led the way to where a large Mercedes awaited them.

Chapman sank into the leather upholstery as Leo drove the car at high speeds through Nantes's winding cobbled streets and then out into open countryside, heading northwest, past neat farms and meadows dotted with Limousin cows. At a roadside village café, a handful of peasants watched expressionless as the Mercedes sped past. After some seven kilometers, Leo slowed and turned right. They passed what appeared to be a factory and crossed over a railway bridge, before coming to a stop in front of a pair of green iron gates with a high wall on either side. A thick screen of poplar trees shielded from view whatever was behind the wall. Leo hailed the uniformed sentry, who unlocked the gates.

Down a short drive, the car came to rest before a large stone mansion. Chapman was led inside and upstairs to a book-lined study. Here a familiar figure in a three-piece pin-striped suit sat hunched writing over a desk. "Welcome to the Villa de la Bretonnière," said Dr. Graumann, rising to shake Chapman's hand. "Come and have a glass of really good brandy."

CHAPTER FIVE

Villa de la Bretonnière

AFTER ROMAINVILLE, the Villa de la Bretonnière was paradise. The three-story building had been built in the 1830s, the same decade as the Paris prison, but it could not have been more of a contrast. It was what the French describe as a *maison de maître:* larger than a mansion, but smaller than a château. It boasted all the appurtenances of a rich man's retreat: oak floors, huge marble fireplaces, crystal chandeliers, and double doors opening onto a large and well-tended garden. The house had belonged to a wealthy Jew, a cinema owner in Nantes, before it was requisitioned and its owner "relocated." The building, surrounded by trees and a high wall, suited Nazi intelligence purposes exactly.

That evening, elated by the brandy and Graumann's welcome, Chapman was shown to a room on the top floor. For the first time in four years, the door was not locked behind him. He slept in crisp linen sheets, and woke to the sound of a cock crowing. Chapman thought he had never seen anywhere so beautiful. To the west, the land sloped gently through woodland and fields to the Erdre River. Waterfowl splashed in an ornamental pond, while a litter of Alsatian puppies played on the lawn.

Chapman was escorted to breakfast by Oberleutnant Thomas. In the dining room, Graumann sat at the head of the table, reading a copy of the *Times* and eating a boiled egg. He nodded to Chapman but did not speak. (The aristocrat, Chapman would soon learn, did not hold with conversation during breakfast.) Around the table, half a dozen men were tucking into a feast of toast, eggs, butter, honey, and fresh coffee, all served on the former owner's best china. Chapman recognized Leo, the chauffeur with the flattened nose, who grinned back through broken teeth.

A French maidservant cleared away breakfast, cigarettes were offered around, and Thomas introduced the other members of the household. Each man, though Chapman could not know it, proffered a false name. A ruddy-faced, well-built fellow with a pearl tiepin was presented as "Hermann Wojch." He was followed by "Robert Keller," a slight, blond man in his early twenties, alongside "Albert," a balding, middle-aged man with a cheery countenance. To Chapman's astonishment, the next person to step forward, wearing plus fours and a gold wristwatch, greeted him in English with a broad Cockney accent. He gave his name as "Franz Schmidt."

Later, upstairs in the study, Graumann adopted his habitual posture, with one finger hooked in his waistcoat, and explained that Chapman was now part of the Abwehr—the German foreign intelligence gathering and espionage service—and that he was attached to the Nantes section, "one of the most important sabotage training centers of the German Secret Service in Europe."

For the next three months, Graumann continued, Chapman would undergo rigorous training, under his direction: Keller would be his wireless instructor; Wojch and Schmidt would teach him sabotage and espionage techniques; Leo would show him how to jump with a parachute. If he passed certain tests, he would be sent to Britain on a mission; and, if successful, he would be handsomely rewarded. There was no word as to what would happen if Chapman failed these tests.

Meanwhile, he was free to explore the grounds of La Bretonnière, but Thomas would accompany him at all times. He should avoid fraternizing with the locals, and under no circumstances should he bring women back to the house. In the presence of French people, he must speak only German, and if any Germans quizzed him, he should explain that he was German by birth but had lived most of his life in America. Officially, he was now part of the

Baustelle Kerstang, a military engineering unit repairing roads and buildings in occupied France.

Chapman would need a spy name, Graumann declared, to protect his real identity. What was the name that the English routinely attached to Germans? Fritz? This, he chuckled, would be the code name for the new Abwehr spy number V-6523.

As he struggled to take in the flood of information, Chapman reflected that Dr. Graumann, with his pin-striped suit, looked more like a "respectable business man" than a spymaster. His tone was brisk but benign, and his eyes under heavy lids twinkled. Each time he spoke, his head jerked slightly, back and forth. His voice struck Chapman as being "surprisingly soft, for a German," but the tone hardened very slightly when the doctor remarked: "Look, you will see a good many things, but you must realise that with our section things must be kept secret. I'm asking you not to be too nosey."

For months, the Abwehr had been searching for an Englishman who could be trained as a spy and saboteur and dropped into Britain. The man must be without scruple, adept at concealment, intelligent, ruthless, and mercenary. Chapman's arrival at La Bretonnière was not some accident of fate. Rather, he represented the latest, boldest stroke in a war between the secret services of Britain and Germany that had raged, unseen but unceasing, for the previous two years.

Before the outbreak of the Second World War, the Abwehr (literally meaning "defense") was reputed to be the most efficient intelligence service in Europe. An early appraisal by MI5, the security service controlling counterespionage in the United Kingdom and throughout the British Empire, described the Abwehr as an "absolutely first-class organisation in training and personnel." This assessment was overly flattering. One of the most striking aspects of the countries' intelligence services was just how little each side knew about the other. In 1939, SIS, the British Secret Intelligence Service (also known as MI6, and operating in all areas outside British territory) did not know what the German military intelligence service was called, or even who ran it. In a frank self-assessment written after the end of the Second World War, MI5 conceded that "by the time of the fall of France the organisation of the Security Service as a whole was in a state which can only be described as chaotic . . . attempting to evolve means of detecting German agents without any inside knowledge of the German organisation."

The Abwehr was equally ill prepared. Hitler had neither expected nor wanted to go to war with Britain, and most Nazi intelligence operations had been directed eastwards. The Abwehr intelligence network in Britain was virtually nonexistent. As Britain and Germany squared up for conflict, a strange shadow dance took place between their rival intelligence services: both frantically began building up spy networks, almost from scratch, for immediate deployment against one another. Each credited the other with extreme efficiency and advanced preparations, and both were wrong.

The first serious skirmish took place over a diminutive, dubious, and aggravating Welsh electrician called Arthur Owens. A manufacturer of battery accumulators, Owens had made frequent business trips to Germany in the 1930s, bringing back small items of technical and military information that he passed on to the Admiralty. In 1936, he was formally enrolled in British intelligence as Agent Snow (a partial anagram of Owens). At the same time, however, Owens had secretly made contact with the Abwehr. MI6 intercepted his mail, but when confronted with evidence of his double game, Owens insisted he was working for British interests. MI6 accepted his explanation, for the time being. On instructions from Germany, Owens picked up a wireless transmitter from the left-luggage office at Victoria Station, providing valuable technical information on German radio construction. Then he vanished to Hamburg, and it was assumed he had "gone bad."

The day after Britain declared war on Germany, the Welshman resurfaced and telephoned Special Branch to arrange a meeting. At Wandsworth Prison, Owens was offered the choice between execution and working as a double agent; once again, he pledged loyalty to Britain. In September 1939, he traveled to Holland, this time accompanied by a retired police inspector, Gwilym Williams, posing as a Welsh nationalist eager to throw off the English yoke. There they met up with Abwehr officer Nikolaus Ritter, and returned to London with valuable information, including the keys to various Abwehr radio codes.

The British still had doubts about Agent Snow, and these deepened after an extraordinary series of events in the North Sea. Ritter had asked Owens to recruit another agent for training in Germany, and agreed to send a submarine to pick them up in the North Sea south of Dogger Bank. MI6, obviously eager to plant a double agent within the Abwehr, duly located a reformed con man and thief called Sam McCarthy, who agreed to play the part. As they motored to the rendezvous in a trawler, McCarthy and Owens each became convinced that the other was, in fact, a German spy. Two days before the meeting, McCarthy locked Owens in his cabin, and they steamed home. When Owens was searched, he was found to be carrying a report describing the operations of the British intelligence services. This was traced to a Piccadilly restaurant manager and sometime MI5 informer called William Rolph. Confronted with the evidence, Rolph admitted he had been recruited by Owens to spy for Germany. As soon as the interrogators had left, he committed suicide by putting his head in a gas oven.

Owens spent the rest of the war in prison, and to this day it is uncertain whether he was a patriot, a traitor, or both. But the Snow case had shown the extraordinary value of running a double agent, and had furnished some vital technical and cryptological clues. The farce in the North Sea demonstrated that the Abwehr was looking to recruit disaffected British citizens, even criminals, as German agents.

In Britain, mounting fears of a German invasion prompted a spy scare of epidemic proportions. The collapse of one European country after another before the Nazi blitzkrieg could only have one explanation: In each country, there must have been a network of German agents behind the lines, aiding the German advance. A similar network, it was assumed, must exist in Britain, plotting to undermine the state, perhaps with the help of pro-appeasement elements within the establishment. The myth of the German fifth column was borne on a most un-British wave of public hysteria, stoked by the press and politicians. "There is a well-defined class of people prone to spy mania," wrote Churchill, who was not immune to the mania himself. "War is the heyday of these worthy folk."

German spies were spotted everywhere, and nowhere. Police were deluged with reports of strange figures in disguise, lights flashing at night, burning haystacks, and paranoid neighbors hearing tapping through the walls. One avid amateur spy catcher reported seeing a man with a "typically Prussian neck." Robert Baden-Powell, the original scoutmaster, insisted you could spot a German spy from the way he walked. Anyone and everyone might be a spy. Evelyn Waugh lampooned the frenzy: "Suspect everyone—the vicar, the village grocer, the farmer whose family have lived here for a hundred years, all the most unlikely people." The spies were said to be spreading newspaper on the ground to give secret signals to airborne Germans, poisoning chocolate, infiltrating the police, recruiting lunatics from asylums to act in a suicide squad, and sending out murderous agents into the British countryside disguised as female hitchhikers.

Vast energy and resources was devoted to following up the reports, with a complete lack of success. The most grievous outcome of the panic was the internment of twenty-seven thousand Germans, Italians, and other "enemy aliens," most of whom were not only innocent, but also strongly opposed to Nazism. The failure to uncover the plotters merely redoubled the conviction that they must be agents of the highest quality. The secret service, wrote an insider, "was left with the very uncomfortable feeling that there must be agents in this country whom it was unable to discover."

The simple truth was that apart from Arthur Owens and his band of imaginary Welsh extremists, the Abwehr had utterly failed to recruit an effective team of spies in Britain before the war. But as Operation Sea Lion, the plan for the German invasion of Britain, took shape, the German secret service set about rectifying this failure with a vengeance. From late 1940, as the air duel between the RAF and the Luftwaffe intensified, the Abwehr began pouring agents into Britain: They came by rubber dinghy, U-boat, seaplane, and parachute; they came disguised as refugees and seamen. Some came armed with the latest wireless transmitters and carefully forged identity documents; others arrived with nothing more than the clothes they stood up in. Between September and November 1940, it is estimated that at least twenty-one Abwehr agents were dispatched to Britain, with instructions to report on troop movements, identify and sabotage targets vital to British defense, prepare for the imminent invasion, and then mingle with the retreating British army. A list of prominent Britons to be arrested by the Gestapo was drawn up, and at the Abwehr headquarters in Berlin there was little doubt that Hitler's storm troopers would soon be marching down Whitehall.

The Abwehr spies were a mixed bag. Some were Nazi ideologues, but most were the human jetsam that tends to float toward the spy world: opportunists, criminals, and a handful of fantasists. The vast majority of the "invasion spies" had one thing in common, though: They were amateurs. Many spoke English badly, or not at all. Few had received more than rudimentary training. They were poorly briefed and often ignorant of English life. One was arrested after he tried to pay £10 and 6 shillings for a train ticket costing "ten and six."

The Abwehr would never find out that its entire espionage program in Britain had been discovered, dismantled, and turned against it. Many of its agents, it is true, seemed to vanish without a trace, but this was only to be expected. Several had begun sending messages by wireless and secret ink, and a few seemed to be flourishing undercover. That, at least, is what Hitler was told. Yet the more professional and experienced German intelligence officers knew that the caliber of spies being sent to Britain was pitifully low. The little information coming out of Britain was low-grade stuff. No sabotage operation of any note had been carried out.

The Abwehr leadership decided that in order to penetrate Britain's intelligence defenses, they would need to look beyond the eager amateurs deployed so far. An altogether superior sort of spy was needed: someone handpicked and properly trained by professionals for a specific, highly dangerous mission. This individual should be dedicated, ruthless, and, if possible, British. For this purpose, in March 1942, the Nantes section (or Dienststelle) of the Abwehr was established as an elite espionage training center. A *Rittmeister* who was also a rising star within the Abwehr was appointed to run the new spy school, and provided with money, expert trainers, staff, and a spacious mansion just outside the city in the little village of Saint-Joseph. The unit would be answerable to the Abwehr headquarters in Paris, but largely independent.

A young English-speaking Abwehr officer named Walter Praetorius had been appointed to find a renegade Englishman worthy of training as a top-class spy. Praetorius was a committed Nazi in his politics, but a confirmed Anglophile in his tastes. His maternal great-grandfather, Henry Thoms, had been a Scottish flax merchant who emigrated from Dundee to the Baltic port of Riga, and married a German woman. Praetorius was fiercely proud of his British blood, and liked to remind anyone who would listen that he was a scion of the "Chiefly line of Clan McThomas."

The young Praetorius had graduated from Berlin University. In 1933, at age twenty-two, he spent a year at Southampton University improving his English as part of an Anglo-German student-exchange scheme. He intended to become a teacher. In England, Praetorius played the flute, rowed for the university, and began to sport the clothes and airs of an English gentleman. But above all, he danced. The most lasting legacy from his year in Britain was an unlikely but intense passion for English country dancing. He learned the reels and sword dances of his Scottish ancestors, but he fell in love with morris dancing. The English tend to mock morris dancing, but Praetorius found the dancers with their odd hats and peculiar rituals quite captivating. During summer vacation, he cycled around England, photographing folk dances and analyzing the dance steps. After months of careful study, he pronounced that morris dancing was the root of all dancing in the world, and therefore a foundation of world culture (a remarkable theory never proposed by anyone else, before or since).

Praetorius was popular at Southampton, where he was nicknamed "Rusty" by his contemporaries on account of the reddish tinge to his receding hair, and remembered as a "kind, gentle type

of personality." But he was also deeply impressionable, one of nature's extremists and liable to fits of excessive and irrational enthusiasm. When he returned to Germany in 1936, his obsession with folk
dancing was soon replaced by an even more extreme passion for fascism. According to British police files, his mother was already a
"rabid Nazi," and young Walter embraced the new creed with characteristic fervor and naiveté, rising swiftly through the ranks of the
Hitler Youth. The "superiority of the German and Anglo-Saxon
races over all others" became an article of faith. The outbreak of war
was an opportunity to demonstrate German strength in the ranks of
the SS. The death of his only brother, Hans, in Poland in the early
days of the war served merely to inflame him further. Rusty, the gentle flutist with the passion for country dancing, had become a committed, unquestioning Nazi.

Adopting the spy name "Walter Thomas" in honor of his Scottish forebears, SS Oberleutnant Praetorius set to work diligently
trawling through paperwork and scouring prisons, refugee centers,
and POW camps in search of ideal spy material. He traveled to Jersey in search of collaborators, and stayed at the Almadoux Hotel. He
interviewed criminals and deserters, British citizens trapped in the
occupied territories, and even IRA sympathizers, Irishmen who
might be recruited to fight against Britain. None would suffice.
Then, in late March 1942, Praetorius sent an excited message to the
newly appointed chief of the Nantes Abwehr station (or Abwehr-
stelle), reporting that he had located an English thief in a Paris
prison who "might be trained for sabotage work," and was going to
interview him at once.

CHAPTER SIX

Dr. Graumann

CHAPMAN BEGAN TO explore his new home, with Praetorius (alias "Thomas") as his guide and guard. Chapman's bedroom, on the top floor of La Bretonnière, was directly above that of Graumann, whose suite occupied most of the first floor. Next door to Chapman slept Keller, whose bedroom was also the radio room. Wojch and Schmidt shared a room, and Praetorius occupied the bedroom next to Graumann. The ground floor consisted of the dining room, an elegant smoking room with wall panels painted in the style of Fragonard, and a large study with desks around the walls and a steel safe in the corner. A pretty gardener's cottage stood alongside the main building, the ground floor of which had been converted into a chemical laboratory for making explosives, with pestles and mortars, scales, and rows of sinister-looking bottles lining the walls.

La Bretonnière had a full contingent of domestic staff: thirty-year-old Odette did the cooking and housekeeping, aided by Jeanette, a teenager. Two gardeners—one a released prisoner—came daily to cut the grass, tend the flower beds, weed the vegetable patch, and feed the chickens, goats, and pigs housed on the grounds.

Chapman's training began at once. A Morse set was produced, and under the tuition of Keller and Praetorius he was taught to distinguish between a dot and a dash. From there he graduated to the letters with two elements, then three, and finally the entire alphabet in German. He was taught elementary radio shorthand, tricks for memorizing sequences of letters, and how to assemble a radio set.

Three days after his arrival, the gardeners were sent home early and Wojch set off a timed explosion in the garden, followed by a demonstration of "chemical mixing" in the laboratory. The red-faced saboteur handled the volatile compounds with extraordinary dexterity, and Chapman, who prided himself on his knowledge of explosives, was impressed: "He just got hold of the stuff, looked at it, tasted it, and started mixing. I don't think he was a chemist, he'd simply been very well trained." Every day, Chapman and Wojch would work in the laboratory, making homemade bombs and incendiary devices from simple ingredients such as sugar, oil, and potassium chlorate. Chapman was set to work memorizing formulas.

Leo began teaching him how to jump and roll in preparation for his parachute drop. A ladder was erected against the tallest beech tree in the garden, and the height of Chapman's jump gradually increased, until he could leap from thirty feet without hurting himself. After the years of imprisonment, he was in poor physical shape, so Leo devised a strict exercise regime: Chapman would chop wood until his shoulders ached, and every morning Praetorius would accompany him on a four-mile run along the banks of the Erdre. Chapman was deeply affected by "the beauty of the river near Nantes," reflecting that it was only since leaving prison "that he had begun to realise how much beauty there was in the world."

For Chapman, these were strangely idyllic days. A bell would summon the men to breakfast at 8:30 a.m., and at 10:00 a.m. Chapman would practice sending radio messages to the other Abwehr posts in Paris and Bordeaux. The rest of the morning might be taken up with sabotage work, coding exercises, or parachute practice. Lunch was at 12:30 p.m., followed by a siesta until 3:00 or 3:30 p.m., followed by more training. In the evening, they might play bridge, or bowls on the lawn, or walk up the road to the Café des Pêcheurs, a small wood-paneled bar in the village, and watch the sun go down over the river, drinking beer at 3 francs a glass. Sometimes, accompanied by other members of the team, Chapman would drive out into the countryside to purchase black-market food: fresh eggs, bread, hams, and wine. The negotiating was done by one of the drivers, a Belgian named Jean, for the French farmers would charge a German more. The food was expensive—a ham could cost as much as 2,500 francs—but there seemed to be no shortage of money.

At La Bretonnière, the alcohol flowed copiously. Dr. Graumann's drinking was particularly spectacular: Chapman calculated that the chief put away at least two bottles of wine a night, followed by glass after glass of brandy. It seemed to have no effect on him whatever. On Saturdays, the household would climb into the unit's four cars, each with French registrations and an SS pass, and drive into Nantes, where they would dine at Chez Elle, dance at the Café de Paris, or visit the cabaret, Le Coucou, where black-market champagne cost 300 francs a bottle. Chapman paid for nothing, and was issued as much "pocket money" as he desired. On these trips in to town, Chapman spotted "V-signs," the mark of the French resistance, chalked on walls in public places. Some diligent Nazi had inserted a swastika inside each V, "thus reversing the propaganda." A few of the men visited the German-controlled brothel in town—pug-faced Albert was a regular at the establishment, and extolled the charms of *les jolies filles* there with such gusto that the others nicknamed him "Joli Albert," a most inapt description.

Chapman found Wojch to be particularly good company: "He liked life, he always had plenty of money, [he was] rather flashy, liked the girls and the drink." He, too, was a former boxer and formidably strong. He would challenge the others to a form of wrestling match in which each contestant would clasp his opponent's hand and then try to force him to his knees. Wojch invariably won.

Chapman began to imagine these men as his friends. He never doubted that the names he knew them by were real. He once heard Thomas referred to as Praetorius, but simply assumed this must be a nickname.

But for all their bibulous bonhomie, his new companions were guarded in their words, furtive in their behavior, and secretive in their activities outside the walls of the compound. From time to time, Wojch or Schmidt would disappear, for a week or longer. When they returned, Chapman would discreetly inquire where they had been. The conversation, he recalled, tended to follow the same pattern:

"Had a good trip?"

"Yes. Not too bad."

"Where did you go?"

"Oh, out of the country."

Chapman learned never to demand a direct answer. Once, when drunk, he asked Wojch if he had ever been to America. Wojch's smile was cold. "What do you want to ask questions like that for?"

Beneath a veneer of informality, security was tight. All important documents were held in the office safe. From time to time, Chapman would observe Graumann go into the garden with a secret document or letter, "take it out and light a cigarette [with it] and burn the whole envelope." At night, two ferocious Alsatian dogs roamed the grounds, keeping intruders out and Chapman in. One morning, Keller found Chapman alone in the radio room, and brusquely ordered him to leave. The door was always locked after that, and rigged with an electric alarm. When Graumann discovered that Chapman had taken to swimming in the Erdre in the early morning, he assembled the staff for a ferocious roasting: "Good God! Is he going out alone? He has no papers on him. What if the French police pick him up?"

Later, the chief took Chapman aside and gently explained: "Look here, if you are going out swimming, take one of the boys along with you. If ever you want to go out, they have orders that you have only to ask, and one of the boys will go with you."

Inevitably, however, Chapman began to glean snippets of information from his housemates. Leo, Wojch, and Schmidt were "more or less reckless, the lads of the village." Wojch boasted that he had been an Olympic boxer before the war. He plainly knew London well, and he waxed sentimental over a former girlfriend, an Irish chambermaid in the Hyde Park Hotel. From casual remarks, Chapman picked up that Wojch had been involved in the dynamiting of a Paris hotel before the invasion of France, an attack in which many Allied officers died. Small but telling details emerged about their earlier lives. Thomas wore his English university boating tie at every opportunity, and boasted that he had been the best oarsman at Southampton. Albert revealed that before the war he had been an agent for a German firm in Liberia. Leo had been a boxer and prize-fighter.

When Chapman asked Schmidt where he got his Cockney accent from, he explained that before the war he had worked as a waiter in Frascati's, the London restaurant. He had visited several of Chapman's old Soho haunts, including Smokey Joe's and the Nest, and recalled the tea dances at the Regal Theatre near Marble Arch. Slowly, it dawned on Chapman that these men must be more than mere instructors; they were experienced, active spies and saboteurs, who had been deployed in France and Britain since before the outbreak of war.

But if some of "the boys" were coming into sharper focus, their leader concealed his past behind steel shutters of politeness that fired Chapman's curiosity. For wireless practice, Graumann would set him the task of transmitting English nursery rhymes such as "Mary had a little lamb" and "This little piggie went to Market." "These were things," Chapman reflected, "which I thought only an Englishman would know"; but Graumann claimed to have visited England only once. When Chapman remarked to Graumann on his "terribly English accent," he batted away the implied question, saying he had been taught by a "very good private tutor."

One night, over dinner, the conversation turned to dogs. "I'll show you a photograph of my dog," said Graumann, rising from the table. Several minutes later, he returned with a torn photograph. The dog was visible, but the face of whoever was holding it had been torn away.

"Dr. Stephan Graumann" was, in reality, nothing of the sort. His real name was Stephan Albert Heinrich von Gröning. He was an aristocrat of impeccable breeding, great wealth, and luxurious tastes; indeed, the "really good brandy" he had poured down Chapman on his first evening at La Bretonnière was a fitting leitmotif for his life.

The von Grönings had been the first family in the northern city of Bremen for some eight centuries, amassing a vast fortune through trading well and marrying better. Over the years, the powerful clan had supplied seventeen members of the Bremen parliament and one notable eighteenth-century diplomat, Georg, who studied with Goethe at Leipzig and then served as ambassador to the court of Napoléon. In recognition of this achievement, he was awarded the aristocratic title "von," and the von Grönings had been getting steadily richer, and grander, ever since.

Born in 1898, Stephan had been brought up in circumstances of extreme privilege. His mother was an American heiress of German extraction named Helena Graue (hence his *nom d'espion:* "Graumann"). At home, the von Grönings spoke English, with an upperclass accent. Home was an enormous town house in the main square of Bremen, a self-satisfied statement in stucco and stone with five stories, a fabled library, several old master portraits, and an army of servants to wait on young Stephan: to polish his shoes, to cook his meals, to drive him to an exclusive private school in a carriage with glass windows and bearing the family crest.

Von Gröning's pampered life very nearly came to a premature end in 1914 when World War I erupted, and he joined the army. But not for young Stephan some dowdy and uncomfortable billet in the trenches; he was commissioned as an *Oberleutnant* in the legendary White Dragoons, perhaps the most elite cavalry regiment in the imperial army. Von Gröning took part in one of the last cavalry charges in history, during which most of the regiment was annihilated by British machine-gun fire. He survived, and was awarded the Iron Cross, second class, for bravery. Von Gröning's war was a short one. He contracted pneumonia, then tuberculosis, and was invalided out of the army. His mother sent him to recuperate at Davos, the fashionable health spa in Switzerland, where he met and fell in love with a Welsh woman named Gladys Nott Gillard, who was also tubercular and highborn, but penniless. They married in St. Luke's church, in Davos, on December 19, 1923.

The von Grönings rented a large mansion in Davos, called the Villa Baby, and then set off traveling, back to Bremen, to Hamburg, and finally to Bavaria. Along the way, von Gröning acquired a coffee business—Gröning and Schilling—which almost immediately went bust. Then he began gambling on the stock exchange, and lost even more money. Had he not considered it vulgar to count one's wealth, he might have realized that apart from the great house at Bremen and some fine oil paintings, he was heading for bankruptcy.

Charming, brave, intellectually gifted but indolent, at the end of the war von Gröning found himself at something of a loose end, which is where he remained for the next seventeen years. He had no desire to study. He collected etchings by Rubens and Rembrandt. He traveled a little, drank a lot, and took no physical exercise of any kind (he rode a bicycle only once in his life, but declared the experience "uncomfortable" and never repeated it). After his failed coffee enterprise, von Gröning would have nothing more to do with business or trade, and fully occupied his time behaving as if he was rich, which he blithely assumed he was. "He was delightful company, and very clever," one member of the family put it, "but he never actually *did* anything at all."

Stephan and his wife shared an interest in lapdogs, strong drink, and spending money they did not have; but not much else. They divorced in 1932, on the grounds of von Gröning's "illicit association with another woman." He was required to provide alimony of 250 marks a month, which was paid by his mother. He then agreed to pay Gladys a lump sum of 4,000 marks, but somehow failed to pay that either. Gladys was reduced to teaching English at a school in Hamburg, while her ex-husband would lie on the sofa in the library of the family home for days on end, reading books in German, English, and French, and smoking cigars. But they remained friends. Von Gröning did not make enemies easily.

Von Gröning had observed the rise of fascism from a lofty distance. He was a patriotic monarchist and an old-fashioned aristocrat from an earlier age. He had little time for the posturing Brownshirts with their extreme ideas. He regarded anti-Semitism as vulgar, and Hitler as an upstart Austrian "oik" (though at the time he kept that opinion to himself).

The outbreak of the Second World War gave new purpose to von Gröning's dilettante existence. At the age of thirty-nine he rejoined the German cavalry—a very different organization from the elegant

lancers of his youth—and served on the eastern front as a staff officer attached to Oberkommando 4 Heeresgruppe Mitte. After a year,
he applied to join the Abwehr. The secret military intelligence service of the German High Command was something of an ideologi-
cal anomaly: It contained its share of Nazi fanatics, but alongside
them were many men of von Gröning's stamp—officers of the old
school, determined to win the war, but opposed to Nazism. The Abwehr was epitomized by its leader, Admiral Wilhelm Canaris, a spy of
great subtlety who ran the Abwehr as a personal fiefdom. Hitler
never trusted Canaris, rightly, for the admiral might eventually have
put out feelers to Britain, seeking to negotiate an end to the war by
removing the Führer.

Espionage appealed to von Gröning, intellectually and ideologi-
cally, while his command of languages and knowledge of English
and American culture made him a valuable asset in the secret service. The years spent lounging in the library at Bremen had not
been entirely wasted: behind the hooded eyes and jovial manner was
a practiced and cynical student of human nature. His outwardly affable demeanor encouraged others to confide in him, but as a von
Gröning of Bremen, he always maintained his distance. "He could
mix in any company, but he always knew who he was." He was swiftly
spotted as the coming man within the Abwehr, and when Canaris
was looking for someone to run his new Nantes spy school, von
Gröning seemed the obvious person to appoint.

Von Gröning liked Chapman. He admired the sheer energy of
the man, so different from his own aristocratic languor. And he
knew he could turn him into a powerful secret weapon.

The photograph he handed Chapman had once shown Gladys
hugging their pet dog, a Sealyham terrier. But before coming downstairs, he had carefully torn Gladys out of the picture. Von Gröning
was not going to run the risk, however small, that Chapman might
recognize his British ex-wife, and thus obtain a clue to the real identity of "Dr. Graumann."

Von Gröning bound Chapman ever closer to the team. The psy-
chology was simple, but effective. The Englishman was flattered and
spoiled, drawn into an intense atmosphere of secretive camaraderie.

Like many brutal men, including Hitler himself, the members of the Nantes Abwehr section could also be sentimental and nostalgic. Von Gröning set up a *Heimecke*—a "home corner"—on the bureau in the smoking room, where the men were encouraged to display pictures of their hometowns, and somehow obtained a photograph of Berwick-upon-Tweed, the nearest town he could to find to Chapman's birthplace of Burnopfield. Birthdays were celebrated with cakes, gifts, and torrents of drink. Von Gröning encouraged informality, and allowed the men to daub graffiti on the walls of the unused attics. One drew a caricature of Hitler as a carrot. It was Chapman who carefully etched the picture of a blond woman with a striking resemblance to Betty Farmer.

Von Gröning was privately amused to see the Führer mocked as a vegetable, but he took pains to remind Chapman that he was now part of a victorious German army that had conquered half of Europe and would soon bring Britain and Russia to their knees. Praetorius, as the most committed Nazi in the group, kept up a steady stream of Nazi jingoism.

Inevitably, the combination of healthy living, good food, group bonding, and propaganda began to have the desired effect. Chapman felt himself drawn to what he called the "German spirit," his vanity fed by the belief that this training school, staffed by hard and hard-drinking men, had been established for him alone. Every meal began with the chorus of "Heil Hitler!" with the Englishman joining in. When Thomas declared that Britain was losing the war, Chapman believed him, though such "gloating" left him feeling "sick at heart."

At the end of a boozy evening, the trainee spy could be found lustily singing "Lili Marlene" with the rest of the crew. "Lili Marlene," he declared, was his favorite song, expressing "the hopes of every man who has left his girl behind."

Chapman's head was being turned by all the attention. But it was not turning nearly so far as von Gröning imagined.

• • •

It is impossible to say when Chapman decided to start spying on his German spymasters. Many years later, he candidly admitted that he did not know quite when, or even why, he began to collect information. Perhaps he was merely taking out an insurance policy against an uncertain future. The instincts of the spy and the thief are not so different: both trade in stolen goods, on similar principles. The value of information depends on the buyer's hunger, but it is a seller's market. Slowly at first, and with great care, Chapman began to build up a stock of secrets that would be of supreme interest to British intelligence.

He noticed the way that von Gröning assiduously read the personal advertisements in the *Times,* and sometimes the *Manchester Guardian,* occasionally underlining passages and taking notes. He overheard that Wojch had been on a sabotage mission to Spain during one of his unexplained absences, and when the door to the small anteroom off the study was left open, he spotted at least fifty pounds of gelignite in neat stacks. Inside a cupboard in von Gröning's bedroom, he saw racks of German military uniforms "of every kind in different lockers with all kinds of numbers." He noted how von Gröning took the codebooks after radio practice and carefully locked them in the safe. Given the opportunity and some gelignite, Chapman knew he could crack that safe.

Chapman claimed to have manufactured a set of skeleton keys to open and snoop inside various locked drawers around the house. This seems unlikely, given how closely he was monitored, but he certainly eavesdropped on his companions, literally, by boring a small hole under the eaves of his bedroom into von Gröning's bathroom. (If challenged, he planned to say he was putting down chemicals from the lab, to poison the rats that ran behind the paneling and kept him awake at night.) By pressing his ear to the hole, he could faintly hear the conversation taking place below, though he learned nothing of interest. He began to make notes: of crystal frequencies, code words, and the times of radio transmission between Nantes, Paris, and Bordeaux. He noted the position of the antiaircraft gun emplacements in the area, and the German military headquarters at the château on the other side of the river, camouflaged with netting. Although he had been instructed not to, he carefully wrote down the chemical formula of each bomb.

As the training gathered pace, senior officials in the Abwehr began to take an interest in von Gröning's protégé, and Chapman found himself being inspected and tested, like a prize specimen at a country fair. In May, Praetorius escorted him to an apartment in the rue de Luynes in Paris to meet a fat man with a red face, who drank champagne and told English jokes, but who asked a series of penetrating questions. From his demeanor, Chapman assumed he must be "a fairly high bug" in the organization. Von Gröning would say only that this individual was "one of our best men."

Soon afterward, a German in civilian clothes arrived from Angers in a chauffeur-driven car. The stranger was extraordinarily ugly and quite bald, save for a fringe of hair at the back of his head, with discolored, gold-filled teeth. He wore a thick coat, carried a leather portfolio, and smoked cigars continuously. Von Gröning treated him with exaggerated respect. Chapman thought he looked "like a gigolo." The bald man grilled Chapman about codes and sabotage. After he had left, Praetorius let slip that the visitor was "an old Gestapo man," the head of counterespionage in western France, responsible for catching enemy spies with a team of radio interceptors working around the clock in shifts to pick up "black senders," clandestine wireless operators sending messages to Britain. The Angers spy catcher had asked that Chapman be transferred to his team for a month, to act as a "stool pigeon amongst Allied agents in the Germans' hands, and as a general aid in counter-espionage work"—a request von Gröning had indignantly refused. "Fritz" was his personal asset, and von Gröning was not about to relinquish him.

In June 1942, Chapman was taken to Paris for his first real parachute jump. He would start at nine hundred feet, he was told, and gradually increase to fifteen hundred feet. After a night at the Grand Hotel and dinner at Poccardi's Italian restaurant on the Left Bank, he was driven to a small airfield near Le Bourget airport, northeast of Paris, where Charles Lindbergh had landed after his transatlantic flight fifteen years earlier. Chapman and his parachute were loaded aboard a Junkers bomber, and minutes later he was floating down over the French countryside. His first jump was a complete success; his second, immediately afterward, was very nearly his last. The parachute failed to open properly, buckling in a gust of wind when he was fifty feet from the ground. He was swung high into the air, and then smashed down, face-first, onto the airfield tarmac. Chapman lost consciousness, one front tooth, one canine, and several molars. A German doctor patched him up. Back in Nantes, von Gröning sent him to the best local dentist, one Dr. Bijet, who set about reconstructing Chapman's battered face. After two weeks of operations, Chapman had a natty new set of gold teeth to replace those he had lost, and the Abwehr had a bill for 9,500 francs. The expense of Chapman's dental work would prompt the first of several heated exchanges between von Gröning and his Paris superiors.

Chapman's wireless skills steadily improved. Praetorius timed him with a stopwatch, and announced he had attained a speed of seventy-five letters a minute, using a hand cipher (as distinct from one encoded on the Enigma machine) based on a single code word: BUTTERMILK. Without the code word, Praetorius assured him, the code was "unbreakable." As he gained in confidence, like most radio operators, Chapman began to develop his own "fist"—individual characteristics that another wireless operator or receiver could become familiar with. Chapman always ended his transmissions with a "laughing out" sign: "HE HU HO HA," or some variation thereof. He called these flourishes "my little mottoes."

Soon he graduated from the German transmitter to a radio of British manufacture, apparently seized from a British agent in France. Usually, the practice messages were coded from German, but he was also required to transmit in English and French. He sent poems, rhymes, proverbs, and sayings. One day, he tapped out a message: "It is very cold here but better than in Russia." He sent Maurice, the long-suffering chief radio operator in Paris, a message asking him to buy Odette, their housekeeper, a wedding present on his behalf. A little while later, he tried out an English joke: "A man went into a shop and asked the price of the ties displayed. The customer was astonished when he heard the high price and said one could buy a pair of shoes for that price. You would look funny, said the shopkeeper, wearing a pair of shoes round your neck. Fritz." It was not a good joke, but then the Paris operators seemed to have had no sense of humor at all. "What silly business is this?" the Paris station responded.

As spring turned to summer, La Bretonnière was a place of quiet contentment, save for the occasional deafening explosion in the back garden. When neighbors complained, they were told that the German engineers were detonating mines found during road construction. In July, von Gröning reported to Paris that Fritz had passed a series of tests, and was responding well to training. The chief of the Nantes spy school was enjoying himself. Managing La Bretonnière was a little like running an exclusive, intensely private men's club, even if the guests were a trifle uncouth.

Chapman was also happy. "I had everything I wanted," he reflected. He also had a new companion. On a black-market expedition in the countryside, Chapman had bought and adopted a young pig, which he christened Bobby. The name was probably a reference to his previous life. The British bobbies (also, less affectionately, referred to as "pigs") had chased Chapman for years; now Bobby the Pig followed him everywhere. An intelligent and affectionate animal, Bobby lived in the grounds of the house. At Chapman's whistle, he would come running, like a well-trained dog, and then lie with his trotters in the air to have his stomach scratched. When Chapman went swimming in the Erdre (von Gröning had by now relaxed his rules on unaccompanied bathing), Bobby would join him, flopping around in the muddy shallows. Then the Englishman and his faithful pig would walk happily home together through the cowslips and yellow irises.

CHAPTER SEVEN

Codebreakers

IN THE SUMMER of 1942, the analysts of Bletchley Park—the secret code and cipher center hidden deep in the Buckinghamshire countryside—decoded one of the most bizarre messages of the entire war. It had been sent from the Abwehr station at Nantes to the Abwehr headquarters in Paris, and it read: "Dear France. Your friend Bobby the Pig grows fatter every day. He is gorging now like a king, roars like a lion and shits like an elephant. Fritz." (The refined codebreaking ladies of Bletchley did not hold with vulgarity; they substituted the word "shits" with a series of asterisks.) Britain's wartime cipher experts had penetrated Nazi Germany's most sophisticated codes and read its most secret messages, but this one was, quite simply, incomprehensible.

For several months, Britain's codebreakers and spy catchers had been following the Fritz traffic with avid interest and mounting anxiety. They knew when this new, highly prized German spy had arrived in Nantes, and when he went to Paris. They knew how many teeth he had knocked out, and what the dentistry had cost. They knew he spoke English, and that he might even be an Englishman. And they knew he was heading for Britain.

The unraveling of Germany's top secret codes by a peculiar collection of mathematical savants in an English country house was perhaps the most spectacular espionage coup of this, or any other, war. The Radio Security Service began picking up Abwehr signals in

August 1940. The wireless set and codes obtained through Arthur Owens, "Agent Snow," had provided the codebreakers with a valuable head start, and the cryptographers at Bletchley Park ("Station X") were soon reading the Abwehr's principal hand cipher, the old-fashioned manual code. By December another team, under the leadership of the inspirationally eccentric Dillwyn "Dilly" Knox, had also broken the code used on Abwehr Enigma machines, the portable German cipher machine used to encrypt and decrypt secret messages. From that moment until the end of the war, British intelligence continuously intercepted and read the wireless traffic of the German secret service.

One member of the team put the success down to "brilliant guesswork and a good slice of luck," but it also came through the application of raw intellectual muscle and sheer hard work. The Abwehr's messages had to be intercepted, sent to Bletchley Park, sorted, distributed, the daily machine and message settings worked out, and finally deciphered and dispatched to the intelligence services. This extraordinary feat was usually performed by Dilly Knox and his team of large ladies (for some reason he employed only women, and only tall ones) within twenty-four hours. Knox himself frequently went about his work clad in pajamas and dressing gown; to relax, he would then go for a terrifyingly fast drive in the country lanes around Bletchley. Knox was one of the greatest cryptographers, and the worst drivers, Britain has ever produced. One day, he returned from motoring through the countryside and remarked casually: "It's amazing how people smile, and apologize to you, when you knock them over."

The successful deciphering of the secret German codes, code named Ultra, was the best-kept secret of the war. Its value to the war effort was almost incalculable. Churchill called the intercepts "My Golden Eggs" and guarded them jealously. The Abwehr never suspected that its messages were being read on a daily basis, and persisted in the mistaken belief that its codes were unbreakable. The wealth of intelligence produced by Ultra decrypts was referred to only as the "Most Secret Sources."

For the purposes of counterespionage, the Most Secret Sources gave early warning of which spies were arriving in Britain, where, and when. As a consequence, most of the "invasion spies" were picked up the moment they arrived in Britain and swiftly imprisoned. Several were executed. The Abwehr's attempt to build a wartime spy network in Britain was an unmitigated failure. Crucially, the German intelligence service never realized this, thanks to one soldier, one Oxford academic, and one inspired idea.

At the height of the invasion scare, Colonel Tommy Robertson, the MI5 officer who had handled the Snow case, approached his commanding officer, Dick White, and pointed out an obvious truth: A dead enemy spy can do no more harm, but neither can he (or she) do any good. A captured spy, however, could be persuaded to double-cross his German employers in exchange for his life, and then work for his British captors. Snow had already demonstrated the potential value of the controlled double agent, who could persuade the enemy to believe he was active and loyal when he was nothing of the sort. More important, over time, the double agent could be used to feed vital disinformation to the enemy. Thanks to the Most Secret Sources, British intelligence could even check whether the ruse was working. Robertson was insistent: Instead of putting enemy agents in prison or on the end of a rope, MI5 should put them to work.

Robertson's suggestion was forwarded to Guy Liddell, the subtle-minded, cello-playing director of "B Division," the branch of MI5 devoted to counterintelligence. Liddell gave his blessing at once, and, with cabinet approval, Robertson was duly appointed chief of a new section for catching enemy spies, turning them, and then running them as double agents. The new outfit was given the innocuously invisible name B1A. At the same time, another linked organization was established, with senior representatives of all the military intelligence services, the Home Forces and Home Defence, to assess the information, true and false, to be sent back via the double agents. This was named the "Twenty Committee," because the two Xs of a double cross make the number "twenty" in Roman numerals. This was precisely the sort of dry classical witticism favored by the man now appointed chairman of the Twenty Committee:

Major (and later Sir) John Cecil Masterman, a distinguished Oxford history don, all-around sportsman, successful thriller writer, and jailbird.

Masterman and Robertson formed the linchpins of the double-cross operation, and they ran it with such dazzling success that after the war Masterman could justifiably claim: "By means of the double-cross agent system *we actively ran and controlled the German espionage system in this country.*" (The italics are his, and deserved.) Theirs was a partnership of equals, and opposites: Robertson was a professional, dealing with the nuts and bolts of running the double agents, while Masterman liaised with the top brass. Robertson was the technician, while Masterman was to become the great theoretician of the double cross.

Thomas Argyll Robertson was universally known as "Tar," on account of his initials. Born in Sumatra to colonial parents, Tar had spent much of childhood parked with an aunt in Tunbridge Wells, an experience that was lonely but formative, for it left him with an ability to chat to complete strangers with disarming frankness. He passed through Charterhouse and Sandhurst without, in his own estimation, learning very much, and became, briefly, an officer in the Seaforth Highlanders, and then, even more briefly, a bank clerk. In 1933, at the age of twenty-four, at the invitation of Vernon Kell, the first director general of MI5, he had given up the staid world of banking to become a full-time intelligence officer, initially dealing with political subversion, arms trafficking, and counterespionage. "Immensely personable and monstrously good looking," in the words of Christopher Harmer, a fellow officer, he had the rare knack of being able to talk to anyone, anywhere, about anything. Bishops, admirals, whores, crooks, and revolutionaries all found it equally easy to confide in Tar Robertson. Masterman pointed out, a touch acidulously, that "Tar was in no sense an intellectual." Tar was no bookworm. Instead, he read people. He excelled in a job that "involved a great deal of conversing with suspect people in pubs . . . meeting, greeting, chatting, charming, chuckling, listening, offering another drink, observing, probing a little, listening some more and ending up with all sorts of confidences the other person never thought he would utter." He continued to wear the distinctive McKenzie tartan trews of the Seaforth Highlanders, a strangely conspicuous choice of attire for someone running one of the most secret organizations in the world. (The tartan trousers earned him another, more appropriately colorful nickname: "Passion Pants.")

John Masterman was cut from very different cloth. It is easiest to imagine him as the antithesis, in every conceivable way, of Eddie Chapman. He was highly intellectual, intensely conventional, and faintly priggish, with a granite sense of moral duty. Masterman was the embodiment of the British establishment: He belonged to all the right clubs, and played tennis at Wimbledon, hockey for England, and cricket whenever possible. Spare and athletic, he had a hard and handsome face, as if carved out of marble. He neither smoked nor drank, and lived in a world of High Tables and elevated scholarship, exclusively inhabited by wealthy, privileged, intelligent English men.

A confirmed bachelor, he might have been homosexual, but if so, in a wholly repressed and contented English way. Women were simply invisible to him; in the 384 pages of his autobiography, only one woman is mentioned with affection, and that is his mother, with whom he lived in Eastbourne during the university vacations. In his spare time, he wrote detective thrillers set in an imaginary Oxford college and starring an amateur British sleuth in the Sherlock Holmes mold. These are somewhat dry and unemotional books, more intellectual puzzles than novels, but that was how this clever, desiccated man regarded human nature—as a conundrum to be unpicked by reason. He seems a peculiar creature today, but John Masterman represented English traits that were once considered virtues: noblesse oblige, hard work, and unquestioning obedience to the norms of society. By his own account, he was "almost obsessively anxious to conform to accepted standards," just as Chapman was equally determined to defy them.

Yet Masterman had one thing in common with Chapman: He had spent four years in a prison. By a stroke of terrible ill fortune, as a newly elected fellow of Christ Church College, Oxford, in 1914, he was sent on a study course in Germany, and was trapped by the outbreak of the First World War. Masterman was interned in Ruhleben prison with a strange assortment of equally unlucky Britons: sailors, businessmen, academics, jockeys from the Berlin racecourse, sportsmen, workmen, tourists, and one Nobel Prize winner, Sir James Chadwick, who lectured his fellow prisoners on the mysteries of radioactivity. The young Masterman emerged after four years without visible scars, but he was weighed down by what he considered to be an inferiority complex. Almost all his friends and contemporaries had perished on the battlefields. "My predominant feeling was one of shame," he wrote. "I had played no part in the greatest struggle in our national history."

Masterman was already in his fiftieth year when the longed-for opportunity to play his part finally arrived with the offer to work in MI5. He seized it gratefully, and it was Britain's great good fortune that he did, for no man was better suited to the job. If Tar Robertson was the "real genius" of the double-cross system, as the historian Hugh Trevor-Roper put it, then John Masterman was its moral conscience, meticulously analyzing the motivations of men, patiently solving the riddle of the double cross, like a vast and complicated crossword puzzle.

Recruitment to MI5 was through the informal old-boy network, and Robertson, with the help of his deputy, a London solicitor named John Marriott, swiftly began putting together a team of gifted amateurs. Section B1A, when finally assembled, included lawyers, academics, an industrialist, a circus owner, at least one artist, an art dealer, and a poet. Tar himself was the only professional in the organization, which started its life in a requisitioned corner of Wormwood Scrubs prison before moving to a large and elegant house at 58 St. James's Street, in the heart of Mayfair. The team's in-house poet, Cyril Harvey, memorialized the building in camp verse:

> At 58, St James's Street
> The door is open wide
> Yet all who seek to enter here
> Must make their motives crystal clear
> Before they step inside,

That none may probe with fell intent
The Secrets of the Government.

Intercepted German spies were first interrogated at a secret military prison in West London, Camp 020. Only then, if suitable for double-agent work, would they be handed over to Tar Robertson and his case officers. If they refused to collaborate, they were either imprisoned or executed. Sometimes the death threat was overt. Masterman was unsentimental on this score. "Some had to perish, both to satisfy the public that the security of the country was being maintained, and also to convince the Germans that the others were working properly and were not under control." All but the most fanatical Nazis agreed to cooperate when faced with this choice, but their motives did not follow any established pattern. Some were merely terrified, desperate to save their skins, but there were also, Masterman found, "certain persons who have a natural predilection to live in that curious world of espionage and deceit, and who attach themselves with equal facility to one side or the other, so long as their craving for adventure of a rather macabre type is satisfied."

If the intercepted spy was considered suitable, then the hard work began, starting with a strenuous exercise of the imagination. In Masterman's words, the case officer must penetrate the world of his adopted spy, to "see with the eyes and hear with the ears of his agent," and create for him a life as close as possible to the one he was pretending to live. If, say, the double agent was claiming to transmit from Aylesbury, then he needed to know what Aylesbury was like and, if possible, to be physically in or very near Aylesbury, since it was suspected that the Germans could pinpoint transmissions, perhaps to within a one-mile radius.

The logistical challenge was immense. Each double agent required a safe house and a staff of at least five people: a case officer, a wireless operator to monitor or transmit his messages, two guards on twelve-hour shifts to ensure he did not run away, and a trusted housekeeper to look after and feed the group. Meanwhile, the case officer had to establish what his agent had been sent to find out, and then reproduce a fake facsimile of it, but without damaging the war effort. An agent who transmitted useless information would be seen as a failure by the Abwehr, and dropped. To maintain German confidence, the double agent must send a mixture of true but essentially harmless information known as "chicken feed," extraneous facts, and undetectably false tidbits, along with whatever disinformation was agreed upon.

Deciding what could or could not be sent to the enemy was the delicate task of the Twenty Committee. Meanwhile, the double agent must be kept busy and happy, because if he turned bad, and somehow managed to inform his German spymasters that he was under British control, then the entire system would be jeopardized. Every double agent, Masterman observed, "is prone to be vain, moody and introspective, and therefore idleness, which begets brooding, should be of all things most carefully avoided." Tar Robertson swiftly discovered that in order to keep these agents sweet, it was sensible to reward them, and not just with their lives. The "principle of generosity" was thus established, and agents who had brought over cash, as many did, were often allowed to keep a percentage.

The ideal case officer needed to be a combination of guard, friend, psychologist, radio technician, paymaster, entertainments organizer, and private nursemaid. It helped if he or she was also a saint, since the individual being cosseted and coaxed in this way was quite likely to be extremely unpleasant, greedy, paranoid, treacherous, and, at least initially, an enemy of Britain. Finally, all of the above had to be performed at breakneck speed, because the longer a spy took to make contact with the enemy, the more likely his German spymaster would suspect that he had been captured and turned.

The results show just how brilliantly Tar Robertson chose the men and women "of high intelligence and clearly defined purpose" who made up his team. Some 480 suspected enemy spies were detained in Britain in the course of the war. Just 77 of these were German. The rest were, in descending order of magnitude, Belgian, French, Norwegian, and Dutch, and then just about every conceivable race and nationality, including several who were stateless. After

1940, very few were British. Of the total intercepted, around a quarter were subsequently used as double agents, of whom perhaps 40 made a significant contribution. Some of these lasted only a short time before their cases were terminated; a few continued to delude their German handlers until the end of the war. A tiny handful, the very best, were involved in the greatest strategic deception of all, Operation Fortitude, by which the Germans were persuaded to believe that the Allied invasion of France would be concentrated on the Pas de Calais, and not Normandy.

As early as 1942, Tar Robertson's team could be justly proud of its efforts. Scores of spies had been rounded up with the aid of the Most Secret Sources, and many had been recruited as double agents. Yet the B1A team remained in a state of deep anxiety, beset by the possibility that a spy could slip through the mesh, attempt to contact an agent already operating in Britain, discover that he was being controlled, and then blow the entire double-cross network.

Those fears were exacerbated when the body of a man named Englebertus Fukken, alias William Ter Braak, was discovered in Cambridge. A Dutch agent, Ter Braak had parachuted into Britain in November 1940. Five months later, after running out of money, he had climbed into a public air-raid shelter and shot himself in the head with his German pistol. If Ter Braak could survive undetected in Britain for so long, then other German agents must be at large. Masterman voiced the nagging fear of every wartime spy catcher: "We were obsessed by the idea that there might be a large body of spies over and above those whom we controlled."

Moreover, MI5 could not ignore the exceptionally low grade of the spies it had caught. Indeed, the level of ineptitude among the captured spies was such that some in the intelligence service wondered if they were being deliberately planted as decoys: "Could any intelligence service, let alone one run by the super-efficient Germans, be so incompetent?" wondered Ewen Montagu, the naval intelligence officer on the Twenty Committee. Perhaps the Germans were training up a troop of superspies to follow the dubious duds they had sent over to date. Perhaps an altogether better class of spy was already lurking undetected in Britain?

Tar Robertson's spy hunters therefore pricked up their ears when, early in February 1942, a reference to a hitherto unknown agent, code-named Fritz, was picked up by British interceptors, decoded by Bletchley Park, and passed on to the intelligence services. To judge from the intercepts, the Germans were taking a great deal of trouble over Fritz, who was also referred to as "C," and sometimes as "E." In May, the Paris branch of the Abwehr was instructed to buy a new set of clothes for Fritz. The following week, Nantes demanded a new wireless set from the stocks of captured British equipment. In June, the listeners discovered, some 9,500 francs had been spent on his teeth, damaged during a failed parachute jump—more money than most German spies were allocated for an entire mission.

The Nantes Abwehr began to refer to Fritz as Fritzchen, the diminutive form of the name, suggesting a certain intimacy with this new recruit. From the Most Secret Sources, it appeared that Stephan von Gröning, already identified by British intelligence as head of the Nantes Abwehr branch, was particularly taken with Fritz. In June, he boasted to Paris that Fritz could "now prepare sabotage material unaided." In July, he insisted that Fritz was utterly loyal, declaring that "any connection with the enemy is out of the question." Paris, more skeptical, replied by wondering if the word "not" had been accidentally omitted from von Gröning's message.

Meanwhile, the Radio Security Service reported that Fritz, plainly a novice wireless operator, was practicing Morse from the Nantes Abwehr branch, using a variation of the Vigenère code known as Gronsfeld. At first, his transmissions had been clumsy, and when he tried to transmit faster he merely succeeded "in making corrupt characters and in fumbling," but he was improving rapidly. "When he arrives in this country," the Radio Security Service reported, "he will send his messages in English." After listening to Fritz "practically every day for several weeks," the interceptor had "learned to recognise his unmistakable style and to record its peculiarities," the telltale "fist." His messages sometimes ended with a cheery "73," shorthand for "Best regards," or "FF," meaning "Is my message decipherable?" He routinely signed off with the laughing sign "HU HU HA HO," then the insulting "99," meaning "go to hell," or words to that effect. Fritz was turning into a first-rate radio operator, even if his messages were rather peculiar, and sometimes positively offensive.

By late summer, MI5 had assembled a thick dossier on Fritz. But they still did not know his real name, his mission, or the date and time of his planned arrival in Britain. And as for the identity of this shadowy associate nicknamed Bobby the Pig, with the regal appetite and the elephantine toilet habits, that, too, remained a mystery.

CHAPTER EIGHT

The Mosquito

ONE MORNING, VON GRÖNING handed Chapman a gun: a shiny American Colt revolver, with a loaded chamber. Chapman had never held a gun before. When he asked why he needed this weapon, von Gröning replied vaguely that he might want it "to shoot his way out of any difficulties he might encounter." Leo taught him how to aim and fire it, using a target erected in the grounds of La Bretonnière, and claimed he soon could hit a franc coin from fifty feet away.

The revolver was just one sign of von Gröning's growing trust. The cadaverous Praetorius no longer shadowed Chapman's every step, and he was allowed to take walks alone with Bobby, though instructed to remain close to the villa. He was permitted to move out of his top-floor room (having carefully disguised the holes in the wainscoting) and into a bedroom in the gardener's cottage, so that he could practice mixing explosives and incendiary mixtures in the laboratory whenever he desired. The homemade bombs were getting bigger and more sophisticated. He practiced making underwater fuses and tossing them into the duck pond. There were various tree stumps on the grounds, and Chapman was encouraged to try blowing them up. On one occasion, he packed too much dynamite into a large oak stump, which exploded with such force that chunks of burning wood were blasted into the garden of the house next door, narrowly missing a neighbor. Von Gröning was livid. Chapman was not quite the explosives expert he thought he was.

While he was attempting to construct a sulfuric acid fuse, the volatile mixture exploded, burning his hand, singeing off a hank of hair, and covering his face with smut. A French doctor bandaged the hand, and Chapman took to his bed. "I was suffering more from shock than anything," he wrote later.

Visitors continued to arrive at La Bretonnière, some to inspect Chapman's progress, others to talk to von Gröning or to undergo training. One of these was a Frenchman referred to only as "Pierre," a collaborator with round glasses who, in Chapman's words, "made all the right Heil Hitler noises." Pierre belonged to a Breton separatist group, Bretagne Pour les Bretons, and he was undergoing training as a fifth columnist in case an Allied invasion forced a German withdrawal. On another occasion, Chapman was allowed to be present during a meeting with two men, one of whom was introduced as "Monsieur Ferdinand" and the other a lad of about eighteen, who appeared quite petrified. These were members of a Gaullist cell, apparently planning to leave France via an established escape route and to join the Free French in London. Monsieur Ferdinand, it seemed, was prepared to smuggle Chapman along with them, for the right price. Von Gröning was clearly exploring alternative ways to get Chapman into Britain.

Von Gröning and his protégé grew closer. Chapman's own father had been distant, when he wasn't absent entirely, and he had not seen him now for a decade. Von Gröning, avuncular and apparently kindly, stepped into the role. The affection was not feigned on either part. In the evenings, while von Gröning soaked up the brandy, Chapman would listen rapt as the older man talked of art, music, and literature. They discovered a shared pleasure in the novels of H. G. Wells and the poetry of Tennyson. Very occasionally, von Gröning would stray into politics or military matters. He remained convinced that Germany would win the war, and that any attempt by the Allies to invade France would result in "a tremendous bloodbath." But his was the assessment of an experienced soldier, not a statement of ideology. To Chapman's surprise, he praised the tactical skill of the Allied invasion of North Africa, and described the British raid on nearby Saint-Nazaire as "very cleverly planned and excellently carried out." In August, the Allies launched the disastrous Dieppe raid on France's northern coast, with the loss of four thousand men killed, wounded, or captured. The German victory was celebrated with a party at La Bretonnière, but von Gröning also raised a toast to the "courage and daring" of the Allied commandos.

If von Gröning's view of the war was nuanced and balanced, then that of his deputy was precisely the opposite. Praetorius and von Gröning had never warmed to each other. Praetorius regarded his boss as the snobbish remnant of an old world, while the younger man was altogether too enthralled by Hitler for von Gröning's liberal tastes. The young Nazi insisted the scale of Russian losses meant victory on the eastern front was imminent. Stalingrad would fall in 1943, to be followed by a "full-scale attack on Britain with all main forces from Europe and the Russian Front." Rommel would conquer all, he insisted, while the prospect of a "terrific Blitz" on Britain, the land he so admired, sent Praetorius into spasms of delight: "You can imagine what it would be like with all of our Stukas and all of the men who have been trained and hardened and toughened," Praetorius exclaimed. "What could the Americans do?" Chapman was beginning to find him extremely irritating.

One morning in midsummer, von Gröning instructed Chapman to pack his bags: He was going to Berlin with "Thomas" for the next phase of his training. In the early hours of a foggy morning, the train from Paris pulled up in a small railway station on the outskirts of the German capital. A car was waiting for them. Chapman asked where they were heading. Praetorius seemed tense and embarrassed. "It is rather awkward at the present moment because if anyone realises you are British we should both be shot without any questions being asked." He then added politely: "Would you mind not asking any more questions?" They seemed to be passing through densely wooded suburbs, but it was still dark outside and the driver had deliberately dimmed his headlights, so that Chapman could see almost nothing. From the faint shimmer of dawn on the horizon, he judged they were heading north.

After a drive of twenty-five minutes, they passed through a pair of iron gates guarded by three sentries in military uniform, down a long drive lined with flower beds, and through a high stone arch, before pulling up in front of a small *Schloss* with a tower, surrounded by trees, a high stone wall, and barbed-wire fences. At the door stood a man in early middle age, short but athletically built, with a dignified air. His wife, rather taller, hovered anxiously in the background; pictures of their children were arranged in the hall. The little man introduced himself as "Herr Doktor." He explained that Chapman was free to wander the castle grounds between lessons, but should on no account try to leave the estate.

Wojch had been a skilled teacher of practical sabotage, but Chapman's new tutor was in a different league. Over the next week, Chapman would be given an intensive course in the very latest explosive technology, by a master of the subject. MI5 later identified him as one Dr. Ackerman, a professional chemist, and one of the most knowledgeable explosives experts in Germany. Chapman was shown into a laboratory, with rows of cork-stopped glass bottles, test tubes, thermos flasks, measuring scales, pestles, and mortars. Patiently, painstakingly, the expert introduced Chapman to an unimagined universe of lethal science, the arcane secrets of explosives, burning mixtures, booby traps, and delayed sabotage.

He taught Chapman how make a time fuse from a cheap wristwatch, by inserting a small screw with two nuts on it into the celluloid face and then attaching one end of electrical wire connected to a flashlight battery via the winding mechanism; when the small hand touched the screw, a charge would pass from the battery into a fuse and ignite the explosion. Next he took an alarm clock and demonstrated how to delay an explosion for up to fourteen hours, by linking the detonator to the winding spring. If no clock or watch was available, he could make a fuse by filling an ink bottle with sulfuric acid and placing a strip of cardboard between glass and lid; the acid would slowly eat away the cardboard, finally making contact with the fuse screwed into the lid, where the heat of the reaction would detonate the explosive charge.

Next, he took a large lump of coal from the scuttle and showed Chapman how to drill a hole in it six inches deep and pack this with explosives and detonator, disguising the hole with plasticine, boot polish, and coal dust. Placed in the coal bunkers of a ship or train, the device would be invisible and inert, until shoveled into the furnace, where the heat would set it off.

Chapman was taught how to dynamite munitions trains and petrol dumps, how to pack an attaché case with explosives and then place pajamas or a towel on top, to muffle the alarm-clock fuse inside. He learned how to construct a booby trap from a package that exploded when the string around a parcel was cut: inside the string were two strands of wire insulated from one another, so that when cut with scissors, an electric circuit was completed, setting off the explosion. Ackerman drew diagrams showing how to connect a series of linked explosives with dynamite wire and detonating fuse, and explained the formula for calculating how much high explosive would be needed to bring down a bridge (length × breadth × depth × 2 = ½ number of grams of explosive required). Some of Ackerman's techniques were diabolically cunning: Placing a dead butterfly over the wire detonator attached to a railway line would ensure that the casual observer would never spot the device. When a train passed over it, the charge would explode, derailing the locomotive.

The little explosives teacher neither smoked nor drank, and paused only for meals. Chapman decided he was a perfectionist: "He insisted on exact proportions, never hurrying, grinding everything very small and mixing it very carefully." The ingredients needed to create a bomb could be bought over the counter at British hardware stores and pharmacies, Ackerman explained: potassium chlorate was a common slug killer, potassium nitrate, a fertilizer, potassium permanganate, a throat gargle; the British used ferric oxide as a floor stain, and ground aluminum as a silver paint powder. The lectures ran on late into the evening. After supper, Ackerman pulled up a chair beside the fire and continued his tutorials, sometimes calling on Praetorius to help translate technical terms.

After five days, the doctor finally seemed satisfied, and Chapman was exhausted. He and Praetorius were picked up by the same driver in the middle of the night and driven back to the station in darkness.

Back at La Bretonnière, Chapman was warmly greeted by von

Gröning, who announced that he had devised a small test for him. A friend, one Major Meier, was responsible for security in the local factories, including the nearby Battignolles locomotive works. Von Gröning had boasted to Meier that he was training up a sabotage agent, a former burglar who could break into anything; he bet he could even place a dummy bomb in the locomotive factory. Major Meier had accepted the wager. A few nights later, Chapman and Leo hauled themselves over the barbed wire surrounding the factory, slipped passed the slumbering guard, and placed a package, addressed to Major Meier, alongside the main office. Von Gröning was delighted; with the money from the wager, he threw yet another party in honor of "Fritz."

Chapman went back to his mephitic potions in the gardener's cottage. The successful raid on the locomotive works had been enjoyable, but after nearly five months in La Bretonnière, he was growing restless and frustrated by the enforced chastity. Leaving aside the whores of Nantes, he had barely seen a woman. The others laughed about the lack of female company, joking that they lived "like bloody monks."

One evening, Chapman, Albert, and Wojch went out on a "spree" in Nantes, where they picked up some girls in one of the official cars. Unluckily, a Gestapo officer spotted the women climbing into their car and an official complaint was filed. When it reached von Gröning's desk, he exploded. "There was a hell of a lot of trouble," Chapman wrote. Wojch suffered the brunt of von Gröning's fury: the rotund saboteur with the pearl tiepin was banished to a unit of the Wachkommando infantry based in distant Rocquencourt, near Paris. Chapman never saw him again. In a message to his bosses, von Gröning noted primly that Fritz, though ideal in every other respect, was apparently prone to what he called "undesirable emotional activity."

As always, when bored and sexually stymied, Chapman lapsed into what he called his "nihilistic" frame of mind. His mood darkened still further when he raised a subject that had been troubling him ever since leaving Romainville. He asked for permission to write to Tony Faramus. Von Gröning refused, but said he would send the young man a food parcel. A little later, Chapman inquired once more: "Could something be done for him?" Von Gröning told him that this was "impossible" and changed the subject. Chapman now descended into a dark depression. He would lie on his bed for hours, smoking and staring at the ceiling. At one point, he even asked "if he could return to the camp at Romainville." Von Gröning realized that unless he moved fast and put Chapman to work, he might lose this mercurial young spy prodigy altogether.

On August 29, 1942, Chapman was summoned to von Gröning's study and presented with a typed sheet of paper. He was told to read it and, if he agreed with the terms, to sign it. The document was a contract, a formally executed agreement to spy on his own country that is surely unique in the annals of legal history. The first section was a list of prohibitions: Chapman must never divulge to anyone the names of his German contacts in Jersey, France, or Germany, the places he had been, or the things he had learned. The penalty for violating any of these clauses would be death. Chapman would undertake to spy in the interests of the German High Command, and faithfully perform whatever mission he was set by the Abwehr. As compensation, he would be paid the following sums: while in France, he would receive 12,000 francs a month; from the date of his departure, he would be paid 300 reichsmarks a month, and payment would continue should he be captured. On his return, having completed his mission to the satisfaction of the Abwehr, he would receive the sum of 150,000 reichsmarks. Chapman estimated this was the equivalent of about £15,000—in fact, the value was nearer to £250, or around $15,000 at today's prices. The contract was not with the German government, but a personal legal agreement between Chapman and his spymaster: von Gröning had already signed it, in the name "S. Graumann (Doktor)."

The final clause was a triumph of German bureaucratic thinking: Chapman would be legally obliged to pay all relevant taxes on these sums in France. The German secret service was about to send Chapman on a mission of treachery in which it was likely he would be killed or executed, and they were worrying about his tax return.

As Chapman was digesting the terms of this extraordinary deal, the German spymaster asked him a question. If Scotland Yard caught him, approximately how many years could Chapman expect to spend in prison? Chapman had considered that question many times himself. He replied that he would probably receive a sentence of between fifteen and twenty years. The older man then turned to Praetorius and observed: "I don't suppose there would be much danger of him surrendering to the police then."

Chapman signed the contract, but later found himself pondering that apparently offhand comment. Graumann, a man he had come to admire, had chosen him not because he was special, but because he was a criminal with a past so crooked he would never dare run to the authorities. Chapman had always known that was part of the German calculation, but the remark stung, and the sting remained.

Filing away the signed contract, von Gröning began, for the first time, to outline Chapman's mission: In a few weeks, he would be parachuted into Britain with a wireless and enough money to survive for a long period. He would then find a place to hide out and gather a quantity of explosives, with help from his criminal associates if needed. There were many important tasks Chapman could perform in Britain, but his primary target was to sabotage the aircraft factory manufacturing the Mosquito bomber in Hatfield, Hertfordshire.

The De Havilland Mosquito—or *Anopheles de Havillandus,* as military wags liked to call it—had proved a lethal nuisance to the Nazis ever since it went into production in 1940. Indeed, its effect on the German High Command was positively malarial. Designed and built at the De Havilland Aircraft Company factory outside London, it was a revolutionary military aircraft. Constructed almost entirely of wood, with a two-man crew and no defensive guns, the little plane could carry four thousand pounds of bombs to Berlin. With two Rolls-Royce Merlin engines and a top speed of four hundred miles per hour, it could usually outrun enemy fighters. The Mosquito, nicknamed "the Wooden Wonder," could be assembled, cheaply, by cabinetmakers and carpenters. It could be used for photoreconnaissance, night fighting, U-boat killing, minelaying, and transport, but its main task was target bombing, and being so light and accurate, it could destroy a single building with minimal harm to civilians. In the course of the war, Mosquitoes would pick off the Gestapo headquarters in Oslo, Shell House in Copenhagen, and the Amiens jail.

Reichsmarschall Hermann Göring, head of the Luftwaffe, was particularly infuriated by the persistent little Mosquito; the mere mention of the plane could send him into a tailspin. "It makes me furious when I see the Mosquito," he once ranted. "I turn green and yellow with envy. The British, who can afford aluminium better than we can, knock together a beautiful wooden aircraft that every piano factory over there is building, and they give it a speed that they have now increased yet again. What do you make of that? There is nothing the British do not have. They have the geniuses and we have the nincompoops. After the war is over I'm going to buy a British radio set—then at least I'll own *something* that has always worked."

For reasons therefore both military and political, the Abwehr had been devising a plan to combat the Mosquito for months. If the De Havilland production line could be stopped, by crippling the factory boilers and generator, this could tip the air war in Germany's favor, demonstrate the worth of von Gröning's new agent, and boost the Abwehr's reputation. It might also mollify the irascible *Reichsmarschall.*

That afternoon, von Gröning sent an exultant wireless message to Paris, reporting that he had conducted "preliminary detailed discussions" with Fritz, and persuaded him to sign a contract. The message was picked up in Britain, where the MI5 officer monitoring the Fritz traffic remarked ominously: "Things seem at last to be coming to a head."

CHAPTER NINE

Under Unseen Eyes

THE CONTRACT IN Chapman's hands may have been legally un-
enforceable, signed with a false name, and frankly absurd, but it had
the desired psychological effect. The prospect of adventure sent
Chapman's spirits soaring once more. The drunken camaraderie of
La Bretonnière was pleasant, to be sure, but at the back of his mind
was Freda and the baby in England; also Betty; also Vera, his ex-wife;
and, if none of the aforementioned worked out, then any number
of Soho sirens.

The days accumulated in a succession of tests, trials, details, and
delays. The ugly spy catcher from Angers returned, in a "terrific
Chrysler with a wireless," to witness a demonstration of Chapman's
sabotage and shooting skills: He shot a line of wineglasses from fifteen paces, one after the other, and set off an acid fuse. The next
performance was for a colonel from a Panzer division, who appeared in a Mercedes: Chapman blew up a tree stump in a timed explosion using batteries and a wristwatch. The same evening, von
Gröning announced that he had tickets for the Folies Bergère, the
music hall that was still playing to full houses in occupied Paris.
Chapman was excited at the prospect of a night out in Paris, although his pleasure palled somewhat when he overheard von Gröning remark on the train that "the chief wanted to see him."
Chapman was not being taken to enjoy the spectacle; once again, he
was the spectacle.

That evening, as they entered the famous opera house in the Ninth Arrondissement, Chapman heard his spymaster whisper to Thomas: "Let Fritz go first, and *he* will just sit behind." The show was already under way in a froth of petticoated dancers doing the can-can when two men in civilian clothes quietly entered and sat directly behind them. One had a mustache and a pronounced limp: "He kept looking at me the whole time, sort of behind his programme," Chapman recalled. This individual was most probably Rudolf Bam-ler, head of Abwehr counterintelligence and one of the few die-hard Nazis in the organization. After the show, von Gröning left by taxi, while Praetorius and Chapman walked back to the hotel, pausing to look in the shop windows: "Each time I looked," wrote Chapman. "I saw these two men very carefully studying me."

Chapman was relieved to get back to the Grand Hotel. As he and Praetorius walked to their rooms, he heard American voices coming from von Gröning's suite. He turned to his minder: "Americans?"

"No, it's just two of our fellows having a game," said Praetorius, quickly. But that evening, by opening a cupboard door and pressing his ear to the folding partition that separated his room from that of von Gröning, he was sure that he could hear his chief talking to two Americans. One of them was saying: "Well, we would like to see the guy." Chapman felt certain the "guy" was him; he recalled that Grau-mann had remarked that if the De Havilland sabotage was success-ful, he would be sent on "a big mission to America."

La Bretonnière had offered a brief feeling of freedom, but now he had the sensation of being watched and monitored as surely as if he had been back in prison with the warders spying through the slot in the iron door. Everyone, it seemed, was keeping an eye on Chap-man: his comrades in Nantes, senior Nazi officials, American spies, and even, perhaps, his own countrymen.

One night, in the Café de France in Nantes, Chapman caught sight of a young man regarding him intently from a corner table. Von Gröning had warned that he was "in all probability being watched by the British," and had shown him some photographs of suspected agents, none of whom he recognized. Now he was convinced he was being tailed. The fellow was in his twenties, well built, with a side parting, a gray suit, and a "West End" look to him that seemed oddly familiar. Chapman looked away, disconcerted, and when he looked back a moment later, the man had vanished. Chapman did not mention the incident to von Gröning, but the urge to escape grew stronger: He must get to Britain, before the British got to him.

In September, Chapman was escorted back to Ackerman's *Schloss* in Berlin, arriving once more in the dead of night. "You have remembered everything," the little German chemist declared, after he had thoroughly tested his pupil. "I am highly satisfied with you." The scientist then launched into a detailed disquisition on exactly how to blow up the De Havilland plant. If the boilers were linked, he should explode the central one using fifteen kilograms of dynamite packed into an attaché case and a delay fuse of at least half an hour. The blast should wreck the other two, and three 80-ton boilers, the scientist explained, would mean 240 tons of matter "exploding in all directions," which should destroy the generator at the same time.

The chemist departed, to be replaced by an older man in civilian clothes, who announced, in English, that he had come to instruct Fritz in the use of "secret ink." From a briefcase, he produced a sheet of white paper, and what appeared to be a matchstick with a white head. Chapman was instructed to place the writing paper on a newspaper, and then clean the paper on both sides for ten minutes using a wad of cotton wool wiped "in a rotary motion." The paper was placed on a sheet of glass, and Chapman was shown how to sketch a message in block capitals using the matchstick, each word separated by dashes. The stick left no visible mark. Chapman was told he could now write in pencil on both sides of the paper, or in ink on the reverse side from the secret writing, as if it was an ordinary letter. The man then vanished, taking the scribbled sheets. When he returned a few hours later, the paper had been immersed in some sort of chemical solution and the secret message had emerged, "a faint greeny color," behind the scrawled pencil. The Professor (as Chapman now christened him) handed over two more matchstick pens and told him to practice his secret writing twice a week. The letters would be forwarded to him, and he would assess their proficiency.

Chapman returned to Nantes by plane and parachute. After taking off from Le Bourget, a Junkers bomber dropped him in a field near the town airfield. The Nantes unit had been deployed in the area as a reception committee, but Chapman made his own way to the airfield and announced himself to the sentry as "Fritz."

Back at La Bretonnière, von Gröning covered the dining table with hundreds of aerial photographs of potential landing spots—Britain was spread out "like a mosaic." They agreed that the village of Mundford, north of Thetford in Norfolk, would be ideal, being rural and sparsely populated, but still reasonably near London. He was then shown aerial photographs of the De Havilland factory in Hatfield, pinpointing the precise location of the boiler room.

In preparation for blending in to a country he had not seen for three years, Chapman listened to the BBC at night, and studied the English newspapers along with a London guidebook to refresh his memory of the city streets. Leo was sent to Dieppe to obtain British equipment left over from the raid, while von Gröning traveled to Berlin in person to collect English paper currency. Chapman was photographed, in a studio in Nantes, to obtain images for his fake identity cards. In the pictures he is leaning forward toward the camera, in matinee idol pose, an oddly intense look on his face. You can almost see the strain of waiting behind his eyes.

The arrangements seemed to gather pace, the final threads weaving together. But then one evening, to Chapman's astonishment, he was taken aside by his German spymaster and asked if he wanted to back out of the mission altogether. "Look, don't think we're forcing you to go to England, because we have other work if you don't want to go."

"No," Chapman replied, momentarily stunned. "I want to go to England."

Von Gröning continued: "If you feel you're not confident that you can do these things, don't go. There's plenty of other work for you here, we can use you on other things."

Chapman protested that he was ready and able: "I think I can do what I was set out to do."

Von Gröning's next suggestion was even more disquieting: Would Chapman like Leo to accompany him on this assignment? Chapman had to think fast. With Leo as a minder, his freedom of action would be seriously curtailed, and if the toothless little thug suspected Chapman's motives, he would kill him, on the spot, possibly with his bare hands.

"I don't think that would advisable," he said quickly. "Probably one could get through whereas two wouldn't, especially as Leo doesn't speak English."

Von Gröning dropped the subject, but it had been an unsettling exchange. Was the German warning him, or trying to protect him? He need not have worried; it was another test of his resolve. On September 24, von Gröning sent a message to Paris headquarters: "Fritz is spiritually and physically undoubtedly absolutely fit."

Like every sprawling bureaucracy, the Abwehr combined nitpicking with inefficiency: First, it obtained the wrong type of parachute; then the Luftwaffe seemed unable to locate the correct plane. A bomber was too noisy for a nighttime drop, so inquiries were made for a transport plane from Russia, or the Middle East. The repeated delays frayed everyone's nerves. Finally, a Focke-Wulf reconnaissance plane was located, at which point somebody pointed out that several agents had been injured during parachute jumps, so perhaps Fritz should instead be taken to the coast by boat, and then rowed to shore in a rubber dinghy. But what sort of boat?

After much argument, it was agreed to send Fritz by plane. That decision soon became bogged down in a new debate over the drop zone. If Fritz aimed for Thetford, it was argued, the plane might be shot down by night fighters operating around London. The Cambrian Mountains were suggested as an alternative by someone who had plainly never been there. Paris duly instructed Nantes: "Show Fritz photos of the Cambrian Mountains." Chapman took one look at these and dug in his heels. Being dropped over the flatlands of Norfolk was alarming enough, but landing on a frozen Welsh hillside in the middle of winter was a different prospect altogether.

Finally, grudgingly, he backed down, and said that if Abwehr really believed these mountains were "safer than anywhere else," then so be it. The Welsh hills became the "new operational objective," and Paris ordered that Fritz be "made familiar in every detail with conditions in the Cambrian Mountains and means of getting from there to London." But a few days later the Paris Abwehr chief, exercising every boss's right of irrational self-contradiction, reverted to the original idea, and Mundford was again selected as the target.

Then, in November, just as it seemed all the wrinkles had been ironed out, the entire mission was put on hold. The war lurched into a new phase, Hitler decided to occupy the whole of France, and Chapman was suddenly drafted into the German army.

For several months, the Nazi leadership had been observing the Vichy regime with mounting concern. Since the French collapse in 1940, the collaborationist French government in Vichy, under Henri-Philippe Pétain, had been allowed to rule the unoccupied portion of southern France as a puppet state under Nazi control. But after the Vichy admiral François Darlan signed an armistice with the Allies in Algeria, Hitler decided to violate the 1940 agreement by invading the zone under Vichy control, in an operation code-named "Case Anton." Every available man would be drafted to aid the new military occupation, including Eddie Chapman.

The members of the Nantes Abwehr section, now Truppe 3292 of Abwehrkommando 306, were formally attached to an SS division and ordered to head south. The spies donned military clothing. Von Gröning wore the full regalia of a cavalry officer, with double-breasted leather trench coat and forage cap; Praetorius, his SS uniform; and the others, a variety of military outfits. They looked like the cast of a Gilbert and Sullivan opera. Chapman himself was ordered to dress up in the field green uniform of a lance corporal in the German marines, with a gold-trimmed collar and a yellow swastika armband. He was faintly disappointed that his uniform had no epaulettes, but he was allowed to carry his gun.

On November 12, 1942, Thomas and the others climbed into the Mercedes, while Chapman traveled with von Gröning in a second car, along with spare tins of petrol, food, and an arsenal of automatic weapons. As they sped south, Chapman passed lines of SS soldiers heading in the same direction and a column of troop-laden trucks that stretched for five miles. French men and women watched from the roadside. To Chapman, some of the bystanders seemed "shocked, frightened and resentful," but most appeared "apathetic." "There were no scenes or anything," he noted, "they just refused to speak and looked very surly as we drove past." At crossroads and checkpoints, the French gendarmes waved them through and saluted smartly, greeting an occupation they could do nothing to prevent. Several times, the Abwehrkommando stopped for refreshments, and by the time they reached Limoges, von Gröning's little war party was, as always, well oiled.

In Limoges, the troop took up billets in a small hotel and linked up with another unit under the command of one Major Reile, a Gestapo officer, who informed them they would be raiding the homes of suspected enemy agents. Armed with pistols and submachine guns, Chapman and the men followed von Gröning to an apartment building, where they knocked down the door of a flat belonging to one Capitaine le Saffre. The suspect had fled, leaving papers strewn everywhere. While the men ransacked the flat, Chapman picked up a handful of papers and stuffed them in his pocket.

At the next house, the troop broke in to find two terrified old ladies cowering under a bed. Von Gröning was dismayed, and even more embarrassed when the women stammered that the man they were looking for had been dead for two years. The German aristocrat had no taste for Gestapo work. By the end of the evening, his troop had raided a dozen houses, most of them empty or occupied by the wrong person, and gathered a grand total of five French suspects, including a seventeen-year-old boy. The terrified Frenchmen, protesting their innocence, were locked in a hotel bedroom without their trousers. Von Gröning later released them all. "Why should I send them to a concentration camp?" he said. "They may be guilty, but they may be innocent." Back at the hotel, Chapman inspected the papers he had gathered from the flat, which appeared to be notes from a diary: "Rendez-vous with so-and-so at such and such an hour . . ." He carefully destroyed them.

Truppe 3292's contribution to the occupation had been insignificant: They had netted some "very small fry" and let them go, looted some booze, and frightened two old women. This still merited a slap-up dinner in celebration. It was Chapman's twenty-eighth birthday. On the way back to Nantes, he wondered if his inclusion in the invasion had merely been another part of his training: "I think it was to see what reaction I would have to the raid." His reaction was a peculiar one: He had thoroughly enjoyed himself. It was perhaps a sign of his moral confusion, and the effect of living among Nazis for so long, that he would later recall this episode—the midnight raids, the smashing down of doors, the terrified people dragged from their beds, the wearing of his first swastika—as "a lovely little trip."

CHAPTER TEN

The Drop

THE INVASION OF Vichy was Chapman's final test. Having dithered for so long, the Abwehr now swung into action with bewildering speed: Von Gröning announced that Chapman would be leaving for Britain within days. He reported that Fritz seemed "visibly relieved" by the news. Paris had sent a questionnaire, a detailed list of the intelligence he might usefully supply from Britain, and together they rehearsed the details of his imminent mission.

He would be dropped over Mundford at around two in the morning. Simultaneously, a bombing raid would be carried out "some place further inland" to draw off any night fighters. On landing, he should dig a hole in an inconspicuous spot and bury his parachute, overalls, helmet, jumping boots, leggings, and entrenching tool. Every item would be British made. Wearing his civilian clothes (they discussed obtaining a British army uniform, but rejected the idea), he should hide out somewhere until dawn and then, using a compass and map, make his way the thirty or so miles to Norwich and take a train to London. Once there, he should make contact with his old accomplice, the notorious Jimmy Hunt, and send his first transmission three days after landing, between 9:45 and 10:15 a.m. Paris, Nantes, and Bordeaux would all be listening for his signal. Von Gröning here remarked that "British red tape" would probably mean that if he were captured, it would take some

time before British intelligence got around to using him for deception purposes. If there was a long delay, said von Gröning, he would
suspect the worst.

Most important, his first message, and all subsequent messages,
should be preceded by five Fs. This was his "control sign," the
agreed signal that he was operating of his own free will. If the message did not start FFFFF, von Gröning would realize that he had
been caught and was transmitting under duress. Naturally, if someone was pretending to be Chapman, he would not know the agreed
control sign, and von Gröning would again conclude that Chapman
had been captured. Likewise, if a message was preceded by PPPPP,
that would be an emergency warning that he was being watched by
the security services or tailed by the police.

Thereafter, Chapman would be expected to transmit every
morning between 9:45 and 10:15, on an all-mains transmitter of
British manufacture taken from a captured British agent, which
could be operated inside a room without an external aerial. He
should transmit at a set frequency, and take five radio crystals in case
of difficulties. All messages should be in English, using the same cipher system but a new code word: CONSTANTINOPLE.* If for any
reason he could not use his transmitter, he was to insert the following advertisement in the personal column of the *Times:* "Young couple require small country cottage near Elstree or Watford with
modern conveniences." He would then send messages, using the secret ink, to a safe house in neutral Portugal, addressed to:

> Francisco Lopez Da Fonseca
> Rua São Mamede 50-51
> Lisbon

These would be picked up by a German agent in Lisbon, and
forwarded to von Gröning.

The sabotage of the De Havilland aircraft factory (code-named

---

*See appendix.

"Walter," a reference to Praetorius/Thomas) was Chapman's primary mission, but not his sole objective. He was also to gather and send information on U.S. troop movements, particularly convoys, and note destination labels attached to railway freight cars, divisional signs, evidence of shipbuilding, and any other military intelligence he could glean. He should also send weather reports to aid bombing raids, specifically describing cloud height, temperature, wind direction and strength, and visibility. To some extent, Chapman could use his own initiative. If the De Havilland premises proved impregnable, he might attack the aircraft propeller factory at Weybridge, in Surrey, or sugar and rubber refineries, or merely do "nuisance work" by leaving bombs in attaché cases in tube-station luggage lockers. Von Gröning was reassuring: "Take your time. Think of things very quietly. It doesn't matter if you don't succeed. Don't run any unnecessary risks. If you can come back we have something else for you to acquit, some other valuable task." He could, if he wished, recruit more members of the Jelly Gang as accomplices.

In order to pay his criminal contacts, obtain the necessary explosives, and live generally, Chapman would be given £1,000 in used notes (worth approximately $60,000 today). That should be "enough to be going on with," said von Gröning, adding that more cash, if needed, could be provided through agents already in Britain. Von Gröning refused to identify these individuals, saying that contact would be arranged by radio. "Of course our agents are there. We have them, we have the connections, but we have to be very, very careful not to take any risks." Chapman wondered if Wojch had already been sent ahead to wait for him, help him, or, quite possibly, to spy on him.

Von Gröning continued his briefing. The day before Chapman was ready to carry out the sabotage, he should send a message stating "Walter is ready to go" and the time of the planned explosion. Reconnaissance planes would then monitor the effectiveness of the attack.

If Chapman was unlucky enough to fall into the hands of the British secret services, said von Gröning, he should "give as little information as possible, offer his services, and ask to be sent back to France." Then he should immediately contact the Abwehr, which would employ him as a triple agent, after staging "a number of small acts of sabotage" to convince the British of his bona fides.

Chapman's mission would last three months, after which he was to make his way back to France, in any one of three ways: A U-boat could be sent to pick him up off the English or Scottish coast, at a location to be arranged by wireless. Alternatively, he could travel to neutral Ireland, where there were "various people who would assist him to return." The third—and, von Gröning stressed, the best— escape route would be to go to neutral Portugal. Once in Lisbon, he could make his way to the safe house on Rua São Mamede, introduce himself as Fritz to Senhor Fonseca, and give the password: "Joli Albert." Chapman's safe passage would then be arranged through the German consulate. Once back in France, he would receive his money, and a hero's welcome.

Von Gröning painted a tantalizing picture of the financial and other rewards Chapman could expect from a grateful Third Reich. After making a report in Berlin, he would be sent on an extended "holiday," with visits to all the major cities in Germany. He might be asked to carry out an important mission in the United States, but he could be posted wherever he wished, and perhaps even receive his own Abwehr command. Chapman had once remarked that he would like to attend one of the great Berlin rallies where Hitler addressed the rapt crowds. Von Gröning promised that this could be arranged. Indeed, he would do more: He would get Chapman a good seat "in the first or second row," even if it meant dressing him in the uniform of a high official. Von Gröning had never shown much enthusiasm for Hitler himself, but seemed only too happy to smuggle Chapman into a Nazi rally and place his spy as close as possible to the Führer.

Chapman judged this a good moment to raise, once again, the subject of Faramus in Romainville. Von Gröning was soothing. "Don't you worry," he said, "we're going to send Faramus a parcel. I haven't had news from him myself but I'm going to look up the question and see what's happening about him—he'll be well looked after."

If Chapman was reassured, he should not have been, for poor Faramus had by now been swallowed up by the Holocaust. No longer a hostage to Chapman's good behavior, he was now a mote at the mercy of a murderous bureaucracy. Chapman believed that he still held his friend's life in his hands; in fact, even if he had failed or defected, no one would have remembered to kill Tony Faramus. He had been selected for death already. At the moment Chapman was packing his bags in Nantes, Faramus was being transported by cattle car to the Nazi concentration camp at Buchenwald.

Faramus had been summoned from his cell in Romainville without explanation. He was taken to a transit camp at Compiègne, and then loaded onto a cattle train with 120 other prisoners, in a truck intended for eight animals. Death came slowly, by suffocation, dysentery, thirst. After a few days, "it was hard to tell the living from the dead, so small had become the margin between them." The living stood shoulder to shoulder with the dead, for there was no room to fall. Five days after leaving Compiègne, the death train drew up at Buchenwald, near Weimar. Of the 120 people packed into the truck, 65 were still alive, and those barely. Among the survivors was little Tony Faramus, who pondered, as he was led away to slavery: "It was hard to believe that such carnage was the work of man."

On December 12, 1942, von Gröning threw a farewell party at La Bretonnière. A goose was killed and roasted, and toast after toast was drunk to the success of Chapman, Fritz, Little Fritz. Everyone sang "Lili Marlene." Von Gröning, who had drunk to excess even by his own extreme standards, was in an ebullient mood: "If you do this for us, you will have nothing more to worry about. Your whole future will be made when you come back. Don't you worry, it will be quite alright. I'll have another bottle of champagne with you."

Praetorius ushered Chapman to one side. He seemed uncomfortable, fidgeting and twitching even more than usual, and whispered: "I have rather an embarrassing thing to do, but for every agent we do it, but it is only matter of form and I hope you won't be insulted."

"What is it?"

Praetorius explained that before heading to Britain, Chapman must be thoroughly searched, for any labels, receipts, tickets, or other items from France or Germany that might indicate he was a spy from occupied territory. Chapman could not be allowed to leave with "anything which could possibly be recognised as coming from us."

"You don't mind?" Praetorius asked.

"Of course not."

Far from objecting, Chapman was grateful for the inadvertent warning from "Thomas." When everyone else had staggered drunkenly to bed, Chapman took all the notes he had made—the radio frequencies, formulas, codes, and names—and burned every scrap.

In the morning, a doctor arrived to give Chapman a full medical examination, and then, with Praetorius and von Gröning standing over him, he packed his British canvas rucksack with everything that a German spy might possibly need in enemy territory, and much that he might not:

1 entrenching tool
1 wireless
1 Colt revolver, loaded, with spare cylinder
2 handkerchiefs
12 detonators, carefully packed in sawdust in case he hit the
   ground hard
chocolate
grape jelly
1 hat
1 razor
1 compass
1 matchbox, with "matches" for secret writing
1 pair spectacles (clear glass)
2 clean shirts
1 British army map
1 ID card in the name of George Clarke of Hammersmith
1 ID card in the name of Morgan O'Bryan of Dublin, electrical
   engineer

Every item was either of British manufacture or made to appear so. Even his wallet was filled with everyday items, taken from the dead at Dieppe: two deck-chair tickets, one Torquay golf-club ticket, one YMCA hostel receipt, and family photographs, all of people Chapman had never met. Here, too, was Betty's love note on Royal Yacht Hotel letterhead paper, now badly creased and frayed—the only authentic item among the substitutes.

With a peculiar expression, von Gröning now handed Chapman a single brown pill, wrapped in a tiny cellophane package, explaining that Chapman could swallow it "if there was any trouble." The word "trouble" did not need defining. Both men knew what happened to captured German spies; what might be done to a spy who was also British did not require elaboration.

Chapman bade farewell to the men of the unit, to Bobby the Pig, and to La Bretonnière, the only "home," as he put it, he had known in ten years. He had found "genuine comradeship" here, albeit with some remarkably nasty people. Before leaving, he handed Praetorius 500 francs, and told him to buy a drink for the boys.

That night Chapman, von Gröning, and Praetorius stayed at the Hôtel des Ambassadeurs in Paris. In the morning, Prateorius searched him as promised, and then handed over a canvas bag sealed with oilskin containing £990 in used notes of varying denominations. Had Chapman looked inside the money bag, he might have spotted that the wads of money were held together by bands stamped "Reichsbank, Berlin," with "England" written on them in pencil. In an unbelievable act of thoughtlessness, the Abwehr had given Chapman a cash package that immediately identified him as a German spy. Having checked every inch of his clothing for clues, Praetorius had handed Chapman a death sentence in used notes.

Waiting at Le Bourget airfield was a Luftwaffe colonel whom Chapman recognized from his parachute practice. The colonel seemed to know all about Chapman's mission, for he discussed with him the merits of the Mosquito bomber, and the importance of halting its production. "You have beautiful planes," he added.

The colonel introduced a pilot, a tall, blond young man wearing an Iron Cross, who then led Chapman across the tarmac toward a sleek black plane, twenty-five feet long with twin engines and machine guns mounted on each side. This, the pilot explained with pride, was a Focke-Wulf of the latest design, adapted for parachuting. A square section had been cut from the floor of the fuselage and replaced by a wooden panel, wedged tight with packing material. Pulling a release handle caused the trapdoor to drop away. Chapman would be taken across the Channel by a three-man crew: the young pilot, Leutnant Fritz Schlichting; Uberleutnant Karl Ischinger, the navigator and commander; and an *Unteroffizier* as wireless operator and gunner. They would be communicating by a tubular intercom "of the larynx type." Chapman noticed that the pilot appeared to be deliberately standing in front of the control panel, as if to prevent his passenger from inspecting it.

At the hut, Chapman slipped his flying overalls on top of his civilian clothes, the old suit that he taken to Jersey all those years ago. As he buttoned up the flying suit, strapped on his kneepads, and laced up his landing boots, Chapman noticed that his hands were shaking.

There was a delay as they waited for a weather report from Britain. Chapman smoked cigarette after cigarette. To make conversation, Chapman asked what the chances were of being shot down by flak or night fighters. The young pilot laughed, and said they could "evade attack" using a device to deflect sound: From the ground, the plane would appear to be at least one kilometer behind its actual position. Chapman realized that none of the crew was wearing a parachute, and he felt a tiny surge of reassurance.

Shortly after 11:00 p.m., the pilot beckoned Chapman toward the plane. Von Gröning and the Luftwaffe colonel walked alongside as he clomped over the tarmac. It was slow going, encumbered by the kneepads and landing boots, the parachute and bulky kit bag strapped to his back. Chapman shook hands with the friend whose real name he did not know, who declared that the moment he received the first message from Fritz he would break out the champagne at La Bretonnière. "We shall be waiting, the Colonel and I," said von Gröning. "We shall definitely be waiting."

Chapman squeezed through the cockpit hatch, and the pilot instructed him to kneel over the floor hole, facing the rear of the plane. The gunner was already seated at the rear. The navigator scrambled in behind.

At 11:25 p.m., the Focke-Wulf took off from Le Bourget into the darkness. The sole illumination inside the cockpit was a tiny flashlight held by the wireless operator. As the plane banked, Chapman caught glimpses of many small lights in the distance. They climbed higher. He thought he could smell sea air. Suddenly, the cockpit was freezing, despite the meager warmth from a heater. The wireless man indicated that Chapman should strap on his oxygen mask. From time to time, the navigator would write something on a small piece of paper and hand it over his head to the pilot. If Chapman lay facedown, the pack squeezed the breath out of him. On his knees, he was unable to straighten his back or turn around. Chapman felt cramp creeping up his body. Something warm and tickling ran over his chin. He had failed to strap the mask tightly enough; blood was seeping from his nose. As they crossed over the English coast north of Skegness, he saw searchlights slicing the sky. The plane seemed to spiral down, the engines in a fighting scream, and then rose again. Passing over the Cambridgeshire fens, the Focke-Wulf performed a strange figure-of-eight dance in the sky. Chapman fastened his helmet, and tied his parachute cord to a bolt overhead. The crew seemed unperturbed: "Far from being nervous or apprehensive, they laughed and joked," as if on a joyride.

Chapman felt the pilot tap him on the back. He tore off the oxygen mask, got to his knees, and yanked the release handle. The trapdoor vanished beneath him, and he jolted downward, but instead of falling through air, he was suspended, head down, on the underside of the plane, the air rushing past him, tearing his breath away. His outsized pack had caught on the sides of the hatch. He dangled, helpless, for what seemed like an age, but was in truth no more than ten seconds. Then he felt a blow in the small of his back—the boot of the wireless operator—and he was somersaulting down. A loud crack, a jolt, and the parachute obediently fluttered open above him. Suddenly, it was utterly quiet. The blood dripped off his chin.

In the far distance, he saw searchlights jousting in the dark. Below he heard the wail of a siren, signaling the all clear. For a strange moment, he wondered if that might be France down there, and not England. Could this be another of von Gröning's tests? For twelve minutes, he drifted down through the still, windless night, toward a spot in the darkness below. He was at least twenty miles from where he was supposed to be.

CHAPTER ELEVEN

Martha's Exciting Night

AT 1:48 P.M. on the morning of December 16, Sergeant Joseph Vail of the Littleport police heard what he thought must be two separate planes, or one with two very powerful engines, over the west side of the town. An alert was immediately relayed to every police station in the area: "Keep a close watch in area Wisbech–Downham Market–Ely as a plane has been spotted circling in the neighborhood having come south from the Lincolnshire coast. Suggest it might be Nightcap, although not in expected area." Another telephone call was made to a number in Whitehall, then another to the home of Colonel Tar Robertson, who got up and put on his tartan trousers. At this point, Eddie Chapman's feet had not yet touched the ground.

Operation Nightcap was the code name for MI5's "Fritz-trap." As early as October, a message had been intercepted revealing that Fritz would "very soon be going on his holiday," and a warning had been sent to security service liaison officers in three different areas of the country to expect the arrival of an enemy agent:

Agent X is probably under 30 and about six feet tall. He may use the name Chapman. He speaks English, French and German. He is a trained wireless operator. It is possible that Agent X may be supplied with means of committing suicide e.g. poison tablets. On arrest he should therefore

be immediately searched, detained pending inquiries and
sent up to London under escort.

For months, British radio interceptors had monitored every dot
and dash of the Fritz traffic, until they imagined they knew the man
intimately. From the Most Secret Sources, the counterespionage
team had obtained a broad idea of Fritz's mission, although not of
the plan to target the De Havilland Mosquito factory. The traffic
suggested that there were three possible drop zones: Mundford,
North Norfolk, and the Cambrian Mountains, with the last named
regarded as the most probable. Robertson had even discovered
Fritz's real surname, although this initially proved more of a red her-
ring since MI5 had spent several fruitless days investigating the
entirely innocent Robert William Chapman, a soldier who had
been reported missing in the Western Desert of Egypt and who
might, it was surmised, have been recruited by the Abwehr while a
prisoner of war.

The spy catchers of B1A knew the details of Fritz's dentistry, the
names on his fake ID cards, and even the approximate length of his
hair after the Most Secret Sources reported: "It may be of intelligence interest that Fritzchen said in clear at 1300 GMT today that
he 'could not keep his schedule this morning as he was having a hair
cut.' " They knew that his password was "Joli Albert," the color of his
boots, and the poisonous contents of the turnups in his trousers.

But MI5 also knew that the chance of catching Fritz, even with
the information from the Most Secret Sources, was slim.

There had been much debate within B Division, the counterespionage branch of MI5, about the best way to ensnare him. A full
police dragnet, with roadblocks and house-to-house searches, was
rejected on the grounds that it offered "too many possibilities of
leakage and subsequent press notices." If an enemy agent was
alerted to the hunt, the Germans might realize that their messages
were being read, and the Most Secret Sources must be protected at
all costs. Another option was to prepare a "flying column" of Field
Security Police—or FSP—the military police attached to the security service, which could be mobilized to the drop zone at short no-

tice. This, too, was rejected, since it might "cause problems with local police and offer only a small chance of success."

Finally, it was decided to set up a combination of traps and hope that at least one was sprung. As soon as the Most Secret Sources received an indication that Fritz was on his way, Operation Nightcap would be mobilized, Dick White would be called at his private telephone number in London, and regional liaison officers and Fighter Command would be placed on alert. An intelligence officer stationed at Fighter Command would track incoming planes, and if an enemy aircraft was spotted that seemed to be heading for one of the three target areas, he would alert the night-duty officer at MI5, who would then contact the chief constable in the area with instructions to scour the countryside, but discreetly. If the plane was shot down, the parachutist would bail out and could then be picked up. If, however, the spy managed to land undetected, the police should "comb out" boardinghouses and hotels. Participants in Nightcap were told sternly: "Whatever you do you should emphasise to all your collaborators the vital necessity of keeping the search as quiet as possible . . . the public must *not* be told that a parachute agent is being looked for." If the police were asked why they were whacking every bush and looking up every tree, they should "pretend to be looking for a deserter."

Despite the elaborate preparations, MI5 was well aware that its net was full of holes. This was clearly a well-trained agent, a "fully fledged saboteur . . . capable of operating his W/T set perfectly." Being English, Fritz was equipped with the finest camouflage a spy could have, and he was about to be dropped in any one of three remote, sparsely populated areas, each up to twelve miles in diameter. He had money, a gun, and, to judge from the Most Secret Sources, plenty of gumption. MI5 was realistic: "We quite realise that our plans do not offer more than a 40% chance of finding our man if he keeps his head and plays his part well."

Fighter Command did pick up the Focke-Wulf, and six fighters from Number 12 Fighter Group were sent in pursuit. One of these got within range, but then "the instruments of the plane packed up for no understandable reason." The German plane got away, and only Sergeant Vail's vigilance ensured that Operation Nightcap happened at all. Because Chapman had struggled for vital moments to extricate himself from a plane flying at 350 miles per hour, he had landed well outside the expected drop zone. In the end, the person who ensured the capture of Agent X was Eddie Chapman.

• • •

Martha Convine could not sleep. She had been woken by a plane, droning loudly overhead, and lay wondering whether it was German. She was getting drowsy, when the all-clear siren had woken her up again. Her husband, George, foreman of Apes Hall Farm, Ely, was snoring steadily, of course, because George could sleep through the Battle of Britain, and recently had. Martha was finally dropping off when she heard a loud banging on the door.

Martha shook George awake, put on her dressing gown, and peered out of the window into the darkness. "Who is it?"

A man's voice replied: "A British airman, had an accident."

It was 3:30 in the morning. For the last hour, Chapman had been stumbling around the wet celery fields in the darkness, dazed and still traumatized from being dangled out of an aircraft at terrifying speed. He had almost hit an empty barn on the way down, and he seemed to have lost his map. Finally, he had found the eighteenth-century stone farmhouse and shone his flashlight through the window in the door. On the hall table lay an English telephone book—a relief since it meant, of course, that the glutinous mud that had been steadily caking his boots for the last hour was British, and not French.

While George sleepily lit the lamp, Mrs. Convine went downstairs and opened the door. The figure on the doorstep might have emerged from a swamp. Martha "noticed he had blood on his face." He was also wearing a lounge suit. You can't be too careful in wartime, so Martha asked him where his plane was. He gestured vaguely at the surrounding countryside: "Across the fields," he said, mumbling that he had come down by parachute.

"I thought I heard a 'Jerry,' " said Martha.

"Yes," the man said, nonsensically. "That would be a cover plane for ours."

Indeed, he really did not start making sense until he was sitting by the range in the kitchen with a cup of tea in his hand. He had asked to use the telephone, and George, who was a special constable and knew the number by heart, dialed the police station at Ely for him. The man spoke very quietly into the mouthpiece, but Martha distinctly heard him say that he had "just arrived from France," which was thrilling.

By the time Sergeants Vail and Hutchings arrived in the police car with two constables, it was 4:30, and the parachutist had drunk three cups of tea, and eaten four slices of toast, and was evidently feeling much better, even cheery.

Convine led the policemen to the living room, where the man was chatting with Martha. Vail reported that "he shook hands with us and appeared agitated, but pleased to see us." He then reached into his pocket and pulled out a pistol, saying: "I expect the first thing you want is this." He unloaded the gun and handed it to Vail, along with another loaded cylinder.

When Vail asked where he had arrived from, the man replied: "France. I want to get in touch with the British Intelligence Service. It is a case for them. I'm afraid I can't tell you much."

An oblong parcel, sewn in sacking, lay on one of the living-room chairs. The man explained that it contained his "radio transmitter, chocolate and shirts." When Vail asked if he had any money, he stripped off his shirt to reveal "a small package strapped to his back between his shoulder blades," which he removed and handed over. Inside, the astonished officer glimpsed wads of banknotes. He also produced his wallet, with an identity card for "George Clarke."

"Is that your real name?" asked Vail. The man just "shook his head and smiled."

While the constables went to find his parachute, the man became "extremely talkative," boasting about the senior German officers he knew and declaring, apropos of nothing at all, that the only way to invade Europe was from Africa via Italy. Vail wondered if he might be "dazed" from his descent. The man smelled slightly of celery.

The exotic visitor and his police escort departed in the police car. George said he was going back to bed; there was work to do tomorrow. But Martha sat in the kitchen as dawn came up, thinking about the strange events of the last few hours. Later that morning, while doing the dusting, she found a British army reconnaissance map down the back of the sofa, which must have fallen out of the man's pocket. When she spread it out on the kitchen table, she saw that Mundford was circled in red crayon. The man had been "very polite," Martha Convine thought, and underneath all that mud and blood he was probably rather handsome. She could not wait to tell her neighbor, but knew she could not. Sergeant Vail had said they must not breathe a word of what had happened to anyone, which was also thrilling.

At police divisional headquarters Chapman was stripped, body-searched, issued with a new set of clothing, and brought before the deputy chief constable, who shook his hand in a friendly manner. Chapman was wary; he did not like being inside a police station, and he was not in the habit of telling the truth to policemen. His answers were cagey.

"Name?"

"George Clarke will do, for now."

"Trade or profession?"

"Well, put me down as independent."

The chief constable picked up the canvas bag containing the radio. "That should not be opened except by the Intelligence Service," Chapman snapped.

The brown pill had been found in the turnup. Did he have any more? "They had better have a look."

Chapman gave a most selective account of his story, starting in Jersey and ending with the "very terrifying experience" of being suspended upside down from a German plane.

Why had had he gone to the Channel Islands? "For a holiday."

Why was he imprisoned in Romainville? "For political reasons."

Then he clammed up. "I have had a rough passage," he said. "I need to speak to the British secret services, when I will have a very interesting story to tell."

The secret services were just as keen to hear Fritz's story. Two men in civilian clothes arrived in a Black Maria. Papers were signed, and Chapman was driven through the morning traffic to London and the Royal Patriotic School in Wandsworth, where he was formally detained under Article 1A of the Arrival from Enemy Territory Order. Then he was loaded back into the car. He did not know, and hardly cared, where he was going. The excitement, fear, and exhaustion of the previous twenty-four hours had drained him. He barely noticed the sandbagged doorways of the city at war, or the scorched gaps where buildings had been destroyed by the Blitz. After half an hour, they turned through a gate in a high wooden fence, topped by double rolls of barbed wire, and drew up in front of large and ugly Victorian mansion.

Two men in gym shoes led Chapman to a room in the basement, with a bench and two blankets, and locked him inside. A man with a monocle opened the door, peered hawkishly at him, said nothing, and then went away. He was stripped again, and ordered to put on flannel prison trousers and a coat, with a six-inch white diamond shape sewn on the back. A doctor appeared and ordered him to open his mouth. The medic spent several minutes probing and tapping at his teeth, particularly the new dental work. Then he tested Chapman's heart, listened to his lungs, and declared him to be in the peak of condition, though "mentally and physically spent." A man with a camera arrived and took photographs from the front and in profile.

Chapman fought to keep his head up. With a supreme effort, he stared into the lens. The face in the picture is drained by fatigue and stress. There is caked mud in the tangled hair, and a trace of dried blood in the moustache. But there is something else in the face. Behind the drooping eyelids and stubble lies the very faint trace of a smile.

CHAPTER TWELVE

Camp 020

LIEUTENANT COLONEL ROBIN "Tin Eye" Stephens, the commander of Camp 020, Britain's secret interrogation center for captured enemy spies, had a very specialized skill: He broke people. He crushed them, psychologically, into very small pieces and then, if he thought it worthwhile, he would put them back together again. He considered this to be an art, and not one that could be learned. "A breaker is born and not made," he said. "There must be certain inherent qualities: an implacable hatred of the enemy, a certain aggressive approach, a disinclination to believe, and above all a relentless determination to break down the spy, however hopeless the odds, however many the difficulties, however long the process may take." Stephens had ways of making people talk, but they were not the brutal, obvious ways of the Gestapo. Behind the tin eye was an instinctive and inspired amateur psychologist.

Born in Egypt in 1900, Stephens had joined the Gurkhas, the legendarily tough Nepalese troops, before moving to the security service in 1939. He spoke Urdu, Arabic, Somali, Amharic, French, German, and Italian. This multilingualism should not be taken to indicate that Stephens was broad-minded about other races and nations. He was ragingly xenophobic, and given to making remarks such as "Italy is a country populated by undersized, posturing folk." He disliked "weeping and romantic fat Belgians," "shifty Polish

Jews," and "unintelligent" Icelanders. He also detested homosexuals. Above all, he hated Germans.

In 1940, the government set up a permanent center for the interrogation and imprisonment of suspected spies, subversives, and enemy aliens in Latchmere House, a large and gloomy Victorian house near Ham Common in West London. Latchmere House had been a military hospital in the First World War, specializing in the treatment of shell-shocked soldiers. In Stephens's words, it had "lunatic cells ready made for a prison." Secluded, forbidding, and surrounded by multiple barbed-wire fences, the interrogation center was code-named Camp 020. Colonel Stephens, extroverted and short-tempered, terrified his underlings almost as much as the prisoners. He never removed his monocle (he was said to sleep in it), and though everyone called him "Tin Eye" as a consequence, very few dared do so to his face. But there was another side to this bristling martinet. He was a superb judge of character and situation; he never lost his temper with a prisoner, and he condemned the use of violence or torture as barbaric and counterproductive. Anyone who resorted to the third degree was immediately banned from Camp 020.

Away from the interrogation cells, Tin Eye could be charming and very funny. He was a frustrated writer, as can be seen from his reports, which have a delightful literary flourish; some of his more extreme statements of prejudice were simply intended to shock or amuse. He thought of himself as a master of the interrogative arts. Some of his colleagues thought he was quite mad. What few disputed was that he was outstanding at his job: establishing the guilt of the enemy spy, breaking down his resistance, extracting vital information, scaring him witless, winning his trust, and then, finally, turning him over to Tar Robertson for use as a double agent. No one could turn a spy like Tin Eye.

At 9:30 a.m. on the morning of December 17, Eddie Chapman found himself in Interrogation Room 3 of Camp 020, facing this strange, angry-looking man with the uniform of a Gurkha and the eye of a basilisk. Stephens was flanked by two other officers,

Captains Short and Goodacre. The three officers made a grim and forbidding tribunal. That was part of Tin Eye's technique. "No chivalry. No gossip. No cigarettes . . . a spy in war should be at the point of the bayonet. It is a question of atmosphere. The room is like a court and he is made to stand up and answer questions as before a judge."

The room was bugged. In another part of Camp 020, a stenographer recorded every word. "Your name is Chapman, is it?" barked Tin Eye.

"Yes, Sir."

"I am not saying this in any sense of a threat, but you are here in a British Secret Service prison at the present time and it's our job in wartime to see that we get your whole story from you. Do you see?"

The threat didn't need to be made. Chapman told him everything, in a great tumbling torrent of confession. He told Stephens about his dismissal from the Coldstream Guards, his criminal past, his time in Jersey prison, the months in Romainville, his recruitment, his training in Nantes and Berlin, and the parachute drop. He told him about the codes he knew, the sabotage techniques he had learned, the secret writing, the passwords, the code words, and the wireless frequencies. He told him about Graumann and Thomas, Wojch and Schmidt, and the ugly man from Angers with the gold teeth. He explained how he had gathered information, and then destroyed it at the last moment.

When Chapman began to describe his decision to take up full-time crime, the interrogation veered close to farce.

"Well, then it gets rather difficult, Sir. I started running around with a mob of gangsters."

"What do you mean?"

"I can't say exactly how I drifted in."

"What made you turn over to these curious people?"

"It's rather difficult to say."

When he described his mission to blow up the machine room of the De Havilland aircraft factory, Stephens interrupted.

"Pretty hazardous undertaking, isn't it?"

"Yes."

"You were rather a favorite. Did they trust you?"

"Yes."

"They said they thought rather highly of you, that you could get in anywhere and do virtually anything?"

"Yes, I could."

Stephens turned the discussion to the contents of Chapman's kit bag. He pointed out that the cash had come wrapped in bands that immediately identified it as German, and "would have cost him his neck" when they were spotted.

"The man who was supposed to search you, proceeds to identify your currency with a German label?" asked Stephens, incredulously.

"That's the fault of Thomas," said Chapman, equally astonished. "In the excitement he probably forgot to take it off."

Stephens made a note. The process of distancing Chapman from his German handlers, by undermining his faith in their efficiency, had begun. So when Chapman recalled the conversation with von Gröning, in which the older man had laughingly said that Chapman would never dare betray them because the British police would lock him up, Stephens again interjected. "That was plain, unvarnished blackmail," he said, in mock outrage, and was delighted when Chapman, "with some bitterness, said he felt that all along."

After two hours of interrogation, Stephens left Chapman in the company of Captain Short, a rotund, owlish figure who was as cheery as his boss was menacing. Today this technique would be called "good cop–bad cop"; in his secret guide to interrogation techniques, Stephens called it "blow hot–blow cold."

"They treated you pretty well, didn't they?" said Short, in a sympathetic tone.

"Yes, I had a very good time there."

"Particularly after having been in prison in Jersey and the other concentration camp."

"How long have I to remain in this one? I mean, I've taken quite a lot of risks getting information which I thought would be of value, and [it is] valuable I think."

Stephens had Chapman exactly where he wanted him. The spy seemed keen to tell all, with apparent honesty. He wanted to tell more. He wanted to please his captors. And he wanted to get out of prison.

In his office, Stephens took a telephone call from the policeman who had accompanied Chapman back to London: "I don't know what this man may tell you, Sir. He came with a German parachute, but I recognised him at once—he was in my platoon some years ago." By an odd coincidence, the two men had been in the Coldstream Guards together, and the policeman now related how Chapman had gone AWOL and was then cashiered. The information tallied precisely with the story Chapman had told. So far, then, he was telling the truth.

The interrogators began to turn up the heat. Chapman was allowed a break, and some food, but then they were back, probing, deliberately misrepresenting what he had already said, worrying away at any fissures in his story to find out if he was lying or holding something back. In Stephens's mind, "No spy, however astute, is proof against relentless interrogation." The MI5 officers worked in shifts, late into the night. "Physically and mentally it will wear down the strongest constitution in the end," Stephens predicted.

The information continued to pour out of Chapman: In the course of forty-eight hours he gave more than fifty descriptions of separate individuals, from Graumann the spymaster to Odette the cook. Chapman described things of vital importance and utter triviality; he described the flak emplacements at Nantes, the location of the Paris Abwehr headquarters, his part in the occupation of Vichy, France, and the price of black-market butter. He described the Breton nationalists, the treacherous Gaullists, and the sundry other dodgy characters that had passed through Nantes. He told them some things they knew, such as the wireless codes they had already broken, which allowed them to test Chapman's truthfulness; but he also told them much that was new, and priceless, creating an astonishingly detailed picture of German espionage methods. He seemed not only eager to impart information, but also offered suggestions as to how it might be used. Surely, said Chapman, by acting on this intelligence, Britain could break the Abwehr code and intercept messages between the various units.

The interrogators offered a vague response, but inside they rejoiced, for Chapman's suggestion showed that the Most Secret Sources were still intact: "It is quite clear from his remarks that he has not the slightest idea that we have been breaking the messages which have passed between these stations during the last few months," wrote the interrogators. It swiftly became apparent that Chapman would not have to be cajoled into acting as a double agent for Britain, but was itching to get to work. One motive for his willingness became clear when he described what had happened to Tony Faramus.

"He is a hostage for my good behavior," explained Chapman.

"For your good behavior in France, or here?"

"Here. The idea was to use him as a kind of lever to make me do my work here." If Chapman could convince his German masters that he was doing their bidding, then, he explained, his friend's life might yet be saved. Stephens made another note.

While Chapman's memory was scoured for valuable information, his luggage was simultaneously being searched for clues. The matches for secret writing and the evil-looking brown pill were sent for scientific analysis; the banknotes were individually examined, their serial numbers noted, to try to establish where they had come from; the fake identity cards were subjected to ultraviolet-light scanning by His Majesty's Stationery Office, their precise chemical composition and typography analyzed and compared to the genuine article; the wireless was sent to the Special Operations Executive (responsible for sabotage and espionage behind enemy lines) to find out if it had come from a British agent operating in France, and if so, which one. Chapman was quizzed about every item in his wallet. He explained that only one was really his own: "That was a private letter written by a girlfriend to me—a girlfriend of mine before the war—I brought that back with me."

Chapman's every statement was compared to the evidence in the Most Secret Sources, to try to catch him in a lie. When Chapman's chronology was erroneous, as it frequently was, they would go over the times and dates again and again, until satisfied that any errors were "natural inexactitudes," not deliberate distortions. Scotland

Yard was asked to provide details of his criminal record, to check out his extravagant claims of villainy; when the record arrived, it was found that many of the crimes Chapman had admitted to were not on it.

Stephens later claimed that Chapman had also "confessed to an experiment in sodomy" during his Soho years. It is hard to know what to make of this: there is no trace of this confession in the interrogation transcripts. Tin Eye, moreover, was an extreme homophobe, and prided himself on his ability to identify and expose experimental sodomites. Chapman may have had a homosexual affair earlier in his youth, but it is certain that he had been heterosexual, to an almost pathological degree, for many years. By way of recommendation, Stephens noted approvingly: "Today there is no trace of sodomy and gone is any predilection for living on women on the fringes of society."

With the evidence Chapman was providing, British intelligence was swiftly building up a picture of the entire Abwehr system in France. The German secret service had been so certain of its unbreakable code that the personnel at the various units often used their own names in wireless correspondence. That information was now merged with Chapman's descriptions, allowing them to identify the different players in the organization. Chapman would have been astonished.

British intelligence had long ago established that the head and deputy head of the Nantes Abwehr section were Rittmeister Stephan von Gröning and Oberleutnant Walter Praetorius. But the man Chapman knew as "Wojch" was really Feldwebel Horst Barton, while "Schmidt" was Franz Stötzner, both suspected saboteurs who had come to England before the war to work as waiters sponsored by an association of British restaurateurs and hoteliers. "Leo" was a known German criminal named Leo Kreusch, and "Albert" a former traveling salesman named Albert Schael. The Gestapo officer from Angers who had tried to recruit Chapman was probably Dernbach, "one of the principal counter-espionage agents in France." Piece by piece, they began to put faces to names; even the pilot of the Focke-Wulf and the beautiful translator at Romainville were identified. Tar

Eddie Chapman, December 16, 1942.
Photographed at Camp 020, MI5's secret wartime interrogation center,
in the hours following his landing by parachute in Cambridgeshire.
KV2 462 © National Archives

Chapman at Camp 020, muddy-faced after landing in a damp celery field. KV2 462 © National Archives

Chapman eating Christmas dinner, 1942, at the MI5 safe house, 35 Crespigny Road. The photograph was taken by Allan Tooth, his police minder. KV2 462 © National Archives

While the previous photograph shows Chapman grinning merrily, another reveals the spy looking more morose—a reflection, perhaps, of his violent mood swings. KV2 462 © National Archives

An Irish identity pass for Chapman created by Nazi forgers, one of two
fake ID cards he carried with him in 1942. The photograph, taken in a
studio in Nantes, shows Chapman in typical matinee-idol pose.
KV2 462 © National Archives

The merchant seaman's pass forged for Chapman by MI5 in the name of
Hugh Anson, a former member of his criminal gang.
KV2 462 © National Archives

Jersey under Occupation:
A British police sergeant takes
orders from a Nazi officer.
© Popperfoto

Norway under Occupation: Vidkun Quisling, collaborator in chief and Nazi
puppet, inspects the "Viking Regiment," composed of Norwegian Nazi volunteers.
© Fox photos/Getty Images

The entrance to Fort de Romainville, the nineteenth-century Paris fortress that was transformed into a Nazi concentration camp. From the collection of Anthony Faramus, in *Journey into Darkness,* Grafton Books, 1990

Faramus (right), age twenty-three, approximately, in the Mauthausen-Gusen death camp. From the collection of Anthony Faramus, in *Journey into Darkness,* Grafton Books, 1990

Anthony Charles Faramus playing a POW in the 1957 film *The Colditz Story.* From the collection of Anthony Faramus, in *Journey into Darkness,* Grafton Books, 1990

The Mosquito bomber under construction at the De Havilland aircraft factory in Hatfield, Hertfordshire. © *Times* (London)

A Mosquito—the "Wooden Wonder"—being prepared for a bombing run over Germany. © *Times* (London)

The De Havilland aircraft factory, with Mosquitoes on the airfield behind.
The two men leaning against the wall may be Allan Tooth and Paul Backwell,
Chapman's MI5 minders. KV2 457 © National Archives

The faked sabotage of De Havilland's: Tarpaulins have been draped over the buildings,
painted to simulate the damage from an explosion, while debris has been spread
around the area. KV2 458 © National Archives

The *City of Lancaster,* the three-thousand-ton merchant vessel commanded by
Captain Reginald Kearon that carried Chapman to Lisbon.
© National Maritime Museum

The coal bomb constructed by Nazi engineers in Lisbon that Chapman agreed to take
on board the *City of Lancaster.* KV461
© National Archives

An X-ray of the coal bomb showing
a block of explosive with cylindrical
fuse that was encased in molded
plastic and painted to resemble a
lump of Welsh coal. KV2 461
© National Archives

The doctored photograph sent to
Lisbon in 1944 for the Operation
Squid deception. The ruler is eighteen inches long but appears to be
only six inches, thus making the
depth charge appear to be one-
third of its real size. KV2 460
© National Archives

Robertson was impressed at the way Chapman had been kept in the dark over the identities of his German comrades: "On no occasion has anyone's real name become apparent to him," he wrote. When one of the interrogators casually dropped the name "von Gröning" into the conversation, Chapman's failure to react proved he had never heard it before.

Establishing a complete picture of Chapman's life in France would take time, but time was already running out. The day after his arrival at Camp 020, Chapman scribbled a message for Colonel Stephens, pointing out that "today was the supposed start of my transmission" and recalling von Gröning's observation about British red tape.

"It is important that we have a connection with the 'Boche' at earliest possible moment," he wrote, perhaps deliberately deploying the sort of language favored by Stephens. "Dr. Graumann especially stressed the point. He may suspect we may be arranging something. He probably thinks it would take much longer for me to commence, if I was arranging anything with yourselves."

The same day, the Radio Security Service began to pick up the German reply station in Paris. Every three minutes, starting at 9:45 a.m., Maurice sent out a message, calling for Fritz to respond. MI5 now faced a quandary. If contact was delayed, von Gröning would suspect something had gone wrong; but if they responded without being absolutely certain that Chapman was playing straight, then the results could be catastrophic. It was decided to wait a day or two, in order to get Chapman, and his motives, "in sharper focus."

By evening, Chapman had still received no response from Stephens. He had been interrogated now for forty-eight hours with only brief intermissions; he was tired and anxious. Unless contact was made soon, the consequences could be dire. He was also torn: between the affection he still felt for von Gröning and the urgent need to betray him; by the desire to save his own skin and that of Tony Faramus; between self-interest and some greater good, as yet undefined; between loyalty to his friends and duty to his country. He wrote another, much longer letter to Stephens. It is an extra-ordinary document, a combination of self-pity, self-examination, and self-assertion, reflecting the internal agony of the spy. It is the statement of a man groping his way through moral darkness toward the light.

> *Mon Commandant,*
>
> *One does not expect gratitude from one's own country—but allow me to draw your attention to a few facts. For thirteen months now I have been under German rule. During this time even when undergoing detention I was treated with strict fairness and friendliness. I made many friends—people who I respect and who I think came to like me—unfortunately for them and for me.*
>
> *I set out from the first day to try to mass together a series of facts, places, dates etc. concerning the German organization, which I think would be a task fairly formidable even for one of your trained experts. From the start I was very much handicapped, my knowledge of German was slight, my French even less—two languages most essential for this work. I studied French until I mastered it, even learning the slang. I read it now as fluently as English. Then, sir, for nine months I listened to every conversation I could hear. I opened many drawers containing documents "geheim" [secret] written on all of them. I bored very small holes from the bathroom to the room of Dr. Graumann, a man very much my friend.*
>
> *Don't think I'm asking for any friendship now, it's a little late—on the other hand this strange thing patriotism. I laugh a little cynically when I think of it sometimes. I have fought the fight and my country won (why I can't explain). I wish like hell there had been no war—I begin to wish I had never started this affair. To spy and cheat on one's friends it's not nice it's dirty. However, I started this affair and I will finish it. Don't think I ask anything for this, I don't. It seems very strange to be working for two different governments—one offers me the chance of money, success and a career. The other offers me a prison cell. There is not a great deal of time left to arrange things.*
>
> *Yours sincerely,*
> *Eddie*

While Chapman was penning this heartfelt note, Stephens was gathering together his four interrogators for a conference on what to do with this remarkable and potentially very valuable crook. As Stephens pointed out, Chapman had accepted that he was in a strange position, wanted by the British police but offering—pleading—to work for British intelligence. "If Chapman is to be believed, he offered to work for the Germans as a means of escape [and] on landing he immediately put himself at the disposal of the British authorities to work against the Germans." The preliminary psychological profile indicated that Chapman's motives, despite his personal affection for Graumann, were "hatred for the Hun coupled with a sense of adventure. There is no woman in the case and no bargain for rehabilitation. He is possessed of courage and nerve."

But there was plainly a problem. If Chapman was allowed his liberty, he would surely be picked up by the police. He had even remarked on it to Stephens: "As I figure it out, with my brilliant past, I am due for a stretch of something like fourteen years." Worse, he might link up with his criminal gang again. But if he was kept under guard in Camp 020, Stephens predicted, "he will go sour and might attempt a break." The only way to operate him safely would be to place him at half liberty, under surveillance but not in prison, "under control in a quiet, country place."

"My opinion," Stephens declared, "is that Chapman should be used for XX [Double Cross] purposes . . . and then sent back to France to join a party of saboteurs already in training to be sent to America for a really big job."

The interrogation team unanimously agreed. There was a risk in sending Chapman back into France. He might be exposed by the Germans, or he might confess all to them; he might even change sides again. But the potential benefits of having a spy at the heart of the German secret service outweighed the dangers. That evening, Camp 020 sent a message to the Double Cross team in St. James's Street: "In our opinion, Chapman should be used to the fullest extent . . . he genuinely means to work for the British against the Germans. By his courage and resourcefulness he is ideally fitted to be an agent."

Tar Robertson had been following every twist of the developing case and agreed to send one of his case officers to take a look at Chapman the next day. Before Chapman could be inducted into the XX fold, he would need a code name. By convention, the names of agents should be plucked from thin air, mere handles that did not connect in any way with their real identities. But the convention was constantly flouted. "Snow," of course, was a partial anagram of Owens; another double agent was called "Tate" because Robertson thought he looked like the comedian Harry Tate; it was said that Dusko Popov, a rather louche Yugoslavian agent, had been named "Tricycle" because of his taste for three-in-a-bed sex. The name selected for Edward Chapman could not have been more apt.

On the evening of December 18, Tar sent a message to all B1A personnel: "We have chosen the name of Zigzag for Fritzchen."

CHAPTER THIRTEEN

35 Crespigny Road

THE MAN DISPATCHED by Tar Robertson to handle Zigzag was Captain Ronnie Reed, a young, unobtrusive radio expert, and an inspired choice. A thin-faced man with a spindly mustache, spectacles, and a pipe, he looked like an archetypal middle-ranking army officer. Indeed, he looked so much like an archetypal middle-ranking army officer that when Tar Robertson needed a photograph to put on a fake identity card for Operation Mincemeat—in which a dead body, dressed in army uniform and carrying misleading information, was deliberately washed up on the coast of Spain—he chose a picture of Ronnie Reed. Reed looked just like everybody else, and nobody at all.

Reed's father, a waiter at the Trocadero Restaurant, had died in the Battle of the Somme in 1916, and his mother brought him up in a tenement in King's Cross. From the St. Pancras Church of England Primary School, he had won a scholarship to the Regent's Park Polytechnic School, where he studied engineering and developed a passion for radios. He could build a wireless from scratch, and with his school friend Charlie Chilton (who went on to become a celebrated radio presenter and producer) he would broadcast to the world from his bedroom with a homemade transmitter: Ronnie would sing a warbling rendition of Bing Crosby's "Dancing in the Dark" while Charlie strummed the guitar.

The outbreak of war found Reed working as a BBC radio engineer by day and flying through the ether by night with the call sign G2RX. One night, Reed and his mother had taken cover during an air raid when a police car drew up. Reed was summoned from the shelter and driven, through the falling bombs, to Wormwood Scrubs. A man was standing at the prison gate. "Ah, Mr. Reed, we've been waiting for you. Come in." He was led through dimly lit corridors to a cell on the first floor.

"In there," said the man.

"W . . . What? Me?" asked Reed, trying to imagine why he was being imprisoned.

"Yes, please."

Inside the cell, flanked by two guards, was a man in flying uniform, his face covered in blood.

"This man is a parachutist," said an officer with red tabs on his uniform, who had entered the cell behind Reed. "He's supposed to transmit tonight back to Germany. We want you to go out into a field in Cambridge, and transmit, and make sure he sends the message we have prepared."

That night, Reed and the parachutist, Gösta Caroli, who was soon to become the double agent "Summer," sat in a pigsty in a Cambridgeshire field and sent a Morse code message to Hamburg: "I'm going underground for a few days, while I sort out some accommodation, and I've arrived safely." So began Reed's career in the secret service.

Shy, gentle, and reserved, Reed was easy to overlook, but he was the "humble genius" of wartime wireless work, perfectly tuned to the arcane mysteries of the radio. He also had the knack of identifying the "fist" of another operator, and then of being able to imitate it precisely—he was probably the best Morse-code mimic in Britain. Reed's skills made him indispensable to Robertson's team, and soon he was monitoring all double-agent radio traffic. One of his tasks was to stand over agents as they transmitted back to the Abwehr, to ensure they were not inserting coded messages. If an agent was unwilling or unable to transmit, then Reed would send the message himself, complete with the agent's telltale "fingerprint." But Ronnie

Reed was more than just an accomplished radio ham; under Robertson's guidance, he was developing into a first-rate intelligence officer. He was incisive, sympathetic, and virtually invisible.

Reed shook hands with his new charge for the first time in Chapman's cell. The young officer had planned to take an instant dislike to this unrepentant criminal with the "lurid past." But like most people, and against his will, he found himself charmed.

Reed frankly explained that if Chapman was to work for MI5, he would need to live a hermitlike existence. Any contact with the police, the Bohemians of Soho, or the criminal fraternity would be forbidden. Instead, Reed explained, he "would have to work for us under strict supervision in almost complete isolation from other members of the community." Chapman laughed and said that after all the recent excitement, a quiet life would be most welcome. Reed said he would return the following day to make the first transmission to Germany, and left Chapman to draft a message, using the Constantinople code and the FFFFF control sign. Reed would then check it, and sit beside him as he transmitted it.

As changeable as ever, Chapman seems to have been buoyed by his conversation with Reed, for he now sent another letter to Stephens. Gone was the peevish, introverted tone. Now he was positively chatty.

> *Mon Commandant,*
>
> *Merci pour votre bonté. As we have little time to get to know each other—let me start and give you a little explanation. At the present moment my story is very difficult to tell. My mind is such a frenzied mass of names, formulas, descriptions, places, times, explosions, radio telegraphy and parachute jumping, small but important conversations, intrigue playing against intrigue. On top of this you must try and imagine a brain—weakened by three years of imprisonment and many months in the punishment cell . . . sometimes in trying to put facts together I really thought I was going mad . . . these things are not untrue, they have all passed— but dates, names, times, are all jumbled in my head higgledy-piggledy, like some giant jigsaw puzzle . . . To conclude Mon*

Commandant. Be a little patient with me if my places and dates and times don't coincide . . . I'm afraid that whole thing has rather passed like a dream: it's for you to try and make it a realisation.

Eddie

Tin Eye Stephens was accustomed to intimidating new arrivals at Camp 020. He was not used to being addressed in this facetious tone or told what to do, let alone by a loutish young burglar in prison garb. But instead of exploding, as he might have done, Stephens just chuckled and tucked the note in the Zigzag file.

The next morning, Chapman was picked up by Reed and two burly Field Security policemen in a Blue Maria and driven 150 yards from the front gate of Latchmere House to the Equestrian Club, a small concert hall within the grounds used as a clubhouse, with a twenty-five-foot flagpole that Reed thought would serve as an aerial. The place was deserted. While the FSPs stood guard, Reed set up Chapman's wireless.

At 10:02 a.m., under Reed's vigilant gaze, Chapman tried to contact his Abwehr controllers. At 10:06 a.m., the reply station responded that it was receiving him "rather weakly" and with interference, but gave the go-ahead. Agent Zigzag then tapped out his first message as a double agent: FFFFF HAVE ARRIVED. AM WELL WITH FRIENDS. O.K. He added his usual laughing coda: HI HU HA.

In the afternoon, the Most Secret Sources reported that the Abwehr stations in France had confirmed that this message was "definitely Fritz" because they "recognised his style of sending and especially the method he adopts for signing off his messages." The deception was up and running.

The following morning, Reed and Chapman found it impossible to renew the contact with Paris. It appeared that the transmissions were being picked up in Nantes, but not at the main receiving station in the capital. A second message was sent "blind": FFFFF GET MORRIS [*SIC*] BRING YOUR SET NEARER COAST. MUST HAVE BETTER RECEPTION. F. OK.

By late December they received the first direct message from von Gröning: THANKS FOR MESSAGE. WISH GOOD RESULTS. OK.

So far, the double cross seemed to be working, although it would be two weeks before the problems of reception and transmission could be ironed out. The radio traffic was code-named ZINC, and filed alphabetically alongside Zigzag.

Chapman seemed more than cooperative, Reed reported, and was still producing a steady stream of valuable intelligence: "Zigzag's powers of observation are extremely good and he is being quite truthful in whatever he tells us." (Reading that assessment, John Masterman noted that he was skeptical that such a man even understood the concept of complete honesty.)

Special Branch set about tracing the rest of the Jelly Gang. Jimmy Hunt, it transpired, had been convicted of warehouse breaking and larceny in 1938; Darry was still in Dartmoor, on a seven-year stretch; the others were all either deserters, doing time, or dead. This was ideal. There was no chance of accidental contact, and with the members of the gang safely out of the way they could be brought into the story with no danger that they might turn up unannounced. Chapman had been instructed to contact his old chums, and perhaps bring one back. Hunt seemed the ideal candidate. As Masterman pointed out, "the Germans had not a photograph of Hunt, but only a general description, [so] it would be possible to impersonate him by someone with a Cockney accent." Hunt the safebreaker would play a central role in the coming drama, without once leaving his prison cell.

Gradually, it was starting to dawn on Chapman's handlers that they had obtained a double agent of potentially huge value. When Camp 020 mistakenly passed the identity of Zigzag to another branch of the intelligence service, there was a loud squeal of protest from Masterman, the master of the double cross, at this "gratuitous" sharing of information. B1A was jealous of its new treasure, and while Tar was happy to pass on his intelligence findings, he was not about to share Zigzag with anyone.

The forensic investigations confirmed how highly the Germans prized Agent Fritz. The quality of his equipment was declared to be first class. The cash he had brought was genuine British currency, not the forged stuff that the Abwehr had often palmed off on lesser agents. The match heads were impregnated with quinine, which the boffins in the science department described as "a very good means of secret writing." The brown pill was potassium cyanide, instantaneously lethal. The wireless was traced to a British SOE agent. Only in the matter of the forged ID cards did the Abwehr seem to have cut corners. The Stationery Office dismissed them as amateur forgeries and liable to be spotted as such by any observant policeman. "It does seem rather extraordinary that the Germans should not take a little more trouble in constructing their documents," Tar complained, as if miffed that the Germans were not trying hard enough. One unsolved mystery was how the Focke-Wulf had managed to escape the pursuing RAF fighters: the Air Ministry could only conclude that "something queer was taking place in connection with the plane and the radio beams associated with it."

Camp 020 was no place to run a double agent. If Zigzag was to be effective, he must be kept happy, and that would require creature comforts at least comparable to those of La Bretonnière. Chapman had been pampered by the Germans: "They pandered to his vanity, granted him liberty and treated him with respect." MI5 must now try to find a red carpet, or the nearest equivalent, and roll it out for Zigzag.

Corporal Paul Backwell and Lance Corporal Allan Tooth were, by common agreement, the two best Field Security policemen in British intelligence. Both had been policemen before the war, and would enjoy successful careers in the intelligence corps after it. They were bright, well educated, and good natured; they were also large and, when they wanted to be, extremely intimidating. Tar Robertson summoned Backwell and Tooth to his office and told them to take a car to Camp 020, where they would pick up one "Edward Simpson," "a dangerous criminal who is wanted by police and who has been released in order to carry out an operation of an extremely hazardous character." They should accompany this man to a safe house in north London where they would live with him until further notice. Robertson was in deadly earnest: "The success of this operation depends upon the utmost degree of secrecy." A photographic pass would be issued in the name "Simpson," indicating that he was performing "special duties for the War Office," which could be produced if they were ever challenged by officials.

"There is no reason to doubt Simpson's loyalty to this country and you are not therefore to regard yourselves as his guards," Robertson continued. "You should look upon yourselves rather as chaperones, whose duty it is to prevent him getting into trouble with the police and with his old criminal associates, to act as a screen between him and the outside world." "Simpson" should never be left alone, day or night. He should not communicate with anyone, use the telephone, or send letters. If he attempted to escape, Tooth and Backwell should not hesitate to "place him under restraint" and then contact either Reed or Masterman. Both policemen would be issued with firearms.

At the same time, they should provide him with companionship. "This regime is bound to be irksome," said Tar, "and you must therefore do your best to make his life as agreeable as is possible in the circumstances." They could take him to the local pub of an evening; each officer would receive £5 as a beer float, and Simpson would also be provided with cash in order to be able to "stand his round." Having gained his confidence, the policemen should note down anything he said of importance, and encourage him to talk about his past. In short, they should guard him, befriend him, and then spy on him. If Backwell and Tooth thought it strange that they were being expected to keep a known crook out of the hands of the police, they were much too discreet to say so.

Days before Christmas, Backwell and Tooth, in plainclothes, arrived at Camp 020, collected Chapman's personal property, and escorted him from his cell. Chapman, without preamble, asked Backwell if he might borrow a pound, as he wanted to give a tip to the sergeant "who had looked after him so well." (Only Chapman would leave Camp 020 as if checking out of a smart hotel.) They drove north. In the car, Chapman's chaperones introduced themselves as "Allan" and "Paul" and explained they would now be his "permanent companions, friends who were protecting him from police and his previous criminal associates." Chapman said little as they drove. "Conversation was strained," Backwell reported.

No one paid any attention to the three men who climbed out of the car and walked up the garden path of 35 Crespigny Road—a nondescript detached house, on a quiet street, in the unremarkable north London borough of Hendon. A few of the neighbors were "digging for victory" in their front gardens, but none looked up. It would have taken a neighbor of exceptional inquisitiveness to spot that Number 35 never took down its blackout curtains (many people did not bother), or that the locks had been changed, or that a man with a thin mustache had arrived that very morning to erect an aerial on the back roof.

Inside Number 35, Backwell locked the door, and the three housemates began, in his words, to "settle in." Reed had set up the radio room on the upper floor; Chapman's bedroom was next door, while the two FSPs shared the third bedroom. The housekeeper, Mrs. West, would not be arriving for a few days, so the policemen divided up the chores: Tooth would do the shopping and Backwell the cooking. When Chapman was out of earshot, they divvided up their other task: "Allan and I agreed to concentrate on different aspects of Eddie. Allan studied his character, likes and dislikes, while I kept to the factual side and noted everything of interest that he said in conversation."

Chapman was anxious. He complained of sleeping badly, and showed no inclination to leave the house. Like a couple of burly mother hens, Tooth and Backwell set about "making Eddie feel at home." Backwell asked Chapman what reading material he enjoyed, and was astonished to discover his love of serious literature. "His taste was unusual for anyone who had lived his kind of life," thought Backwell, who bought him some German novels, the works of Alfred, Lord Tennyson, and the plays of Pierre Corneille, in French.

Gradually, Chapman seemed to relax. His days were filled with further interrogations, sending wireless messages under Reed's supervision, and making plans. In the evenings, he read, smoked, listened to the radio, and chatted with his amiable guards. Privately, Backwell and Tooth compared notes on their ward. They were struck that German propaganda seemed to have had an "enormous" effect on him; at first he dismissed BBC reports of Allied advances, claiming that he knew Germany was winning the war, that Russia was exhausted. The Allies, he insisted, would never succeed in invading France. Backwell decided to mount his own propaganda campaign, by exposing him to such patriotic literature as *I, James Blunt,* H. V. Morton's novel imagining a Britain under Nazi rule. "Gradually we made him realise that German propaganda, however convincing it had been, was far from the truth."

After a few days of communal living, Backwell and Tooth reported that Chapman now appeared "quite happy" and was "a mine of information." Their companion seemed to know all about sabotage, and "often speaks of various methods of destroying pylons, bridges, petrol tanks, etc." Often he insisted on conversing in French. The policemen agreed they were living with a most peculiar fellow. One moment he was reading classical literature in the original French and quoting Tennyson, and the next he would be discussing the best way to blow up a train.

One night, as they were relaxing after dinner, Chapman wondered aloud "what it was that made him leave Germany to come over here." He continued musing in the same vein: "In Germany he could have lived well, both now and after the war. He was not forced to come." The two policemen pondered the same question. His politics seemed to be based on a close reading of H. G. Wells: "He has no sympathy with nationalism and in the post-war reconstruction he would like to see a world federation." Tooth decided that deep down Chapman was a patriot: "He is proud to be British and wants us to win the war." On the other hand, he was apparently impelled by some internal recklessness. "It seems that he is a man to whom the presence of danger is essential," Tooth wrote. "I feel that it is for this reason that he would be undertaking his return to France, for he is virtually a man without a country."

Some days later, Chapman let slip that he had a private plan of his own, but then he changed the subject, remarking: "It is such a wild scheme it would not be thought feasible." Tooth duly reported Chapman's remarks to Reed and Robertson, adding: "I can only glean that the success of these plans depends entirely on Dr. Graumann keeping a promise that he should visit Berlin, when I gather something of great importance was to take place."

Chapman showed no remorse for his past, and regaled his new companions with extravagant tales of his own villainy, such as the time he broke into the Grimsby pawnbrokers and the raid on Express Dairies. The information was duly added to MI5's growing list of Chapman's undetected crimes. "I think we should keep these new adventures entirely to ourselves, but have it on record," wrote Reed.

The interrogators, spy catchers, and double-crossers of MI5 (Reed excepted) were usually upper class and the products of English public schools. Most had never encountered a man like Chapman before, and their first instinct was to despise this uncouth fellow with his flamboyant manner. Yet in almost every case they came first to like, and then to respect him, though never entirely without misgivings.

The horrific bloodletting of the war elsewhere in the world was reaching a climax. In a few weeks, the Battle of Stalingrad would end with German surrender after the most expensive battle, in terms of human life, ever known: 2 million killed or wounded, including civilians. The extermination camps continued to belch out human smoke; the Battle of the Atlantic raged between the U-boat and Allied convoys; U.S., British, and Free French forces had launched Operation Torch, to wrest control of North Africa away from the Germans. But away from the guns and noise, the spy controllers of both sides continued their silent, deadly, unseen war: As Christmas approached, espionage experts all over London wondered what to do about Eddie Chapman, and what made him tick.

When he was not thinking up new ways to deceive and double-cross Nazi Germany, John Masterman, historian and athlete, liked to think about cricket. Sometimes he thought about espionage and cricket at the same time. "Running a team of double agents," he reflected, "is very much like running a club cricket side. Older players lose their form and are gradually replaced by newcomers. It is not always easy to pick the best players to put into the field. Some of the players required a good deal of net practice before they were really fit to play in a match." In Chapman, he seemed to have discovered a batsman of astonishing natural ability, who needed no additional training and who might well knock up a fantastic innings. If, that is, he did not stalk off the pitch, and then reappear to open the bowling for the other side.

Masterman entertained these thoughts as he lay on the floor of the barbershop in the Reform Club on Pall Mall. At the start of the war, he had resided in the United University Club; then, when a bomb blew the roof off, he had moved in to the Oxford and Cambridge. Not long after that, the barber at the Reform Club had died and his salon had closed; Masterman was invited to make his digs there instead, an offer he readily accepted since the club was only a few minutes' walk from B1A headquarters. And so now he spent his nights on the floor where the hair clippings of "great and clubbable" men had fallen ever since 1841.

Sleeping on a thin mattress on the hard tiles was not easy. The cook at the Reform did his best with the rations, but the food was seldom anything but grim. The electricity shut down with monotonous irregularity. Baths were doled out in strict rotation, and were always cold. But Masterman loved living at the Reform: "I had, with my memories of my uselessness in the First War, a kind of unconscious wish for trials and discomfort." He watched his fellow men at war (the women were, as ever, invisible to him) and reflected on their stoicism. One night, the Carlton Club was hit by a bomb. The members of the surrounding clubs, in pajamas and slippers, formed long lines to save the library from the flames, passing books from hand to hand and discussing the merits of each as they passed. Such people, thought Masterman, "made defeat seem impossible." This strange warrior-monk would spend the rest of his war in this masculine world of institutional food, hard floors, and cold baths. And now, with a new, intensely fit, first-class batsman to send to the crease, John Masterman was as happy as he had ever been in his life.

On the other side of London, in Latchmere House, the commandant of Camp 020 was also thinking about Agent Zigzag. Tin Eye Stephens regarded most enemy spies as "the rabble of the universe, their treachery not matched by their courage." But Chapman was different—the "most fascinating case" to date. Unlike every other captured agent, he had not displayed even a flicker of fear. He seemed to crave excitement, and very little else. "What manner of man is the spy?" Stephens pondered. "Is he patriotic, brave? Is he of the underworld, a subject of blackmail? Is he just a mercenary? Spies who work for money alone are few, but they are dangerous." For a crook, he observed, Chapman was strangely uninterested in money. He seemed genuinely patriotic, but not in the Hun-bashing, jingoistic way that Stephens epitomized. What Chapman seemed to want was another breathless episode in the unfolding drama of his own life. If MI5 could stage-manage the next act with enough flair, Tin Eye reflected, then Zigzag might be their biggest star yet.

On Christmas Eve of 1943, Maurice, the German wireless operator in Paris, sent a message to Agent Fritz: PLEASE COME AT NINE FORTY FIVE AND FIVE PM QRQ. (The sign "qrq" was ham shorthand for "send more quickly.") The Germans were still apparently having difficulty picking up Chapman's transmissions. Ronnie Reed had fiddled with Chapman's radio and could find no fault, but he was not too alarmed. The patchy link would buy them some more time.

Far more worrying was something that Chapman had said. Soon after arriving in Crespigny Road, he asked Reed to find Freda Stevenson, his former lover and the mother of his child. Chapman had only vaguely alluded to Freda before. Now he explained that he had never held his own daughter, now three years old, that he was still in love with Freda, and that he wanted to see them both, urgently. Reed said he would try to find her.

Freda was an unknown quantity. Allowing Chapman to contact her might lift his spirits, Reed reflected, but it would complicate the case. If Chapman was serious about his feelings for a woman he had not seen for years and a child he had never met, would that affect his willingness to return to France? Perhaps Freda had remarried; perhaps she had given the child up for adoption. Reed concluded: "We should know the exact situation concerning them before Zigzag visited them, rather than that he should run his neck into what might be an extremely awkward situation." But as the days passed, Chapman's requests to see Freda and Diane grew more urgent. Reed stalled, and every time he did so, Chapman's face would fall, and he would shuffle off to his room. Backwell and Tooth treated him like a particularly fractious and unpredictable teenager. "Eddie had moods," wrote Backwell. "If things did not go as he planned, he would go upstairs to bed and stay there for hours on end and refuse to eat. He never got annoyed with Allan and me on these occasions. But we left him alone when he felt like this."

Chapman's deteriorating temperament cast a pall over the Christmas celebrations at 35 Crespigny Road. Backwell roasted a chicken with sausages. Tooth took some photographs around the Formica-topped kitchen table. The series offers a strange reflection of Chapman's volatile mood swings: In one snap he is drinking beer and grinning at the camera, in the next he appears sunk in misery.

Another reason for Chapman's frustration was the continuing difficulty in communicating with his German spymasters. His wireless could pick up messages sent from France, but he was unable to make direct contact and had to send his replies blind. Soon after Christmas, Reed announced that he had solved the problem. Chapman had casually remarked that during his time in La Bretonnière he had noticed a loose switch on the wireless, which he had fixed by soldering it with a hot poker. This, noted Reed primly, is "a method not calculated to provide a really satisfactory electrical connection." He took the machine home, mended the switch himself, and returned it the next morning, saying he was sure it would now work.

Chapman had written and encoded a simple message overnight. Reed checked it over, approved it, and switched on the wireless. At 9:45, a connection was made with the Paris receiving station. Everything was working perfectly. But in their haste and excitement to see if the repair had worked, they made a mistake. It was the first error of the entire case, but it was also the very worst mistake they could have made. At 9:47 on December 27, Chapman tapped out the following message: CALL AT 1000 IF PARIS UNABLE RECEIVE ME. OK FRITZ. HU HA HU HO. The acknowledgement came back that the message had been clearly received. Reed and Chapman were jubilant.

Ten minutes later, they were sitting over a cup of tea in the kitchen when Chapman suddenly turned pale, and stammered: "My God, I believe I forgot the Fs."

CHAPTER FOURTEEN

What a Way Out

THE WRATH OF Tar Robertson was terrifying to behold. Tin Eye Stephens was angry so much of the time that his underlings had become used to it; but Tar practically never lost his temper. "He was non-judgmental," said one friend. "He saw the best in everyone." On the morning of December 28, when Reed stutteringly informed his boss that he had just sent a message on the Zinc traffic without the agreed "all OK" sign, Robertson did not see the best in Reed. He saw red.

By omitting the five Fs from the start of the message, Chapman and Reed had accidentally indicated to von Gröning that Fritz was being controlled by British intelligence. Not only had this probably compromised one of the most promising double agents of the war, there was a risk it could tip off the Abwehr to the fact that other supposedly loyal agents were being similarly controlled. The entire Double Cross system might be in danger.

Reed was crippled with embarrassment and contrition. For a wireless operator of his experience, this was a mistake so elementary as to be almost unforgivable. Part of Reed's job was to watch for so-called control signs that an agent might surreptitiously insert into his traffic to alert a German handler that he was working under duress. Sometimes these tip-offs were minuscule: omitting a word of greeting, the addition (or omission) of an X or a full stop. But Chapman's agreed sign, to indicate that he was still a free agent, was obvious and unmistakable; MI5 knew what it was; it had been used in each of Zigzag's messages to date.

Young Reed fired off a volley of painful excuses. "From the fact that both Zigzag and I completely forgot about them [the five Fs], it can be seen that they are a very easy thing to omit," he groveled. He pointed out that Chapman would "undoubtedly have done the same thing if he had been operating as a free agent," which was hardly the point. He also claimed that since "Zigzag has already sent two messages including the five Fs, I personally do not feel that this omission is as bad as it would have been had it occurred earlier during his traffic." This was the flailing shame of a man desperately trying to mollify his incandescent boss.

The same evening, at the second agreed receiving window of 5:00 p.m., Chapman and Reed sent another message, this time making no mistake: FFFFF SORRY DRUNK OVER XMAS FORGOT FFFFF. HAPPY XMAS. F.

"They may forget about the inclusion of the five F's themselves," wrote Reed, with a confidence he did not feel. For the next twenty-four hours, MI5 anxiously scanned the Most Secret Sources, expecting to see a flurry of transmissions indicating that von Gröning now knew that his agent had been caught and was transmitting under British control. Finally, the interceptors picked up a laconic message: "Message of 14 letters from Fritzchen deciphered. It was found that this did not begin with 5 enciphered F's." Von Gröning had believed the second message. A stupid mistake on one side had been canceled out by an equally foolish error on the other, and poor, frazzled Reed could breathe again. Much later, he would claim the mistake was merely "annoying." At the time, it was mortifying.

Chapman was relieved but increasingly restless. A life of domesticity locked up in a suburban house with two ex-policemen was not quite how he had envisaged the role of a spy. He began to agitate for a decision about what would be done with him. He drew up a note, under the heading "Work I could possibly do in France" and gave it to Reed.

Preparations should now be put in running order for my return. I have been given to understand that my liberty is to be given to me on my return to France—It has been suggested by Dr Graumann I should make a tour of Germany. But of course I think I can also stay in Paris. There are many points which could be attacked and I can give fairly good schemes for attacking them . . . I can supply detonators and small quantity of dynamite and details of places to be attacked. If I were given two or three good men and allowed to train them myself, allowed to fix things up for them in France, allowed a free hand in my own methods, I am sure I can accomplish good work. On the other hand if we only want information then again I must be trained more thoroughly in German as my knowledge is not enough and also in different army and navy specialities. This is rather a long job and if the people who are preparing the things for my departure will come and see me and take down my ideas I am sure good results will be obtained.

Laurie Marshall, Reed's deputy, was duly dispatched to Crespigny Road to hear Chapman's ideas, which ranged from the simple and effective to the dramatic and bizarre. If he was returned to Nantes, Chapman explained, he could conceal coded information in the "silly joking messages" he sent in his radio transmissions; more ambitiously, if the British sent out a sabotage team, he could try to supply them with explosives and detonators from the stock in Graumann's office in La Bretonnière. "The men must be very resolute and prepared to lose their lives," Chapman insisted. Among the possible targets would be Gestapo offices, Abwehr HQs, and SS officers. Chapman had noticed that senior Abwehr officers often sent one another gifts of cases of cognac; it would be comparatively easy to make a booby trap from one of these, and pack it with "sufficient explosive to destroy a whole building." Marshall found Chapman's enthusiasm "a little sinister," but reported that the discussion had provided "an excellent indication of the way Zigzag's mind is working."

There was no sign, as yet, that the Abwehr suspected anything was amiss, but to sustain von Gröning's faith in his agent, some sort of demonstration of Chapman's skills would soon be required. "We should do all that we can to arrange a speedy and spectacular explosion of some kind at the De Havilland works," wrote Masterman. This staged act of sabotage should then be widely reported in the press, and certainly in the *Times*—von Gröning's British newspaper of choice.

It was an article of faith among the Double Cross team that a double agent should, as far as possible, live the life the Germans believed he was living, and do the things he claimed to be doing. Masterman called this "the principle of verisimilitude, the imperative necessity of making the agent actually experience all that he professes to have done." It is far easier, under interrogation, to tell part of the truth than to sustain a latticework of pure lies. If Chapman was going to pretend to have blown up the De Havilland factory, then he must go and case the joint, precisely as he would if he were genuinely bent on sabotage.

Chapman and Backwell made the ten-mile journey to Hatfield by bus, and got off at the stop just beyond the factory. Chapman carefully surveyed the target as they walked slowly around the perimeter fence. Near the main entrance, as arranged, Backwell stopped and stood with his back to the plant, while Chapman looked over his shoulder and described, while pretending to chat with his friend, everything in sight: The gate appeared to be manned by a single police guard, and inside the compound Chapman thought he could see three possible powerhouses. In the field, he counted twenty-five aircraft, Chapman's first sight of the sleek wooden Mosquitoes. Even to the eyes of an amateur they were beautiful little planes, which "also conveyed an air of warlike viciousness." A little farther along, the fence ran behind the garden of the Comet public house. Next door to the pub was a small café. The morning shift was just arriving, and the guard plainly knew all the factory workers by sight, for he nodded to each as they passed, entering the names on a list.

Chapman and Backwell repaired to the café for a cup of tea. In the corner of the tearoom sat a man in uniform, a lance corporal, who stared at them but said nothing. Could he be an Abwehr spy, sent to see if Fritz was performing his mission? Or was he just a vigilant serviceman on leave, wondering why two men were chatting in undertones next to an important military factory in the middle of a war? Would he give the alarm and have them arrested? Backwell rejected the thought: "He seemed more nervous than suspicious." Perhaps the corporal was just late back from leave.

That night, with the agreement of the factory owner, who had been brought into the plot by MI5, Backwell and Chapman returned and inspected the area more thoroughly. Four large transformers were housed inside a walled yard. Nearby was a building beside an empty swimming pool. In their reconnaissance photographs, the Germans had incorrectly identified this as a subsidiary powerhouse, when it contained only an old boiler and pump for the disused swimming pool. At night, the main entrance was still guarded, but a smaller gate, alongside the pub, was simply left locked. Chapman explained that if he was really trying to cripple the factory, he would climb over this small gate in the middle of the night, clipping the barbed wire on top and using the pub as cover. He would then plant two suitcases, each filled with thirty pounds of explosives: one under the main bank of transformers, and the other in the supposed subsidiary powerhouse. Each of these would be primed with a wristwatch fuse on a one-hour delay. If such an attack were mounted in reality, it "would completely ruin the output of the whole factory." Of course, not even a superspy would be able to lug sixty pounds of explosive and two suitcases over a barbed-wire gate on his own; for this fictional feat of sabotage, Chapman would need an equally imaginary accomplice. Jimmy Hunt would be the ideal man for the job, and since he was still firmly incarcerated, he was in no position to object.

· · ·

On New Year's Eve, Chapman sent a message to von Gröning: FFFFF WENT DOWN AND SAW WALTER. IT IS VERY DIFFICULT JOB. IT CAN BE DONE. I HAVE CLOTHES TICKETS ETC.

The inside of the De Havilland plant was only one picture Chapman would have to be able to paint with confidence on his return to France. If he was to convince von Gröning that he had reestablished contact with his Soho criminal friends, then he would have to go to Soho; if he was going to claim that he had landed near Ely and then taken the morning train to London, he would have to be able to describe what the place looked like in daylight. His German spymaster had asked for additional information such as troop movements and defensive measures, and if he was going to maintain his credibility he would have to start delivering—or at least appearing to deliver— what they wanted. Clearly, he could not do this cooped up in Hendon. He would need to go and do some snooping; John Masterman and the censors on the Twenty Committee could then decide what could be safely sent to von Gröning.

MI5 sensed that the Abwehr was becoming impatient. Fritz had been in Britain for three weeks when a message arrived demanding: PLEASE SEND SPECIFIC INFO ON MAIN GOVERNMENT AND WAR OFFICES. A few days later another message landed: PLEASE GIVE NAME PLACE AND SHORT DESCRIPTION OF YOUR ARRIVAL.

Chapman swiftly replied: FFFFF LANDED TWO MILES NORTH OF ELY AND BURIED GEAR. TOOK TRAIN NEXT DAY WITH TRANSMITTER TO LONDON AND LATER CONTACTED FRIENDS. ALL OK. FRITZ. But von Gröning had plainly had enough of cheery but vague reassurances. He wanted some particulars. So Backwell and Tooth now instituted a series of away days for their housemate. They took him back to Ely, to the spot where he had landed, and traced his notional walk to Wisbech railway station, where they ate fish and chips. They visited the spots that a German spy might visit: They walked around the Hendon airfield, the London railway terminals, and the parts of the City of London that had suffered recent bomb damage. They began to drop in more often at the Hendon Way pub, where the three men became "well known and accepted." No one asked them questions; there was something about the two older men, sitting in front of their beer in the corner of the snuggery, that did not invite familiarity.

They went clothes shopping in the West End, keeping a lookout for military transport vehicles, U.S. Army signs, bomb damage, government offices, and criminals who might recognize Chapman. "Eddie soon began to regain his confidence," Backwell reported. "In spite of this he never tried to lose either Allan or myself, and seemed nervous if we were away from him for a short time." Such trips were vital background for Chapman's cover story, but more than that they "helped to keep his mind occupied." As Backwell and Tooth were discovering, Chapman's mind, when left unoccupied, tended to turn to dark thoughts, dwelling on Freda and his daughter, and his own sexual frustration.

Chapman could appear "terribly restless." He remarked that he did not know how to translate the technical German words used in bomb making, so a German teacher, Mrs. Barton, was sent to Crespigny Road to provide personal tuition. John Masterman, like a don with a demanding student, suggested he be given the four-volume Muret-Sanders German dictionary, to study in bed. More books and magazines were provided, but Chapman could not sit still for more than a few minutes. One night he confessed to Tooth that he had "feelings of nihilism—when he feels his life is empty and nothing really matters." Reed was becoming increasingly alarmed by Chapman's depressive outbursts, his fidgety impatience and re-peated references to sex. "His inherent boisterousness and vitality soon turned to the path of the inevitable feminine relaxation . . . Many attempts were made to sublimate these emotions and direct his energy into more profitable channels."

Reed, Tar Robertson, and John Masterman held a planning meeting and agreed that Chapman's restlessness made it "quite im-possible to run him as a long term double agent in this country," for he was temperamentally unsuited to the "cloistered life." A broad strategy was laid out: the sabotage of the De Havilland factory would be faked, as elaborately, loudly, and convincingly as possible; Chap-man would claim credit with his German spymasters, and then re-turn to occupied France, probably via Lisbon; he should not take back accomplices, or contact other Allied agents in France, but carry out intelligence and perhaps sabotage work on behalf of Britain, to be specified at a later date.

That evening, Reed visited Crespigny Road to explain the decisions that had been made. Chapman was sitting in a chair looking "very pale." Tooth explained in an undertone that he had been listening to the radio, when Chapman had walked in and heard a "reference to secret inks and troop movements." The news referred to some entirely unconnected event, but for a ghastly moment Chapman—as ever assuming a central role in any drama—had thought the report must be about himself, and was still in shock.

Reed initiated a general conversation about the future. He pointed out that if the simulated attack on the De Havilland plant worked out as hoped, then the Germans would be delighted and might want to keep him in Britain. Would Chapman be prepared to stay, and perhaps carry out other faked acts of sabotage?

Chapman shook his head. "I have another, more personal matter to conduct on my return, in Berlin."

"Any individual enterprise, on your part, no matter how commendable, would probably be less satisfactory than our recommendations," said Reed.

Chapman was tart: "Since you don't know my plans, how can you judge?"

"I think you should tell us exactly what you propose to do."

"I will not do that. You would think it absurd and impossible. As I am the sole judge of whether I can pull it off, it is best if I keep it to myself."

Chapman was stubborn, but with "a great amount of patience and sympathy," Reed pressed him, again and again, to say what was on his mind. Finally, Chapman relented, and took a deep breath.

"Dr. Graumann has always kept his promises to me, and I believe he will keep the promises he made about what will happen when I return. He believes I am pro-Nazi. I always said 'Heil Hitler!' in the presence of groups of people and expressed admiration for Hitler as a man and for the Nazi philosophy. Whenever Hitler was speaking on the radio, I always listened with rapt attention, and I told Dr. Graumann how much I would like to be present at a Nazi rally where Hitler spoke." Graumann had promised to obtain Chapman a seat near the podium, "in the first or second row," even if it meant dressing him in the uniform of a high official.

"I believe Dr. Graumann will keep his promise." Chapman paused. "Then I will assassinate Hitler."

Reed sat in stunned silence, but Chapman was still talking. "I am not sure yet exactly how I will do it, but with my knowledge of explosives and incendiary material it should be possible."

Reed recovered his composure sufficiently to protest that it would be extremely difficult get close enough to the Führer to throw a bomb. "Whether or not you succeeded, you would be liquidated immediately."

Chapman grinned. "Ah, but what a way out."

Reed did not try to dissuade him. Late into the evening they discussed the possibilities. Chapman explained that he could never lead a normal life in Britain, given his past; nor could he remain in occupied France forever. Here was an opportunity to give meaning to his life, albeit by forfeiting it.

Writing up his report that night, Reed tried to divine what drove this latest, extraordinary twist in the Zigzag affair. In part, the offer to assassinate Hitler seemed to spring from the suicidal nihilism that sometimes weighed on Chapman. But he was also hungry for fame, seeking "the big way out." Reed remembered how Chapman had once hoarded newspaper clippings of his crimes: "He can think of no better way of leaving this life than to have his name prominently featured throughout the world's press, and to be immortalised in history books for all time—this would crown his final gesture." There was something desperate about this self-appointed mission: a crooked man's offer to assassinate a truly evil one. Yet there was also something else, a strange spark of heroism, a sense of moral obligation in a person whose only duty, hitherto, had been to himself. Reed was moved. "I believe he has a considerable amount of loyalty towards Great Britain."

CHAPTER FIFTEEN

Freda and Diane

WHERE WAS FREDA? Chapman's inquiries were persistent. What had been a request was now a demand. He was petulant and becoming confrontational. One night, he confided to Backwell that the care of Freda and Diane was the only thing that now mattered to him. He must make amends. The policeman reported: "He wants to provide for the [child] in whom, he has said, his one interest lies." He even spoke of taking custody of Diane, if Freda was in difficulty, but conceded that this was "impossible" in the current circumstances. He asked Tooth, in the event of his death, to give Diane the complete works of H. G. Wells on her sixteenth birthday. But at the same time he wondered if it would be better for his daughter never to "know of his existence, [since] he would only handicap her and cause her pain and trouble."

"Personal matters occupy a great deal of his attention," Backwell reported. If killing Hitler was one self-appointed mission for Chapman, then caring for Freda and Diane was the other.

One night, he lost his temper and scribbled a furious note to Tar Robertson: "My sources of information have practically run dry. I can be of no further service here, and for many, many personal reasons I don't wish to stay here one day longer." Backwell passed on the letter, with an accompanying note: "He feels his present position is intolerable, being in the country again, and yet unable to see old acquaintances and do as he pleases . . . E is essentially a man of

action who cannot by nature follow a stereotypical form of living."
Backwell was convinced that only a meeting with his former lover
and their daughter would put Chapman back into a reasonable
frame of mind. "The question of Freda always seems to be at the
back of his mind," he wrote. "The arrangement of a meeting with
Freda would almost completely solve his problems."

Reed was doubtful. There was no telling how Freda might react
to a reunion. The security risk was too great, since "if she bore any
malice and realised Zigzag was back in the country she would probably go to the police and cause an embarrassing situation." Even if a
reunion went well, Freda would somehow have to be incorporated
into Chapman's cover story, possibly putting her and the child at
risk. He told Chapman that the police were still trying to trace Freda
while the "authorities" considered his request. Chapman reacted
badly. He became even more "truculent and moody," and took to his
bed. Reed was now alarmed. Chapman plainly believed MI5 had already found Freda, but was deliberately keeping them apart. And he
was right.

Police had tracked down Freda Elsie Louise Stevenson almost
immediately, because for some years Freda had been trying to find
Eddie Chapman "in connection with an application for a maintenance allowance." She was now living with her daughter in a
boardinghouse at 17 Cossington Road, Westcliffe-on-Sea, Essex.

Freda's life had grown steadily bleaker in the years since Chapman left her at the age of nineteen. She had been living in the flat in
Shepherd's Bush when he vanished in 1939, a few weeks before she
discovered she was pregnant with Diane. She had tried to find
Eddie, first through a parade of Soho barmen, then by asking
around his criminal associates, and finally by going to the police.
This was how she learned that he was in Jersey, in prison. She sent
letters and photographs. There was never any reply. Then came the
invasion, and there was no longer any point in writing. A rumor
went around the London underworld that Chapman had been shot
by the Germans while trying to escape from Jersey.

Freda moved on. She had trained as a dancer, but when war
started there was less and less dancing to be done. She moved to

Southend, to be near her mother. A pale, frail creature, with large brown eyes and a small, downturned mouth, she was trusting and gentle by nature; but also astonishingly resilient, and a ferociously protective mother. Her father, a bus driver, had died before she was born, so she, too, had been raised fatherless. She did not ask, or expect, much from life, and with what little life gave her, she made do. In August 1941, she had met and married a much older man called Keith Butchart, the manager of a balloon works. The marriage foundered almost immediately. One night, when Butchart was out drinking, Freda gathered up little Diane, burned her new husband's suit in the fire, and moved out.

She was working part-time as a firewoman when the two officers from Special Branch caught up with her. In the front parlor of the boardinghouse, they asked her lots of questions about Eddie Chapman. When they went away, Freda hugged Diane, and felt a small glimmering of hope.

Back at Crespigny Road, Tooth and Backwell found that their role had expanded to include the care and maintenance of Chapman's libido. Not only did they have to cook, clean, and find entertainment for their ward, they were now expected to help him find women of easy virtue. The two policemen accepted this new duty with cheerful resignation. Up to now, MI5 had sought to steer Chapman away from what Reed had delicately termed "feminine relaxation." Now they were instructed that if Chapman wanted to relax, he should be encouraged to do so.

On January 15, 1943, after dinner at the Landsdowne pub, Chapman and Backwell went to a part of New Bond Street known to be a red-light area. After a hurried negotiation in a doorway, Chapman picked up a prostitute, who took him to a flat above a shop. "Luckily there was a pub just opposite," reported Backwell, "and he promised to meet me there in about half an hour. He was as good as his word." A few days later, the crook and the policemen went out "relaxing" together. In Lyons Corner House, they met two girls, Doris and Helen, and invited them out to dinner. The men agreed beforehand that if anyone asked what Chapman did, they would say he was a member of the armed forces "just back from abroad"—a cover story that would also explain why he was so unfamiliar with life in wartime Britain.

Chapman had last lived in London in 1939, and the city had changed almost beyond recognition. The Blitz had stiffened British resolve, but it had left livid scars across the capital, inflicting some forty-three thousand deaths, destroying more than a million houses, and damaging such landmarks as the Houses of Parliament and St. James's Palace. Chapman had left a swinging, prosperous London. The one he returned to was shabby and toughened, crouched in self-defense, festooned in barbed wire, inured to deprivation, and braced for the next assault. It would take Chapman weeks to adapt to this transformed world of coupons and rationing, blackouts and bomb shelters.

The visit to New Bond Street, perhaps inevitably, afforded only temporary relief. Soon, Chapman was more depressed than ever. His minders came up with more elaborate diversions. One night, with Chapman wrapped up in coat, hat, and scarf, they took him to see the stirring wartime film epic *In Which We Serve,* starring Noël Coward, Chapman's old acquaintance from his Soho days. Chapman was warned to be alert, and if he saw anyone he knew to make himself scarce and then meet his minders at a prearranged place. For a while the system worked well, and several times Chapman was able to spot former associates before they saw him. "There was one amazing thing about Eddie," Backwell reported. "When it came to faces and descriptions he was superb. Often in London he would single out faces that he had seen before in a quite different place."

But Chapman's own features were also distinctive. One evening, at the entrance to Prince's restaurant in the West End, Chapman came face-to-face with a "cat-burglar" in a brown, double-breasted suit, whom he had known before the war. Flushed and "slightly drunk," the man thrust out a hand and said: "Hullo, stranger, fancy seeing you." Tooth prepared to intervene, but Chapman "looked hard at the man, said a formal 'Hullo,' and continued down the stairs." The man followed, apologizing for his mistake but still insisting that Chapman was the "split [*sic*] image of someone he knew." Chapman now broke into French—"some jocular remark about having a twin"—and left the astonished man in the doorway. Back-well believed the bluff had worked: "The man apologised and left, somewhat bewildered but, I think, fairly sure he had made a mis-take." Chapman claimed that he had forgotten the man's name; none of his minders believed him. "I suppose it is natural for Zigzag not to reveal the identity of this cat-burglar out of a sense of loyalty to his previous criminal associates," reflected Reed. "After all, it is re-ally not our concern."

The incident merely served to reinforce Chapman's frustration with his semicaptivity, in which he could observe the London he knew, but never be a part of it. He demanded to see Winston, his younger brother, whom he believed to be in the army, but was told (falsely) that "so far our inquiries indicated that his brother was in India." One night, he contemplated climbing out the window at Crespigny Road and heading to the West End, but a flash of con-science stopped him, the realization that "it was not in the interests of his work or of his companions." Yet he hankered for his old friends, and asked Reed to find Betty Farmer. Reed was not certain whether this was for amorous purposes, or to apologize for having abandoned her so spectacularly in a Jersey hotel dining room three years earlier. As always, Chapman's motives were hard to read: Here was a man who kept every option open, who seemed congenitally in-capable of taking a bet without hedging it. The last trace of Betty Farmer was her tearful statement to the Jersey police back in 1939. She had vanished. Reed thought this was just as well. Chapman's emotional life was already complicated enough.

It was decided to arrange a meeting with one of the very few peo-ple of Chapman's acquaintance who could be trusted: Terence Young, the filmmaker who was now an intelligence officer attached to the Field Security Section, Guards Armoured Division, in the Home Forces. In the intervening years, Young had become some-thing of a celebrity as an up-and-coming film director, and there were moves afoot to take him out of uniform to make propaganda films. Churchill was said to have taken a "personal interest" in the project. Young was approached by Marshall of B1A, and asked, over tea at Claridge's, whether he would meet Chapman, in conditions of strict secrecy, to "talk to him about some of his old friends" and "build up his morale." Young was delighted to agree, saying he had often wondered what had happened to his wicked old friend. "He said that Zigzag was a crook and would always be one," Marshall reported, "but an extraordinary fellow."

Young went on to describe the glamorous, roué world Chapman had inhabited before the war, the people he knew from "the film, theatrical, literary, and semi-political and diplomatic worlds," and his popularity, "especially among women." Could Chapman be trusted with intelligence work? Marshall inquired. Young was adamant: "One could give him the most difficult of missions knowing that he would carry it out and that he would never betray the official who sent him, but that it was highly probable that he would, incidentally, rob the official who sent him out . . . He would then carry out his [mission] and return to the official whom he had robbed to report." In short, he could be relied on to do whatever was asked of him, while being utterly untrustworthy in almost every other respect.

Chapman and Young were reunited over a late dinner in a discreet corner booth at the Savoy, with Marshall as chaperone. They seemed "delighted to see each other and conversation was very animated," Marshall reported. As the drink flowed, however, the discussion turned to the war, and Young expressed the view that an Allied victory was "inevitable." Chapman shot back that this was "smug and complacent," before launching into a paean about "Hitler's idealism and the strength and efficiency of the German soldier." Despite the reeducation efforts of Tooth and Backwell, the effects of living among Nazis for so long still lingered. On the way home to Crespigny Road, Marshall warned Chapman of the "folly of expressing such views, no matter how true they might be."

Chapman's faith in German military efficiency was being undermined in another way: The Abwehr was still having technical difficulty with its wireless receivers. The Most Secret Sources revealed that a new radio station, code-named "Horst" and manned by a full-time operator identified as Leutnant Vogy, had been set up specifically to receive Fritz's messages at Saint-Jean-de-Luz. But on

January 14, Maurice sent a message saying Chapman should continue to send his messages blind, because the new aerial had blown down. This new proof of ineptitude offered an opportunity to put the Germans on the defensive. The next message from Fritz to von Gröning was, in Chapman's words, "a stinker": FFFFF DISGUSTED AND WORRIED BY LACK OF RECEPTION. THIS IS A HOPELESS BUNGLE. HAVE BEEN PROMISED FULL SUPPORT AND MUST HAVE IT. WORK GOING SPLENDIDLY. HAVE FULL LIST OF ALL YOU WANT. YOU MUST DO SOMETHING TO CLEAR UP THE TROUBLE. F.

For the next few days, Abwehr radio traffic was studied to gauge the effects of this broadside. There was nothing. Plainly, the radio operator had simply decided to suppress the irate message in order, in Reed's words, "not to reap the wrath" of von Gröning. Not for the first time (or the last), the smaller cogs in a large machine took a unilateral decision to prevent the boss from finding out about their own incompetence. A few days later, Maurice sent a meek message saying that the aerial had been fixed and "new arrangements have been made." From that moment on, transmission and reception worked perfectly.

Backwell took Chapman shopping for bombs. If Chapman was going to convince the Germans he had wrecked the De Havilland factory with explosives, then he must test whether it was possible, in reality, to obtain the necessary ingredients. It was astonishingly easy. At Timothy Whites, they bought potassium chlorate in the shape of weed killer. At Boots in Harrow, they picked up potassium permanganate and nitrate of saltpeter. J. W. Quibell in the Finchley Road was happy to sell Chapman sulfur powder, moth crystals, and aluminum powder in the form of silver paint. Flour and sugar could be bought, for a price, at any grocer. Britain might be in the grip of rationing, but buying the materials for a homemade bomb was a piece of cake. (In fact, obtaining the ingredients for a decent cake would have been rather harder.) Chapman's shopping list was never queried: when he mistakenly asked for "Kalium" (German for potassium), a pharmacist's assistant merely thought he was being asked for calcium. Back at Crespigny Road, Chapman experimented "on a small scale" with mixing various explosives. This time he did not

practice blowing anything up; unlike the neighbors at La Bretonnière, the good people of Hendon would certainly not have toler-
ated lumps of burning tree stump whizzing around their back
gardens. "This kept Eddie busy," wrote Backwell, but "he was terribly
restless, and could not concentrate for long on any one thing."

Perhaps Chapman should have been content, making bombs,
brushing up his German, meeting old friends, sending sharp little
notes to his German masters, and gathering together the strands of
a cover story, but he was miserable. His longing to see Freda and the
child had become an obsession. He talked of little else. Reed realized that a problem was about to ignite a crisis: "In this frame of
mind he might easily have gone bad on us when he returned, and
revealed to the enemy his association with us. Even if this did not
happen he would probably have been unwilling to carry out any of
our instructions and would have acted entirely on impulse and his
own fancies."

Marshall, Reed's deputy, was sent to Crespigny Road to have a
heart-to-heart with Chapman over a bottle of whiskey. Marshall was a
sympathetic character, and an excellent listener. As they drank and
talked, Chapman began to open up as never before. He spoke entirely in French, which "tends to break down his natural reserve and
to lead him to express his innermost thoughts," Marshall noted.
Chapman talked of his harsh childhood, his resentment at his lack
of education, his impatience and his desire to make amends for the
past, and of his desire to find a rationale for living, or dying.

They talked until three in the morning. Marshall's nine-page account of this "serious and intimate" conversation is one of the most
revealing documents in the Zigzag files: a complete character study
of a man wrestling with differing elements in his own nature.

"He is endeavouring, perhaps for the first time, to understand
himself and the meaning of life," wrote Marshall. "During the last
three years he has discovered thought, H.G. Wells, literature, altruis-
tic motives and beauty. Although he does not regret his past life he
feels he has no place in society and it would be better if he dies—
but not needlessly. He wishes to make retribution for the bad things

he has done. He cannot be satisfied that he has done something of value unless he actually performs some concrete action himself."

He confessed that he was torn between patriotism and egotism, and "fighting against himself." Hitherto, he had always "acted for himself and had done what he wanted to do," but he had changed. "Now he had realised that he must consider other people and he was finding it very difficult." At one stage, Chapman turned to his companion with a pained expression and asked: "Do you consider that personal life is more important than one's country or ideals?"

Marshall replied that he did not.

The next question was still more profound: "What do you think is the purpose of life?"

This time Marshall had his answer: "I said that I believed that man was climbing to some high destiny, that he had struggled from his ape-like existence to his present state of civilisation, that he was gradually climbing and that it was the duty of every one of us to help man onwards in his ascent."

Realizing how high-minded this must sound, Marshall added quickly: "This does not necessarily mean we have to be 'goody-goody.' War is a bestiality."

Chapman pondered Marshall's words, and remarked that this credo was similar to that of H. G. Wells and, insofar as he had one, his own philosophy. They spoke of socialism and capitalism, patriotism and duty. "It rather seemed," thought Marshall, "as if he had come on these things for the first time, and thought them great discoveries, as indeed they are."

Now it was Marshall's turn to ask a question: "What personal part do you propose to play in helping man in his struggle?"

Chapman's reply was bleak: "My life is of little value and it would be better for me to die—not to throw my life away needlessly, but to do something by which I could make retribution [*sic*] for the wrongs I have committed."

Marshall shot back that this was "the coward's way out. If you cause yourself to die now, that is an admission of defeat. You are now a thinking man. Man must progress, and you must play your part in making that progress possible. It is for you to decide whether a British victory would help mankind in his upwards progress, or whether it would be better if Nazi principles prevail."

Chapman replied that he had already made his mind up on that score: "England cannot be allowed to lose the war."

Marshall reflected that Chapman "has seen too much brutality and horror, the cowed French population [and] the brutality of the Gestapo," to be able to stand aside. Marshall made his way home from Crespigny Road in the freezing London dawn, convinced that Chapman would now "play his part."

• • •

Reed was fascinated by Marshall's report of his evening with Chapman, describing it as "a most valuable character study." It revealed a man anxious to do his duty, but also determined to find some sort of resolution to his inner turmoil. Finding Chapman's "higher destiny" in the war against Hitler would not be possible until he had made peace closer to home. It was time to unleash Operation Freda.

On January 26, 1943, Freda and Diane were driven up to London and lodged at the Brent Bridge Hotel. The reunion took place that night. Backwell and Tooth, such gentle jailers, provided flowers, a bottle of champagne, and babysitting services. While Freda Stevenson and Eddie Chapman got reacquainted in an upstairs room, the policemen played with three-year-old Diane in the hotel lobby. Eddie had been coached to tell Freda that he had escaped from Jersey, and that in return the police had dropped all charges. "He would now join the army and be posted overseas." She accepted the explanation without question. The following day, Freda and Diane moved into Crespigny Road, to become, in Backwell's words, "part of the household," which now was comprised of one crook and double agent, one dancer-turned-firewoman, one energetic toddler, and two long-suffering policemen.

Freda had reentered Chapman's life as abruptly and completely as he had left hers, almost four years earlier. In this bizarre parody of domesticity, Chapman no longer demanded trips to the West End or meetings with his former cronies, but seemed "quite content to limit himself to our own circle." Of an evening, the young couple would walk, arm in arm, to the Hendon Way, while one policeman followed at a discreet distance, and the other looked after Diane and did the chores.

Of course, the twin tasks of running an expanded household while operating an untested double agent did present logistical challenges. Freda had moved into Chapman's bedroom. The challenge was, therefore, "to get Freda up, dressed and downstairs before 9:45 am, as the tapping of the key could be heard in the bathroom or on the stairs." There was the additional difficulty that Mrs. West, the cleaner, came in during the mornings, but had to be prevented from operating her vacuum cleaner when Chapman was transmitting.

One evening, at around seven, Chapman announced that he and Freda were retiring to bed. "Eddie, we're on the air at 9 o'clock," whispered Reed as the couple left. "Don't forget."

At eight, Reed tiptoed up the stairs and knocked gently on the door. "You've got an hour, Eddie." There was no reply.

At 8:45, Reed banged on the door. "You've only got fifteen minutes, Eddie."

Chapman poked his head around the door. "Oh no, not just fifteen minutes," he said, and vanished inside again.

Reed was wondering whether he would have to go in and insist on coitus interruptus himself when, with minutes to spare, a tousled Freda finally emerged.

Freda responded to the subterfuge with an impressive lack of curiosity. Her lover was seldom out of sight of one, and usually two, burly men who monitored his every move. More men, usually in civilian clothes but including one with striking tartan trousers, came and went at odd times of day, and Freda was often told to take a long walk with the toddler. Sometimes Eddie could be heard practicing German nouns. There were some very odd-looking chemicals in the kitchen cupboard. "Freda must have got very used to the strange happenings," Backwell reflected. "But she never asked any questions." When she and Chapman had lived together in Shepherd's Bush, there had been unexplained comings and goings and peculiar men whose presence and business was never explained, so it may have seemed just like old times. "Although she knew very little of what was going on, she accepted things without question and became quite accustomed to the three of us always being together," wrote Tooth.

The transformation in Chapman's mood was immediate. "Since he has seen Freda and the child, E has been in very good spirits and says that his whole outlook toward the future has changed. He now has a 'raison d'être.' He has lost interest in other women and in going to the West End, and says he is quite prepared to remain in this neighborhood, working on his cover story and preparations for his return to France." In place of the gloomy grouch of before, the new Chapman seemed positively ebullient. He doted on his daughter, a bubbly child whose vitality and noise filled the house. Chapman's black nihilism gave way to an equally extreme optimism and an exaggerated self-confidence. He even began to discuss what he might do when the war ended, something he had never done before. He talked of moving to Poland with Freda, and setting up a cabaret, or simply returning to crime, since he doubted "his capacity to live a law-abiding life." But he also wondered whether there might be a place for him in the secret services, as this "would fulfill his need for excitement."

Tooth privately doubted very much whether MI5 would welcome Chapman as a permanent addition to its ranks, but noted that at least the young man was feeling positive: "Previously, he had no faith in the existence of a future for him, and had little desire for it." Having achieved one mission—reuniting with Freda and his child—Chapman was now eager to complete the next, the fake sabotage of the De Havilland factory.

"What a man!" wrote Ronnie Reed, on learning that Operation Freda had succeeded beyond all expectations. "It is extraordinary how obvious a course of action seems after it has been taken. The introduction of a specific woman into the case overcame nearly all difficulty and re-orientated the whole picture of his emotional problems and his attitude to life." By an odd coincidence, it was discovered that Chapman's divorce from Vera Freidberg had been made absolute during his time in prison. He promptly proposed to Freda, who sensibly suggested that they might wait until after he had returned from active service.

There was more than mere altruism in MI5's pleasure at the turn of events: An Eddie Chapman with a fiancée and child in Britain was far less likely to defect to Germany. Given his previous record, Chapman's marriage proposal today might well be forgotten tomorrow, but as Reed noted sagely, "this resolution provides a strong incentive for him to return to Allied Territory." Chapman's British spymasters were, on the whole, honorable and upright men, but they knew a useful lever when they saw one. Just as the Germans held Faramus as a hostage for Chapman's loyalty, so MI5 could now be expected to look after Freda, just so long as Chapman behaved himself. Of course, the matter was never expressed in such bald terms. There was no need to be so vulgar.

As for Freda, perhaps she genuinely never realized her pivotal role in the unfolding drama, nor imagined that the polite gentleman visitors who treated her so courteously had an ulterior motive; maybe she never asked any questions because she really never suspected a thing. But then again, Freda was a born survivor, and if she did understand the part she was playing, she was far too canny to say so.

CHAPTER SIXTEEN

Abracadabra

PERSUADING THE GERMANS that the De Havilland aircraft factory had been wrecked, without causing any real damage, would require some powerful magic. So a magician was summoned. Enter Jasper Maskelyne: professional conjurer, star of the West End, and Britain's most flamboyant secret weapon. Maskelyne came from a long line of magicians, alchemists, and astronomers (his grandfather had been a celebrated stage conjurer in Victorian Britain), and by the 1930s he was already well known as a master illusionist, specializing in sleight of hand and exposing the fraudulent claims of spiritualists. He was also a skilled inventor (one of his most lasting gifts to humanity is the coin-operated toilet door. When you "spend a penny," you owe it to Jasper Maskelyne). He looked as a conjurer ought, with a lacquered center part in his hair, film-star mustache, top hat, and magic wand. He was very clever, and insufferably vain.

When he first offered to contribute his magical skills to the war effort, he was dismissed as a showman (which he was) and put to work entertaining the troops. But eventually General Archibald Wavell, the imaginative commander of British forces in North Africa, realized that Maskelyne's talents might be applied to the battlefield. Maskelyne was sent to the Western Desert, where he assembled "the Magic Gang," possibly the most eccentric military unit ever formed, whose members included an analytical chemist, a cartoonist, a criminal, a stage designer, a picture restorer, a carpenter, and a lone professional soldier to fill out the military paperwork. The gang set about bamboozling the enemy. They built fake submarines and Spitfires, disguised tanks as trucks, and successfully hid part of the Suez Canal using a system of revolving mirrors and searchlights that created a blinding vortex in the sky nine miles wide.

For his greatest trick, Maskelyne helped to win the Battle of El Alamein by creating an entire array of "tricks, swindles and devices" to convince Erwin Rommel that the British counterattack was coming from the south, rather than the north. In 1942, the Magic Gang built over two thousand dummy tanks and constructed a bogus water pipeline to water this phony army. The half-built pipeline was easily spotted from the air, and the slow progress of its construction seems to have convinced the Germans that no attack was possible before November. Rommel went home on leave, and the attack started on October 23. After the victory, Churchill praised the "marvellous system of camouflage" that had helped to make it possible.

This, then, was the ideal person to help make the De Havilland factory disappear in a puff of smoke. According to Charles Fraser-Smith, a supplier of military gadgets to the secret services who would later be immortalized as "Q" in the James Bond novels, Maskelyne was called in to make it "look, from the air, as if the place had been blown to Kingdom Come." In consultation with Tar Robertson and Colonel Sir John Turner, head of the Air Ministry camouflage section, a plan for faking the sabotage of the factory began to take shape.

At first, the planners contemplated laying asbestos sheets across the roof and then simply starting a large fire, which would surely be spotted by German reconnaissance. Masterman vetoed this idea, pointing out that the flames would make a very tempting target for the Luftwaffe, with the "danger that the Germans may try to bomb the factory while the fire is burning." Instead, it was decided to erect a veil of camouflage so convincing that it would seem, from the ground as well as from the air, as if a very large bomb had exploded inside the factory power plant.

The camouflage technicians constructed four replicas of sub-transformers out of wood and papier-mâché, painted a metallic gray. Two of these would be rolled over, as if blown sideways by the force of the blast. Meanwhile, the real transformers would be covered with netting and corrugated iron sheets painted to look, from high above, like a "vast hole" in the ground. On the night of the deception, the large green wooden gates to the transformer building would be replaced by a pair of mangled and broken green gates. The walls of the smaller building would be draped with tarpaulins, painted to look like the half-demolished remnants of a brick wall, while the other walls would be covered in soot, as if blackened from an explosion. Rubble and debris would be spread around the compound to a radius of a hundred feet. Colonel Turner assured Tar that the reconnaissance pilots, as well as any German agent sent to inspect the damage, would be utterly fooled.

Chapman tapped out a message to von Gröning: FFFFF WALTER READY TO GO. BEGIN PREPARATIONS FOR MY RETURN. F.

Military meteorologists studied the weather forecast and the passage of the moon, and decreed that the attack would be best staged on the night of January 29–30, when there should be little cloud cover (allowing the Germans to see what had been done) but long hours of darkness. That night, the moon would not rise until 2:30 in the morning, giving the conjurers at least three hours of darkness in which to perform.

Building a convincing stage set was only half of the production. To convince the Germans, the press reviews would have to be fixed as well, and for that only one newspaper would suffice: the *Times*—"The Thunderer," the organ of the British establishment. Chapman had arranged to send Stephan von Gröning messages through the *Times;* MI5 would now employ the same direct method of communication to feed him a lie.

The editor of the *Times* was Robert Barrington-Ward, a pillar of press probity who shared the same alma mater as John Masterman. Even so, Masterman warned that getting Barrington-Ward to play ball might be "extremely difficult." Masterman briefly laid the situation before him, emphasized the importance of the deception, and then asked if the newspaper would agree to "publish a small paragraph on the Saturday morning following the incident." Barrington-Ward refused, politely, regretfully, and adamantly, observing that "though he would like to help, the suggestion that he should insert what was in fact a bogus notice in *The Times* cut across his whole policy. Not only the reputation but the public utility of *The Times* depended entirely on the principle that it should never insert any items of news which it did not believe to be true." Masterman remonstrated. The single paragraph deception was such "a small thing in itself." But Barrington-Ward did not budge: "The answer is respectfully no."

The editor of the *Times* was technically right: When an independent newspaper, even in wartime, deliberately publishes falsehoods, it ceases to be either independent or a newspaper. Barrington-Ward also dissuaded Masterman from trying to "plant" the false story in the press via the Ministry of Information, since this would either involve lying to the newspapers or, worse, letting journalists in on the ruse, a strategy certain to end in disaster since most hacks are, by nature, incapable of keeping a secret. Instead, Barrington-Ward advised Masterman to make a "private approach" to others of his profession who might adhere to less firm ethical principles: the *Daily Telegraph*, perhaps, or the *Daily Express*. Masterman was not used to being lectured on ethics. Somewhat embarrassed, the two men shook hands and agreed they would both regard the negotiation as "not having taken place."

Arthur Christiansen, editor of the *Daily Express*, was either less fastidious or more patriotic, or both. He, too, pointed out that the hoax "meant him deliberately publishing something in the paper which he knew was not true," but he was happy to oblige. Indeed, he relished the idea of pulling the wool over German eyes, but pointed out that under wartime censorship rules he was not supposed to publish anything likely to encourage the enemy. Reporting the destruction of a vital aircraft factory was firmly in the category of unprintable news, and if he did so, "the censors, as soon as they saw the paragraph, would be shouting down his 'phone." They struck a compromise: Christiansen would publish the fake report, but only in his earliest edition, which was sent to Lisbon, from whence it would be distributed, via the German consulate, to Germany and the occupied territories. If the Germans ever discovered that the notice had appeared only in the first edition, they would simply conclude the censor had spotted it and forced the editor to cut it out of later editions. Masterman drafted a one-paragraph account of a news event that had not happened, and never would. Christiansen, chuckling, translated it into journalese.

Chapman sent a message alerting von Gröning to the planned date of the sabotage: FFFFF ARRANGEMENTS FOR WALTER ARE NOW COMPLETE. OBJECTIVES ARE SUBSTATIONS.

The last elements of the elaborate deception were slotted into place. Fighter Command was instructed to watch out for reconnaissance planes over the Hatfield area, but on no account to attack them. If any factory employees asked about the painted tarpaulins, the factory owner would say that this was part of a test "to see if high altitude photography can pick up minor damage." If the press turned up, they should be told that "something had occurred, but very small and not worthwhile reporting." That should get the rumor mill grinding.

As darkness fell, a team of camouflage experts slipped into the De Havilland aircraft factory and set about perpetrating the fraud. It seems likely that Maskelyne led the team, though he may simply have watched from the wings. That was typical of the man: Now you saw him, and now you didn't. This was prestidigitation on an industrial scale, yet in a few hours the camouflage team was finished, and Ronnie Reed watched them disappear into the "inky blackness." Shortly before midnight, the people of Hatfield were woken by a loud explosion.

Dawn broke on a panorama of devastation. The site of the bogus blast was "surrounded by chaos," in Reed's words. Brick, rubble, bent iron, lumps of concrete, and splintered wood were spread around the substation courtyard. From the side, the smaller building appeared to have been struck with a giant mallet, while the dummy transformers lay smashed among the debris, like the guts of some vast disemboweled animal. Even the boiler-room operator was convinced, for he arrived at the factory office "in a state of great excitement," shouting that the building had been struck by a bomb. A screen was swiftly erected, as if to keep out prying eyes.

Tar Robertson surveyed the conjurer's handiwork and professed himself delighted. "The whole picture was very convincing," wrote Reed. "Aerial photography from any height above 2,000 feet would show considerable devastation without creating any suspicion." The weather conditions were not ideal, with thick cloud cover, but if "the other side paid a visit" they would witness a "scene of destruction," a con trick painted on canvas. This, wrote Fraser-Smith, was "Maskelyne's masterpiece."

Chapman dispatched a triumphant wireless message: FFFFF WALTER BLOWN IN TWO PLACES. That night, an exultant Stephan von Gröning ordered "champagne all round" at La Bretonnière. A reply duly arrived: CONGRATULATIONS ON GOOD RESULT OF WALTER. PLEASE SEND INFO ON NEWSPAPER REPORTS. WILL DO ALL WE CAN ARRANGE YOUR RETURN. STATE PROPOSITIONS.

The Daily Express

Monday, February 1, 1943

FIRST EDITION

FACTORY EXPLOSION

Investigations are being made into the cause of an explosion at a factory on the outskirts of London. It is understood that the damage was slight and there was no loss of life.

The very terseness of the newspaper report was designed to imply there was more to the story. The first edition was printed at 5:00 a.m., and copies were dispatched, as usual, to Lisbon.

By a pleasing coincidence, the day after the bombing, Hermann Göring, who had boasted that no enemy aircraft could fly unscathed over Berlin, was due to address a military parade in the German capital. Before he had begun speaking, Mosquitoes from 105 Squadron droned overhead and began pounding the city, disrupting the procession and enraging the head of the Luftwaffe. The same afternoon, Mosquitoes from 139 Squadron inflicted similar indignity on a parade being addressed by Dr. Goebbels. Once more, the Mosquito had demonstrated its worth. With what satisfaction the German High Command must have received the news that the Mosquito factory was now in ruins, thanks to a German sabotage agent.

•   •   •

The tone of von Gröning's congratulatory message to Agent Fritz suggested that the Abwehr was in no hurry to bring him back, given the excellent results achieved so far. MI5, however, wanted to return Chapman to France as soon as possible, before the police found out that they were sheltering a known criminal. As Tar remarked: "The Security Service is, as matters stand, compounding two felonies at least, and a great many more which it believes to have been committed." Chapman, buoyed with newfound confidence, was just as keen to get to work, either as a spy, a saboteur, or an assassin.

Chapman's offer to kill Hitler was rejected, without fanfare or explanation. MI5's files are suspiciously silent on the subject. Although the proposition must have been debated at the highest levels, in the declassified documents there remains no trace of this. The official report on the Zigzag case describes in detail Chapman's proposal to blow up the Führer, but the passage immediately following—which presumably records the response to the offer—has been blanked out by MI5's internal censor.* Perhaps the veto came

---

*See National Archives, File KV2/459. Document 254 B, paragraph 50.

from Churchill himself. In May 1942, British-trained Czech partisans had killed Reinhard Heydrich, Hitler's potential successor and the head of Reich security, but the hideous wave of reprisals that followed had persuaded the British cabinet to rule out further assassination attempts. Perhaps Chapman was too loose a cannon to be fired at such a moving target. It is equally possible that Chapman, now he had discovered love and fatherhood, was no longer so keen "to depart in a blaze of glory."

Reed believed that von Gröning's promise to send Chapman to a Nazi rally had been "vague." On the contrary, it had been most specific. Despite his own reservations about Hitler, von Gröning had responded enthusiastically to the idea of placing Chapman in close proximity to the Führer, even if that meant disguising him as a German officer. This raises another, intriguing possibility. Von Gröning, like many members of the Abwehr, was fundamentally opposed to the Nazi regime. Some Abwehr officers had been plotting to bring down Hitler since 1938, and the July plot to assassinate the Führer the following year would lead to the abolition of the Abwehr and the execution of Canaris himself. Had von Gröning seen in Chapman a potential tool for assassinating Hitler? Did the German aristocrat himself cherish an ambition "to be immortalised in history books for all time"? Had he divined that his prize spy, for all his apparent commitment, might have an ulterior motive for wanting to get alongside the Nazi leader? Were Chapman and von Gröning secretly working together to this end? The answers will probably never be known, because British intelligence quietly quashed the idea. John Masterman seldom made, and almost never admitted, a mistake. Yet after the war he still wondered if a grave error had been made when MI5 "declined to encourage" Chapman's proposal to kill Hitler: "Perhaps we missed an opportunity, for Zigzag was an enterprising and practical criminal."

Within MI5, debate still raged over what to make of Chapman. Reed, Masterman, and Robertson were certain that he was "frank and straightforward," though mercurial. "His sincerity can hardly be doubted," insisted Reed. The Cockney scholarship boy from the tenements of King's Cross understood Chapman's harsh background and could speak his language. Others were unconvinced. Captain Shanks, one of Reed's brother case officers, decided Chapman was a fraud, "a man whose stock-in-trade is the attractive, suave and agreeable manner, a superficial elegance . . . He gives the impression of the rolling stone who has gathered no moss, but acquired a certain amount of polish." Shanks thought it "possible" that Chapman's character contained "a spark of decency," but he was doubtful. Here was a profiteer and a pirate who had agreed to work for the Germans out of pure self-interest, and was now offering his services to Britain with the same base motives. "Chapman is no fool, he may have decided to run with the hare and hunt with the hounds. It is difficult to accept that a man who has all his life been an enemy of society should be actuated by any patriotic sentiments." Shanks conceded that "whether a patriot or opportunist, Chapman has undoubtedly done this country a service," but he could not conceal his distaste.

Such observations were partly true, but they also reflected the gulf between the predominantly upper-class and well-educated doyens of the secret services and the working-class, unschooled crook with whom they were now in league. It had not escaped the notice of the more snobbish case officers that Chapman tried to cover up his Northern accent with "a refined manner of speaking," but that he struggled to sound educated. "His natural and instinctive speech is at times ungrammatical," noted one interrogator. "But I think it is to be admired that a man of his background and character should have acquired even the rudimentary culture which he has."

In no instance was the social gulf wider than between Eddie Chapman and Victor, Lord Rothschild—peer, millionaire, scientist, and the head of B1C, MI5's explosives and sabotage section.

Lord Rothschild was the product of Eton, Cambridge, the clubs of Mayfair, and the topmost drawer of British society. He had an inherited title, everything money could buy, and an IQ of 184. Malcolm Muggeridge, the journalist and writer who worked in intelligence during the war, found him unbearable, suffused with "the bogus certainties of science, and the equally bogus respect, accorded and expected, on account of his wealth and famous name." But he was also oddly shy, and entirely fearless, with a boyish love of explosions. As head of B1C (with a staff of exactly two secretaries) Rothschild's role was antisabotage: to identify parts of Britain's war effort vulnerable to attack, and to defeat German sabotage plots. One of his tasks was to ensure that Winston Churchill's cigars were not booby-trapped. Another, far less amusing, was to dismantle German bombs: explosives concealed in coat hangers, bombs disguised as horse droppings, thermos flasks packed with TNT. This he did with astonishing coolness in a private laboratory paid for out of his own capacious pocket. "When one takes a fuse to pieces," he wrote, "there is no time to be frightened." Most people were happy to take Lord Rothschild's word for this.

As a trained German sabotage agent, Chapman obviously needed to be dismantled and examined by Lord Rothschild as carefully as any bomb. They met twice, talked for hours, and got on famously: the crook and the peer, two men with nothing in common save a shared interest in loud bangs. They discussed booby traps and incendiary devices, coal bombs, train bombs, and the various ways to scuttle a ship. Chapman explained German techniques for making fuses out of wristwatches, ink bottles, and electric bulb filaments. He showed Lord Rothschild how to conceal a rail bomb with a butterfly, how to hide dynamite in blocks of marzipan, and how to make a detonator from a patented stomach medicine called Urotropin.

Rothschild absorbed it all with astonishment and admiration: "I think it's terrific what you've kept in your mind. It's a hell of a sweat committing things to memory."

"I've had quite a lot of experience of setting these things," Chapman replied.

"Of course you knew a certain amount about this business before, didn't you?"

"I've had quite a little experience getting into places."

"Are you an expert on electrical matters?"

"Not an expert, but I did start my hectic career as an electrical engineer."

"The trouble about you is that you're too good at this sort of thing . . . I mean the average chap who presumably the Germans would get hold of wouldn't be so skilled with his fingers as you are."

And thus they burbled on, delighting in one another's expertise, a highly trained scientist and an equally well-trained burglar.

"How do you open a safe then?" asked Lord Rothschild.

"Well, you stick the dynamite in the keyhole and you don't damage the safe, only sometimes you put a little too much in and blow the safe door up, but other times you're lucky and the safe just comes open."

Thus the scion of a great banking dynasty learned how to rob a bank.

When the conversation turned to the faked sabotage of the De Havilland factory, Rothschild grew wistful. "I'd like to have done it with you," His Lordship sighed. "It would have been fun wouldn't it?"

When they had finished with the past, they turned to the future.

"What are you going to do when you go back?" Rothschild asked.

"Well, I'm rather waiting for suggestions. I mean if I can be of any help, I want to do everything I can to assist."

Lord Rothschild had a suggestion: He would like to get his hands on some German bombs, detonators, and other gizmos. "I think they ought to provide us with a little equipment."

"Well, what would you like?"

"Some of their gadgets. If you do ever think of paying us a visit again, we'd rather like to have some German equipment instead of our own, you know. It's more interesting in some ways, isn't it?"

When Ronnie Reed appeared, in the middle of a discussion about how to make a bomb out of a piece of coal, Lord Rothschild turned to him with all the enthusiasm of a child: "We were just saying that we two would rather like to do a little show together—blow something up."

Finally, with reluctance, Rothschild wound up an interrogation that reads like a chat between two old friends with a shared hobby. "We've been gassing away for a hell of a long time," he said happily.

Chapman rose and shook hands with the chubby, beaming peer he knew as "Mr. Fisher." "Well, many thanks, goodbye," said His Lordship. "And good luck in case I don't see you again before you go off on one of your trips." He might have been sending Chapman off on a jolly holiday, instead of a mission into the heart of Nazi Germany.

CHAPTER SEVENTEEN

The Greater the Adventure

COLONEL TAR ROBERTSON came in person to congratulate Chapman on the success of the fake sabotage operation. They sat in the front room of 35 Crespigny Road, while Backwell and Tooth busied themselves in the kitchen, and Freda took Diane for a walk, again.

"I consider you to be a very brave man," Tar declared. "Especially in view of the fact that you are prepared to go back to France and carry on working for us." Of the many spies that had passed through Camp 020, only a "few, a very few," could be considered genuinely stouthearted. Chapman, he said, was the bravest so far.

Tar then set out the broad lines of his mission. Once he had learned his cover story, he would be returning to occupied France as a long-term counterintelligence agent with the principal aim of acquiring information about the Abwehr. He should accept any mission offered to him by the Germans, and then contact Allied intelligence as opportunities arose. Chapman would not be provided with a wireless, since this could too easily lead to his exposure, and nor would he be put in contact with British agents operating in France, being "far too valuable to risk by any such link-ups." Arrangements would be made to enable him to pass on messages, but he should not attempt to communicate, unless he had information of the highest urgency, until contact was safely reestablished.

"I am not at all keen for you to take any action in France which might get you into trouble with the German authorities, and I am most anxious for you not to undertake any wild sabotage enterprises," Robertson declared. Killing Hitler was not on the agenda.

Before Tar could continue, Chapman raised a question that had been troubling him since his conversation with Lord Rothschild. If he returned with an accomplice—Leo, say, or Wojch—"people for whom he had a certain liking," then presumably he would be expected to hand them over to the police on arrival, "knowing that in doing so these people would be sentenced to death." He was not sure he could do that. He had never betrayed an accomplice yet. Tar responded that although this was a matter for the law, he was "pretty certain that we would take every possible step to see that his wishes were granted." Chapman would not have to deliver his friends to the hangman.

Tar resumed: "We are preparing a cover story as near to the truth as possible so that if you are cross-examined in detail by the Germans, you need only tell them the truth." The chief of Double Cross had studied German interrogation techniques; he knew the dangers Chapman would be facing, and he had even drawn up a checklist of ways to withstand the pressure: "Always speak slowly, this enables hesitation to be covered when necessary; create the impression of being vague; do not appear to be observant; give the impression of being bewildered, frightened or stupid; feign drunkenness or tiredness long before they actually occur." Chapman might well face physical torture, drugs, or anesthetic, Tar warned, but German interrogators generally preferred to get results by "procuring *mental* breakdown . . . by making the witness uncertain, uncomfortable, ridiculous or embarrassed, by stripping him naked or dressing him in women's underwear, making him stand facing the wall, making him sit on a three-legged chair so that it is a constant effort to keep his balance." Chapman would probably face two interrogators: "one with a brutal manner, the other suave." Above all, he should stick to his cover story, and never tell an unnecessary lie.

For all his expert advice, Robertson also knew that if Chapman fell into the hands of the Gestapo, and they chose to disbelieve him, they would break him. And then they would kill him.

The first task was to get Chapman back behind enemy lines, but the Abwehr seemed in no hurry to remove him. Despite Chapman's request to be picked up, the Most Secret Sources revealed that the matter was not even being discussed across the Channel. In response to the request for "propositions," Chapman sent a message: FFFFF PICK UP BY SUBMARINE OR SPEEDBOAT. WILL FIND SUITABLE POINT ON COAST. TRYING TO GET SHIPS PAPERS. SEE BACK PAGE EXPRESS FEB 1.

The response, a few days later, was blunt: IMPOSSIBLE PICK YOU UP BY SUBMARINE. Instead, it said, Chapman must return by the "normal" way—in other words, by ship to Lisbon. This had always been von Gröning's preferred route, but there was nothing normal about booking a passage to neutral Portugal in the middle of a war. "The suggestion was absurd," said Reed, "for Zigzag, being in the possession only of a poor identity card, aged 28 and having no business whatsoever, could not possibly go as a passenger." The Germans probably knew this, and the suggestion was merely a ruse to keep him profitably in place. It was clear, said Reed, that "any attempt to return to occupied territory would have to be made by Zigzag alone." To Chapman's way of thinking, the refusal to send a U-boat was evidence that his German bosses were "not over-anxious to pay him the £15,000 they had promised."

Masterman believed there was a chance the Germans might eventually send a submarine but was "not prepared to offer any odds," and trying to keep Chapman out of trouble while awaiting that distant possibility was an "unenviable and practically impossible task." Chapman must make his own way to Lisbon, with the help of MI5. Reed asked an MI5 agent in Liverpool to find out how a man might be shipped, under a false identity, as a crewman aboard a British merchant vessel sailing to Portugal. The agent reported that such a scheme was feasible, "provided the man could look and behave like a seaman."

While Reed began planning Zigzag's departure, Chapman made his own preparations. A handwritten note duly arrived on Tar's desk under the heading *"Points I would like to have done."* It was his last will and testament. "The Germans have given me a contract for £15,000," he wrote:

this contract is at present in Berlin. I am to be given the money on my return to France. If anything happens to me I want the things which I have arranged for my daughter Dianne [sic] Chapman to be carried on—for this I appoint two of my friends—Allan and Laurie [Tooth and Marshall] to see [that] what I want doing is carried out. Freda Stevenson is to divide the money equally between herself and daughter. If it is not possible for me to get the money out of the country, then I hope that when the Allies enter Germany they will make the Germans pay up "Quoi meme." This I have explained to Ronny [Reed]. In return I offer to do my best and obey any instructions given to me.

Some £350 had already been made over to Chapman from the money he had brought from France; from this, he asked that Freda be paid a regular weekly stipend of £5. When the money ran out, he hoped that MI5 would continue to pay the money until he was "in a position to repay and continue the payments." If he came by additional cash in France, he would try to channel the money back to Freda via a watchmaker he knew in Nantes who made regular trips to neutral Switzerland, whence money could be transferred to Britain.

"Zigzag is fully convinced that the Germans will pay him," wrote Laurie Marshall. "He does not ask the British authorities to pay any money to him or to his descendants."

This was all most confusing for the more literal-minded members of MI5. Here was a grasping thief who seemed to have no interest in money for himself. Backwell had also noted that while Chapman was keen "to get as much money as he can from the Germans, he does not seem very interested in the financial side of the undertaking." He was scrupulous in paying his share of expenses, and once remarked wryly that with the cash he had brought over, he was "paying for his stay" at Crespigny Road.

Under Masterman's "principle of generosity," double agents should be compensated. But how much? Laurie Marshall, an accountant in peacetime, now began totting up Chapman's net worth as a spy. First, there was "the risk to his life which he will incur on our behalf: he will do his utmost not to betray us [but] if his betrayal of the Germans is discovered he will pay with his life." An additional factor was the value of the information he might obtain in the future: "If Zigzag successfully reinstates himself with the Germans, he will be in a unique position to give us full information on the activities of the German SS in France, as soon as we are able to catch up with him." Yet there was also an entry on the other side of the ledger: "We cannot be absolutely certain that Zigzag, once returned to his friends in Nantes, will maintain 100% loyalty to us, nor can it be sure that he will fully carry out the mission given to him—he may carry out some individual task of his own. It is not considered that he will fail us, but we cannot have complete certainty."

The equation was therefore: Chapman's life plus the value of his intelligence, minus the possibility that he might turn traitor, fail, or head off on some wild freelance mission. The accountant carefully added it all up and advised that "substantial payment be made now to Zigzag [and] a further substantial payment should be promised after the successful completion of his mission or our obtaining information that although he had worked loyally for us, his mission had been unsuccessful owing to his being suspected by the Germans." The money should be added to the cash already paid over, and if Chapman failed to return the total would automatically be paid to Freda and her daughter. In the meantime, a savings account would be opened, and the money invested in a 3.5 percent war loan. That way, the man being sought by British police and employed by two rival secret services would not only be profiting from the war, but investing in it. The money would be held in the London Co-Operative Society. Chapman had always favored co-ops, though more for what he might take out of them than for what he could put into them.

So far, Zigzag's double cross had gone without a hitch, and that, to Reed's cautious mind, was a cause for concern: "It was almost too good to be true and much more reasonable that arrangements should go a little wrong." Chapman agreed: Everything was "going rather too smoothly." Von Gröning would surely appreciate him even more if matters appeared to go slightly awry. Jimmy Hunt, or his fictional doppelgänger, would be the fall guy.

Chapman had already informed the Germans that he had re-cruited Hunt as an accomplice, and that he owed him £15,000 for his notional part in the De Havilland factory sabotage. Since it had been decided that Chapman would be returning alone, the fictional Hunt now needed to be disposed of, preferably in such a way as to put the wind up the Germans.

On the morning of February 9, midway through sending a mes-sage to France, Chapman and Reed deliberately broke off the trans-mission with PPPPP, the agreed-upon danger signal. Once again, the Germans failed to spot the warning. Reed was incensed: "After mak-ing such careful arrangements for Zigzag to indicate that the police were on his track, they had failed him in practice." The stakes would have to be raised.

The following day another message was sent: FFFFF DANGEROUS TO CONTINUE TRANSMITTING. THINGS GETTING AWKWARD. ESSEN-TIAL COME BACK WITH JIMMY. HAVE IMPORTANT DOCUMENTS. SHIPS PAPERS HARD TO OBTAIN.

The story Chapman would tell the Germans was this: Jimmy Hunt had seen the German message refusing to send a submarine and, suspecting that he might not be paid, had begun to make trou-ble, demanding that he accompany Chapman back to France; the PPPPP signal had been sent, he would explain, because Jimmy had spotted a police car, which they suspected might be intercepting radio transmissions.

Once again, the German reply was complacent, ignoring the awkwardness Chapman had referred to and requesting more infor-mation on the bombing of the factory. Chapman sent a terse mes-sage saying that the substations at the factory had been "completely destroyed" by placing "60 lbs. of gelignite under the transformers." This was followed by another message saying that he had "seen a chance to return to Lisbon and asking if preparations had been made to receive him." To this, there was no reply. Clearly, the Ger-mans must be made to sit up and pay more attention.

On February 12, the *Evening Standard* carried a news item under the headline GELIGNITE INQUIRIES on the front page: "A man was questioned at Shepherd's Bush police station last night in connection with the possession of gelignite." The *News Chronicle* carried a similar story, reporting that "185 names have been taken during a club raid in Hammersmith." Both stories were, of course, fake, placed in the newspapers with the connivance of their editors.

Chapman now sent his last wireless message: FFFFF JIMMY ARRESTED. SEE EVENING STANDARD FEBRUARY 12TH FRONT PAGE. CLOSING TRANSMITTER AT ONCE. WILL TRY AND GET TO LISBON. FRITZ. In an internal memo, Reed ordered: "No further transmissions are to be made on Zigzag's transmitter." The fictional Jimmy Hunt had served his purpose and could now be liquidated. The ZINC traffic was ended.

Chapman's last, panicky message seemed to have the desired effect. The Most Secret Sources picked up a worried transmission from von Gröning, ordering radio operators in Paris and Bordeaux to continue scanning the airwaves for any word from his agent; to do anything else, he said, would be "absolutely inexcusable."

In a single blow, MI5 had convinced the Germans that a prize agent was now in mortal danger and that Hunt had been removed from the picture, and thus a little more time had been bought in which to prepare Chapman's return trip to the Abwehr.

For a month, Chapman had been allowed, in Reed's words, "to live as man and wife with Freda and his illegitimate child." Now the time had come to break up the strange domestic arrangements at Crespigny Road. Backwell and Tooth were almost as sorry to see Freda and Diane leave as Chapman himself. Theirs had been a strange, homely world, a cocoon from the grim realities of the war. Tar Robertson arranged for Eddie and Freda to spend their last night together not in Crespigny Road, but in the grander surroundings of a bedroom in the St. James headquarters. There is an oddly touching exchange in the transcript of one of Lord Rothschild's interviews with Chapman. The two men were in the middle of a complicated discussion about detonators when Ronnie Reed interrupted.

"Victor, do you mind if Eddie just has a word with Freda on the telephone?"

"No, rather not, of course not."

When Chapman had left the room, Reed explained to Rothschild: "As it's her last night in London we thought it would be advisable for her to spend her last night here. He's just getting her to bring some clothes."

"Beautiful," said Lord Victor.

It *was* rather beautiful.

"Freda returned home," wrote Backwell in his diary, "and we settled down to some concentrated grilling."

Chapman's life would depend on his ability to tell his cover story "unhesitatingly." Hour after hour, day after day, Chapman was coached on every detail of the tale he must tell the Germans, from the instant he landed to the moment of Hunt's "arrest." After a week of this, a Field Security policeman named Hale was brought in to play the part of a German interrogator. He aggressively pummeled Chapman with questions: Where had he lived, who had he seen, how had he obtained explosives, and what had he discovered? Hale repeatedly tried to trip him up with strange questions such as "What shoes was Jimmy Hunt wearing?" He tried to bluff him, accusing him of being a British spy, and alarming him by claiming that there had been a German observer at the factory on the night of the explosion, whom they would shortly produce. Chapman was "not shaken in any way." When Hale demanded to know what had happened to the members of the Jelly Gang, Chapman did not miss a beat: "Poor Freddy Sampson, he was taken as a deserter by the RAF; Tommy Lay is still serving four years in Wandsworth and Darry is doing seven years in Dartmoor. I am not sure what George Sherrard is up to, but he is living in Kilburn and probably mixed up in some monkey business." As for Hunt, Chapman would say he had been released on bail after his arrest on explosives charges.

Reed, who monitored the trial interrogation, was pleased at the way Chapman had withstood the bullying tactics. He was a natural liar: "We can rely upon his ingenuity to fill in small details and

incidents of an amusing character which always give an added basis
for believing that a man's story is true . . . Zigzag is not easily rattled
during an interrogation and unless the enemy have some knowledge of his having worked for the British Intelligence during his stay
in this country (something which is highly unlikely) I do not believe
he will experience any real difficulty in persuading them that he has
carried out his mission to their satisfaction."

Part of that mission had been to collect military and other information. If Chapman was to convince his German bosses of his bona
fides, he must not only tell a convincing story, but also bring back
some goodies. Chapman drew up a list of all the things he had seen
that the Abwehr might be remotely interested in; from this, Reed removed anything that might be useful to the enemy; then they added
some additional information, interesting but essentially harmless,
and, finally, some believable fictions that would set the Abwehr
guessing. The resulting mixture—chicken feed garnished with
grains of truth—was approved by the Twenty Committee, and then
written out on fourteen sheets of plain writing paper with the secret
ink matchsticks. Chapman sketched out a series of army divisional
signs, some accurate, some imaginary: "Blue starfish with curling
tentacles on yellow background," "blue hands and white clouds over
top of shield," and so on. He also revealed that Llandudno, in
Wales, was home to the Inland Revenue office (a building even MI5
officers might be happy to see bombed), and that the Ministry of
Agriculture had a branch at Africa House, Kingsway; he sketched a
map of the military airfield at Hendon, and described the defenses
around Green Park and Hyde Park in central London: "AA guns
camouflaged and concreted. Few lorries or troops. Piquet guards,
ATS, some huts. Four masts, possibly radio, near trees, approx 24
rockets stand and iron and stone ammunition shelters, empty."
Reed calculated there was information here of sufficient interest to
persuade the Abwehr that Chapman was in earnest, and in sufficient
quantity to show he was keen.

Among themselves, the officers of MI5 discussed what additional
information Chapman might reveal to the Germans if he was exposed as a double agent or, worse, turned traitor. Chapman had al-

ways been driven in and out of Camp 020 and other sensitive military installations at night. Stephen thought he might have "picked up the names of officers or warders," but nothing of any great value. Robertson was also sanguine: "There is no information in Zigzag's possession which we should in the least mind him imparting to the Germans should he be disposed to go bad on us," he wrote, adding quickly, "we do not in fact consider that he would go bad."

There was one secret, above all others, that Chapman must never know. "It is imperative that no hint should be given to him about Most Secret Sources," wrote Reed. Chapman had no inkling that the Abwehr codes had been broken. But in some ways, his information had been *too* good: He had provided clues that he believed would help Britain to break those codes—which indeed they would have done, had the codes not been broken already. If he was forced to reveal what he had told MI5, then the Abwehr might conclude that its codes were now vulnerable and change them, providing Bletchley with a new headache. Chapman must be made to believe the Abwehr codes were still invulnerable, by painting a "gloomy picture . . . regarding the capabilities of our interception organization to pick up and decode radio messages." Reed told Chapman that MI5 could gather German wireless transmissions, but found it difficult to trace enemy agents transmitting in Britain, and almost impossible to crack German codes without "a vast number of intercepts." Even with the information Chapman had provided, Reed said sadly, "the successful solving of any cipher must take a very long time." This was all untrue, but Chapman replied that Reed's assessment confirmed what he had been told by von Gröning, "that the code in use by their radio stations was a most difficult one and practically impossible to break." If he was exposed, Chapman could be relied on to confirm the Abwehr's belief that its wireless transmissions were secure. Ultra was safe in Zigzag's hands; the deception agent was effectively deceived.

Having recited his cover story until he was bored stiff, Chapman was set to work memorizing a questionnaire listing all the information he might usefully acquire when back in occupied territory. This, too, had to be carefully vetted. MI5 interrogators had gathered much useful information from the questionnaires of captured German spies, since these often revealed gaps in Abwehr knowledge and areas of particular concern. Tar Robertson was insistent: Chapman must only be given "instructions which, if he were captured and forced to reveal them to the other side, would not convey information to the enemy." Chapman's questionnaire was astonishingly broad, covering just about every aspect of the Abwehr organization, including its codes, personnel, buildings, relations with the Gestapo, favorite hotels, and plans in the event of an Allied invasion. SOE wanted to know about counterespionage techniques, most notably the wireless interception station run by Dernbach—the bald spy catcher of Angers. Rothschild asked if Chapman would be kind enough to dig up information on sabotage targets in the United Kingdom, chemicals used by saboteurs, and camouflage techniques.

Chapman agreed to all the requests, even the impossible ones, for he was in the highest of spirits. The prospect of peril seemed to work on him like a drug, with Backwell noting that "in spite of the fact that he has quieted down in many ways, it seems that he is a man to whom the presence of danger is essential." Robertson agreed, reflecting that this "deep-seated liking for adventure, movement and activity is more likely to be the cause, than the effect, of his criminal career."

The mission was to be open-ended, in time as well as content, for as Rothschild observed: "You may see lots of openings, which at the moment are a closed book." He might bring back a team of saboteurs, or go to America, or volunteer to train a team of German fifth columnists to remain in France in the wake of an Allied invasion and German retreat. "Obviously if he were to gain control of such an organization the value to the Allied cause would be immense," wrote Reed. Chapman should use his own initiative: "It all depends on the opportunities that you see presented to you when you go back," Rothschild told him. MI6, as the service operating outside British territory, might have had a claim to Chapman's services, but MI5 was already running Agent Zigzag, and intended to continue doing so.

For reasons both practical and personal, the B1A team was con-

fident that Chapman would not turn traitor, not least because of the
rekindled emotional bond with Freda and their daughter. Soon
after they parted, Freda sent Chapman a passionate letter, which
MI5 intercepted and copied, before passing it on. "You will see that
the incentive for him to return to this country is quite strong," Reed
remarked, as he showed the letter to his boss. Then there was the
money: He might be about to be rewarded with a small fortune by
the Germans, but his first priority was providing for his family in
Britain, and that would depend on remaining loyal. But most important was the character of Chapman himself. Robertson believed him
to be "genuinely inspired with patriotism," and though he might be
a criminal, the potential intelligence windfall from having a spy at
the heart of the German secret service was an opportunity too good
to squander on the basis of mere morality. Tar concluded that given
"the excellent personal relations which Zigzag appears to enjoy with
various officers, it would be of the greatest possible value to get him
back into those circles with the added prestige of having successfully
completed a mission on their behalf." Reed was emphatic: "He will
be greeted as a hero."

As the hour of departure loomed at the beginning of March, the
case officer reported that Chapman was as ready as an agent could
be. "Zigzag is confident that he can put over his story and his morale
is extremely good . . . While his interrogation in Berlin may be ardu-
ous, after the first few days he should have no difficulty in continuing the old life he used to lead before coming here."

If, "by some unhappy chance," his collaboration with the British
was uncovered, he could probably survive by playing triple agent.
But to do that, he would have to explain why he had included the
FFFFF message, the sign that he was acting freely, *from the outset*. In
Tar's words, "it is very important to have an alternative cover story
for a final emergency, which satisfactorily explains the deliberate
untruth of the primary cover story." Reed came up with an inge-
nious solution.

If Chapman was exposed, he should say that MI5 "had detained
Freda as a hostage and had forced him to return to France" by threatening to "shoot this woman." As proof that he had tried to warn

von Gröning he was under control, he could point to the message, sent after Christmas, in which he had omitted the FFFFF signal. He could claim that the British had then spotted the omission, and forced him to include it thereafter. In this way, a mistake might just be turned to Chapman's advantage. Reed admitted that this explanation was a long shot, to be deployed as "a very last resort," but if Chapman found himself backed into a corner, it "might possibly enable him to escape with his life."

The safe house on Crespigny Road, Chapman's unextraordinary home for three extraordinary months, was packed up. His wireless set was stacked away in a cupboard—he planned to tell von Gröning he had buried it—along with the fake ID cards, the cash, and the poison pill. He solemnly shook hands with Paul Backwell before climbing into the waiting Black Maria with Reed and Tooth, who would accompany him to Liverpool for the next stage. Robertson had told him: "Except in special circumstances we do not expect to hear from you, if at all, for a considerable time." What Tar did not say, and both men knew, was that there was a strong likelihood, once he left British shores, that they would never hear from Zigzag again.

It fell to Lieutenant Colonel Stephens to write the final report that sent Chapman on his way, and he rose to the occasion magnificently, pulling out all the literary stops. Tin Eye wrote with professional pride and frank admiration, in prose of the deepest purple.

> The story of many a spy is commonplace and drab. It would not pass muster in fiction. The subject is a failure in life. The motive is sordid. Fear is present. Patriotism is absent. Silence is not the equipment of a brave man, rather it is the reaction to a dread of consequence. High adventure just means nothing at all.
>
> The story of Chapman is different. In fiction it would be rejected as improbable. The subject is a crook, but as a crook he is by no means a failure. His career in crime has been progressive, from Army desertion to indecency, from women to blackmail, from robbery to the blowing of safes. Latterly his rewards have been large, and no doubt he de-

spises himself for his petty beginnings. The man, essentially vain, has grown in stature and, in his own estimation, is something of a prince of the underworld. He has no scruples and will stop at nothing. He makes no bargain with society and money is a means to an end. Of fear, he knows nothing, and he certainly has a deep-rooted hatred of the Hun. In a word, adventure to Chapman is the breath of life. Given adventure, he has the courage to achieve the unbelievable. His very recklessness is his standby. Today he is a German parachute spy; tomorrow he will undertake a desperate hazard as an active double agent, the stake for which is his life. Without adventure, he would rebel; in the ultimate he will have recourse again to crime in search of the unusual. The risk is considerable, but so long as there is a chance of success I think the risk should be taken.

For Chapman, only one thing is certain, the greater the adventure, the greater is the chance of success.

CHAPTER EIGHTEEN

Stowaway Spy

CAPTAIN REGINALD SANDERSON Kearon, master of the merchant ship MV *City of Lancaster,* had spent his war being shot at by German torpedoes. He had taken command of the MV *Assyrian* in 1940, only to have it sunk under him by a U-boat. Then he took the helm of the MV *Belgravian,* until that was also torpedoed. On both occasions, he had been the last man to leave his sinking ship.

Kearon was one of thousands of unsung heroes of the Merchant Navy who continued to ply the oceans throughout the war transporting vital supplies. The merchant ships traveled in convoys, often undergunned and ill-defended. This was not like other forms of warfare: It was dirty, often boring, and enormously dangerous. The enemy was usually invisible.

The three-thousand-ton *City of Lancaster* had been built by Palmers of Jarrow in 1924 as a coal ship; now she carried food, building supplies, munitions, and anything else needed to sustain the war effort, wherever the empire required it. Her thirty-man crew were mostly Liverpudlian Irishmen, hard men who worked their hearts out at sea and drank themselves insensible on shore. The *Lancaster* was as battle-scarred as her captain. She had evacuated twenty-five hundred people from Saint-Nazaire in 1940, and seen the ship alongside her bombed and sunk with all hands. She had been stalked by German U-boats and attacked by Heinkel bombers, and she had fought back with her 10- and 12-pounders, two antiaircraft guns, and a pair of machine guns, fore and aft. No one pretended it was a fair fight.

A big, bluff Irishman born in Arklow on the coast of County Wicklow in 1905, Kearon looked like Neptune in uniform. His hair had gone gray, but the edges of his wide beard were still rust-red, as if corroded by salt spray. A strong mixture of seawater, rum, and rage ran in his veins. He was entirely fearless, beloved and feared by his crew in equal measure, and blessed by an almost mystical capacity for survival against the odds. Having spent three years as a floating target, and having had two ships sunk under him, this sea dog was longing to bite back.

The *City of Lancaster,* bound for Freetown, Sierra Leone, via Lisbon, was at Liverpool docks taking on a cargo of pipes, mail, and parcels for British POWs when Captain Kearon was summoned to the shipping office on the quay. Waiting for him was a thin, slight man in civilian clothes with an inadequate mustache. He introduced himself as Major Ronald Reed (he had been promoted). Politely, but authoritatively, the little man explained that he worked for British intelligence. Captain Kearon, he said, would soon be taking on a new crew member, one Hugh Anson, as an assistant steward. This man was a double agent, performing a vital secret mission for the British government, and Kearon would be responsible for his well-being on board. In Lisbon, he would jump ship. The desertion would leave the *City of Lancaster* shorthanded, Reed said, but this was unavoidable. Kearon should report the incident as normal, just as he would for any other crew member. The crew should be told that Anson was a former criminal who had served five years in prison in Lewes, but who had been released early, with the help of the Prisoner's Aid Society, on condition that he join either the Merchant Navy or the armed forces. His cover—as "a man who had a bad record but who it was thought had turned over a new leaf"—would help explain his lack of nautical experience, and when he vanished in Lisbon, it would simply be assumed that he had turned over an old leaf.

Reed was grave: "From now on this man's life is in your hands. It is absolutely essential that no word of his mission should become known to the crew." Finally, he produced a large bulky envelope, tied with string, sealed with a blue seal, and stamped "OHMS," On His Majesty's Service. The package should be locked in the ship's safe, and then handed to "Anson" on arrival in Lisbon. Inside was Chapman's Colt revolver with a spare loaded chamber, fifty £1 notes, and a ration book and a clothing book made out in the name of Hugh Anson. There were also press clippings, describing an explosion at a factory in northern London.

Back in his hotel room, Reed wrote that Captain Kearon "impressed me as being discreet." Reginald Kearon, in truth, was thrilled to have a British spy on board his ship.

Chapman and Tooth had checked in to the Washington Hotel. Reed was staying at the rather more comfortable Adelphi. Even in the secret world, the officer class had privileges, and it was safer that the three conspirators not be seen together, just in case anyone was watching.

Hugh Anson was the name of the petty criminal who had been the driver of the Jelly Gang's getaway car. In his cover story, Chapman would explain to the Germans that he had paid Anson £100 for all his identity cards, and had then substituted his own photograph for that of Anson, who agreed to "lie low" for two months before reporting the missing documents. Chapman would claim that he had obtained his seaman's papers by bribing one Frani Daniels, a criminal contact at the shipping office. The real arrangements for shipping out Chapman had proved far more intricate. The MI5 counterfeiters had put together a "complete set of forged civilian papers," including a National Service registration form, a National Health Insurance card, and an unemployment book. But obtaining the correct seaman's papers was proving a "vast and complicated" business. Finally, with the help of a local MI5 operative named Hobbes, Reed decided to steal a selection card from the catering department of the Merchant Navy. Hobbes walked into the Liverpool shipping office pretending to be inspecting the fire precautions, and walked out with the necessary papers—which Reed then fraudulently filled out over a beer in the corner of the Flying Dutchman pub next door. "This course, though morally incorrect, was practically suitable," Reed reported.

That evening was spent going over arrangements for communicating with Britain when and if Chapman gained access to a German radio. Reed decided that the best way to send simple messages was by means of a simple code embedded in Chapman's "ham chat," the little flourishes he had always added to his messages, notably his "laughing out" signs.

The message QLF is a jocular sign meaning "please send with your left foot," and 99 means something a little more insulting. If Chapman sent QLF, it would indicate that his German spymasters were "completely satisfied"; if he sent 99, it would mean they were "suspicious." More complex messages could be sent using the various combinations of the laughing sign:

> HU HU HU: No information to impart.
> HA HA HA: Nantes Abwehr unit is closing down.
> HI HA HU: I am going to Berlin.
> HA HU HI: I am going to Paris.
> HU HI HA: I am going to Angers.
> HE HE HE: I am going to America.
> HE HE HE HA: A group of Americans have gone to the USA and are operating there.

"The 'laughing out' sign occurred throughout Zigzag's traffic [and] it is not thought that any question will be raised by the enemy," wrote Reed.

If he gained unsupervised access to a wireless, he should send messages in the usual way but encoded on the word "DELIGHTFUL." Chapman had been invited by the Germans to invent a code word for his first mission, and had come up with CONSTANTINOPLE. If, in the future, he was asked by the Germans to think up another code word, it was agreed that he would select POLITENESS. Unbeknownst to Chapman, Bletchley Park could already read any message he sent, but having the code word beforehand would make the lives of the codebreakers even simpler. "We shall not have the bother of having to attempt to solve his messages but will be able to do so immediately," wrote Reed.

Von Gröning had always passed on his copies of the *Times* to Chapman. When a message from Zigzag had been safely received, Reed would post a message in the personal columns of the newspaper, on either the Tuesday or Thursday after receipt, stating: "Mrs. West thanks the anonymous donor of the gift of £11." The second digit of the number would describe the number of the message received. So if MI5 had picked up six messages, Mrs. West would thank her unknown benefactor for £46. With luck, the fictional Mrs. West (a small tribute to the housekeeper at Crespigny Road) should end up a wealthy woman.

Finally, Reed and Chapman laid an "elephant trap." Chapman was instructed to tell his Abwehr masters that before leaving Britain, he had made arrangements "that if any other members of the German secret service require assistance," they could contact the safecracker Jimmy Hunt at the telephone number Gerrard 4850. When the phone was answered, the caller should say: "It is Lew Leibich speaking, and I would like to speak to Jimmy." The number would be directly linked to a telephone on Ronnie Reed's desk at B1A, who would arrange an appropriate reception committee.

With a map of Lisbon, Reed and Chapman located the German safe house on the Rua São Mamede, and the German consulate. Reed also made Chapman memorize a Lisbon telephone number, to be called in case of emergency. Ralph Jarvis, the MI6 representative in Lisbon, had already been alerted that an important agent was en route. The Radio Security Service and Bletchley Park were instructed to keep a watch for any reference to Fritz in the Most Secret Sources.

At the end of the evening, Chapman announced that he wished to write a farewell letter to Freda. Reed suggested he send it via Laurie Marshall, who would forward it. The letter was copied and duly sent on to Freda. The letter of adieu remains classified, but the covering letter to Marshall reads: "Goodbye for the present, I shall soon be back with you at 35—thank you for your kindness to me—please give or forward this letter to Freda." This was not the tone of a man in fear for his life.

The following day, Chapman presented himself at the Board of Trade office. The clerk accepted the forged paperwork without demur, merely remarking that the shipping company had sent another assistant steward to the *City of Lancaster* and clearly "did not know what they were doing." Chapman was told to report to the ship and prepare to sail the following day. They returned to the hotel, where Tooth packed Chapman's belongings, including two new white steward's uniforms and fourteen sheets of what, to the naked eye, appeared to be plain white writing paper, and searched his clothing for anything that might betray him, just as Praetorius had done so many months before. Chapman then set off for the docks, Reed reported, "in the approved style with kitbag over his shoulder."

Tooth and Reed followed "at a very respectable distance." Possibly the distance was too respectable, for "somehow or other, after trudging for a number of miles around the docks, Zigzag disappeared." One moment he had been walking ahead, doing a very reasonable impression of a jolly jack-tar, and the next he had vanished. Reed wondered if Chapman had suddenly had second thoughts and absconded. With rising anxiety, they searched the docks but could find neither Chapman nor, infuriatingly, the *City of Lancaster.* Finally, they gave up, and began walking dejectedly back to the hotel. They had told Chapman to meet them at the Adelphi, but "some sort of feminine intuition" told Reed that his spy might just have returned to his own, less classy hotel: "Sure enough Zigzag was in the bar, with a prostitute."

They decided not to interrupt him, but tiptoed away, leaving him to finish his negotiations. From the Adelphi, they called the bar of the Washington and got Chapman on the line, who cheerfully reported that he had found the boat, left his kit on board, and been instructed to return the next morning at 8:00 a.m. "He did not wish to dine with us as he was 'busy,' " Reed reported, delicately. They agreed to rendezvous in Reed's room at the Adelphi at 9:00 p.m.

Reed and Tooth dined at the hotel, and just before the appointed hour climbed the stairs to Reed's suite. On opening the door, they found Chapman inside: "Zigzag had, in some way, managed to obtain entry and was reclining on the bed awaiting dinner which he had ordered on my telephone, together with a number of bottles of beer." In the space of a few hours, Chapman had confirmed all the qualities that made him a great crook, a superb spy, and a most fickle man: He had written a love letter to the mother of his child, vanished, slept with a prostitute, broken into a locked room, and helped himself to room service at someone else's expense. He had also, it emerged, stolen Reed's gold-plated scissors and nail file, "which he had coveted for a time." This was all as Young had once predicted: Chapman would do his duty, while merrily picking your pocket.

Reed could not bring himself to be angry. Indeed, the incident deepened his affection for this strange young man he had known for all of eight weeks. "Zigzag is himself a most absorbing person. Reckless and impetuous, moody and sentimental, he becomes on acquaintance an extraordinarily likeable character. It is difficult for anyone who has been associated with him for any continuous period to describe him in an unbiased and dispassionate way. It was difficult to credit that the man had a despicable past. His crimes of burglary and fraud, his association with 'moral degenerates', and his description as a 'dangerous criminal' by Scotland Yard is difficult to reconcile with more recent behavior."

Chapman's past *was* despicable; his recent actions had been almost heroic (with lapses); but his future remained quite unknowable. At the docks, Chapman waved, and headed up the gangplank of the *City of Lancaster,* leaving Reed to reflect: "The case of Zigzag has not yet ended. Indeed, time may well prove that it has only just begun."

CHAPTER NINETEEN

Joli Albert

ON MARCH 15, 1943, the *City of Lancaster* steamed out of the Mersey to join the convoy assembling in the Irish Sea, forty-three merchant vessels in all, escorted by three destroyers and four more lightly armed corvettes. The ships formed into lines, with the escorts on either side, ahead and astern, like sheepdogs, moving the flock forward, wary for predators. Hugh Anson, the new assistant steward, was told to find a berth with the gunners and then report to the captain's cabin. As the convoy sailed south, Chapman and Kearon held a hushed and hurried consultation. The captain, "fearing prying fingers," offered to safeguard any of his passenger's secret spy equipment, and was rather disappointed to be handed some ordinary sheets of writing paper. He locked them away in the safe, being careful not to get his fingerprints on them. Kearon explained that he would treat Chapman like any member of the crew, but in the course of the passage he would expect him to behave in an unruly fashion, since this would confirm his cover story as a "bad lad" and help explain his disappearance when they reached Lisbon.

If they reached Lisbon. That afternoon, a lone German bomber streaked out of the sky and released its payload, narrowly missing a five-thousand-ton cargo boat carrying explosives and ammunition. High above, the Focke-Wulf reconnaissance planes circled. "Nervous expectancy showed on every face," and Chapman noticed that the crew slept fully clothed. Not that he had time to notice much, as

Snellgrove, the chief steward, put him to work scrubbing out, serving meals, and generally doing the dogsbody work expected of a
rookie. Chapman complained, loudly. Snellgrove noted that "Anson
was seasick most of the time and quite useless at his job."

That night, as the convoy headed into the Atlantic, Chapman
was woken from a queasy sleep by the ship's alarm. On deck, still
fumbling with his life belt, he was sent staggering by a huge explosion, followed by another. Two merchant ships and a tanker were
burning furiously, and by the light of the flames Chapman could
make out the dark shapes of the other ships. A torpedo had struck
the ammunition ship. Captain Kearon shut down the engines, and
starbursts lit up the sky. The U-boats, it seemed, had slunk away
again. The windows of the ship's bridge had been blown out, and
glass lay around the deck. There was no further attack that night,
but Chapman could not sleep.

The next morning, Captain Kearon told him that seven ships
were missing from the convoy, three of which had been sunk by col-
lisions during the night, or from damage incurred by the exploding
munitions ship. Chapman reflected that this was just the sort of information he might usefully pass on to the Germans in Lisbon, since
it would confirm what they already knew, but demonstrate keenness
on his part. For the same reason, Chapman began making daily
notes of the ship's position and course. Since German reconnaissance planes were already tracking the ships, "no harm would be
done by giving the position of the convoy to the enemy." The captain agreed, and offered to let Chapman see the ship's logbook in
order to chart their exact position. With his remaining secret ink,
Chapman carefully wrote down the information on a sheet of writing paper.

Captain Kearon was relishing his new role as spy's assistant. But
the rest of the crew did not know quite what to make of the new
steward. Word of Anson's prison record spread quickly, and it was
agreed that he clearly was "a high-class burglar." He seemed to have
plenty of money, had a gold monogrammed cigarette case, and wore
an expensive wristwatch. Anson's nickname in Soho, he confided,
was "Stripey," on account of the time he had spent in striped prison

garb. But for a crook, he was surprisingly polite and cultured; he read books in French "for pleasure." "Several members of the crew were impressed by his good education," Kearon later reported. "The gunlayer summed up the general opinion that he was man of good family gone wrong." One evening, Chapman astonished the ship's company by announcing that he would compose a poem, there and then. With a pencil and an envelope he set to work, and then declaimed the result.

> *Happy go lucky, come what may*
> *Three cheers for Stripey, hip hip Hooray.*

As poetry goes, this little spasm of doggerel may not be up to much, but to the ears of Chapman's messmates it was Shakespeare, further evidence that they were in the presence of a genuine gentleman robber. Anson was certainly bolshie enough to be a poet, for he grumbled unceasingly. The captain duly noted down his poor attitude in the ship's log: "He said he did not like sea life as no one did their share of work, he said he did most of the work. This is definitely untrue, as I, master, have observed."

On the eighteenth, the *City of Lancaster* steamed into Lisbon port and tied up at Santos Quay. Portugal was still neutral, though its dictator was inclining to the Nazis, and Lisbon was a boiling cauldron of espionage, awash with refugees, smugglers, spies, hustlers, arms dealers, wheeler-dealers, middlemen, deserters, profiteers, and prostitutes. It was Chapman's kind of town. John Masterman described Lisbon in his postwar novel, *The Case of the Four Friends,* as a "sort of international clearing ground, a busy ant heap of spies and agents, where political and military secrets and information—true and false, but mainly false—were bought and sold and where men's brains were pitted against each other." The Allied and Axis powers maintained safe houses, dead drops, fleets of informants, and small armies of competing spies, as well as official consulates and embassies, all under the thin veneer of neutrality. The Abwehr even ran its own bars and brothels, for the express purpose of extracting information from sex-starved and drunken British sailors.

The crew of the *City of Lancaster* assembled on deck for a lecture about avoiding strong drink and loose women while on shore. The bosun, Valsamas, distinctly overheard Anson whisper: "Pay no attention. That's just a lot of bullshit."

On land, the assistant steward joined four of his crewmates at the British Seaman's Institute in Rua da Moeda, where all proceeded to get loudly drunk, in the traditional manner. Anson declared that he would pay, but after an hour of steady drinking at MI5's expense, the new assistant steward told one of the gunners he had "business to attend to" in town with an old acquaintance.

"If I find this friend I am well away," he confided.

When Gunner Humphries pressed him about the identity of his friend, Chapman merely winked and remarked mysteriously: "No names, no packdrill." He agreed to meet them later at George's, a brothel-bar on the dockside.

A few days earlier, Bletchley Park had decoded an Abwehr message to another double agent, code-named "Father," indicating that the safe house at 50 Rua São Mamede had been "brûlé," or "burned." MI5 had no way of warning Agent Zigzag that his contact address had metaphorically gone up in smoke.

Chapman's taxi dropped him at a large, dirty building, deep in the working-class district of the city. The door was answered by a young girl, who fetched her mother. *"Joli Albert,"* said Chapman brightly, and then in halting Portuguese: "My name is Fritz. May I see Senhor Fonseca?" This declaration was met with "blank faces." He tried again in German, English, and French. Finally, he wrote the name "Fonseca" on a piece of paper. This provoked a flicker of recognition, and from the ensuing mime he understood that Senhor Fonseca was not in. He wrote down the word "telephone." After some more gesticulating, the girl led him to a nearby café, dialed a number, and handed the receiver to Chapman. A man's voice answered. *"Joli Albert,"* said Chapman. The password was no more effective, but at least the man spoke a form of French. He agreed to meet Chapman at the café next door. With deep misgivings, Chapman waited, smoking heavily and drinking foul Portuguese brandy.

Finally, a slim young man in his late twenties appeared, with a much older man, who spoke German. Once more Chapman gave his password, and explained that he needed to see a senior Abwehr officer. Their alarmed expressions indicated how badly the plan had gone awry. Clearly, they "did not know anything about the matter," and with every word he uttered, Chapman was putting himself in greater peril. He apologized for his mistake and told the two men to "forget the whole business." Then he ran.

Back at George's Bar, the party was in full swing. Chapman slipped into the throng of sailors and tarts, his return almost unnoticed, and was soon in conversation with an English-speaking Portuguese barmaid called Anita. She was twenty-six, thin, with a dark complexion, wavy black hair, and deep-brown eyes. She was also a prostitute and a paid MI6 informant. She would later tell British intelligence that the man everyone knew as Anson had confided that his real name was Reed. Ronnie would have been scandalized.

Chapman spent the night with Anita in a small hotel near the harbor, wondering if the Germans had given up on him, whether he was heading into a trap, and whether his career as a double agent was already over.

Early next morning, Chapman entered the smart lobby of the German Legation on Rua do Pau de Bandeira and told the sleepy man at the front desk that his name was Fritz, that he was a German agent, and that he would like to see the senior Abwehr officer. The man yawned and told him to come back in two hours. When he returned, the receptionist was markedly more alert, even attentive. An official of some sort appeared, and told Chapman to go to a house in the nearby Rua Buenos Aires. Outside the address he had been given, a Fiat car was waiting with the engine running and two civilians in the front seat. Chapman was told to sit in the back and was driven in silence to yet another address, a flat at 25 Rua Borges Carneiro. There he was escorted upstairs, where the two men politely invited him to explain his business. Chapman told the story he knew by heart, for the first of what would be many recitations. The taller of the two, clearly senior, nodded and occasionally asked questions, while the other, a small, fat man, took notes. When Chapman had finished, the tall man thanked him politely, and told him to remain on board his ship but to kindly return to this address the following day.

That evening, Captain Kearon could be heard roasting Steward Anson for spending a night ashore without permission and warning him bluntly about the perils of venereal disease. When Anson told the captain to "mind his own business," Kearon exploded and told him "any future offence must entail prosecution at home." The crew agreed: Anson was on very thin ice.

Though Captain Kearon put on a grand show of fury, the master of the *City of Lancaster* was deeply relieved to see Chapman return. When they were alone, Chapman described how he had spent two days being ferried and shunted from place to place, and added that if and when he came to make a report to MI5, he could tell them that the Abwehr was a bureaucratic nightmare. Kearon would later state: "He instructed me to report that the organization worked just the same as it does in London. He said Ronnie would be pleased to hear that!" Kearon made a suggestion: When Chapman was ready to leave the ship, he should start a fight. This would allow the captain to punish him, and provide the obvious rationale that Anson had jumped ship to avoid another prison sentence in Britain.

When Chapman returned the next day to Rua Borges Carneiro, he was ushered into the presence of an elegant young man in horn-rimmed spectacles, who introduced himself as "Baumann" in excellent English and "apologised for the inconvenience" of the previous day, as well as Germany's failure to welcome him with due fanfare. The man offered Chapman a cigar and a glass of brandy, then invited him to tell his story once more. The identity of Chapman's suave interrogator is uncertain: MI5 would later identify Baumann, alias Blaum, alias Bodo, as an officer who had served as chief of the Abwehr sabotage section in Lisbon since 1942. But it is equally possible that Baumann was Major Kremer von Auenrode, alias Ludovico von Kartsthoff, the head of the Lisbon Abwehr station. Chapman himself believed that Baumann was "connected with Johnny," the German code name for Agent Snow. Owens's German controller had been a Major Nikolaus Ritter, alias Doktor Rantzau.

Whoever he was, Baumann seemed to know a great deal about Chapman's time in France, his mission, and its results.

Chapman handed over the sheets of paper with the secret writing, and then made Baumann an offer he had been mulling ever since setting sail for Lisbon. During his sabotage training in Berlin, Chapman explained, he had learned how to construct a coal bomb by drilling a cavity into a large lump of coal and then packing it with high explosive. Placed in the bunkers of a ship, the device would remain unnoticed until shoveled into the furnace, whereupon it would explode, sinking the vessel.

If Baumann would provide him with such a bomb, said Chapman, he would hide it among the coal on the *City of Lancaster,* then jump ship as planned, and send the boat, her captain, and her crew to the bottom of the Atlantic Ocean.

•   •   •

Tar Robertson was unflappable. But when the latest batch of wireless intercepts arrived from the Most Secret Sources on the morning of March 21, he almost took flight. Agent Zigzag had been in Lisbon two days, and already he seemed to be contemplating an act of gross treachery by offering to sink the ship that had taken him there.

In a top secret message, the Abwehr station in Lisbon had informed Admiral Wilhelm Canaris that Agent Fritz was in a position to sabotage a British merchant vessel with a coal bomb, and requested authorization to proceed. The operation required permission from the Abwehr chief himself, since it "contravened the established policy of the Abwehr not to undertake sabotage in or from Portugal." To make matters worse, the same message described the precise route to Lisbon taken by the *City of Lancaster,* and how many ships had been sunk in the attack on the convoy: This information could only come from Chapman. At the very least, he had "told the Germans more about his convoy than he should have done." At worst, it was further evidence of treachery.

Robertson convened a crisis meeting and drew up a series of goals, in order of priority. First, to protect the ship and its crew; second, to preserve the Ultra secret and the Most Secret Sources; and, finally, "not to interrupt Zigzag's mission unless he was, or it seemed probable that he was, double-crossing us."

Reed could not believe that Chapman would turn traitor so swiftly. Had he been forced or instructed to carry out the sabotage, or was it his own idea? "Whatever view we took of Zigzag's character and patriotism we could not run the risk of taking it for granted that he would not, in fact, commit the sabotage," he wrote. While the meeting was still in progress, Berlin sent a message approving the sabotage of the *City of Lancaster.*

MI6 had also read the cables, and offered to use its own people in Lisbon to neutralize Zigzag. Robertson told them to wait. The *City of Lancaster* was not due to leave port for a few days, and since Chapman was planning to jump ship just before she set sail, there was probably still time to intercept him and the coal bomb.

Major Reed, wrote Tar, was "acquainted with the relevant facts and considerations." Moreover, "the master and Zigzag both know Mr. Reed and it is therefore easier for him to approach them with less chance of arousing German suspicion." Reed must fly to Lisbon at once, where he should find Chapman and interrogate him immediately. Unless Chapman volunteered information about the sabotage plot, freely and without prompting, he should be arrested at gunpoint and "brought back in irons." Chapman might be surprised to see Reed pop up in Lisbon, but there was no reason he should deduce that the Abwehr's messages had been intercepted: "It would be quite natural for us to send Mr. Reed out to ascertain if he had contacted the Germans and what they had said."

Little Ronnie Reed, the radio ham who had joined up because he liked to play with wirelesses, was about to find himself a leading player in a rapidly unfolding drama that might require him to bring a known criminal back to justice at the point of a gun.

While Reed was scrambling to catch the next passenger flight to Lisbon, Chapman went back to Rua Borges Carneiro to pick up the bombs. A few days earlier, he had handed Baumann a sample lump of coal from the ship's bunkers. Welsh coal has a distinctive grain and color, and the German forgers had achieved remarkable results. Baumann now presented him with two irregular black lumps about six inches square—in shape, weight, and texture indistinguishable from real Welsh coal. Rather than drill out an existing piece of coal, as the Doctor had done, in order to pack in more explosive Baumann's engineers had taken a canister of explosive with a fuse attached and molded a plastic covering around it, which had been painted and covered in coal dust. The only clue to the lethal contents was "a small aperture, the diameter of a pencil, in one face."

Chapman was impressed: The bombs, he declared, "could not possibly be detected." He told Baumann that he would plant them in the bunkers that night and jump ship the following morning. Baumann confirmed that all the necessary paperwork was ready to get him out of the country, including a new passport with a photograph taken in Lisbon two days earlier.

That evening, Chapman walked up the gangplank of the *City of Lancaster*, somewhat gingerly, with two large coal bombs in a rucksack strapped to his back. He did not know that Ronnie Reed was hurtling toward Portugal as fast as wartime air travel could carry him; nor did he know that Captain Jarvis of MI6 had posted an agent to watch the ship, and was standing by for orders to seize and, if necessary, kill him.

But Chapman was not going anywhere near the furnace, and he had no intention of blowing up the ship. He was simply using his initiative, as instructed. His friend and fellow bomb enthusiast, that courtly and well-bred "Mr. Fisher," had asked him to obtain some German sabotage "toys," and that was precisely what he intended to do. Mr. Fisher, he reflected, would be thrilled to get his hands on the two beauties in his backpack.

Once on board, Chapman carefully stashed the rucksack in his locker. He then approached a large gunner by the name of Dermot O'Connor, who was dozing on his bunk, and punched him hard on the nose. The brawny Irishman had been identified by Chapman as the crew member most likely to be goaded into a brawl without asking awkward questions. This conjecture was proven entirely accurate.

O'Connor erupted from his berth like a surfacing killer whale, and the two men set about thumping one another with enthusiasm, noise, and any weaponry that came to hand. There are two versions of how the fight ended: According to Chapman's self-flattering account, he finished off O'Connor by whacking him on the head with a half-empty bottle of whiskey; according to Captain Kearon (and every other witness), O'Connor neatly felled Chapman by head-butting him in the eye. Chapman was carried off to the sick bay, bleeding profusely and shouting that the Irishman had violated "the Queensberry rules." When they had been patched up, both men were fined half a day's pay by Captain Kearon, who loudly told Chapman that he was now in serious trouble.

A farcical staged scene followed:

CAPTAIN KEARON: "Have you met a better man at last?"
ANSON: "After fighting him fairly and beating him by the Marquis of Queensberry rules he head-butted me in the face. The people on this ship are hooligans."
KEARON: "Are you the only decent one on board then?"
ANSON: "Yes."

At dawn the next day, Assistant Steward Anson, the left side of his face cut and badly bruised, was detailed to take Captain Kearon his early morning tea. Chapman knocked on the door of the captain's cabin and slipped inside, carrying a tea tray in one hand and a rucksack with two large bombs in the other. Chapman had earlier explained to Kearon that he was "trying to get a special bomb on board for transport to home," and he now thrust the coal bombs into the captain's hands, explaining that "he had put to them the proposition that he should sabotage the *City of Lancaster* and the enemy had agreed." Kearon was no shrinking violet, but even he quailed at being handed ten pounds of high explosive in his bed by a man with a face that seemed to have gone through a meat grinder. He announced that he would weigh anchor immediately and head home. Chapman insisted that the bombs were safe unless heated, and that any change of plan would only attract German suspicion. The captain was eventually "persuaded to carry on his usual route and act as though nothing had happened." Now wide awake, Kearon opened the safe, extracted Chapman's package, pushed the two evil-looking bombs inside, and shut the door, quickly. Chapman stuffed the papers and money in his rucksack and handed the revolver back to the captain, "as a present." In return, the captain gave Anson the address of his sister-in-law, Doris, who lived in Porto, just in case he had any trouble. They shook hands, and Chapman slipped away into the dawn.

Captain Kearon's cameo role in British military espionage was over. The British spy had acted his part superbly, the captain reflected. "He lived up to his reputation as a jail-bird very realistically." This was not, perhaps, entirely surprising.

· · ·

That afternoon, the Most Secret Sources picked up a message from the Lisbon Abwehr station confirming that Fritz had completed his mission. The news was relayed by Captain Ralph Jarvis of MI6 to Ronnie Reed of MI5 when he arrived at Lisbon airport at 5:30 p.m. on Tuesday, March 23, traveling under the name Johnson, an official with the Ministry of War Transport. Reed's heart sank. If Chapman had planted the bomb, he was a traitor guilty of attempted murder, and the tons of coal in the ship's bunkers would somehow have to be sorted through, piece by piece. Jarvis explained that Captain Kearon had been interviewed by his agents at the shipping office and "denied emphatically that Hugh Anson had any connection whatsoever with British intelligence." Reed replied that the captain probably thought he was protecting a British agent, and obeying orders to "tell absolutely no one about the connection."

Captain Kearon and Ronnie Reed met, alone, at the Royal British Club in Lisbon. The MI5 case officer could tell immediately from the captain's buoyant and conspiratorial expression that his fears were unfounded. Kearon explained that Chapman had "behaved magnificently," that the "plot" to sabotage the ship had been a ruse to obtain the bombs, and that two lumps of exploding coal were now sitting in the safe of his ship, which he would be only too happy to pass on as soon as possible. Anson had specifically told him that "the coal was High Explosive and was to be given to Ronnie," and had suggested that MI5 should stage some sort of fake explosion on board, "in order to send up his prestige" with the Germans.

Kearon also described how he and Chapman had agreed that the ship's course and the attack on the convoy could be reported to the Germans without endangering British shipping, and how Chapman had valiantly allowed himself to be followed by a large Irish gunner for the sake of his cover story. When the waiter was not looking, he passed over the names and addresses in Lisbon Chapman had left with him, and a revolver.

Reed sent a jubilant telegram to Tar Robertson: "Convinced Z playing straight with us."

The relief was shared in London. Not only had Chapman demonstrated his loyalty, but British intelligence now had two intact bombs of a type they had never seen before. "This is typical of the risks that Chapman has been prepared to undertake on our behalf," wrote Tin Eye Stephens. He had offered to carry out a sabotage mission knowing that when the *City of Lancaster* did not sink at sea, he would inevitably be suspected of double-dealing, "with possibly fatal results to himself." Yet he had been prepared to take the chance. "He thought that the value to the British of getting examples of the devices used by the Germans justified the risk to himself."

Slightly less thrilled by the outcome was MI6. Relations between the sister services were often strained, and the men of external espionage did not appreciate the men of internal security encroaching on their patch. MI6 flatly refused to contemplate staging a fake sabotage of the *City of Lancaster* in Lisbon, pointing out that this would be "politically complicated."

Ralph Jarvis of MI6, in civilian life a merchant banker, rattled poor Ronnie Reed by pointing out that the coal bombs might be activated by a delay fuse rather than heat, and could explode at any moment. Reed did not share Lord Rothschild's insouciant approach to high explosive. He thought better of packing the bombs in his luggage: "It would be most unfortunate if an explosion were to take place in the plane on my return journey home, both for the plane, the political consequences, and myself . . ."

Rothschild instructed that the bombs should be photographed, x-rayed, placed in a heavy iron box padded with cork, and then sent to Gibraltar on the next British vessel, addressed to "Mr. Fisher" c/o ANI, Whitehall. In Gibraltar, the package would be picked up from Captain Kearon by an MI5 agent who would say: "I come from Ronnie." Rothschild was insistent on one point: The bombs should be sent "if possible intact and not sawn in half." Only someone like Rothschild could imagine that anyone else would *want* to saw up a lump of coal packed with high explosive.

CHAPTER TWENTY

Damp Squib

NO ONE PAID much attention to the Norwegian sailor with the livid black eye who boarded the afternoon flight from Lisbon to Madrid, and sat quietly at the end of the airplane. He carried a Norwegian passport in the name of Olaf Christiansson, describing him as a seaman, born in Oslo. There was a party of Norwegians on board, but their quiet compatriot did not engage them in conversation. Indeed, he could not, because he did not speak a single word of Norwegian.

At the Madrid airport, a stocky little man with rosy cheeks emerged from the waiting crowd. "Are you Fritz?" he whispered. "Yes," said Chapman, *"Joli Albert."* At the Hotel Florida, Chapman dined on roast pork, drank a bottle of sticky Spanish wine, and slept for twelve hours. The next five days passed in a blur. Chapman lost count of the nameless German visitors who came and went, asking the same questions, or very slightly different questions. Sometimes the interrogations took place in his hotel room, or in the lounge, or nearby cafés. The rosy-cheeked German gave him 3,000 pesetas and told him he might want to stock up on clothes, tea, coffee, and "other articles difficult to obtain in Occupied Europe." So he was going back to France. Through the Madrid streets, Chapman was followed, discreetly, by a smiling little shadow.

The man who had first interviewed him in Lisbon, later identified by MI5 as Abwehr officer Konrad Weisner, reappeared at the

Hotel Florida and announced that he would be accompanying Chapman to Paris. In a private sleeper compartment, Chapman lay awake as the stations rumbled by in the darkness: San Sebastian, Irun, Hendaye, Bordeaux. At dawn on March 28, the train pulled into the Gare d'Orsay: waiting on the platform was Albert Schael, Chapman's moon-faced drinking companion from Nantes, the original Joli Albert and the first familiar face he had seen. They embraced like old friends, and as they drove to the Abwehr apartment on the rue Luynes, Chapman asked where Dr. Graumann was. Albert, speaking in an undertone so the driver could not hear, hissed that he had been sent to the eastern front, "in disgrace."

The cause of von Gröning's banishment is unclear. Chapman later learned that his spymaster had quarreled with the head of the Paris Branch on an issue of "policy," and von Gröning's prodigious intake of alcohol had then been used as an excuse for removing him. Von Gröning later claimed that he had wanted to send a U-boat to pick up Chapman but had been overruled, sparking a furious disagreement. It is equally possible that like other members of the Abwehr, von Gröning's loyalty to Hitler had come under suspicion. Whatever the cause, von Gröning had been stripped of his post in Nantes and ordered to rejoin his old unit, the Heeresgruppe Mitte, in Russia.

Chapman considered Dr. Graumann an "old friend," but more than that, he was a protector and patron. If anyone could shield Chapman from the Gestapo, it was Dr. Graumann. His disappearance was a serious blow. The interrogations continued: The Luftwaffe colonel who had seen him off at Le Bourget airport and the pilot, Leutnant Schlichting, quizzed him about his jump and landing. They were followed by an army officer, unnamed and unfriendly, and then a civilian, who rattled off a series of "about 50" technical questions about British military installations and weapons, none of which Chapman could answer. Whenever Chapman inquired after Dr. Graumann, he would receive "vague replies" to the effect that he was "somewhere on the Eastern Front." Finally, Chapman screwed up his courage to announce that he wanted to see Dr. Graumann immediately and that he "would not give his story or work for anyone else." The request, and the accompanying fit of pique, was ignored, or so it seemed.

The general tenor of the questions was affable but persistent. Chapman was allowed to "amuse himself" in the evenings, but always accompanied by Albert and at least one other minder. But his request for an "advance" on the money owed him was flatly rejected. After an angry protest, he was given 10,000 francs to spend, which was later increased, with evident reluctance, to 20,000. This was not the hero's reception and untold riches he had been hoping for. The disagreement left Chapman feeling distinctly uncomfortable.

Chapman memorized the faces of his interrogators, and the few names he could glean. But most of his mental energy was devoted to telling and retelling the story, half-truth, half-fiction, that had been seared into his memory over the days and weeks in Crespigny Road. The story never altered, and Chapman never faltered, though he was careful to offer only vague timings and dates, mindful of Tar Robertson's warning: "Timing is the essential factor to conceal, the cover story must not be too precise." He knew the story so well that at times he believed it himself. We know the story, because a verbatim transcript survives.

I landed at about 2:30, in a ploughed field. I was at first stunned by my descent, but on recovering my sense I buried my parachute under some bushes by a small stream running along the edge of the field. I undid the package which had been strapped to my shoulders, taking with me the transmitter and putting the detonators in my pockets. I could see a small barn not far away and, after approaching this cautiously, I realized that it was deserted and entering through a window I climbed up into the loft and slept until daybreak. I was not aware of the time I awoke, because my watch had stopped. It had apparently been broken by my descent. I left this barn and walked along a small road and on to the main road, traveling in a southerly direction, until I saw a signpost which said Wisbech. A study of my map showed me I must be somewhere near Littleport, and when I arrived in the village I saw the name on the railway station. Inspection of the times of trains to London showed that one was leaving at 10:15. I caught this and arrived at Liverpool Street at about a quarter to one. I entered the buffet there, had a drink and bought some cigarettes and, after staying for a few minutes, went to a telephone booth in the station and called Jimmy Hunt at the Hammersmith Working Man's Club. Whoever answered the phone said that Jimmy would be in at about 6 o'clock, so I took the underground train to the West End and went to the New Gallery Cinema, where I saw "In Which We Serve." I thought it best not to walk about the West End in daylight so soon after arriving.

I stayed at the cinema until blackout time and then phoned Jimmy again at the club. He was very surprised to hear my voice, but arranged to meet me at the underground station at Hyde Park. When he arrived we went into a nearby public house and I told Jimmy that I had managed to escape from Jersey and that I had so many things to talk over I thought it would be better if we could go somewhere quieter. I was especially anxious that the police should not know that I was back in the country, so Jimmy said that we had better go to one of his cover addresses in Sackville Street where he was living with a girl. I told him I did not want anyone else to see me, so he phoned her and told her to go out for a time as he had a business friend calling on him. She was used to disappearing when Jimmy had "shady" business to transact so this did not appear unusual.

On arrival at the flat in Sackville Street I explained the whole thing to Jimmy. I told him that when I was imprisoned in Jersey I had decided to work for German Intelligence; that they had treated me extremely well and had promised me a considerable amount of money if I would carry out a mission in Britain. I had brought £1,000 with me and had been promised £15,000 if I succeeded in sabotaging De Havillands. It was an invaluable opportunity for

Jimmy to obtain quite a lot of money and the protection of the German government to get him out of the country. I showed him the radio transmitter I had brought with me and said that I required some place where I could work this. Jimmy told me that the police had been after him quite a lot lately and that he had been considering renting a house in Hendon. Meanwhile, however, it would be advisable for me to stay at the flat in Sackville Street and keep pretty quiet.

I went along to the house in Hendon on Saturday and I transmitted from there for the first time on Sunday morning.

I explained to Jimmy how necessary it was for me to start straight away and obtain the materials for my sabotage at De Havillands. We agreed it would be unwise for me to go out very much, in case the police were on my track, but Jimmy said that there remained some gelignite at St. Luke's Mews which we had used on jobs before the war.

I went to De Havillands with Jimmy one day round about the new year, and we surveyed the whole factory from the road nearby. We saw that there were three places which we thought should be our primary objectives. We decided to hold a reconnaissance at night time and entered by an unguarded gate, which had only a small amount of barbed wire attached to it. Near the boiler house, we came across six huge power transformers in a yard. By climbing over a wall, it was possible to gain access, and we realized that an explosive charge under one, or perhaps two of the transformers would completely ruin the output of the whole factory. We looked around and found another subsidiary power house near a building which was by the swimming pool; it was bounded by a high fence and contained two more transformers which obviously handled considerable power. We decided it would be necessary to place about 30 lbs. of explosive under each transformer, and thought it would be possible to fit this into two suitcases.

On the night arranged we went up there at about 7 o'clock and parked the car behind a garage in the front of the factory. We had some coffee at a place nearby and then crept through the gardens of a house at the back of the 'Comet' and slipped through the barbed wire at the unguarded gate. Jimmy made for the transformers near the swimming pool and I tackled the one near the power house. We left one hour's delay on each of our explosive mixtures, and stopped our car on the bypass about two miles away from De Havillands. Fifty-five minutes after, we heard two immense explosions, about 30 seconds apart. As soon as this occurred we came straight back to London.

The day after we had arranged for the sabotage, I had arranged to meet a girl at The Hendon Way called Wendy Hammond, who worked at a subsidiary of De Havillands. She told me that there had been an awful mess and that people at the factory were trying to hush it up and say that nothing had occurred. It was clear that there had been considerable damage, and some people were injured, but no one wanted to admit it.

Jimmy was often with me in the bedroom when I transmitted and he took a great deal of interest in the radio messages which we received. He was especially interested to know whether there was any chance of receiving his £15,000 and when you sent the message to say that it was impossible to pick me up by submarine he became somewhat truculent and thought that the chances of receiving the money were extremely remote. He said that he would come back with me to Lisbon and see that he was paid. Unfortunately, as you know, he was arrested on suspicion of possessing gelignite, and later the Hammersmith Club was raided to see if he had any other confederates. He was released by the police after he had been detained for about a week, but I did not have very much contact with him after that. Owing to the arrest of Jimmy it was not possible for him to come with me, and it would have been very much

more difficult to obtain two sets of documents to get out of
the country, so of course I had to come alone.

Sticking to the broad lines of the cover story was easy enough;
the challenge was to remain alert while seeming relaxed, to maintain consistency, to anticipate the thrust of the interrogation and
stay one question ahead. What was it Robertson had said? Speak
slowly; be vague; never tell an unnecessary lie. The rules were all
very well in the living room at Crespigny Road, but under the relentless probing of expert Abwehr interrogators, Chapman could feel
his grip slipping, as the truth and lies merged. The donnish Masterman had warned him: "The life of a secret agent is dangerous
enough, but the life of the double agent is infinitely more precari-
ous. If anyone balances on a swinging tightrope it is he, and a single
slip can send him crashing to destruction." No one could balance
forever, with so many hands tugging at the rope.

After ten grueling days in Paris, Chapman was told he would be
traveling to Berlin. The journey would take him to the heart of
Nazism, but something also led him to suspect that it "would bring
him nearer to Graumann." That suspicion was confirmed when Albert took him aside and suggested that whatever might happen in
Berlin, he should "reserve the more interesting details of his experiences in England for the time when he might meet Graumann."
The ingratiating Albert asked Chapman to put in a good word for
him with Dr. Graumann.

The train to Berlin was packed with soldiers, but a first-class
compartment had been reserved for Chapman and his new minder,
an officer he knew as "Wolf." When an army major insisted on taking a seat in the reserved carriage, Wolf summoned the train police
and the furious man was ejected, shouting that he would report the
offense to Himmler himself.

From Berlin station, Chapman was whisked to a small hotel, La
Petite Stephanie, off the Kurfürstendamm. The grilling continued.
Chapman was getting tired. The anxiety was fraying his confidence.
He slipped. An interviewer, apparently from Abwehr headquarters,
casually asked him to describe how he had constructed the suitcase

bomb used in the De Havilland sabotage. Chapman explained again how flashlight batteries attached to a detonator had been strapped to the right side of the suitcase using adhesive tape. The man pounced: In earlier interviews, in Paris and Madrid, Chapman had described how he had attached batteries to the *left* side. Chapman forced himself to think quickly but answer slowly, as Tar had instructed: "I had two suitcases—one set of batteries was fixed to the right side, and one to the left." A sweaty moment passed.

The next day, a tall, slim naval officer appeared at La Petite Stephanie, introduced himself as Müller, and presented Chapman with a brand-new German passport made out in the name "Fritz Graumann." His place of birth was given as New York; his father's name was given as Stephan Graumann. It was the strongest hint yet that his old spymaster was back in the game. Müller told Chapman to pack and be ready to leave in an hour; they were going to Norway.

•   •   •

Back in Bletchley, the codebreakers charted Zigzag's meandering route as he crisscrossed Europe from south to north. They passed on Chapman's new passport names, Norwegian and German, and noted that the supposed sabotage of the *City of Lancaster* had "certainly raised his stock" with his German bosses.

There was only one hitch: The bombs had not gone off, and though the Germans did not appear to suspect Chapman, they were becoming impatient. "The Germans have shown the greatest interest in the *City of Lancaster* and are naturally anxious to discover if the act of sabotage actually took place," Masterman warned. Anita, the prostitute from George's Bar, reported that Jack, an indigent black beachcomber who lived under a nearby bridge, had been approached by two Germans who offered him 2,000 escudos for information about sailors from the British ship. The Abwehr had broken all the rules to smuggle the bombs aboard the *City of Lancaster,* but the ship was still intact: Canaris wanted results. Ewen Montagu, the naval representative on the Twenty Committee, the panel ruling what information might safely be passed to the Germans, issued a warning: "There must either be an explosion or Zigzag is blown."

Some sort of incident would have to be staged on board the ship. Thus, Operation Damp Squib was born.

Victor, Lord Rothschild, was a little disappointed to be told he could not blow up a "perfectly good merchant ship," but he settled for "as big a bang as possible, together with a lot of smoke." The prospect of even a moderate explosion aboard the *City of Lancaster* sent his blue blood racing: "A good decent bang would be a good idea. I do not know how much of a bang one can make without doing damage. I suppose it depends where the bang takes place."

Together, Rothschild and Reed cooked up an elaborate scenario. When the ship docked in Britain, Reed would go aboard, disguised as a customs officer, accompanied by another agent in similar disguise carrying an explosive device in an attaché case. This agent, "who will previously have been to MI5 head office for tuition in working the bomb," would pretend to search for contraband, plant the bomb in the bunker, light the fuse, and then get out of the way, quick. When he heard the explosion, the agent would "fall down and pretend he has hurt his arm, which will be bandaged by the master." He would then explain that "he was poking the coal in the bunker when there was a hissing noise, followed by an explosion which blew him over." The crew would then be interrogated and sailors' gossip would do the rest. "The story of the sabotage will get back to the enemy through some members of the crew," Reed predicted.

The operation required a special bomb that would make plenty of noise and smoke without killing the MI5 agent who set it off, igniting the coal, or sinking the ship. Rothschild turned to his friend and fellow explosives enthusiast, Lieutenant Colonel Leslie Wood of the War Office Experimental Station, who duly produced a device guaranteed to make a "sharp explosion, accompanied by a puff of reddish smoke, approximately three minutes after ignition." Wood sent a parcel to Rothschild by courier: "Herewith your three toys: one for you to try yourself, *not* in the house! The other two for your friend to play with."

Operation Damp Squib was a very silly plan. It was complicated, risky, and involved far too much playacting ("binding up a notional injury is fortuitously introducing unnecessary 'business' of a dangerous kind," warned Masterman). Damp Squib was vetoed, much to Rothschild's annoyance, and he vented his frustration by blowing up all three toys himself.

Instead, the bomb would have to be "discovered" when the ship reached Glasgow; this would be followed by a full interrogation of everyone on board. "When the *City of Lancaster* next touches at Lisbon, German sub agents will certainly try to get in touch with members of the crew and will get the impression (probably in most cases from some intoxicated seaman) that something curious had happened on the voyage because there was a formidable inquiry when the ship returned to the UK. This is all that is necessary in order to build up Zigzag."

Sure enough, when the ship put in at the Rothesay docks on April 25, a small army of Field Security Police clambered aboard and began rummaging through the coal bunkers, tossing the coal over the side, piece by piece. The gawping crew noticed that "as each piece of coal was thrown into the dock they all ducked." Finally, after some five hours, an officer, "who was very dirty and smothered in coal dust," was seen emerging from the bunkers, triumphantly "holding in his hand an object which looked like a lump of coal." Every member of the crew was then interrogated, with particular emphasis on the voyage to Lisbon and the disappearance of Assistant Steward Hugh Anson.

Autosuggestion worked its magic: Sailors who had noticed nothing out of the ordinary about their former shipmate now declared that they had suspected Anson was a German spy from the moment he came on board. They recalled his gold cigarette case, his wads of cash and "swanking" manner, his general incompetence at sea, his good manners, and his apparent education "beyond his station." Under interrogation, all sorts of sinister details emerged: the way he had boasted of his crimes, bought drinks for everyone, and then slipped away from George's Bar. Why, he even wrote poetry and read books in French. One of the crew produced Chapman's poem as conclusive proof of the man's fiendish brilliance. "The standard of the poetry does not come up to the flattering adulation of the crew," one of the interrogators remarked dryly, but to the men of the *Lancaster*, the accumulated evidence pointed to one conclusion: Anson was a multilingual, highly educated Nazi spy who had tried to murder them all with an "infernal machine" hidden in the bunkers.

As "a spur to rumor-spreading," the crew was solemnly sworn to secrecy. The gossip raged through Glasgow docks like a brushfire, to Reed's delight: "Approximately 50 people now regard Zigzag as an enemy agent and know about this bomb business, and it will grow in the telling, which is precisely the result [we] wish to have." The rumor was passed to other seamen, and from there, through countless bars, to different ships and other ports, and from thence across the seas. It even reached the ears of the owner of the *City of Lancaster*, who was livid: "He has no objection to helping put agents on board, but he thinks it is going a bit far when they leave explosives around on the ship."

From the lowest bars of Europe, the story of how a top German spy had tried to sabotage a British ship reached German High Command, the FBI, and the highest levels of the British government. A copy of the Zigzag file was sent to Duff Cooper, the former minister of information now supervising covert operations, who in turn showed it to Winston Churchill. Cooper reported that he had "discussed Zigzag at some length with the prime minister who is showing considerable interest in the case." MI5 was instructed to give the case the highest priority and to inform Churchill immediately "if and when contact is reestablished with Zigzag."

J. Edgar Hoover, the FBI chief, was also watching Zigzag's trail. Through John A. Cimperman, the FBI liaison officer based at the American embassy in London, Reed and Rothschild channeled "comprehensive memoranda" on the Chapman case to the American government. "I promised Mr Hoover that I would let him have appreciations of the sabotage aspects in return for their co-operative attitude," wrote Rothschild. Chapman was fast becoming a secret star worldwide: In Washington and Whitehall, in Berlin and Paris, his exploits, real and unreal, were discussed, admired, and wondered at.

But then Zigzag/Fritz, the most secret spy in the Most Secret Sources, vanished from the wireless traffic, abruptly and completely.

Rittmeister Stephan von Gröning (alias Doctor Graumann), Chapman's aristocratic German spymaster. Courtesy of Ingeborg von Gröning

Stephan von Gröning as a young officer in the White Dragoons, ca. 1914. Courtesy of Ingeborg von Gröning

Oberleutnant Walter Praetorius (alias Thomas), Chapman's principal German minder and a Nazi fanatic with a taste for English folk dancing.
© National Archives

Franz Stoetzner (alias Franz Schmidt), the German agent with the cockney accent who spied in Britain before the war while working as a London waiter. Courtesy of MI5

Karl Barton (alias Hermann Wojch), the principal sabotage instructor at La Bretonnière. Courtesy of MI5

Colonel Robin "Tin Eye" Stephens, commander of Camp 020: interrogator, martinet, and inspired amateur psychologist. © BBC

Lord Victor Rothschild: peer, millionaire, scientist, and head of MI5's wartime explosives and sabotage section. Rothschild and Chapman discovered a shared passion for blowing things up. © Topfoto

John Cecil Masterman: Oxford academic, thriller writer, sportsman, and spymaster; the intellectual behind the Double Cross operation. National Portrait Gallery, London

Jasper Maskelyne, the professional conjuror employed by the War Office to baffle and deceive the Germans. © British Library, London

Major Ronnie Reed, the unobtrusively brilliant BBC radio engineer who became Chapman's first case officer. Courtesy of Nicholas Reed

Reed operating Chapman's German radio set. Courtesy of Nicholas Reed

Dagmar Lahlum, the
Norwegian girlfriend
unofficially recruited by
Chapman into MI5.
Courtesy of Bibbi Røset

Freda Stevenson, pictured here with
baby Diane, her daughter fathered
by Chapman. This was possibly the
image sent to Chapman in Jersey
prison. KV2 462 © National Archives

Betty Farmer, the woman
Chapman abandoned at
the Hotel de la Plage in
1938. "I shall leave, but I
will always come back."
© News International Syndication

Graffiti in the attic at La Bretonnière, the German spy school in Nantes, including what appears to be a likeness of Betty Farmer, Chapman's girlfriend, probably drawn by the apprentice spy himself. Courtesy of the author

Hitler caricatured as a carrot in the attics of La Bretonnière: evidence that von Gröning may have actively encouraged a disrespectful attitude toward the Führer. Courtesy of the author

La Bretionnière. This photograph, taken by Stephan von Gröning in 1942, remained in his wallet for the rest of his life. Courtesy of Ingeborg von Gröning

Chapman after the war.
© News International Syndication

Chapman pictured in a West End drinking den with Billy Hill, crime baron and self-styled "King of Soho," and the boxer George Walker (right). © News International Syndication

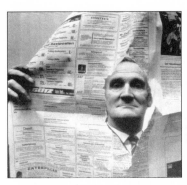

Chapman protesting in 1952 after his attempts to serialize his memoirs in a newspaper were stymied under the Official Secrets Act.
© Topham/AP

Hamming it up for the camera in full SS uniform, an outfit he never wore in real life.
© Popperfoto.com

The Iron Cross awarded to Chapman by a grateful Führer for his "outstanding success." No other British citizen has ever received the medal.
Courtesy of Nicholas Reed, photo by Richard Pohle

Chapman in his pomp, posing with his Rolls-Royce. As honorary crime correspondent for the *Sunday Telegraph,* Chapman specialized in warning readers to steer clear of people like himself. © *Daily Telegraph*

CHAPTER TWENTY-ONE

The Ice Front

STEPHAN VON GRÖNING never spoke of the horrors he witnessed during his second stint on the eastern front, but he was "deeply affected" by the experience. He recalled one episode only: being sent to reopen a church that had been closed by the Communists, in some small town that the Germans had overrun. He remembered how the village people entered the building and fell to their knees. Von Gröning was not a religious man, but he had been moved by the expression of profound piety in the midst of a pitiless war. In the last few months, he had aged by several years. His hair was now gray, his face more sallow and drooping. His hands shook until stilled by the first drink of the morning. Much of his dissipated hauteur had dissolved in the freezing winds of Russia. At the age of forty-five, von Gröning had begun to look like an old man.

But the erect figure in the military greatcoat waiting behind the barrier at the Oslo airport was still instantly recognizable. "Thank God you are back," said von Gröning. "He appeared really moved." As for Chapman, he was genuinely delighted to see "the old man," his affection undimmed by the months he had spent betraying him, and his intention to continue doing so. Von Gröning introduced the chubby, balding figure in naval uniform beside him as Kapitän Johnny Holst—his real name, for once. The man grinned cheerily and welcomed Chapman to Norway in execrable English.

As they drove into the city, von Gröning explained that Chapman would soon be free to "enjoy a well-earned holiday," but before that, he must be interrogated one last time, and a full, definitive report had to be sent to Berlin.

Von Gröning had arrived only a few days earlier and taken up residence in a smart "bachelor flat" at 8 Grønnegate, near the presidential palace, where he now opened a bottle of Norwegian aquavit to celebrate Chapman's safe arrival. The party began. An attractive young woman named Molli was the first guest to arrive, then a tough and shrewd-looking German called Peter Hiller, and finally Max, a Pole with long hair and flashy jewelry. Chapman remembered little of his first night in Oslo, but he recalled that the guests seemed "pleased to see him and were very enthusiastic about his success in England," and none more so than von Gröning. When Chapman asked for news of the rest of the Nantes team, the German was vague. Walter Thomas, he said, was currently in Berlin, and would shortly be traveling to Oslo to resume his duties as Chapman's "companion." Inwardly, Chapman groaned; the young Nazi with the passion for English country dancing was such grim and earnest company. The "hard-drinking Holst," currently dissolving into the sofa to the strains of a German drinking song, seemed a far more jovial chum. Soon afterward, a fight broke out between Holst and Hiller over Molli's charms, and Chapman passed out.

The interrogation started the next morning, despite the seismic hangovers of both interviewer and interviewee. Von Gröning was a masterful inquisitor. For a start, he knew his subject intimately and the best ways to feed Chapman's vanity, ignite his anger, and prick his pride. Behind the heavy lids, he seemed half asleep at times, but then he would dart a question under Chapman's guard that would leave him scrambling. The interrogation continued for two weeks with every word recorded and transcribed by Molli Stirl, the woman at the party, who was secretary of the Oslo Abwehr station. Von Gröning was unrelenting and meticulous, but there was something different about the way he questioned Chapman, something far removed from the harsh grilling in Spain, France, and Berlin. Von Gröning wanted Chapman to get it right; when he made an error, of chronology or fact, he would gently lead him back, iron out the inconsistency, and then move on again. Von Gröning was on Chapman's side; he was willing him to succeed, for Chapman's sake, but also for his own.

Chapman sensed the shift in their relationship. In Nantes, he had been dependent on von Gröning's goodwill, eager for his praise, flattered by his attention. The roles had not quite been reversed, but equalized. Chapman needed von Gröning to believe him, and von Gröning needed Chapman to succeed, forging a strange, unspoken complicity. At times, the older man seemed almost "pathetically grateful" to Chapman, without whom he might still be wading through the slush and blood of the eastern front. Von Gröning was "proud of his protégé," but he was also reliant on him, and that, Chapman reflected, was his "best security." Von Gröning's status had plummeted when Chapman disappeared; his return had raised von Gröning's stock in the Abwehr once more. Chapman was more than just another spy: He was a career investment, the "man who had 'made' him in the German Secret Service," and they both knew it.

The mutual dependence of spy and spymaster was not peculiar to Chapman and von Gröning; it was the central defining flaw of the German secret service. The Abwehr's decentralized structure allowed individual officers to control their own networks of spies. Wilhelm Canaris sat in judgment over all, but the separate branches, and even individual officers within the same branch, operated with a degree of independence, and in competition. In the British secret services, case officers shared responsibility, since a spymaster whose self-interest was bound up with the success of his own agent could never see that agent clearly. "Absolute personal integrity and the exclusion of all personal considerations is the first and fundamental condition of success," insisted Masterman. In the Abwehr, by contrast, each spymaster was ambitious for his own spy to the point where he might suppress his own suspicions and insist on the loyalty or efficiency of an agent despite evidence to the contrary. Even when a spy was useless, or worse, the spymaster would be unwilling to admit the failure, on the assumption, logical but fatal, that it was "better for selfish reasons to have corrupt or disloyal agents than to have no agents at all."

Did von Gröning see Chapman clearly through those watery blue eyes? Several times, Chapman noticed his "watchful" expression and wondered if his yarn had been unraveled by this man who knew him better than any other. As one associate put it: "Stephan made up his own opinion, he was secretive, and he did not tell people what he was thinking unless they asked." If von Gröning suspected he was being lied to, that the entire tale of sabotage, heroism, and escape was a monstrous fabrication, he said nothing, and the heavy-lidded eyes chose not to see.

Chapman was installed at the Forbunds, a large and comfortable wood-built hotel in the Oslo city center, which had been commandeered by the Abwehr and the Luftwaffe. Von Gröning handed over 500 kroner as spending money and told him he could have more "as and when he required it." The reward would be paid when the report had been written up, taken to Berlin, and approved.

Chapman came face-to-face with the war of occupation for the first time. In France, he had mixed with a handful of tarts, collaborators, and black marketers, but he had little contact with other French citizens. In London, his conversations outside the security service had been few and strictly supervised. Now he observed Nazi rule at unpleasantly close proximity.

The invasion of Norway, in April 1940, had been swift and devastating. The nation was decapitated, and King Haakon fled into exile in London. The Norwegian Nazis, led by Vidkun Quisling, assumed office as a puppet government under German rule. Hitler had simple ambitions for Norway: to defend it against the expected British counterinvasion, to bleed the country white, and to convert it to Nazism. The Norwegian people, however, declined to be bullied into fascism. Pressure and threats gave way to outright coercion. In the spring of 1942, Goebbels declared of the recalcitrant Norwegians: "If they will not learn to love us, they shall at least learn to fear us." Many had learned to fear the Nazis in the ensuing Gestapo-led terror, but more had learned to hate them. A few collaborated, as a few always will; the more extreme or ambitious joined the Norwegian Nazi Party, or volunteered for the Viking Regiment—the Norwegian legion deployed by Hitler on the eastern front. Quisling, vague, inefficient, and fanatical, won the rare distinction of being so closely associated with a single characteristic—treachery—that a noun was created in his name. At the opposite moral pole, an active Norwegian resistance movement organized protests, strikes, sabotage, and even assassinations.

Between the extremes of collaboration and resistance, the majority of Norwegians maintained a sullen, insolent loathing for the German occupiers. As a mark of opposition, many wore paper clips in their lapels. The paper clip was a Norwegian invention; the little twist of metal became a symbol of unity, a society binding together against oppression. Their anger blew cold in a series of small rebellions and acts of incivility. Waiters in restaurants would always serve their countrymen first; Norwegians would cross the street to avoid eye contact with a German and speak only in Norwegian; on buses, no one would sit beside a German, even when the vehicle was jampacked, a form of passive disobedience so infuriating to the occupiers that it became illegal to stand on a bus if a seat was available. Collaborators were shunned by former friends, neighbors, and family. They were seldom openly rebuked, but they were socially ostracized. The resistance groups called this the "Ice Front," Norwegian society's collective cold shoulder intended to freeze out the enemy.

The Germans and their Norwegian collaborators sought refuge from the hostility in a handful of places where they could socialize, such as the Ritz Hotel and a large restaurant renamed the Löwenbräu, which admitted only Germans and collaborators. But even here, Chapman recalled, sealed off from the rest of Norway, "it was an uneasy feeling." Norwegians assumed that Chapman was German and avoided him. They answered in monosyllables, or eyed him with ill-veiled contempt from behind what he called a "wall of hatred." He had experienced none of this antagonism in France. A naturally sociable man, Chapman was learning what it feels like to be loathed.

Chapman's discomfort was compounded by the sensation that his German handlers also regarded him with some distrust. The grinning Johnny Holst accompanied him everywhere, friendly but vigilant. The German officials who came and went at the Forbunds Hotel "appeared somewhat suspicious and were not communicative."

His disingenuous questions about intelligence operations met with silence. Von Gröning had promised him "complete freedom." Both knew that Chapman's freedom was far from complete. The Abwehr officials he met never gave their names. Not once did he cross the threshold of Abwehr headquarters, a large block of flats at Klingenberggate. Von Gröning instructed him to relax and "not to work." He had assumed this was a reward, but gradually the realization dawned that this enforced leisure was a security precaution, a way of keeping him at arm's length.

He was told to carry a pistol, to report if he felt he was being followed, and to ensure that he was never photographed. British agents were doubtless watching him, von Gröning warned, and might even target him. But the Germans were also watching him. And so were the Norwegians.

Chapman had been in Oslo a few days when Praetorius, the man he knew as Walter Thomas, finally arrived, dirty and disheveled after a three-day train journey via Sweden, and more than usually grumpy. Praetorius, newly married to Friederike, his childhood sweetheart, had been undergoing training in Berlin for officers intended for the eastern front. He was furious at being ordered to babysit Chapman instead. Unlike von Gröning, who had been only too delighted to escape the carnage, Praetorius saw himself as knightly warrior in the old tradition. An ardent Nazi and anti-Communist, he was itching, he said, to do "battle against the Reds" and was determined to win himself an Iron Cross. (Chapman concluded that Thomas had a "hero complex.") Alternately spouting Nazi propaganda and practicing his English country dancing steps, Praetorius was once again a constant presence—eccentric, humorless, and profoundly aggravating. After just a few days, Chapman begged von Gröning to make him go away, but the spymaster, who found Praetorius no less annoying, said he had no choice: Berlin had specifically ordered that the young Nazi should be present at the debriefing and act as Chapman's "companion." Unbeknownst to either of them, Praetorius was compiling his own report.

After two solid weeks of interrogation, von Gröning boarded the plane to Berlin with the final version of Chapman's story, neatly typed up by Molli Stirl, in his briefcase. Chapman could finally relax, unaware that his fate was being furiously debated at Abwehr headquarters in Berlin, where one faction of the German secret service wanted him rewarded, and another wanted him eliminated. The argument can be partially reconstructed from postwar interrogations of Abwehr personnel. Von Gröning, naturally, led the supporters' club, pointing out that Chapman had performed "the only successful sabotage ever carried out" by the sabotage branch of the Paris Abwehr. His most vigorous opponent was the officer newly appointed to head the Paris station, von Eschwege, who insisted that Fritz was either "controlled by the British" or a fraud. Far from carrying out a successful mission, he claimed, "when [Chapman] went to England he did nothing, and lied about his activities."

The argument was complicated by an internal turf war and a personality clash. According to an Abwehr officer present during the debate, von Eschwege "apparently had the idea, which is not unknown to any of us, that nothing which had been done before was any good." Von Gröning, on the other hand, was described as "one of those 'don't-tell-me-what-to-do-I-know' types." The dispute raged for five days until, finally, judgment was passed, presumably by Canaris himself. The Abwehr needed a success story; there was nothing to prove that Chapman was double-dealing, and there was plenty of evidence, including English newspaper reports, to back up his account. He had shown exemplary bravery in the service of Germany and should be rewarded, congratulated, pampered, and closely watched.

Von Gröning returned to Oslo "beaming with pleasure." The Abwehr, he announced, had decided to award Chapman the sum of 110,000 reichsmarks: 100,000 for his "good work in England," and an additional 10,000 for the plot to sabotage the *City of Lancaster*. This was some 27 percent less than the 150,000 reichsmarks he had been promised in the original contract, but it was still a large sum, and an accurate reflection of circumstances; the Abwehr was only about 73 percent sure Chapman was telling the truth. Like any experienced contract criminal, Chapman asked to be paid "in notes," but von Gröning said that the money would be held for him "in credit" at the Oslo Abwehr headquarters, where Chapman could "draw on it when necessary." He did not need to add that this way Chapman would be less tempted to abscond with the cash. He would also receive a monthly wage of 400 kroner. Chapman signed a receipt, which was countersigned by von Gröning—now not only his spymaster, but also his private banker.

The scene that followed marked perhaps the oddest moment in the entire saga. According to Chapman, von Gröning then rose "solemnly" to his feet and handed him a small leather case. Inside, on a red, white, and black ribbon, was an Iron Cross—*das Eiserne Kreuz,* the highest symbol of bravery. First awarded in 1813 to Prussian troops during the Napoleonic Wars, the Iron Cross was revived by the kaiser in the First World War, and by the Second World War had become a central element of Nazi iconography, the stark symbol of Aryan courage. Hitler himself proudly displayed the Iron Cross he was awarded as a corporal in 1914. Göring won two, one in each war. The mystique of the cross was such that postcards of the most famous recipients were printed and avidly collected by children and adults alike. The medal, von Gröning said, was in recognition of Chapman's "outstanding zeal and success." No other British citizen has ever received the Iron Cross.

Chapman was astonished and privately amused by this extraordinary presentation. He reflected wryly to himself: "If I stay with this mob long enough, I might end up a Reichsmarschall . . ."

As the Nazi occupation weighed ever more heavily on Norway, Chapman, under orders to enjoy himself, lived a lotus life: "You are free to explore the countryside," von Gröning told him. "Go yachting and bathing." Chapman did what he was told. During the day, he was left to explore his new home, always with Johnny Holst or Walter Praetorius in tow. At night, they would go drinking at the Löwenbräu or the Ritz. It was hinted that his next mission might involve a sea crossing, and so Holst "was put at his disposal to teach him yachting, whenever he needed him." Holst was a wireless instructor, yet he was available to go sailing or drinking at a moment's notice, "postponing classes whenever he felt so inclined." Chapman's new companion was a strange man, cultured and refined in many ways, but a slob in others. He spoke Danish and Norwegian, loved music and the sea. When very drunk (which he was much of the time), he could be belligerent and morose; when merely tipsy (which he was the rest of the time), he was sentimental and lachrymose. He suffered from acute delirium tremens, and his hands shook violently. Holst was having an affair with another of the Abwehr secretaries, a German woman named Irene Merkl who had been a fifth columnist in Norway before the invasion. "If the British ever come to Norway, she would be shot," Holst would remark with pride.

Von Gröning, aware of Chapman's propensity for boredom, told him to "brush up on his Morse," and so he was escorted one morning to the wireless training school, lodged in a large Oslo town house, the upstairs rooms of which had been divided into cubicles, each with a locked door. Trainee spies were brought in at different times, and locked in, to ensure they never spotted one another. Chapman's telegraphy was tested, and declared to be good, though "rusty." He was then "hustled" out. Plainly, he could not be trusted to be left alone with a radio.

Life in Oslo drifted pleasantly by. Chapman, it seemed, was not expected to learn, or do, anything very much. A photographer named Rotkagel, the former manager of a Leica factory, was detailed to teach him photography, and he was issued with his own camera and film. Chapman found it strange to be "regarded as an expert"; from time to time, he was consulted on matters of sabotage, "asked to give advice as a result of his exploits," and presented to visiting German dignitaries by a proud von Gröning as "the man who has already been over there for us."

One day, Chapman half jokingly declared to von Gröning that he wanted "to buy a boat." Instead of dismissing the idea, the German promptly produced a wad of cash. From Evanson's boatyard, with Holst's help and advice, he purchased a Swedish yawl, an elegant little sailing vessel with a small cabin ideal for navigating through the fjords. As the days passed, the surveillance regime seemed to relax; Holst and Thomas no longer dogged his every step. He was even allowed to sail alone, with consequences that were almost disastrous when he put out into the Oslo fjord against Holst's advice and lost his sails in a storm. He was towed back to harbor, but instead of being mocked for his foolishness, this escape only seemed to "enhance his stock" among the Germans.

Chapman was fêted, a free captive, rich and idle; he should have been happy. But the Ice Front had chilled him. The wintry stares of the Norwegians, the sense of unreality, compounded by his own double-dealing, had wrought a change. In Nantes, he had been content to take advantage of the situation; but now, living a life of fake bonhomie and stolen luxury with his German companions, he found himself affected by the oppressive contempt of the Norwegians, a "truly brave, patriotic people."

The Ritz Hotel, a classical-fronted, cream-colored building with wrought-iron balconies in the exclusive Skillebekk neighborhood, had once been the preserve of Oslo's wealthy; now it was the chosen retreat of a different elite composed of occupiers and collaborators. Every evening, officers of the SS, the Gestapo, and the Abwehr mingled with recruits to the Viking Regiment and members of the Quisling government.

One evening in late April, Chapman was drinking at the mahogany bar of the Ritz when he spotted two young women at a corner table, laughing together. When one of them took out a cigarette, Chapman sauntered over and offered a light. *"Bitteschön."* The girl shook her head, shot a glance of acid disdain, and lit her own cigarette. Chapman noticed that up close she was "most attractive," with delicate features and large eyes with almost colorless pupils. Undaunted, Chapman drew up a chair. He was French, he lied, a journalist writing an article for a Paris newspaper. He bought more drinks; he made the girls laugh. Holst joined the group and began chatting to the other girl, whose name was Mary Larsen, in Norwegian, while Chapman set about charming her blond friend in French and English. Finally, she conceded that her name was Dagmar. Slowly, almost imperceptibly, the ice began to thaw. Chapman invited her to dinner. She refused point-blank. Chapman persisted. Finally, she relented.

Only much later did Chapman pause to wonder why a beautiful girl who hated Germans should choose to drink in the city's most notorious Nazi hangout.

CHAPTER TWENTY-TWO

The Girl at the Ritz

DAGMAR MOHNE HANSEN Lahlum was born in Eidsvoll, a small, rural town in southeastern Norway, where the Norwegian constitution was signed in 1814. The daughter of a shoemaker, Dagmar was anything but straitlaced, and from an early age she was regarded by local gossips as altogether too pretty and opinionated for their respectable town. The neighbors muttered that she had fancy airs and would come to no good. Dagmar loathed living in Eidsvoll, claiming, with some justification, that nothing interesting had happened there since 1814. She would pore over magazines sent to her by an aunt in Oslo and try to reproduce the latest fashions with her needle and thread, while dreaming of escape. "She was young, she wanted to explore the world, to learn English, and dance," a relative recalled.

Shortly before the war, at the age of seventeen, Dagmar packed up her few belongings, headed for the city, and found work as a receptionist in a hotel in the capital. She enrolled in evening modeling classes and learned to sashay and swivel her hips. She had watched, appalled and a little excited, as the solid ranks of invading German troops marched down Karl Johans Gate, but at first the occupation hardly touched her. At night, in her tiny flat at Frydenlundsgate, she read books about art and poetry, and painted elaborate clothing designs. "She wanted to improve herself." She, like Chapman, "wanted adventure."

Her first she quickly regretted. She met a much older man

named Johanssen who seemed worldly and sophisticated and married him with a 20,000 kroner dowry from her father. Johanssen expected Dagmar to cook and clean like an obedient hausfrau, which was not what Dagmar had in mind at all. She left him and demanded her dowry back; Johanssen refused. On the night she met Chapman, Dagmar was celebrating her twenty-first birthday with her best friend, Mary, and toasting the start of her divorce proceedings.

Dagmar would be the grand passion of Chapman's war, but few love affairs can have started more inauspiciously. She thought Chapman was an enemy invader, though she conceded he was charming. With her Craven A cigarettes, long ebony holder, high heels, and fashionably risqué dresses, he imagined she was just a good-time girl. Both were utterly mistaken. For Dagmar Lahlum, model and dressmaker, was also secretly working as an agent for Milorg, the spreading Norwegian resistance network. Though neither knew it, Eddie Chapman and his "beautiful and adorable" new lover were fighting on the same side.

Chapman quickly became infatuated. He adjusted his lie, dropped the pretense of being a French journalist, and claimed to be a German, born and raised in the United States. He wined and dined Dagmar with every luxury that occupied Oslo could supply. No longer did she sew her own clothes, for he bought her anything she desired. He took her sailing on the fjords; they swam naked in the icy water, and made love in the woods. As always, Chapman's love and loyalty moved on the shifting tide of his moods. He was loyal to Britain, but happy to be courted by the Nazis; he was loyal to his MI5 spymasters, but considered his truest friend to be von Gröning, the man he was betraying; he was still betrothed to Freda, but besotted with Dagmar. Von Gröning observed the blooming love affair with shrewd approval. A spy in love was a spy who might be manipulated, and Dagmar—of whom they had no suspicion—might be a most useful bargaining chip. It was precisely the same calculation MI5 had made over Freda.

Though Dagmar seemed to be in love, Chapman sensed tension and a little fear in her, something private and alert. She plainly disbelieved his claim to be German-American, and often asked how he had developed such a strange accent. She refused to accompany him to restaurants used by Norwegians. In the street, her fellow countrymen would stare at them, a Norwegian girl holding hands with a German, and she would blush deeply. The gossips noted sourly how Dagmar smoked black-market American cigarettes and sported an expensive new wardrobe. "Because she had nice clothes everyone assumed she was Nazi. It was the rule: if you had money, you must be collaborating." Chapman saw how her compatriots subtly slighted Dagmar; he sensed her hurt and embarrassment, and bristled on her behalf. One night, in the Löwenbräu, a legionnaire from the Viking Regiment made a barbed remark about Dagmar within earshot. The next moment, the Norwegian was flat on his back, with Chapman beating the glue out of him for this "fancied slight." Johnny Holst had to drag him off. From her comments, it was obvious that Dagmar was "anti-Quisling," but he knew that behind her back the Norwegians called her a "Nazi's tart." Trapped in his tangle of lies, Chapman longed to tell her the truth, but he held back, knowing the truth could kill them both.

The precariousness of the situation was underlined when Chapman was summoned to von Gröning's flat one evening and presented to a tall, gray-haired man in an expensive-looking English suit. He introduced himself as "Doktor König," in excellent English with an American accent, and he seemed to know Chapman's story alarmingly well. There was something about the intensity of his clinical manner and "hawk-like" gaze that was deeply unnerving. Chapman concluded he must be "some kind of psychologist." Without preamble, König launched into a detailed interrogation that had clearly been prepared "with a view to testing his reliability." Chapman was being hunted.

König: "Where could you leave a valuable package safely in London?"

Chapman: "The Eagle Club, Soho."

"Who would you leave it with?"

"Milly Blackwood," said Chapman, thinking quickly. Milly had indeed been the owner of the Eagle, but she was now, he knew, safely dead.

"Where would you conceal a secret message for another agent?"

"In a telephone booth or a public lavatory."

"Where did you leave your wireless?"

"I have the address of a house, in the garden of which, near a certain tree, I buried it."

The interrogator paused and gave Chapman a long look: "I am in charge of an agent who will shortly be going to England on a mission. The agent might need the wireless."

Suddenly, with a lurch, Chapman sensed the trap. The wireless, of course, was stashed away in a cupboard in Whitehall, and he had no way of contacting his British handlers to arrange for it to be buried. He could give an invented address for the hiding place, but if the Germans did send an agent to find it and turned up nothing, his entire story would unravel. No one in MI5 had spotted this flaw in his story. Even von Gröning had missed it, or chosen to overlook it. Was it a bluff? Dare he counterbluff? He was first vague, and then petulant, complaining it was "unfair" to give his radio to another agent. "I myself expect one day to be sent back to England," he blustered. It was hardly a convincing argument. The Abwehr could easily find him another transmitter. The gray-haired interrogator eyed him coldly. It was, Chapman said with thumping understatement, an "uncomfortable moment."

That evening, the gray-haired man escorted Chapman to a quiet restaurant and began to ply him with cognac, while "periodically asking awkward questions." Chapman got drunk, but not nearly as drunk as he appeared. By the end of the evening, the hawk-faced man was also slurring his words and seemed more "benign," but as Chapman staggered to his feet, the man fixed him with an unblinking look. "You are not absolutely sincere," he said.

Chapman held the stare for a second, and then grinned: "I know I am not."

When Chapman returned to the flat in Grønnegate the next morning, the gray-haired visitor had vanished, and von Gröning was in a buoyant mood. "The doctor was quite satisfied with your answers and information," he said breezily. "You passed the test."

There were other tests. A few nights later, Chapman was sitting alone in the Löwenbräu, waiting for Dagmar, when a Norwegian woman aged about forty-five sat down beside him and introduced herself as Anne. They began chatting in German. Anne remarked on his accent. Chapman replied that he had been raised in America. They switched to English, which she spoke perfectly. In an undertone, she began to complain about the occupation, the lack of food, and the swaggering German soldiers. Chapman listened but said nothing. She invited him to dinner. He politely declined. As soon as Dagmar arrived, Chapman rose swiftly and announced they were leaving. A few nights later, he saw Anne again at the Löwenbräu. She was very drunk. Chapman looked away, but she spotted him, weaved up, and hissed: "I think you are a British spy." The remark was loud enough to be heard at the next table. When Chapman related the incident to von Gröning, the German remarked simply: "Leave it to me." Chapman told himself that this Anne must have been an agent provocateur for the Germans; but perhaps she had been a genuine member of the resistance, testing his loyalties, and he had exposed her. He never saw her again.

The underground war raged, for the resistance was gaining in confidence, coherence, and skill. From 1942, British-trained Norwegian saboteurs launched a series of attacks on the Vemork hydroelectric plant to prevent the Germans from acquiring heavy water, which could be used to produce nuclear weapons. These operations, combined with Allied bombing attacks, effectively put the plant out of production and crippled the Nazi nuclear program in Norway. Each act of resistance, however, was followed by a terrible reprisal. After two Gestapo officers were shot in the fishing village of Televäg, the entire male population was murdered or sent to the Sachsenhausen concentration camp, the village was razed, and the livestock were confiscated.

One afternoon, as Chapman and Dagmar drank a cup of tea in his room, a shattering explosion rocked the hotel. Chapman stuffed his few belongings into a suitcase, then he and Dagmar clattered down the staircase to join the throng in the street, staring in wonder as the top floor of the hotel blazed. The Norwegian fire brigade arrived and began putting out the fire, as slowly and inefficiently as possible, spraying water everywhere while the Norwegian crowd jeered and cheered. Chapman thought the scene worthy of a Marx brothers script. By the time the firemen had completed their leisurely work, the Forbunds Hotel was in ruins. Dagmar disappeared from Chapman's side and returned a few moments later: "It is the work of the British," she whispered.

Chapman and his minders moved into new quarters, Kapelveien 15, a safe house in the northern suburb of Grafsin that would become the Oslo equivalent of Crespigny Road, with Holst and Praetorius playing the parts of Backwell and Tooth. In an echo of the domestic arrangements with Freda, Chapman urged Dagmar to live there, too. At first, she resisted. Her countrymen would spurn her even more as a "kept woman," and who would pay the rent? Chapman laughed, explaining that there was "sufficient money for them both." Dagmar moved in.

The money was indeed plentiful, but not endless, and Chapman was burning through it at an astonishing rate. Von Gröning was only too happy to dole out cash on demand; indeed, he encouraged Chapman to spend as much as possible, to host parties, buy Dagmar whatever she wanted, and foot the bill for every occasion. There was a method to von Gröning's profligacy by proxy. Once Chapman had spent his money, he would need to go back to work; an impecunious spy, like a spy in love, was easier to handle.

Chapman, typically, had no idea how much money was left, but he was not so careless that he failed to spot another aspect of von Gröning's financial arrangements: The German was skimming his cut. If Chapman asked for, say, 10,000 kroner, von Gröning would agree, give him a chit to sign, but then hand over perhaps half that sum. However much he requested, von Gröning always produced less, and "pocketed the balance." Von Gröning's speculations on the stock market had been disastrous, but in Chapman he had found an investment offering a substantial return, and not just in terms of career development. Hitherto, Chapman had regarded von Gröning as his mentor: upright, aristocratic, and unassailable. Now he had demonstrated that he was also an embezzler, but Chapman was happy to let his spymaster "help himself." Neither man alluded to

what each knew was going on, their tacit understanding forming yet
another strand in the web of complicity.

• • •

Kapelveien 15 could have been an illustration from a Nordic book
of fairy tales—a large wooden house set back off the road in a large
garden dotted with fruit trees and currant bushes. Roses clambered
over the roof. "It was a delightful spot," Chapman reflected. On the
door was a nameplate: "Feltman." Like La Bretonnière, his new
home had once had Jewish owners. Idly, Chapman wondered what
had happened to them.

Joshua and Rachel Feltman had emigrated to Norway from Russia in the 1920s. They had opened a barbershop, and then a clothes
shop. They had done well. In 1927, Joshua bought the house at
Grafsin. Rachel could have no children of her own, but she adopted
a nephew, Herman, and raised him as her own son. The neighbors
welcomed them. Then came the horror.

Like everyone else, the Feltmans witnessed the invasion with
mounting disbelief and deepening fear. Joshua was a big, placid
man who believed the best of everyone. The Nazis were human too,
he said. At first, it seemed he might be right. But then, early in 1942,
the Feltmans were summarily ordered to leave their home. They
moved into a flat above the shop. Herman, now twenty-four years
old, urged his parents to take refuge in neutral Sweden; the Germans were beginning to round up Jews, and tales of frightful atroci-
ties had begun to filter northward from Europe. Joshua hesitated,
and Herman decided to go alone, to prepare the way for his mother
and father. With a Jewish friend, he boarded a train for Stockholm.
As the border approached, Nazi soldiers climbed aboard and began
demanding documents. Herman's papers declared him to be Jewish. He jumped from the moving train, breaking an arm and fractur-
ing his spine. He was still in a hospital when the Germans arrested
him and shipped him to Poland.

Unaware of their son's fate, still Joshua and Rachel wavered, but
then, when the Nazis began to corral the small community of Norwegian Jews, they ran. Milorg offered to help smuggle them to Swe-

den; a group of partisans would take them, on foot, to the border, and see them safely across. Joshua loaded their possessions onto his back, and they set off. No one knows exactly what happened next. Perhaps the partisans coveted the few chattels in Joshua's sack. Perhaps their guides were secret collaborators. Soon after Chapman and Dagmar moved into Kapelveien 15, the dead bodies of the Feltmans were found in woods near the Swedish border. A few weeks later, their only son, Herman, was gassed and cremated in Auschwitz.

Seventeen-year-old Leife Myhre, who lived at Number 13, watched the new neighbors move in. He had run errands on Saturday mornings for Joshua Feltman, and Rachel Feltman had given him biscuits. He liked the Feltmans—"they were fair, hardworking, straightforward people"—and he hated the Germans. At first, some German officers had moved into Number 15, but now a new set of neighbors had taken their place. They wore civilian clothes, and over the fence he heard them speaking English. They had big parties, and afterward they would line up the bottles and shoot them, one by one. Sometimes they shot rats in the garden. "They were in extremely good physical condition. One day the telephone rang, and I saw one of them run all the way up the garden and then dive straight through an open window to answer it." Leife was impressed, in spite of himself. He never spoke to anyone in the house, except once, after the Norwegian woman moved in. "She was very attractive, and not much older than me. Once, when I saw her on the street, I stopped her and said: 'You shouldn't be mixing with these Germans you know.' She looked around and blushed and then she whispered to me: 'I am not working for them, you know.' " There was something in her expression—embarrassment, defiance, fear—that Leife never forgot.

Chapman, his lover, and his minders settled happily into the pretty house stolen from the murdered Feltmans. Chapman took photographs of the domesticated evening scene: Dagmar sewing a button on his jacket in the living room, her face shyly, or perhaps intentionally, averted; Holst, unconscious from drink on the sofa, his hand thrust down his trousers, wearing a smile of stupefaction. Chapman invariably won the shooting competitions in the back garden because Holst could not hold a gun straight on account of the DTs. Meanwhile, Praetorius would practice English country-dance steps on the back porch. Sometimes von Gröning would come to dinner. Dagmar was told that the paunchy visitor was a Belgian journalist.

One morning in May, von Gröning appeared at the house and told Chapman that they would be leaving for Berlin in a few hours, to see "certain people, connected with sabotage organisation, [who] were interested in his story." That evening, they checked into the Hotel Alexandria on Berlin's Mittelstrasse, and then drove on to a flat where three men were waiting: a *Hauptmann* in a Wehrmacht uniform, a Luftwaffe lieutenant colonel, and an SS officer in civilian clothes who was plainly drunk and "applied himself freely to a bottle of cognac" throughout the meeting. They asked Chapman some vague questions about the De Havilland plant and other potential sabotage targets in Britain, in particular the location of "vital machinery, requiring replacement from America." Chapman pointed out, sensibly, that any such military factory would be heavily guarded. While the panel absorbed this sobering thought, another bottle of brandy was opened. When that was finished, the meeting broke up.

Von Gröning was livid, declaring that he was "disgusted with the whole affair." The colonel was a fool, and the SS man was plastered, he said. Chapman was also somewhat baffled by the strange encounter, but the meeting had provided one useful piece of intelligence: The higher powers were evidently planning to send him on another mission to Britain. If that were the case, he would need something to present to MI5 on his return.

Chapman had not been entirely idle during those lazy days on the fjords, for as he cruised around Oslo, he had been quietly filling out the questionnaire he had brought in his head. He noted down possible RAF targets—ammunition dumps, the huge tanks where the Luftwaffe stored petrol on the Eckberg isthmus, the harbors where the U-boats docked and refueled. He memorized the faces of the officials he met, the names he picked up, the addresses of key German administration buildings, and descriptions of the informers and collaborators who milled around the bars. "It all depends on the opportunities that you see presented to you," Rothschild had told him. Slowly, surreptitiously, Chapman drew a mental map of the German occupation of Oslo.

One afternoon after his return from Berlin, Chapman and Dagmar untied the little yawl from its mooring and set sail, slipping out under the shadow of Akershus Fortress and heading into the expanse of Oslo Fjord. With Chapman at the tiller, they sailed past the Aker shipyards toward the Bygdøy peninsula, the finger of land that curls into Oslo's bay like a question mark. A mile from the harbor, Chapman dropped anchor, and they waded onto a small pebble beach, empty except for some deserted fishing huts.

Bygdøy was Norway's most exclusive preserve, a gated, guarded enclave divided into a series of estates, including one of the royal properties. Now it was the home of Vidkun Quisling. The pair climbed through a patch of dense woodland and found a path leading to the hilltop, on which stood a huge stone mansion, once home to a Norwegian millionaire, and now Quisling's private fortress and administrative headquarters. He had named it Gimli, after the great hall in Norse mythology where righteous souls dwell for eternity. Leading Dagmar by the hand, Chapman kept to the woods skirting the estate until they came in sight of a machine-gun tower guarding a gated entrance. Beyond it, an avenue of lime trees led to the villa. Chapman mentally measured the barbed-wire fences and counted the armed guards.

Back on board, Chapman opened a bottle of cognac, then set sail. As they scudded through the waves, he gave the helm to Dagmar, while he sketched a map of the Quisling estate and its defenses; Tar Robertson would be most interested. Chapman could never explain when, or even quite why, he decided to confess his true identity to Dagmar. Perhaps he simply could not bear to lie any more. He later denied that he had been "under the influence of drink at the time," which suggests that he was at least a little tipsy. Undoubtedly, the Ice Front played a part. Dagmar had been ostracized by her own people as a "Nazi whore"; she, Chapman, and a handful of others within the Norwegian resistance knew otherwise, but he could see the effect it was having on her. Chapman knew that "he risked losing her if he continued to impersonate a German," and holding on to Dagmar seemed more important than anything else.

Farther down the coast, Chapman anchored the little yawl. At dusk, with Dagmar in his arms, he made his declaration: He told her he was a British spy, that the Germans believed him to be a German agent, and that he would shortly be returning to Britain on a mission. Dagmar was intrigued; she had always suspected that he was not German. Above all, she was relieved, for the discovery gave her a means to untangle her own motives and feelings. She had allowed herself to be picked up by a man she believed to be German because she thought he might have information useful to the resistance, but also because he was handsome, charming, and generous. Now, having discovered his real identity, she could love him without shame. She was curious to learn the "details of Chapman's work for the British," but Chapman insisted that she should know as little as possible. He swore her to silence. She agreed, and took his secret to the grave.

Thus was Dagmar Lahlum recruited, unofficially, into the British secret service. "You could be of use," Chapman told her. Von Gröning seemed to like her; she should take every opportunity to be "alone with him" and get him to talk freely; she could also help to gather information on the other members of the Oslo Abwehr.

Chapman's declaration to Dagmar was an act of faith, but it was also a wild gamble. Her hatred of the Germans seemed as genuine as her feelings for him; he did not believe that she had been planted by the Germans at the Ritz as a honey trap. But he could not be certain. He set her a small test: to locate the Oslo headquarters of the Abwehr, which Chapman already knew. If she found the Abwehr HQ, it would be proof of her commitment; if she failed it, well, he would probably already be in a Gestapo prison, or dead. Dagmar accepted the challenge with gusto.

The next few days were anxious ones. Chapman deliberately left Dagmar alone in the company of Praetorius, Holst, or von Gröning, and then carefully studied their faces for any "change of attitude" that might indicate a betrayal. He detected not a flicker of suspicion. Two days after his confession, Dagmar whispered that she had found the information he wanted: the Abwehr headquarters was at 8 Klingenberggate, and the head of station was a naval officer, with four rings on his sleeve. Chapman began to breathe easier. Not only was Dagmar apparently faithful; she might also prove a first-class subagent, a formidable new branch of Agent Zigzag.

Dagmar seemed to be privy to all sort of interesting information; moreover, she was a vital prop. A man taking a photograph of a military installation would arouse suspicion, but what could be more natural than a young man taking snapshots of his Norwegian girl-friend? Von Gröning threw a party for Chapman's twenty-ninth birthday at his flat: Thomas gave him a radio; Holst, an ivory ashtray; and von Gröning, a van Gogh print. Dagmar baked a cake and took lots of photographs of the revelers, as souvenirs. That night, Chapman climbed into the attic of Kapelveien 15, peeled back the metal sheet that protected the wooden girder next to the chimney stack, and hid the film inside: Here was a complete photographic record of the Oslo Abwehr team, "obtained discreetly" by a vague, pretty Norwegian girl no one could ever suspect of spying.

The espionage partnership of Eddie Chapman and Dagmar Lahlum was also an alliance, at one remove, between the British secret services and the Norwegian underground. Dagmar had hinted at her links with the resistance movement, which subsequent events confirmed. One summer evening, they found themselves near the university, where a student demonstration was taking place, a protest against the latest attempt to Nazify the education system. Suddenly, the police attacked and began hauling off the student leaders. Dagmar pointed to a young man being hustled away, and whispered that he was a member of Jossings, another underground resistance group. Brandishing his SS pass, Chapman intervened and "obtained the immediate release of Dagmar's young friend," but not before a loud "argument with a German soldier and a German officer in the street."

On July 10, 1943, as they were walking arm in arm through Oslo, Dagmar told Chapman to wait in the street, and then darted into a tobacconist. She returned a few minutes later, empty-handed, looking flushed and excited, and whispered the news: "The Allies have invaded Sicily." In the early part of 1943, Allied military planners, concluding that France was not yet ripe for invasion, had opted to deploy troops from the successful North African campaign to the island of Sicily. Code-named "Operation Husky," it was the largest amphibious assault of the war so far, and opened the way for the invasion of Italy. The news of the invasion had not been broadcast on Norwegian radio, and Dagmar could only have obtained the information through the underground. Under Chapman's questioning, "she intimated, without revealing the names of any of her contacts, that this information came through the patriotic Norwegian Jossings."

Not for the last time, Chapman wondered who had caught whose eye at the Ritz bar.

CHAPTER TWENTY-THREE

Sabotage Consultant

AT THE END of the summer of 1943, with the first chill settling on the fjords, Chapman was summoned to von Gröning's flat and presented with a contract for "new sabotage work" in Britain. Chapman should sign on the dotted line, the German blandly declared, shoving a piece of paper across the desk and unscrewing the lid of his silver fountain pen. The contract was similar to the first, and promised the same financial reward. Chapman read it carefully, and handed it back, politely observing that he "did not consider the proposition of sufficient importance." He had plenty of money already.

Von Gröning was astonished, and then enraged. A furious row erupted, with the German bitterly pointing out that without his support Chapman would still be rotting in Romainville prison, or dead. Chapman declined to budge, saying that the job was too imprecise, that mere sabotage was an unworthy task, and that the money was insufficient. His refusal was partly a ruse to buy time and delay the parting from Dagmar, but also a bid for a more explicit mission that he could take back to his British spymasters. Robertson's instructions had been clear: Find out what the Germans desire, and we will know what they lack. Von Gröning's authority had been fatally compromised by his dependence on Chapman, and this was a defining moment in the relationship between patron and protégé. Von Gröning now needed his spy more than Chapman needed his spymaster. The older man raged and sputtered, threatening all manner of punishment, until his face had turned an alarming scarlet and the veins stood out on his neck. Finally, he dismissed Chapman, telling him that his allowance would be cut. Chapman shrugged: If his own income was reduced, then von Gröning would also find himself out of pocket.

The "deadlock" persisted for a week. One by one, the other members of the station—Praetorius, Holst, and even the secretaries—approached Chapman and told him of von Gröning's fury, and the dire consequences of his refusal to sign the contract. Chapman held fast, insisting he was "after some bigger and better job and would not accept anything so vague." When von Gröning cut off his funds altogether, Chapman responded with an angry letter, saying that if he persisted, he was prepared to go back to Romainville and face his fate.

Von Gröning caved in, as Chapman knew he must. The German flew to Berlin, and returned the following day in "good spirits." The Abwehr chiefs had earmarked an important new espionage mission for Chapman, for which "there would be a large reward." Chapman would be sent back to Britain to find out why the enemy was winning the war under the sea.

For the first three years of the conflict, Germany's U-boats had ravaged Allied shipping with brutal success. Prowling in "wolf packs," the submarines struck with terrifying efficiency, as Chapman knew from personal experience, before gliding away unseen and often unscathed. The U-boats usually patrolled separately across likely convoy routes, and when one located the prey, they would swarm in to the kill in a mass attack. In the course of the war, U-boats would destroy twenty-nine hundred ships, sending 14 million tons of Allied shipping to the seabed. Winston Churchill himself observed: "The only thing that ever really frightened me during the war was the U-boat peril." Recently, however, the balance of the conflict had altered, and U-boats were being successfully attacked at an alarming rate. In May 1943, some forty-one U-boats were sunk, killing more than a thousand German sailors. The Germans remained ignorant that the Enigma code had been broken, and never knew that the hunters were being hunted through their intercepted radio messages. Rather, Berlin decided that the British must have developed some sophisticated form of submarine-detection system that enabled them to track U-boats from the surface, and then take action, evasive or aggressive. Chapman's mission was to identify this submarine detector, find out how it worked, photograph it, steal it if possible, and then bring it back. For this he would be rewarded with 600,000 reichsmarks, an additional 200,000 marks in the currency of his choice, and his own Abwehr command in occupied Europe.

Here was an almost unbelievable fortune, a prize for a virtually unattainable mission, and a ringing declaration of German faith in Chapman's abilities and loyalty. At first, he hesitated, pointing out that he knew nothing of the technicalities involved and would "need coaching in what he was to look for." This would all be arranged, said von Gröning, with the complaisance of a man whose investment might be about to produce a quite astonishing dividend.

To find this fabled weapon, Chapman would be exposed to the deepest secrets of Germany's underwater war. A document arrived from Berlin containing all the information, "known or surmised," about this supposed submarine detector. A few days later, he was escorted by Holst and von Gröning to the Norwegian port of Trondheim, where three intensely suspicious officers of the marine branch of Abwehr reluctantly described what little they knew about Britain's submarine-tracking capability. The British, they explained, seemed to be using some sort of parabolic reflector with a "rebounding ray" to pick up the submarines; the detonators used on British depth charges also appeared to have an built-in device for measuring the distance from the target, and thus exploded with maximum devastation. Quite how the British asdic (later sonar) system worked was a mystery to them: perhaps, they speculated, it used an "ultra-red ray device," or television, or a technique for detecting and measuring heat from the U-boat exhaust.

Chapman was left with the "impression that these people knew very little about our U-boat detection devices" and were "extremely worried" about this secret weapon able to track a submarine, night or day, from a distance of "up to 200 miles." One U-boat, they said, had been "attacked in bad weather in thick fog," something hitherto thought impossible. U-boat casualties were "extremely high," and mounting. The officers conceded they had no idea where the device came from, but offered "the address of an engineering depot in Kensington that might be making it." Throughout the interview, as Chapman took notes, the senior naval intelligence officer "continually stared at him and remarked that he had seen him somewhere before."

Back in Oslo, Chapman was summoned to see Kapitän-zur-See Reimar von Bonin, the chief of the Abwehr in occupied Norway. It was the first and only time that they would meet. Over lunch at von Bonin's grand apartments in Munthesgate, the balding German officer, clad in full naval uniform with four gold bars on his sleeve, explained that the British antisubmarine device was so sensitive that it could detect a U-boat lying on the seabed with its engines off, and surmised that the British must be using "x-ray apparatus of some sort."

The mission was scheduled for March 1944. As before, Chapman would be parachuted into a remote area of Britain with all the necessary equipment. When he had identified or, better still, obtained the device, he should steal a small fishing boat from the southern coast of England and sail ten miles out to sea, where he would be "picked up by five seaplanes and escorted to the coast of Europe." The Abwehr apparently believed that Chapman would be able simply to steal a boat, in the middle of a war, and set sail; this was either a measure of ignorance or faith in Chapman's criminal talents, or both. He was taken to Bergen, and spent three days being trained by the harbormaster in "the use of a compass on a small fishing cutter."

The preparations to pitch Chapman into the war at sea were interrupted, however, by a slightly different outbreak of hostilities: another turf war, this time within the German High Command. In December 1943, an unidentified senior German air force officer arrived from Berlin, declaring that "Chapman was just the type of man the Luftwaffe was looking for to send on a mission." The Luftwaffe had its own plans for the celebrated British spy, and its own paranoia. A second, rival mission was now unveiled. Just as Germany's U-boats were suffering from some new detection device, so British night fighters seemed to be winning the war in the air with secret new technology. British aircraft had been downed that contained a hitherto unknown radar system; not enough hardware had survived the crashes to reconstruct the equipment, but there was sufficient to alert the Luftwaffe that it was facing a dangerous new weapon. The technology in question was probably the American-designed radar system known as AI 10 (Airbourne Interceptor Mark 10), in use by British fighters and bombers, most notably the Mosquito, since late 1943. "No reward would be too great if he could obtain a photograph or the plans of this device," Chapman was told.

Just a few months earlier, Chapman had been the object of profound suspicion. Now, it seemed, with Nazi Germany on the defensive, he was the golden boy of the Abwehr, courted by both navy and air force, "each wanting their part of the mission to have priority." Von Gröning intervened in the internal tussle: The naval mission would take precedence (and the navy would pay for the operation); the night-fighter radar would be a subsidiary target.

Chapman found his skills being put to practical use: Like some emeritus lecturer in espionage, he gave seminars as a "kind of honorary consultant in sabotage methods" to a select audience of spooks, using the fictional attack on the De Havilland plant as a textbook case. Before he had been kept away from wireless operations, but now he was asked to teach telegraphy to two young Icelanders, Hjalti Björnsson and Sigurður Norðmann Júlíusson.

Germany was becoming increasingly concerned that Iceland might be used as the launchpad for an Allied invasion of the Continent, and so the Abwehr had begun to forge an Icelandic espionage network. Björnsson and Júlíusson had been recruited in Denmark by one Guðbrandur Hlidar, a slightly peculiar Icelandic vet who was "more interested in practicing artificial insemination, in which he was a specialist, than espionage, in which he was not." Hlidar's recruitment of Björnsson and Júlíusson suggests that he should have stuck to his test tubes, for these two were not the stuff of spies: Though thoroughly willing, they were also remarkably dense. Several weeks of intensive instruction was needed before they had mastered the most basic wireless techniques.

The last remnants of the La Bretonnière gang began to break up. The relationship between von Gröning and Praetorius, never friendly, was steadily deteriorating, with Praetorius, neurotic and touchy, accusing von Gröning of plotting to keep him in Oslo to deny him the heroic military future he craved. Finally, after repeated lobbying to higher authorities to deploy him elsewhere, he got his wish. Praetorius was delighted with his new appointment, although his new position was not one normally associated with the fearsome Nazi war machine, let alone the Teutonic heroes of old. Praetorius had long been convinced of the therapeutic physical and cultural effects of English folk dancing. Somehow he had persuaded the German authorities of this and was duly appointed dance instructor to the Wehrmacht.

When Chapman asked where the young Nazi had gone, von Gröning said, with a look of disgust, that he was "touring Germany instructing the German forces in sword-dancing, reels etc, which he had learned when in England." Von Gröning was amused but amazed: The decision to deploy his deputy on the dance floor was yet further proof that the German High Command was in the hands of fools. A few weeks later, Praetorius sent a photograph of himself giving a dance lesson to the troops (sadly, this has not survived). The man Chapman knew as Thomas had been an irritating and pedantic companion, but a fund of entertaining eccentricities. Chapman felt a flicker of regret as the Nazi dancer packed his white suit and dancing shoes, and twirled out of his life forever.

• • •

Alone in the evenings, Chapman and von Gröning plotted the future: not the details of espionage, but the sort of plans old friends make together to boost morale in bad times. They agreed to set up a club or a bar together in Paris; Chapman would act as the manager, and Dagmar could be the hostess. Such an establishment, von Gröning hinted, would make "useful background for carrying on his activities" after the war. They both knew it was make-believe. With Praetorius out of the way, von Gröning relaxed and became more outspoken. He no longer seemed obliged to proclaim a jingoism he did not feel, nor to conceal his feelings about Nazism. "Hitler is by no means in charge of the direction of military operations any longer," he said. "It is entirely in the hands of the German general staff, and one no longer reads 'I, Hitler, command . . .' on army orders . . ." He confided in Chapman that he had always admired Churchill, and that he secretly listened to the BBC every night in bed. When it was reported that a number of British officers had been shot in Stalag 3, he openly "expressed disgust." He even "aired his anti-Hitler views in public," and told Chapman of his revulsion at the mass murder of European Jews. His sister Dorothea, he revealed, had recently adopted a Jewish girl to save her from the gas chambers.

Von Gröning was an old-fashioned German patriot, committed to winning the war, but equally determined to oppose the horrors of Nazism. Such views were not uncommon within the Abwehr. Wilhelm Canaris had made sure to appoint men who were loyal to him rather than to the Nazi Party, and there is evidence that from an early date he and others within the Abwehr were actively conspiring against Hitler. Canaris had employed Jews in the Abwehr, aided others to escape, and is believed to have provided intelligence to the Allies revealing German intentions. The intense rivalry between the Abwehr and the SS had been steadily building, amid accusations that Canaris was defeatist, if not actively treacherous. The Abwehr unit was extruded from actual command, and would soon fall foul of Nazi loyalists in dramatic fashion.

As the day of departure approached, Chapman and Dagmar also made plans. From the moment he had confessed to her on the boat, Dagmar "knew he would one day leave her to return to England." They, too, built fantasies out of the future, imagining the club they would run in Paris, the children they would have, and the places they would go after the war. Dagmar should continue to act as his agent after he had gone, Chapman told her. She should maintain contact with the various members of the Abwehr, and generally "keep her eyes and ears open for information that might later be of interest." He would arrange for the British to make contact with her as soon as it was safe, but she should "trust nobody unless she was

approached by somebody who gave, as a password, her full name—
Dagmar Mohne Hansen Lahlum." Since she would be working as a
British agent, Chapman grandly announced, Dagmar must be paid.

Just as he had left instructions for MI5 on looking after Freda,
Chapman now set about making provision for Dagmar. Through
von Gröning, she should be paid a monthly allowance of 600 kroner
from his account until further notice. She should also be provided
with somewhere to live. Von Gröning readily agreed: So long as Dagmar was under German protection, then Chapman's loyalty might
be assured. Holst was sent to find suitable accommodation, and Dagmar was duly lodged in a comfortable little flat at 4a Tulensgate.
Chapman now had two different women, under the protection of
two different secret services, on opposing sides of the war.

On March 8, 1944, eleven months after coming to Norway,
Chapman boarded a plane bound for Berlin, the first stop en route
to Paris, and then England. His parting from Dagmar was agonizing.
Chapman faced an uncertain future, but he left Dagmar in multiple
jeopardy, employed and secretly paid as an unofficial British agent,
but ostensibly "kept" by the German Abwehr. If Chapman's betrayal
was discovered, then she, too, would fall under German suspicion. If
Germany lost the war, her countrymen might seek reprisals against
her for "fraternising." Dagmar wept, but insisted she was not afraid.
If Norwegians mocked her, she would tell them to "mind their own
business." If the "Mrs. Gossips" back in Eidsvoll wanted to cluck and
mutter in their kitchens, so be it. They exchanged promises: She
would keep her word, and he would come back for her, one day.

• • •

As they sped toward Berlin, von Gröning and Chapman went over
the details of the mission. His code, as before, would be the "double
transposition operation type," based on the code word ANTI-
CHURCHDISESTABLISHMENTARIANISM (Chapman was never
one to make life easy for the German receivers). The days and times
of transmission would be worked out using a formula based on a
fragment of a line from the First World War song "Take Me Back
to Dear Old Blighty": "Liverpool, Leeds, or Birmingham, well, I

don't [care] . . ." All that remained was to establish a control signal, a word or phrase that would indicate he was operating freely. Chapman had already made his choice. Free messages would always contain the word "DAGMAR," the equivalent of the FFFFF sign used on his first mission. Von Gröning duly informed Paris and Berlin: "If the message does not include the word Dagmar, the agent is operating under control."

Implicit in Chapman's control signal was a coded warning to his German handlers: If anything should happen to Dagmar, then all bets were off.

CHAPTER TWENTY-FOUR

Lunch at the Lutétia

ZIGZAG HAD VANISHED, and was presumed dead. There had been a brief surge of hope when the Most Secret Sources reported that the Lisbon Abwehr station had been asked to "provide a cover address for Fritzchen at Berlin's request." But the request was never followed up, and there was no further mention of Fritzchen. The radio listeners and codebreakers of Bletchley continued to scour the airwaves for any trace of the agent. Churchill himself demanded to be informed if and when he resurfaced. But there was nothing: nothing from Chapman himself, no indication from the Most Secret Sources that the German agent Fritz was still operative, and no sightings reported by the network of SOE spies spread throughout occupied France. The Nantes station seemed to have closed down, and von Gröning's name no longer appeared in Abwehr wireless traffic. Chapman had probably broken under interrogation. Perhaps the failure to blow up the *City of Lancaster* had brought him under suspicion, or perhaps he had been betrayed by a British mole. Men like Masterman and Robertson were not sentimental, yet the thought of what Chapman may have endured before execution gave them pause for thought.

· · ·

On the freezing morning of May 5, 1944, on the rocky coast of Iceland, a seal hunter spotted three men "whose appearance and activities seemed to him suspicious." They did not look like seal hunters, they were not hunting seals, and no other sane person would be trudging through the snowy dawn at ten degrees Fahrenheit below zero. The hunter informed the local sheriff, who told the American commander stationed nearby, who sent out an expedition "into the wastelands" to investigate. They found the three men quickly, which was just as well, for they had almost frozen to death. The leader of the luckless little band was German, and the other two were Icelanders who admitted, after some "guttural protestations of innocence," that their names were Björnsson and Júlíusson.

The German, Ernst Christoph Fresnius, claimed to be gathering meteorological information for a German shipping institute, but it did not take long to persuade the bovine Björnsson to confess that they had hidden a radio transmitter and a pedal-operated generator in a nearby cave. All three were shipped to Camp 020 in London, where Stephens swiftly extracted the truth, playing Fresnius off against his "unsubtle retainers." It was only a matter of hours before Stephens learned that the trio had been sent to monitor and report on troop movements, confirming that the Germans were "worried still about the possible use of Iceland as a base for continental invasion."

So far the case seemed predictable, but when Björnsson and Júlíusson began to describe their training at a spy school in Norway, Stephens suddenly sat up and paid attention. The wireless instructor in Oslo, they said, had been a "mysterious figure, speaking bad German in a rather loud high-pitched voice, clad in a pepper-and-salt summer suit, displaying two gold teeth and enjoying the amenities of a private yacht." There was only one person in the world with that combination of dentistry and sartorial taste. Photographs of Chapman were produced, and Björnsson and Júlíusson identified their Oslo radio instructor without hesitation. The Double Cross team was overjoyed. Even dry, hard John Masterman hailed the return of "an old friend" from his monkish cell at the Reform Club. Zigzag had darted back onto MI5's radar. But what—with his sharp new suit and private yacht—was he up to?

• • •

Since Chapman's last trip to Berlin, the German capital had been thrashed and crushed by repeated and ferocious aerial bombardment. Between November 1943 and March 1944, Britain's Bomber Command had launched 16 massed attacks on the German capital, deploying up to 800 long-range bombers. Some 4,000 Berliners were killed, 10,000 injured, and 450,000 rendered homeless. A quarter of the city's living accommodation was gone, along with Kaiser Wilhelm Church, the SS Administrative College, Charlottenburg Castle, and the Berlin Zoo. The city was barely recognizable as Chapman and von Gröning drove down shattered streets through "mountains of rubble," rank with the stench of leaking gas, smoke, and putrefaction. "The whole city reeked of fire. It was like the ruins of Pompeii," Chapman reflected. The faces of the Berliners were gouged with "resignation and misery."

Chapman and von Gröning checked into the Metropol Hotel on Friedrichstrasse, and after a meager meal of tinned meat, they were driven, past the bombed remnants of the Berlin Bank and the Kaiserhof Hotel, to the Luftwaffe headquarters—a huge concrete monolith of a building on Leipzigerstrasse. On the fifth floor, a Luftwaffe captain displayed the fragments of electrical instruments retrieved from British aircraft, including a dashboard-mounted screen with which, he explained, the enemy could apparently "locate our night fighters and bombers with the greatest of ease." The intelligence officer had only a vague notion of where these machines might be found, suggesting that Chapman might try "Cossors of Hammersmith," the military manufacturer, or else locate a fighter base in England and obtain the device by theft or bribery.

Again Chapman was struck by the faith in his criminal talents: "The Germans left it entirely to [my] sagacity to get through, with the aid of former pals." Moreover, with every official he met, the scope of his mission to England expanded. He was now introduced to another officer who explained that the Luftwaffe command believed that bombers at certain British airfields were assigned to bomb specific German cities. As a subsidiary mission, Chapman, or one of his gang, should spy on the air bases in Cambridgeshire and try to ascertain the RAF's bombing schedule. A civilian named Weiss then gave Chapman a four-hour lecture on "radio-controlled rockets and flying bombs." This was the first Chapman had heard of these terrifying pilotless bombs intended to blast Britain, finally, into submission. All countries were now racing to deploy such weapons, Weiss explained, in what would be the war's fiery finale. Chapman's task would be to find out if Britain had yet produced flying bombs, and when it intended to use them.

That night, in the hotel on Friedrichstrasse, Chapman and von Gröning gazed out of the window of the Metropole Hotel, the only building still standing in the neighborhood, "an island in a sea of rubble." From the exhaustion on the faces of Berliners, the appalling wreckage of the city, and the fantastical expectations pinned to Chapman's assignment, both men had reached the same conclusion: Germany was facing defeat and desperately attempting to turn the tide before the imminent continental invasion. Von Gröning now "made no secret of the fact that he expected Germany to lose the war," and he confided that he had begun "converting much of his money into articles of value"—assets that could be moved easily in the unpredictable aftermath of defeat—and stashing them in his mansion in Bremen. The flying bombs represented a last reckless gamble, von Gröning said, but the Nazi propaganda machine was still predicting total victory. "If their weapons are not successful," he added soberly, "the reaction will be enormous."

Chapman and von Gröning were ordered to proceed to Paris and await instructions: Chapman was lodged once more at the Grand Hotel, while von Gröning stayed at the Lutétia, the SS headquarters on the boulevard Raspail. Agonizing suspense followed. The delay, von Gröning explained with frustration, was "due to the inability or reluctance of the Luftwaffe to find a plane." Chapman wandered the streets of Paris and beheld a city broken in morale and spirit, racked by oppression, with the black market, hunger, and disease thriving. There was growing French resentment at the Allied bombing raids that killed Germans and ordinary civilians indiscriminately, and little enthusiasm for the expected invasion. In the cafés,

Chapman heard people mutter: "Life under the Germans is prefer-able to having no homes."

In mid-April, word came through that Chapman would fly from Brussels. He and von Gröning scrambled to Belgium by train, only to learn that the flight had been called off "owing to the danger of interception by night-fighters." They trailed disconsolately back to Paris. In May, there was a fresh flurry, when Chapman was informed he would be dropped near Plymouth during a German bombing sortie, but again he was stood down. The Allied invasion could begin any day, von Gröning told him, and "if he landed in England before it started, his first and most important mission would be to discover the date and place [of the attack]." Although von Gröning expected Germany to lose the war eventually, he, along with most Germans in occupied France, remained airily confident that Germany's Chan-nel defenses could "repel any attack."

Adding to the tension, Chapman had been allocated a new "shadow," in the shape of a young, slightly built man from the Luté-tia known as Kraus, or Krausner. Von Gröning warned Chapman that Kraus, a homosexual who frequented the Paris underworld, had a reputation as a spy catcher and had trapped more enemy agents than anyone else in German counterespionage, and was "as-tute in posing off-hand questions." Like every other German officer, he had a task for Chapman—the delivery of a camera and money to an agent already established in Britain.

One evening after dinner, Kraus asked nonchalantly if Chapman knew Dennis Wheatley, the British thriller writer. Chapman said he had met him. "Is he working for British Intelligence?" asked Kraus. Chapman pretended to be indignant: "How the hell should I know?" Chapman did not know, as Kraus evidently did, that Wheat-ley had become a key member of the London Controlling Section, the top secret nerve center organizing strategic deception under the direction of Lieutenant Colonel John Bevan.

On a Sunday morning in the place Pigalle, Chapman recog-nized a fellow former hostage from Romainville, a young Algerian named Amalou. That evening, they met in a café in the Latin Quar-ter called Le Refuge, where Amalou explained that he had been released from the prison after Chapman; he didn't know why, nor why he had been arrested in the first place. When Chapman asked for news of Anthony Faramus, Amalou shrugged sadly. Faramus had been taken from the prison a few months after Chapman. No one knew if he was alive or dead.

Faramus was now in the Mauthausen concentration camp. At Buchenwald, he had been starved, frozen in his ersatz tunic and wood-soled shoes, beaten, and worked in the slave gangs until he collapsed. "If and when I come to my end," he had reflected, "the remains of my body will be dragged across the muck to the outside and dumped at a spot from which, later on, the crematorium wagon will come to fetch it." Faramus had calculated that he might have "approximately six months of natural life left" when, for no reason he could discern, he was loaded on to another train, and transferred to Mauthausen, the vast labor camp in Upper Austria.

Here, conditions were, if anything, worse than in Buchenwald, for this was truly, in the words of Faramus, "an extermination camp, a boneyard." The Mauthausen-Gusen complex of camps was intended to be the most hideous of all: Here, the "Enemies of the Reich," the intelligentsia, and others could be exterminated by lethal labor. Disease, violence, brutality, and the gas chambers killed relentlessly. Over fifty-six thousand people perished at Buchenwald; as many as three hundred thousand may have died at Mauthausen. Some workers sought death: Skeleton-slaves working in the quarries at Mauthausen would wait for their guards to be distracted, find the heaviest boulder they could lift, and hurl themselves off the cliff sides. Others, like Tony Faramus, his leg ulcerated and poisoned, his body riddled by disease, waited listlessly for the end. While Chapman wondered what had happened to his friend, Faramus was also racked by wonder: "All the time, I wondered—why? Why such bestiality? What was the purpose of it all?"

A few days after the meeting with Amalou, Kraus casually remarked to Chapman that he would like to visit Le Refuge in the Latin Quarter. Chapman was stunned. He began "to think furiously." Had he been followed to the café? Had he said anything to Amalou that could expose him? Had he put himself, or Faramus, in deeper danger by inquiring after his friend? Was Amalou an informer? Chapman suggested that they go to the Lido instead, and an unpleasantly "knowing" smile darted across the face of Kraus.

Shortly afterward, a letter from Dagmar arrived, saying she was "having a good time and had met a certain Sturmbannführer," the agreed-upon code that she was still being paid and was not under suspicion. The letter had already been opened.

On June 6, 1944, the Allies invaded northern France in the largest seaborne invasion ever launched. Operation Overlord was supported by Operation Fortitude, the deception carried out by the Double Cross team. For months, the double agents of B1A had been feeding disinformation to the Germans indicating that the invasion would be aimed at the Pas de Calais region. In addition, leaked diplomatic misinformation, false wireless traffic, and fake infrastructure in the form of wooden tanks and landing craft were all used to bolster German belief that the attack would be aimed at the southern part of the coast, while Fortitude North sought to plant the expectation of a simultaneous assault on Norway. German reserves were kept back in preparation to defend Calais from an attack that never came. Instead, Allied troops poured into Normandy, wrong-footing the enemy in one of the most successful wartime deceptions ever achieved.

D-Day changed everything, including Chapman's mission. MI5 had come to believe Chapman could achieve "the unbelievable"; in parts of the Abwehr, there seems to have been a growing belief that he could work miracles. In the fervid days following the invasion, the German spy chiefs even discussed infiltrating Fritz into the Normandy beachhead to operate behind the lines, with "any uniform he liked (that of a padre was suggested), any money he wanted, and the assistance of other agents." Berlin sent instructions that he should find the code used in transmissions between ships "for the shelling of coastal towns by the navy in support of the land forces." The plan foundered when it was pointed out that even a spy of Chapman's resource would find it hard to swim out to a ship in the middle of a bloody conflict disguised as a military chaplain, and then steal top secret codes.

It was agreed that Chapman should instead train a team of fifth columnists to be left behind in Paris if the Germans retreated. He was set to work teaching Morse to two women volunteers who proved entirely unsuited to the task: one, an excitable Italian ballet dancer called Monica; the other, a former typist named Gisella. Chapman noted with admiration Monica's "dimples," but he began to suspect that he was now marooned within the frantic German military bureaucracy.

Von Gröning was also depressed. He told Chapman that he was convinced he would "never leave," but he had other reasons to worry: The Abwehr was no more. Following yet further evidence linking Abwehr officers to anti-Nazi activities, Hitler had pounced. He had summoned Canaris and accused him of allowing the secret service to "fall to bits." Canaris had shot back that this was hardly surprising as Germany was losing the war. Hitler fired Canaris immediately, shifting him to a meaningless position. The Abwehr was abolished, and its operations absorbed into the RSHA—the Reichssicherheitshauptamt ("Reich Security Main Office")—under Himmler's SS. Von Gröning found himself no longer working for the liberal Canaris but under the control of Walter Schellenberg, chief of the SS foreign intelligence service.

In his gloom, von Gröning even contemplated his own spy mission, declaring that he would volunteer to stay behind in the event of a retreat and pose as a French antiques salesman to coordinate the fifth column. Chapman put this plan down to an "excess of brandy." Chapman tried to cheer him up, and for his birthday he bought him an engraved ivory statuette as a memento of their stay in Paris.

In June, Germany produced its long-feared counterpunch, unleashing on London the first of its flying bombs, or V-1s (the "V" standing for *Vergeltungswaffe*—"reprisal weapon"). "Terrible devastation will ensue," von Gröning predicted, "since nothing could survive the explosion within a 4,000 meter radius." The destruction would be such that if Chapman ever did reach Britain, he might be unable to use his radio, since all power plants would be destroyed. On the thirteenth, the first day of the flying-bomb barrage, the German and the Englishman tuned in to the BBC to hear the reports of the damage. Von Gröning's face fell: The bombing was the last item of news, the reference to Hitler's new weapon "slight," even nonchalant. There had been "few casualties." The broadcaster was lying (more than six thousand British civilians would die from V-1 attacks over the next nine months) but it was a fine piece of propaganda. Von Gröning dismissed it as such, but he admitted that the flying bombs would prove "a flop" unless their effectiveness could be properly assessed.

Chapman had finally convinced himself that Germany would lose the war without his help when, once again, the spymasters sprang into unexpected action. A message arrived from the new bosses in Berlin announcing that a plane was now "at Chapman's disposal"; he would fly from Holland on June 27. The reason for the sudden activity lay in the flying-bomb campaign. Uncertain of the effects of its mighty barrage due to the fog of British propaganda, Germany needed reliable eyes and ears on the ground. Chapman's new mission was to assess the extent of the destruction caused by the V-1s and send back details, along with weather reports and barometric readings. He would act as target spotter and damage assessor, to enable the gunners to aim their flying bombs from launchpads in northern France with greater precision.

• • •

In the paneled splendor of the Lutétia Hotel, von Gröning ran through Chapman's mission. In order of priority, his tasks were to obtain details of Britain's U-boat tracking apparatus; to locate and steal the device used in night fighter aircraft; to report on the effects of the V-1s, giving precise timings and the resulting damage; to provide weather reports; to locate the various U.S. air bases in Britain; to identify which German cities were being targeted by each air base, and to employ another member of his gang to monitor them and report using a second radio.

The sheer complexity of Chapman's multiple mission reflected a mounting desperation on the part of German intelligence, a realization that only a truly spectacular breakthrough could affect the momentum of the war. The Germans, unaware that their entire spy network had been turned against them, believed that they had several active agents in Britain. Some of these were held in high regard. None had ever been asked to undertake a mission of such difficulty and danger. Fritz had attained near-mythical status, and somewhere in the upper echelons of the German High Command it was believed, in a triumph of wishful thinking, that this lone British spy could yet help win the war for Germany.

For this exalted purpose, Chapman was issued with the best espionage kit Germany could provide, including a miniature Wetzlar camera, a Leica camera (to be passed on to the unnamed spy in Britain), a Leitz range finder and exposure meter, and six rolls of film. No longer was there talk of Chapman unearthing his old radio in Britain; he now had two brand-new sets complete with aerials, headphones, five crystals, and a Bakelite Morse code key. For self-defense, and possible self-destruction, Chapman was handed a Colt revolver with seven rounds, and an aluminum phial containing a white liquid and several pills, poison with instant effects that "might come in useful, should anything go wrong." Finally, Chapman was presented with a bulky canvas bag containing £6,001 in used notes of various denominations (the equivalent of almost $360,000 today), separated into envelopes—the most money Chapman had seen since the smash-and-grab raids of the 1930s. As part of his cover, he carried two fake letters: one addressed to Mr. James Hunt of St. Luke's Mews, London; the other signed by "Betty" and filled with "harmless chatter."

• • •

The Abwehr might have been disbanded, a failed organization in many ways, but nobody could fault its officers' hospitality and sense of occasion. Von Gröning announced that a farewell luncheon would be held at the Lutétia Hotel for the departing Fritz, spy number V-6523. With every hour, the Allies drew closer to Paris, but in von Gröning's convivial universe, there was always time for a party.

And so, on June 25, 1944, a celebrated German spy and secret British double agent was guest of honor at a lunch party at the SS headquarters in occupied Paris. The guests were von Gröning, the sinister Kraus, two attractive secretaries from the typing pool, and an intelligence officer from Bremen who was a friend of von Gröning's. In a paneled private dining room, around a table loaded with food and wine, the guests drank to Chapman's health and wished him good luck. Even Chapman found the occasion "unreal." Midway through the main course, the telephone rang and he was handed the receiver. It was a senior SS officer, conferring his personal best wishes and sending up "two bottles of cognac and cigarettes for the party." Von Gröning rose tipsily to his feet and gave a farewell speech, extolling Chapman's past exploits and predicting that his mission would have "a profound effect on the war." Was there, perhaps, just a glimmer of irony in von Gröning's voice when he raised a glass to Chapman's future "triumph"? Chapman noticed that Kraus wore his unnerving "half-smile" throughout.

The bibulous farewell party spilled onto the pavement of the boulevard Raspail, as von Gröning, Chapman, and a large leather suitcase containing his equipment were loaded into a waiting car. "The last glimpse I had of the chiefs of the Lutétia was the group of them standing waving from the front steps as we drove away."

CHAPTER TWENTY-FIVE

The Prodigal Crook

As a blustery dawn rose over Cambridgeshire on the morning of June 29, three weeks after D-Day, a man in civilian clothes could be seen walking, unsteadily, down Six Mile Bottom Road, with a large leather suitcase balanced on his head, swearing to himself. Eddie Chapman was in a spectacularly bad mood. In the last twenty-four hours, he had been wined and dined, shot at, and hurled out of a plane at nearly four thousand feet; he had thrown up over his parachute overalls, and banged his head on a hard East Anglian road. And now he had been screamed at by a farmer's wife, who threatened to set the dogs on him.

A few hours earlier, after shaking hands with von Gröning, Chapman had been strapped into a harness in the back of a German Junkers 88 at the Soesterberg airfield, near Utrecht in Holland. The bomber pilot was a fresh-faced lad of about twenty-one. Schlichting, the pilot on his earlier flight, had, it seemed, been shot down in his "invisible" Focke-Wulf. This was not news to inspire confidence. Shortly before midnight, the bomber had climbed into the sky, crossed the North Sea at an altitude of just fifty feet, and then flew parallel to the coast, keeping "out of the direct light of the rising moon."

Once over the coast, the Junkers had come under attack from night fighters and antiaircraft batteries. The engines screamed as the pilot took evasive action, spiraling up to four thousand feet, and then plunging back down again. Chapman's stomach rolled with every twist. His guts lurched again as flak thudded into the plane's tail.

Over the drop zone, Chapman tumbled out of the hatch into the darkness and drifted to earth for a dozen hideous minutes, buffeted by a strong wind and desperately trying to cling on to a large suitcase filled with radio and photographic equipment. Somewhere over Cambridge, clutching his cumbersome luggage, he had vomited the remains of the banquet from the Lutétia.

Chapman's second landing had been even worse than his first. Swinging wildly in the wind, he had narrowly avoided a hedge, and then landed hard on a country road between Cambridge and Newmarket, knocking himself out. For fifteen minutes, he lay stunned, before staggering to his feet. Groggily, he cut loose his pack, wrapped his overalls, gloves, kneepads, belt, and entrenching tool into the parachute, and hid the bundle under a hedge. Still dazed, he had knocked at the door of a nearby cottage and explained to the woman who answered it that he had just made a forced landing. The woman took one look at his civilian clothes, screeched in terror, and slammed the door in his face. Chapman had set off as fast as his jellied legs would carry him, fearful of a shotgun blast in the back. This was not the welcome he had been hoping for.

At a smallholding, Chapman steeled himself to try again. This time, the reception was more cordial. He telephoned the nearest police station, and got through to the night-duty officer, who began, with plodding precision, to take down "the details": name, place of birth, date of birth, married or single . . .

"Peeved," Chapman brusquely instructed the man to contact his chief constable immediately and explain that a British double agent had landed. "Don't be silly," said the policeman on the other end. "Go to bed."

Enraged, Chapman shouted: "That's exactly what they told me last time. Ring up your station in Wisbech. They'll remember me."

Finally, a sleepy Ronnie Reed was roused from his bed by a ringing telephone. "It's Eddie," said a familiar, high-pitched voice. "I'm back, with a new task."

Two hours later, Chapman found himself back in Camp 020, staring at his own reflection in the glinting monocle of Tin Eye Stephens. Two weeks earlier, the Most Secret Sources had intercepted a message from Paris to Berlin, signed by von Gröning, asking "whether operation possible?" B1A was alerted: If von Gröning was back in business, then perhaps Zigzag was also about to resurface. An agent in Paris reported seeing a British man in the Lutétia Hotel answering to Chapman's description, "a wiry type, a pure adventurer."

And here, to Stephens's delight, was the rogue himself, "expansive in his conceit," relating an almost impossible tale of survival, and describing the "splendid time" he had had in occupied Norway. "The courageous and ruthless Chapman has given satisfaction to his no less ruthless German employers," wrote Stephens. "He has survived who knows what tests. He was apparently able to match their best drinkers without giving the show away, and to lead a life as hard as any of them."

After an hour of conversation, Chapman was "tired beyond the point of useful investigation," but even a cursory interrogation suggested that "he will have a vast amount of intelligence of the highest order to impart." Chapman was put to bed in a safe house in Hill Street in Mayfair, and fell into an exhausted sleep. Stephens, however, remained awake, writing and pondering. Tin Eye was possibly the least sentimental officer in the entire secret service, and Chapman scored highly in the three categories of human being he most despised: as a spy, a rake, and a "moral degenerate." Yet he was impressed, even moved, by this strange young man: "The outstanding feature of the case is the courage of Chapman. Yet there is something more to the story than that, for Chapman has faced the searching inquiries of the German secret service with infinite resource. He has rendered, and may still render his country great service. For that, in return, Chapman deserves well of his country, and a pardon for his crimes." A general instruction was circulated to all MI5 officers connected with the case stating that Zigzag should be "greeted as a returned friend to whom we owe much and who is no way under suspicion or supervision of any kind."

The next morning, Chapman was driven to the Naval & Military Club, where he was reunited with Tar Robertson and Ronnie Reed over a substantial breakfast. The warmth of their welcome could not have been more heartfelt. Reed was particularly delighted to see his friend "back safely, and roaring like a lion." For the second time in two years, Chapman unburdened himself to his British spymasters. But this time his story was not the incoherent torrent of half-remembered facts he had brought from La Bretonnière, but the detailed, precise, minutely memorized dossier of a trained agent. He produced an undeveloped roll of film with photos of senior Abwehr officials, and a scrap of rice paper on which he had noted the code word used by Oslo for radio traffic— PRESSEMOTTAGELSETRONDHEIMSVEIEN—and the various crystal frequencies. He described in detail the people he had met, the places he had seen, and the various sensitive military sites he had identified as potential bombing targets. His observations were as meticulous and precise as his earlier reports had been vague and inchoate, offering a complete picture of the German occupying force: the location of the SS, Luftwaffe, and Abwehr headquarters in Oslo; tank depots; the U-Boat signals center; air supply bases; naval yards; German divisional signs; and flak defenses. From memory, he sketched a map locating Vidkun Quisling's mansion in Bygdøy and described how he had "purposely put ashore there whilst yachting to view the house."

After breakfast, Chapman was given a medical examination by Dr. Harold Dearden, the psychiatrist at Camp 020, who pronounced him "mentally quite fit though physically tired." At first, his listeners were inclined to believe that he was stretching the truth, but as the information poured out of Chapman, all skepticism evaporated. "All the evidence appears to prove his complete innocence affirmatively and conclusively," wrote Stephens. "It is inconceivable [that], if he had revealed any part of the truth concerning his adventures in this country on the occasion of his previous visit, the Germans would have allowed him his freedom, still less have rewarded him with the very large sums of money which they paid him and even still less that they would now have sent him over once more."

There was a simple way to check whether he was telling the whole truth. MI5 knew he had been involved in training Björnsson and Júlíusson, but Chapman himself had no idea that the two hopeless Icelandic spies had been caught. If he volunteered information about the Icelanders without prompting, wrote Stephens, "it would be a first-rate check on his good faith." Chapman did precisely that, offering a detailed account of the spies, their appearance and training, that tallied exactly with what his interrogators already knew. "I think this goes far to indicate that Chapman is playing straight," wrote Stephens. Chapman was genuine; even the suicide potions he brought were the real thing—pills of potassium cyanide made by Laroche of Paris, and also in liquid form. "The only safe place for it is down the drain and well washed away," concluded MI5's scientific department.

Another indication of Chapman's good faith lay in the revelation that the Leica camera and £1,000 from the fund he had brought were intended for another German spy in Britain, "a man whom they undoubtedly believe to be one of the most valuable agents they have operating in this country." Chapman's spymasters had taken pains to ensure that he did not discover the name of this other spy. But MI5 knew it: His code name was Brutus.

Roman Garby-Czerniawski, alias Armand Walenty, was a Polish fighter pilot who had operated a secret anti-Nazi group in France until he was captured by the Germans in 1941. After eight months in prison, the Germans believed that they had turned him, and allowed him to "escape" in order to forge a Polish fifth column in Britain. Garby-Czerniawski had turned himself in, and was now being operated, very successfully, as Double Agent Brutus.

For some time, Garby-Czerniawski's German handlers had been promising to supply him with more money and better photographic equipment. Shortly before Chapman landed, the Most Secret Sources had picked up an Abwehr message between Paris and Wiesbaden, which said that Fritz had been given "money and a Leica" to pass to "Hubert," the German code name for Brutus. When Chapman announced that he was acting as a courier, he was merely confirming what MI5 already knew.

Here was fresh evidence that Chapman was "safe." But the supposed handover of the equipment from Zigzag to Brutus could pose a serious headache: It would require stage-managing and correlating not one but two separate streams of false information, and the two agents would be no longer be able to operate independently thereafter. "Zigzag will be given, and will have to appear to carry out, instructions which would link Zigzag to Brutus. It does not suit us to have these two agents linked, but it is going to be very difficult to avoid."

The extraordinary breadth of Chapman's mission offered multiple opportunities for deceiving the Germans again, but MI5 was cautious. "Although no one thinks for a moment that [Chapman] might be double crossing us, if he is to be used for any form of deception, this issue must, of course, be placed beyond all possible doubt."

There were just two aspects of Chapman's story that troubled the meticulous Stephens: Chapman's loyalty to his German spymaster, von Gröning, the man he called Dr. Graumann, and Chapman's relationship with Dagmar Lahlum.

Chapman's friendship with von Gröning had intensified in the intervening months, and Chapman's loyalty to Britain might be tempered by his affection. "It must always be borne in mind that he had a very close connection and high regard for Graumann," wrote Stephens. "He regards him as being anti-Nazi and liberal in his outlook." Chapman was quick to defend Graumann, insisting that he was "a very able man, cautious and resourceful, but was handicapped by the poor material in the way of personnel that he had at his disposal." He also pointed out that his spymaster's sister had adopted a Jewish child, although the more cynical heads in MI5 wondered whether, if true, this was simply "a form of insurance for the future."

Stephens had to consider the possibility that von Gröning and Chapman might be in league together. There was always something unknowable and fickle in Chapman's makeup. The opportunist and the man of principle were one, as Stephens observed: "Chapman is a difficult subject and a certain percentage of his loyalties is still for Germany. One cannot escape the thought that, had Germany been winning the war, he could quite easily have stayed abroad. In England, he has no social standing; in Germany, among thugs, he is accepted. It is not easy to judge the workings of Chapman's mind: he is bound to make comparisons between his life of luxury among the Germans, where he is almost a law unto himself, and his treatment here, where he still has the law to fear." Those doubts were echoed by Len Burt, the head of Special Branch and the senior police officer liaising with MI5. On the basis of Chapman's past record, Burt remained "quite convinced that Zigzag is a man without scruples who will blackmail anyone if he thinks it worth his while and will not stop even at selling out to the opposition if he thinks there is anything to be gained out of it."

The riddle could not be solved immediately. Chapman must be watched, his relationship with von Gröning probed: he should be handled with kid gloves. MI5 could not match the munificence of his Nazis handlers, but they could try: "Although we do not propose to and cannot supply him with champagne for his meals, this is the sort of thing with which we have to compete."

Of greater concern was Chapman's relationship with Dagmar Lahlum—"the inevitable girlfriend," as one MI5 officer sighed. By confiding in this untested woman, Zigzag had, in Stephens's view, "blundered badly." She could betray him at any moment with disastrous consequences: If von Gröning realized he was being double-crossed, any information Chapman sent to Germany would then be interpreted, rightly, as the opposite of the truth. Zigzag would then be providing real, not false, intelligence to the enemy.

Chapman insisted, loudly and repeatedly, that Dagmar was not only loyal to him, but a skilled spy in her own right and vigorously anti-German. He described how he had wooed her, and how he had debated with himself for months before telling her the truth. "She is not a 'fast' girl," he protested, "and I am quite satisfied that she was not 'planted' by the Germans in the café when I first met her." If she had betrayed him to the Germans, "he would have at once observed a change of attitude of the Germans towards him." If the Germans had suspected Dagmar, or himself, they would not have agreed to provide her with a free apartment and a monthly stipend. Dagmar had his "complete confidence." But for Chapman's British handlers, "the unofficial introduction of this girl into the service of the British government" added an unexpected and unwelcome complication.

Chapman's interrogators noted that he was "anxious at every opportunity to talk about Dagmar Lahlum." He returned to the subject again and again, insisting that he had made a promise to "ensure her financial position" and clear her name after the war. "One of his objects will be to reinstate her with her compatriots by asserting that she had double-crossed the Germans," wrote his case officer. Chapman's passion seemed genuine enough, but then MI5 had not forgotten Freda Stevenson, who was still being supported by the British secret services. "There was some sort of understanding, of which ZZ has by now doubtless repented, that if he ever came back he would marry Freda," noted a skeptical interrogator.

As his trump card, Chapman described how Dagmar had learned of the Sicily landings through the Norwegian underground, and how she was linked to the resistance movement. What better proof could there be of her bona fides? MI5 did not quite see it that way. British intelligence services were in contact with Milorg, one of the main Norwegian resistance groups, but regarded the organization as inefficient and unwieldy, and prone to leaks. That Dagmar was apparently part of Milorg and may have told them of Chapman's real identity only served to muddy the waters further. Dagmar was working for one secret organization, in league with another, and being paid by a third. From the British point of view, the lady had too many suitors for comfort: "Dagmar is in contact with the Norwegian underground movement, at the same time has the confidence of a British Secret Service Agent, and is at present being maintained by the German Secret Service."

Stephens's faith in Chapman was undimmed, but he urged caution: "I do not wish to be held wanting in admiration of a brave man [but] I must issue a warning about this strange character. In England, he is wanted for crime. In Germany he is admired and treated royally by the German Secret Service. It is not unnatural, therefore, in the years, that he has come to dislike the English in many respects and to admire the Germans. Indeed, there is more than admiration, there is a genuine affection for his spymaster Graumann. His present ambition is to settle down with Dagmar Lahlum in Paris at the end of the war. Where do the loyalties of Chapman lie? Personally, I think they are in fine balance."

Chapman's supporters, including Tar Robertson, pointed out that he had thoroughly demonstrated his loyalty already. But set against this was his criminal past, his affection for von Gröning, and now the problem of yet another romantic entanglement. After long debate, the spymasters agreed. There would be a final installment in what Stephens described as "one of the most fascinating chapters of contra-espionage history in the war." Chapman would be given one more chance to prove his mettle.

On June 30, two days after landing, Chapman sent his first radio message to von Gröning, while Ronnie Reed looked on approvingly: HARD LANDING BUT ALL OK. FINDING BETTER PLACE. COMING AGAIN THURSDAY. DAGMAR.

CHAPTER TWENTY-SIX

Doodlebugs

BRITAIN, PUMMELED AND pounded for so long, was braced for Hitler's flying bombs. Nazi propaganda had given early warning of a new weapon that would wreak vengeance for the bombing of the Fatherland and finally crush British resistance. Early in 1944, the Germans began instructing their agents that they should soon evacuate London for their own safety. The first robot bombs, powered by a jet engine, with a crude guidance system, had whined over the city on the night of June 13. The bombs, each carrying eighteen hundred pounds of explosive, flew at around four hundred miles per hour with a buzzing drone like a venomous insect that would abruptly stop when the fuel ran out, leaving an eerie, empty silence as the bomb plummeted to earth, followed by the explosion.

At first, the flying bombs came in ones and twos; then in swarms. On the night of June 15, 217 missiles hammered into Britain, with 45 dropping on central London. Unpredictable and hard to shoot down, the V-1s gave a horrible new twist of uncertainty to civilian life. People on the ground would stop to listen anxiously to the engine overhead, waiting for the sudden silence. Typically, the British found a comic nickname to blunt the fear of these atrocious weapons— "doodlebugs."

The bombs flew blind, and this was both a strength and a weakness. There was no one to report where the payload had been dropped, and no way to aim them with confidence. A pattern emerged in London. The German gunners appeared to be targeting the heart of the city, but most of the bombs were dropping two or three miles short of Trafalgar Square. John Masterman made the obvious deduction: "It was clear that the Germans could only correct their aim and secure results by adjustments based on experiment, and that their data must rest in the main upon reports from this country." If those reports could be doctored, then the V-1s could be diverted to where they would do less damage.

By the time Chapman arrived in Britain with orders to report on the flying bombs, a rudimentary deception plan was in place. If the double agent's reports exaggerated the number of bombs in the north and the west of London, but minimized those in the south and the east, the Germans at the launchpads would logically assume that they were overshooting, and reduce the range. The flying bombs were already falling short, and with a careful stream of false reports they might be lured even farther south and east, away from the densely populated areas of central London and even into the countryside, where they would fall mainly in fields and woods. Clearly, there were limits to this form of deception: "If St Paul's was hit, it was useless and harmful to report that the bomb had descended upon a cinema in Islington," since the Germans would swiftly discover the truth, and the credibility of the double agent would be compromised. Masterman ruled that the Twenty Committee must "decide what measure of useful deception was possible without blowing the agents."

To the hardheaded men of military intelligence, the plan was clear and logical, but persuading the British cabinet that it should authorize a ruse that would spare some Londoners but might condemn others to death was far harder. The politicians argued, somewhat bizarrely, that public morale would be damaged if the flying bombs were diverted to new, hitherto unscathed areas of the country, since the bomb-scarred residents of central London had "learned to live" (and die) with the devastation, and they were best able to cope with a fresh bombardment. The ministers balked at the "terrible responsibility . . . for directing the attack against any part of London." Despite their qualms, the deception went ahead.

The barrage intensified. By the end of June 1944, some 660 V-1s had landed on London. The Germans seemed to be aiming for the Charing Cross area, but the mean point of impact was calculated to be the Dulwich station in southern London. Juan Pujol, the cele-brated Spanish double agent code-named "Garbo" by the British, had volunteered to provide his German spymasters with accurate in-formation about where the bombs were landing: "I might take on the work of making daily observations . . . and let you have by radio an exact report on objectives hit so that you will be able to correct any possible errors of fire." Garbo spiced up his reports with charac-teristic eruptions of Nazi fervor: "I am certain you will be able to ter-rify this very pusillanimous people who will never admit that they are beaten."

The Germans were hungry for more, and the arrival of Zigzag, with specific instructions to monitor bomb damage, was the clearest indication that the Germans were short of accurate intelligence, and thus vulnerable to being misled. Chapman also brought evi-dence of Berlin's faith in a weapon that "his German masters confi-dently believe has reduced London and the South coast to a shambles."

Chapman sent his first report, misrepresenting the location, timing, and damage inflicted by the bombs, on July 1. He continued to transmit disinformation in a steady stream for a month. The data had to be carefully coordinated so the double agents involved—most notably Zigzag and Garbo—"should report actual incidents in North West London but give as the times of those incidents the ac-tual times of incidents in South East London. If this is done skilfully it is hoped the enemy will identify the bomb which fell in South East London with the incident in North West London and plot it there." The Germans must be persuaded that they were consistently over-shooting. In the words of Dr. Reginald Jones, the brilliant physicist assigned to Air Intelligence: "We could give correct points of impact for bombs that tended to have a longer range than usual, but couple these with the times of bombs that had actually fallen short." When the enemy corrected their aim, they would therefore "reduce the av-erage range." The resulting disinformation then had to be carefully vetted, before being sent over on Zigzag's wireless. All this took time. "It is essential," wrote Chapman's handler, "that it should not be apparent to recipients that there is always a substantial time lag." The gamble was huge. If Chapman was discovered, then instead of taking his reports at face value, the Germans would read them for what they were: the obverse of the truth. Instead of shortening their aim, they would extend it. Rather than draw the flying bombs away from the target, Zigzag might inadvertently lead them to it.

To bolster Chapman's credibility, photographs were taken of the doodlebug damage at various points around London, so that he could send these on to the Germans via Lisbon. But Air Intelligence vetoed the move: "I am afraid we cannot approve of their being sent over, since they would be of considerable value to the enemy, and naturally those that would be of no value to the enemy would stand Zigzag himself in very little stead." Here was the essential dilemma of running a double agent: how to send information that appeared accurate, but could do no harm.

Chapman had been instructed to provide daily weather reports with barometric readings. MI5 asked the Twenty Committee whether he might send these without compromising security. Chapman had been provided with more than enough money to buy a barometer, after all, and therefore had little excuse not to send the readings to his German masters. Reluctantly, the authorities agreed. Chapman could send barometer readings, but with "slight errors introduced."

Chapman's deception messages have survived only in fragments. MI5 was careful to destroy the traffic, aware of the potential repercussions if the inhabitants of southern London realized they were being sacrificed to protect the center of the city. German intelligence in Oslo picked up Chapman's coded messages every morning, and Paris in the evening. At first, reception was poor and patchy, but it improved after Chapman sent a volley of abuse. "The outgoing traffic, apart from complaints of poor service, has consisted almost entirely of reports on the times and places of impact of flying bombs," reported Chapman's case officer. There was no hint in the Most Secret Sources that Chapman's bomb reports were regarded with suspicion. His British handlers were delighted: "The

Zigzag channel was considered indispensable to the bomb damage deception scheme."

The success of that scheme is still debated. At the very least, the Germans never corrected their range, and the bombs continued to fall short, in the suburbs and countryside, where they killed and destroyed, to be sure, but on a far lesser scale. Chapman has "held his place in German confidence," wrote John Masterman. Masterman knew what it was like to be bombed. He had lain awake on the floor of the barber's shop at the Reform Club, listening to the doodlebugs overhead, wondering, in the thudding silence, if the next one would destroy him. "I was as frightened as the next man of the bombing," he admitted. But the "shambles" predicted by German propaganda had not materialized. St. Paul's Cathedral, the Reform Club, and Masterman himself all survived the onslaught of the doodlebugs, and owed their survival, in some measure, to a double agent tapping out lies in Morse code on a German wireless.

Masterman was exultant: "The deception was a very real triumph . . . saving many thousands of lives."

· · ·

On July 25, the bomb deception scheme was suspended. Evening papers had begun to print maps showing where bombs had fallen, potentially threatening the deception. But in any case, radar-controlled antiaircraft batteries from the United States had begun to shoot down V-1s in large numbers, and a month later the threat had effectively been neutralized, though the bombs had killed 6,184 people. Chapman told his German handlers he was going in search of the "secret equipment for which he was promised high reward." Chapman's low boredom threshold was well known, as was his venality: The announcement that he was going in search of more lucrative espionage targets appears to have aroused no German suspicion.

Chapman had spent a month in his safe house, dutifully "tapping out such messages as the Air Ministry want to put over," but he was becoming restive: "If this state of affairs continues he will go bad on us," warned one case officer. "He will turn his tortuous mind to working out schemes for making more money, which will almost certainly bring him to the notice of the Police. It would be extremely embarrassing for us if he should be arrested while still on our hands." As ever, Chapman's libido was in constant need of exercise. One evening, Reed accompanied him to a notorious pickup bar in Cork Street and handed him a £20 note: "Take your pick! But be back in half an hour."

Chapman still could not walk the city's streets alone in case he was arrested, for Scotland Yard had a long memory. MI5 wondered whether that memory should now be erased. "I do feel his exploits to date have amply earned him a pardon for the various outstanding crimes he is alleged to have committed," wrote John Marriott, one of MI5's lawyers and Robertson's deputy. "I agree," wrote Tar. Under constitutional law no one may be pardoned for a crime unless already tried and convicted. Instead, police forces around the country with an interest in prosecuting Eddie Chapman were simply informed through Special Branch that the home secretary "desired that no such proceedings should be brought." This was a pardon in effect, if not in name. "No action should be taken against him, at least not without prior consultation with us," MI5 insisted. Chapman, however, was not informed that his slate had been wiped clean; the threat of prosecution remained a useful leash.

The spy chiefs now debated how best to employ Zigzag. Chapman himself volunteered to return to France, saying he could help "comb out any German underground movement which may have been left behind." That idea was vetoed; Chapman was too valuable as a double agent in Britain, feeding lies to the enemy. "Any question of Zigzag's return to the Germans at this stage of the war is out of the question," his handlers decided. Ronnie Reed took him to lunch at the RAC Club, and marveled at his guiltless internal contradictions. In one breath, Chapman would be describing his love for Dagmar, but in the next proclaiming he was "anxious to write to Freda to tell her he was back in London." Reed agreed to pass on the message, but advised Chapman to tell her he was "very busy and would communicate with her in a few days time." More worrying, Chapman was talking about writing up his adventures as an "autobiography," an idea that MI5 quashed immediately, pointing out that it would be "impossible for him to disclose during the war, and in all probability for a long time thereafter, anything about his work for the Germans or for ourselves." Chapman grumpily replied that he wanted to write up an account "while it was still fresh." He promised to confine his reminiscences to "his old criminal activities." MI5 was not convinced.

Chapman had brought ample evidence of German anxieties over the vulnerability of its U-boat fleet. Tar concluded that the best way to "stimulate Zigzag's interest," and baffle the enemy, would be to exploit those fears by sending over "deceptive material about anti-submarine devices." A new plan was formed: Chapman would dispatch a message to his handlers, saying that he had located the factory in the north of England where a new submarine detection device was being manufactured, but had been unable to obtain the device itself because the factory was "in continual active operation." He would then claim that he had managed to "steal a document and photographs from an office in the building"; the document could be transcribed and sent over by wireless, and the photographs sent via Lisbon. Both, needless to say, would be fake.

Through the Most Secret Sources and traditional espionage, the British knew that the German navy was alarmed by the rising U-boat toll, and that it feared some new weapon must be in use. In fact, the Germans were wrong. As Ewen Montagu of Naval Intelligence observed, "the increasing number of U-boat kills was due to other devices, most notably the Mark XXIV mine, and by intercepting and decoding U-boat signals using Ultra." The most important British weapon in the underwater war was the ability to pick up and read the U-boat radio traffic. However, if the Germans believed there was some other new and powerful underwater weapon in use, that fear should be encouraged and expanded. As always when practicing to deceive, MI5 stuck as close to the truth as possible while planting a deception.

British destroyers, frigates, and corvettes had recently been fitted with a device called a "hedgehog," a mortar bomb that exploded on contact with a submarine. The Most Secret Sources revealed that German intelligence had found out about the hedgehog through "careless talk by merchant seamen." Since they knew something about the weapons already, a great deal of misinformation, wrote Montagu, could be loaded onto a little information: "While we should not disclose details of their design and construction, we should notionally increase their range and explosive effect and, more important, try to convince [the Germans] that they were fitted with proximity fuses which would go off on a near miss without actual impact." This "proximity fuse" would supposedly trigger other depth charges once it had located the submarine. There was, of course, no such thing, but by making the humble hedgehog appear to be a beast of terrifying ferocity, Naval Intelligence hoped further to erode German morale, and make the U-boat fleet more wary of attacking convoys. Most important, if U-boat commanders feared that the Royal Navy had a rocket-propelled device that could hunt them at the bottom of the ocean, then they would be less likely to dive deep. Nearer the surface, they were easier to kill.

Chapman duly sent out a message saying that he had heard about this proximity fuse, smaller than a normal depth charge and developed by Cossor's to attack deeply submerged U-boats. The response was encouraging: "After passing the information on to the German navy, the Abwehr came back to Zigzag with much praise and an insistent demand that he should get more details." Chapman reported (incorrectly) that "all secret manufacture by Cossor's is now done in St. Helens," and announced that he was heading north to try to gather more information. The stage was set for Operation Squid.

While the Admiralty worked out the details, Chapman was encouraged to enjoy himself. Agent Zigzag was still "worth keeping sweet," yet a distinct sourness had begun to creep into the relationship between Chapman and the British secret services, for reasons that had little to do with the war and everything to do with personality—the warp and weft of espionage.

Ronnie Reed's role in the Zigzag case came to a sudden end when he was posted to the American forces as intelligence liaison officer in France. Reed's reputation (and, for that matter, his mustache) had grown over the previous two years, and he had eagerly embraced the "wonderful experience" of seeing France for the first time. For Chapman, however, Reed's departure was a heavy blow. The two men had grown deeply fond of one another, sharing so many anxious moments hunched over the wireless. On the day of Reed's departure, Chapman presented his departing case officer with a small parcel, wrapped in tissue paper: inside, still in its leather case, was Chapman's Iron Cross. It was a typically spontaneous Chapman gesture of admiration and friendship. Reed was profoundly touched.

To replace Reed as the Zigzag case officer, in a rare but calamitous misjudgement, Tar Robertson appointed a man who could not have been more different, or less to Chapman's taste.

Major Michael Ryde was a crisp, by-the-book professional, with an overdeveloped sense of moral rectitude, an underdeveloped sense of humor, and a drinking problem. The son and grandson of chartered surveyors, Ryde had married the only daughter of Sir Joseph Ball, a notorious political fixer and the head of MI5's investigative branch. Ball had steered his son-in-law into the security services just before the outbreak of war, and for three years Ryde had performed an exceptionally boring desk job as regional security liaison officer in Reading. Newly promoted to B1A, he was clever, fastidious, and moralizing; Ryde could be charming when sober, but was invariably unpleasant when drunk. He and Chapman loathed one another on sight. In the tangle of Chapman's loyalties, there was now an ironic symmetry. His closest friend, a German spymaster, must be betrayed out of a duty to his country; but the man who should have been his ally in that enterprise would soon become his sworn enemy.

Ryde regarded his vulgar new ward as an encumbrance and an embarrassment, and within hours of taking on the case he had made it his personal goal to expel Chapman from the British secret services at the first opportunity.

CHAPTER TWENTY-SEVEN

Going to the Dogs

THE WAR STAGGERED toward its finale. Paris was liberated on August 25, 1944, and the Allies advanced steadily eastward while the Red Army marched west. With victory in sight, the British secret services looked to the future and began to see their spy networks in a new light. Wartime espionage was a dirty business, and Chapman was by no means the only person of dubious character to find a home in MI5. But with victory in prospect, an element in the intelligence hierarchy now wondered whether there ever could—or rather should—be a place in it for a scoundrel like Eddie Chapman.

Chapman's new case officer, Major Ryde, was now his constant companion. It was torture for both, for few partnerships were more ill-matched than that of the roistering crook and his patrician shadow. Chapman insisted on going out on the town at every opportunity and MI5's expense. The £80 spending money and fifty clothing coupons he had been given on arrival evaporated in a few days. Chapman demanded more, pointing out that he had brought £6,001 in his suitcase when he parachuted into Britain the month before. Ryde tartly informed him that the £10 notes were out of date and unusable. Chapman was "disagreeably surprised" but quite unabashed, and demanded that he should allowed to keep the rest of the cash he had brought. MI5 watched the money pour into the hands of various Soho casino owners and barmen "with some apprehension."

Ryde trailed after him resentfully. "I have spent a good deal of time with Zigzag at the cost of a certain amount of boredom and a certain amount of money expended on entertaining him," he complained. Ryde had nothing against strong drink; indeed, quite the reverse. He just did not want to drink in the company of men like Eddie Chapman.

Early in August 1944, Ryde called a meeting with Tar Robertson to discuss the Zigzag case and, if possible, to end it. Ryde reported that Chapman seemed "most discontented at the moment"; he was expensive, moody, and entirely disreputable. "He has been keeping the bad company of some professional pugilist with whom he has been hitting the high spots" and was "always in the company of beautiful women"—a fact that seems to have vexed Ryde in a way that suggests envy more than disapproval. The case officer wrote a report, ending with the conclusion: "The Zigzag case must be closed down at the earliest possible moment." Ryde was immediately slapped into line by his superiors. John Masterman insisted that the word "earliest" be replaced by "latest," and Tar agreed: The case should be closed only when it was "convenient" to do so. Stung, Ryde backed off. But he was now gunning for Chapman, and collecting all the ammunition he could.

Robertson took Chapman to lunch at his club, and found him in a state of seething resentment toward Ryde, complaining bitterly about "the way his case was being run." When asked about his future plans, Chapman "did not seem to have any very clear ideas on the subject," Tar reported, though he spoke vaguely of setting up a club, or running a pub, or working for MI5 after the war. "He is quite clearly restless and is likely to be so, as long as he is asked to perform the rather humdrum business of tapping a key at our instructions."

Relations between Chapman and Ryde might have been reaching a crisis point, but in other respects the Zigzag case was ticking along most satisfactorily. The Germans seemed as devoutly trusting as ever. Early in August, von Gröning had sent a message asking Chapman to suggest a method for delivering the camera and money to his fellow spy, and instructing him to find "a suitable person" who could monitor bomber formations at airfields in East Anglia. The Air Ministry had vetoed any deception in this latter area, so Chapman stalled, saying he was still searching for a recruit since "the friends he hoped to employ for this purpose are in prison or otherwise not available."

Operation Squid, the plan to convince the Germans that Britain had some new and devastating weapon able to detect and destroy U-boats, moved into its next phase. The deception would take two forms. The first was a "stolen" photograph purporting to show an underwater antisubmarine "proximity fuse" that did not, of course, exist. This would have to be smuggled to the Germans via Lisbon. A real hedgehog depth charge was photographed alongside a ruler a foot and a half in length, which had been adapted to appear as if it was only six inches long, thus making the weapon appear one-third of its actual size. Chapman would tell the Germans that he had bribed a merchant seaman bound for Lisbon to act as a "mule," by hiding the photo "in a French letter in a tin of Epsom Salts," and that he would convince the sailor he was smuggling drugs. In reality, MI6 in Lisbon simply acted as "postman," and arranged for the fake photograph in its tin to be delivered to the Germans by one of their agents disguised as a seaman. The German reaction was precisely as hoped: "After they had received the photo the Abwehr were avid for full details of the fuse," wrote Ewen Montagu.

Zigzag duly obliged. With the help of Professor Geoffrey J. Gollin, the brilliant scientific adviser to the Naval Intelligence Division, Montagu drew up a bogus letter from Professor A. B. Wood, an expert in underwater acoustics at the Admiralty Research Laboratory at Teddington, to a scientist at Cossor's munitions factory named Fleming. In it, he extolled the virtues of a new, top secret antisubmarine device. Chapman told his German handlers that he had found the letter in the Manchester offices of Cossor's and had copied it. He now sent the fake letter by radio, verbatim.

Dear Fleming,

I feel sure that you will be as pleased as I was to hear the results of the latest squid trials.

A standard deviation of plus or minus 15 feet is a wonderful improvement on the old method of depth-finding and my only regret is that our present target is incapable of greater speeds. Doubtless 13 knots is as much as the enemy is likely to reach in this war but we must always keep a 'jump' ahead, preferably two jumps!

I thought you might like the enclosed photos of the standard re-mote setting depth charge fuse for coupling direct to the squid Mk J indicator controller (as suggested by the late Captain Walker).

I hope to visit Manchester again soon and am looking forward to having another of our discussions which have proved so fruitful during the last three years.

Yours sincerely,
A.B. Wood
Professor

"Captain Walker" was a reference to Captain Frederic "Johnnie" Walker, a naval officer famed for having sunk more U-boats during the Battle of the Atlantic than any other British or Allied comman-der. Captain Walker had recently died of a cerebral thrombosis. There was no "Mk J indicator controller," and certainly no depth charge capable of detecting a submarine at a distance of fifteen feet and then pursuing it at a speed of thirteen knots. There was, how-ever, a Fleming—Ian Fleming, the future creator of James Bond—who was then working in Naval Intelligence. Fleming may have been party to this subterfuge, designed to breed maximum anxiety among German U-boat commanders and keep them as close as pos-sible to the surface. Ewen Montagu proclaimed the operation a tri-umph. "We never found out what the assessment of this information by the German navy was, but the actions of the Abwehr [*sic*] made it seem that they must have been very favorable."

Despite the success of Operation Squid, Ryde did his best to undermine the achievement. "I do not myself believe there is any substantial chance of these photographs reaching Berlin," he wrote. "Unless the Admiralty press us to carry on the case, I am convinced that we ought to close it down and part company with Zigzag as soon as possible, giving him such financial bonus, if any, as he is thought to deserve . . ." Ryde seemed more determined than ever to expel Chapman, and the preparations for handing over the camera to

Brutus offered an opportunity. It was decided that Zigzag would arrange to leave the money and camera in a marked package at a railway-station cloakroom, but while the handover was being organized, the Germans sent a radio message hinting at doubts over Chapman's loyalty. Brutus's German handler wrote that he did not wish his agent to make direct contact with Fritz, since the latter was, in his opinion, "not quite reliable." This may have reflected no more than internal rivalry, one spymaster questioning the dependability of another's agent, but it was enough for Ryde to declare that the Germans were "dubious about Zigzag's integrity."

German suspicions, Ryde wrote, may have been further stoked by widely reported statements made in Parliament about the V-1s by Duncan Sandys, the minister who chaired the War Cabinet committee on flying bombs. Sandys had let slip certain crucial details about bomb-damaged parts of London. "The messages sent by Zigzag, if compared in detail with the recent speech made by Duncan Sandys in the House, show very serious discrepancies, and there is a possibility that the case will be blown on these grounds." Then there was the question of Dagmar. "Zigzag is liable to be compromised through the girlfriend he left behind in Oslo," wrote Ryde, slowly but implacably chipping away at his own agent's credibility. When it was mooted that Chapman might continue to work for MI5 after the war, Ryde was scornful: "It is unlikely that his private life will be such that he will remain suitable for employment." He also pointed out that Chapman's value was dependent on his relationship with von Gröning and that this link would become worthless with the end of the war.

Chapman, unaware of Ryde's machinations, had discovered a new and lucrative pastime. Through some of his old criminal contacts, he learned that dog races in southern London were being "fixed." With the connivance of the owners, certain dogs were being fed meatballs laced with Luminal, an antiepileptic drug. A mild hypnotic, the Luminal had no visible effect until the animal, usually the favorite, had run some distance, when it would slow down. For a consideration, Chapman arranged to receive a tip-off when a dog had been knobbled; he then bet heavily on the second favorite and usually collected a tidy profit, which he would split with his criminal informant.

One evening in August 1944, Chapman turned up at his safe house several hours late for an appointment to transmit to Germany, and explained casually that he had been at the dog track. "Zigzag himself is going to the dogs," his case officer puffed, gleeful to have been provided with such a convenient double entendre. Chapman, Ryde reported, was "making quite large sums of money by backing the winners of races which have already been fixed." When confronted, Chapman angrily insisted that he was merely profiting through information gathered from his contacts, a technique not so very far removed from espionage. Ryde, of course, did not see it that way. "To take advantage of other people's dirty work to fleece the bookmakers cannot be regarded as a desirable occupation," he sniffed.

Reluctantly, and under intense pressure, Masterman and Robertson accepted that Chapman might soon have "served his purpose." Yet they balked at cutting him adrift. Tar insisted that Chapman had "done an extremely good and brave job," and if the case was shut down, then he should be properly looked after "by giving him a fairly substantial sum of money." With the avuncular concern he had always shown, Robertson wondered whether Chapman might be coaxed toward the straight and narrow by means of a legitimate job. Chapman was duly told that "if he could put up some firm business proposition it might not be impossible for us to help him with the capital." He had seemed enthusiastic, and talked of running a club in the West End or a hotel in Southend (the Ship Hope Hotel was for sale, he said), in order to be near Freda and Diane. Ryde declared that it would be a "waste of money" for someone with such a long criminal record to open licensed premises, since the police would simply "close them down as soon as they find out that he is in fact behind the business." The only way to set up Chapman as an hotelier would be to alert the local chief constable, and explain the situation: "If the latter, notwithstanding Zigzag's past record, appears willing to give his venture a fair chance so long as the hotel was properly conducted, then it might be worthwhile for Zigzag to go on with it." Ryde doubted that any chief constable would agree to this proposition, or that Chapman would keep his nose clean: "It is obvious that we cannot assist him financially if his idea of business is to work the dogs."

Just as Ryde had predicted, Chapman was drifting back to his old haunts—the Shim-Sham Club and the Nite Lite—and his old ways. The pull of the criminal brotherhood was growing stronger, yet his years as a secret agent had changed him: His primary allegiance was still to Britain, and the other secret fraternity of which he was now a part. When Ryde hinted that Chapman's days as an agent might be numbered, he had responded crossly, declaring that "if we no longer require his services" he would "get in touch with the Americans."

Safe from prosecution thanks to the home secretary's unofficial "pardon," Chapman was allowed to move around London more freely, though Ryde followed at a distance, tutting, watching, and gathering evidence. The spy manager was now actively spying on his spy: "I have seen Zigzag walk up to a Norwegian and address him in Norwegian, I have seen him in the company of highly undesirable characters, speaking to a German Jewess in German, a Frenchman in French. I have heard him discussing with a man with a known criminal record conditions in Paris in such a way that it must have been apparent that he has been there within the last few months." Chapman, Ryde reported to his superiors, was keen to write a memoir of his exploits: How soon before his natural swagger got the better of him and he bragged to his nasty friends? he speculated. "I am able to curb these indiscretions when I happen to be present," he wrote, "but there is no knowing what form these conversations take when I am not there."

Ryde was overruled again. Whatever his personal behavior, Chapman was still a trusted asset: "The war may end at any moment and all contact with the Germans be lost and his case may die a natural death." If this happened, Chapman should be let go with tact and generosity, and told that "the necessity of closing the case was no reflection on him, but forced upon us by the war situation."

Ryde grumbled and plotted: "It is becoming increasingly clear to me that there are a number of serious security dangers which, in the case of a character like Zigzag, it is impossible to avoid." Zigzag was proving harder to kill off than Ryde anticipated; every time he believed he had Chapman on the ropes, the man would bounce back with another demonstration of his worth. Von Gröning continued to send messages of support, demanding ever more intelligence: "Try to get latest editions of monthly antisubmarine report issued by antisubmarine warfare division of Admiralty . . . Very important." Von Gröning repeatedly congratulated Fritz on his performance: "General report [is of] great interest."

On September 8, Germany launched its first V-2 attacks against Paris and London. The V-2 was a quite different creature from its predecessor. An early ballistic missile driven by liquid oxygen and alcohol, the rocket bomb had a range of two hundred miles, flew at ten times the speed of the V-1, and carried a nose cone with a ton of high explosive. Chapman had learned of these weapons back in France, and warned British intelligence of a "radio controlled rocket which will be bigger, very costly in fuel and not at all economical in construction." Von Gröning instructed Chapman to act, once again, as a target locator for the new bombs: "Continue giving data about place and time of explosions. Are they more frequent now?" The V-2 attacks were often devastating—160 people were killed in a single explosion when a bomb fell on a Woolworth's department store in southern London—but Chapman sent a reply downplaying the effects: "Heard many rumors of explosions of gas works and mains but no information of the cause. Making inquiries."

During his visit to the Luftwaffe headquarters in Berlin, Chapman had been shown fragments of British night-fighter radar equipment, and noticed that the pieces had serial numbers. He now asked von Gröning to transmit a complete list of those serial numbers, notionally so that he could steal the correct device, but in fact to give the Air Ministry a clear idea of exactly what the Germans had salvaged. It was also decided that a display of petulance would keep von Gröning keen. Chapman sent an angry message, complaining that he was not receiving sufficient backup and urgently needed more money. He also asked, pointedly, whether the German secret service intended to support him when the war was over.

Chapman could not have known it, but during his absence Hitler had destroyed the remains of the Abwehr. On July 20, Claus von Stauffenberg, a German officer, tried and failed to assassinate Hitler by planting a bomb in an attaché case in the conference room at Hitler's "Wolf's Lair"—his command post for the eastern front in Rastenburg, Prussia. The device exploded against the heavy leg of an oak table, which probably shielded the Führer from the full force of the blast. Chapman would never have made such an elementary mistake. Five thousand members of the German military were arrested in the aftermath of the failed July plot, including Canaris and his deputy, Hans Oster. They were tried, convicted of treason, and then hanged. Von Gröning does not appear to have been implicated in the plot, but as an Abwehr officer of the old school with anti-Nazi views, he was undoubtedly under suspicion.

Von Gröning's response to Chapman's complaint arrived on August 28, after a gap of several days. It was an odd—and oddly moving—message, the statement of a proud man whose world was falling apart: "War situation need not and will not affect your return you must make suggestions in good time and you will have every support whatever happens. Was home, my house destroyed by bombs, otherwise would have answered sooner. Graumann."

The von Gröning family home in Bremen, that great five-story symbol of aristocratic eminence, had been flattened by Allied bombers. The house had been empty: the cook, the chauffeur, the valet, the gardener, the maids, and the other servants had been laid off long before. The gilded carriage had been stolen, the family cars commandeered. Von Gröning's pictures, antiques, china, silver, and other valuable objets d'art—the remains of his great inheritance—had been stored in the attic. All had been destroyed. The only item of value recovered from the rubble was a singed silver plate engraved with the names of his fallen comrades in the White Dragoons.

CHAPTER TWENTY-EIGHT

Case Dismissed

CHAPMAN IMAGINED HIS old friend, sitting in the bombed-out wreckage of his privilege, drinking himself into amnesia. He was touched by von Gröning's plight: SORRY YOUR BAD NEWS DON'T DRINK TOO MUCH. AM GOING TO MANCHESTER TO DO JOB. WHAT ABOUT PICKUP OFF NE COAST? CAN YOU LEAVE ME COVER ADDRESS IN FRANCE ALSO RADIO POSSIBILITY FOR JIMMY OR MYSELF TO GO THERE. NEED FRENCH MONEY ALSO. DAGMAR.

Von Gröning's message had hinted at a plan to continue espionage operations with Chapman, "whatever happens." The Allies were acutely conscious of the danger of postwar resistance groups emerging in Germany—the so-called Werewolves, SS fanatics who might be determined to continue the war by other means. Ryde grudgingly conceded that the message put the Zigzag case in a different light: It showed that the German spymaster "has a post-war plan in mind and there is now a real purpose in keeping the case running" in order to find out "whether Graumann intends to continue to work after the complete and final German collapse." If Chapman could "get the Germans to lay on an expedition to meet him somewhere in the North Sea," Ryde reported, then an ambush might be set.

As promised, the next day, von Gröning sent over a complete list of all the serial numbers obtained from the equipment in downed British aircraft, "a collection of words, figures, stops and dashes" that added up to another intelligence bonanza. The Air Ministry set about identifying the various bits of machinery. Montagu of Naval Intelligence was overjoyed: "The Germans have told the Agent highly secret information about the state of their knowledge . . . there are also points in it of which we did not, in fact, know that the Germans were aware, even from our knowledge gained from Most Secret Sources." A proposal to launch yet another deception plan based on the night-fighter intelligence was ruled out, however, on the grounds that "German knowledge is too near the knuckle for us to try to tamper with it at this stage."

Ryde fumed. Chapman had escaped again. To make matters worse, Robertson had instructed him to discuss compensation with this unpleasant young man and decide whether "we should out of our own funds supplement what ZZ has received from the Germans." The money was disappearing fast. "I still maintain that we are bound to give Zigzag a square deal," wrote Tar, "as he has done a very considerable service for this country." The sum of £5,000 was suggested, as a "settlement of our indebtedness to him [and] to impress upon Zigzag that we value the work which he has done for us at least as high as the Germans value that which he has done for them."

One evening, in strained conversation with Ryde, Chapman remarked that he expected to be "dealt with fairly" by the secret services.

"Could you give me some idea of what you have in mind?" Ryde asked, through gritted teeth.

"Well, the Germans gave me £6,000 when I came back here," Chapman replied.

Ryde responded that "of the £6,000 he had brought with him, £1,000 was for someone else and that being the case he had £5,000 from the Germans."

Ryde could hardly believe that he was having to haggle with such an individual. He pointed out that Chapman had also kept the money from his first mission, and should be grateful. "This argument did not seem to impress Zigzag," who tersely pointed out that the entire case had so far "only cost the British government about £200."

"I think that is a matter about which you should feel gratified," said Ryde, with all the considerable pomposity at his disposal. But Chapman was "not at all impressed." The discussion ended in deadlock, acrimony, and even deeper mutual antipathy.

The Germans, it seemed, were in a much more generous mood. Chapman had sent a message demanding "at least £6,000 to be delivered to him by parachute." In reply, the Germans had said that they would rather send the money through Lisbon, perhaps via the "reliable sailor" who had delivered the photographs. But if that proved impossible, then they pledged to drop the money by air. "Such promises are generally empty," insisted Ryde, at the same time scenting another opportunity to put an end to his agent.

The Abwehr had often made a practice, in the past, of providing agents with forged British currency. This was an economy measure, but a foolish one, since several Nazi spies were uncovered trying to spend the fake cash. "I think it would be important in closing the Zigzag case to destroy his faith in the Germans," wrote Ryde. "Zigzag's only interest in the case is the money he can make out of it, and if we were able to get the money and then prove to him that it was forged, we shall have gone a long way towards shattering the very high esteem which he undoubtedly has for Graumann and others . . . If the money is in fact counterfeit, Zigzag will probably send an unprintable message, closing the case himself."

In the meantime, Chapman sent a message to von Gröning saying that he was heading to the Liverpool docks to try to find a courier to bring the money back.

Ryde wanted to sack Chapman without a penny. He wanted to see him off the premises in such a way that he could never come back, never demand anything else of the intelligence services, and never work as a spy again. For this, he needed to demolish his credibility. Just one serious blunder would bring Chapman down. In the end, Ryde discovered two, furnished by Chapman's closest allies: von Gröning, the newly homeless aristocrat, and Jimmy Hunt, a newly released convict.

Ryde was intrigued by the close relationship between Chapman and von Gröning: "Zigzag has always spoken of Graumann in the highest terms and has expressed something akin to affection for 'the old man.' " But there was something more to the mutual admiration in this case, something about von Gröning he felt that Chapman was holding back. Ryde was a prig and a snob, but he was also a talented spy, with the intuitive ability to spot a lie.

One morning in the safe house, after Chapman had transmitted his morning message to Germany, Ryde deftly steered the conversation toward "Dr Graumann," and wondered "whether the Germans have any suspicion that he was being worked under control." Before Chapman could answer, Ryde continued, as if thinking aloud: "If Graumann did suspect this, it is unlikely that he would reveal his suspicions as it is in his own personal interests to keep the case going as long as possible." Chapman agreed, "without a moment's hesitation."

"Graumann is my best security," he added.

"What do you mean?" asked Ryde.

"He has made a great deal of money out of the case. For example when I ask for £6,000, Graumann probably draws £12,000 and pockets the change."

Slowly, it dawned on Ryde that Chapman was putting out enough rope to hang himself. If Chapman and von Gröning were in league embezzling money from their German masters, then it was also probable that Chapman had confided that he was working for the British. If so, then von Gröning, for reasons of greed and ambition, was betraying his own country with an agent he knew to be false. This evidence of financial collusion, wrote Ryde, "increases my suspicion that he has at least told Graumann, his German spymaster, of his connection with us in this country."

Seeing Ryde's expression, Chapman changed the subject. "My impression was that Zigzag knew perfectly well what was in my mind but was not going to admit it, and my earlier suspicions were strengthened."

Ryde conceded that the possible risks from a joint conspiracy involving Zigzag and his German boss might be limited, since von Gröning's self-interest would probably ensure that he kept Chapman's secret. "If it is true that Graumann is aware of Zigzag's position in this country it is very unlikely that anyone other than Graumann knows and there is probably little danger to us at present." But more important to Ryde's campaign, if Chapman had revealed himself to his German spymaster but had kept the fact from the British, this was a major security breach, proof that he had lied. Ryde was elated: "It may show that Zigzag has withheld from us this very important piece of information and it is against our principles to run a case with anyone who is found not to be absolutely open with us."

If Chapman had told von Gröning he was working for British intelligence, then who else had he let in on the secret? The question was soon answered.

Ryde was still debating how best to deploy this new evidence of Chapman's unreliability, when Jimmy Hunt accidentally administered the coup de grâce. One late October evening, Ryde's deputy, an MI5 officer called Reisen, paid an unannounced visit to Chapman's flat and found a debauched scene. Chapman was throwing a party. Characters from his seedy past and increasingly dubious present were ranged around the sitting room in various states of inebriation, including the boxer George Walker, a jobbing journalist named Frank Owens, and sundry other denizens of the Soho underworld. As Reisen entered the room, a large individual with the pallor of long-term imprisonment rose unsteadily to his feet. Here was Jimmy Hunt, the safecracker who had played such a crucial role in Chapman's early criminal life and then, as a figment of MI5's imagination, in his second career as a spy.

"I suppose you have come to take Eddie away on a job," Hunt said, grinning knowingly. Reisen made a noncommittal reply, determined not to betray his astonishment "in the presence of so many others." The implication of Hunt's remark was clear, and Reisen was "quite certain that Hunt knew the nature of the job to which he referred." Chapman had held his state secrets close for five years, but now, it seemed, his innate braggadocio had reemerged to trip him up. He had not merely spilled the beans: He had spilled them to a newly liberated, extremely drunk convict, and in so doing he had served up his own head, on a plate.

Ryde, delighted and vindictive, marshaled his evidence and moved in for the kill, as remorseless as if he had been terminating an enemy spy. Chapman had faced so many inquisitors in the past: Tin Eye Stephens, Praetorius, von Gröning, Dernbach, and a beautiful woman in a designer coat in Romainville jail. He had survived interrogations by the Gestapo, the Abwehr, and MI5; an agent provocateur in an Oslo bar; an inquisitive SS spy catcher in Paris; and any number of agents posing as spies had all tried to trip him up. But it was the bean counter of Whitehall who trapped him in the end.

Ryde's denunciation was a masterpiece. "I have long suspected that Zigzag has no regard whatever for the necessity of observing complete silence regarding his connection with us," he wrote. By confiding in Hunt, Chapman had "broken the most elementary security rules." With malice aforethought, Ryde methodically laid out the case for the prosecution: Chapman had already confided in one unauthorized individual, Dagmar Lahlum, and was probably in league with his German spymaster. He had attempted to extract money from MI5, gambled in fixed dog races, and kept the company of professional criminals. He had threatened to work for a rival secret service, and he was costing a small fortune to maintain in a lifestyle of champagne and loose women. Leaving aside von Gröning, who clearly had a vested interest in his success, the Germans were uncertain of their spy's loyalty, and the speech by Duncan Sandys had probably undermined his credibility anyway. Finally, and fatally, he had bragged to a known criminal about his work for the British secret services. "This act of Zigzag's does of course provide a first-class excuse for closing the case with him in the wrong and for administering a very firm rebuke," said Ryde, with relish. "In view of the inflammable situation caused by Zigzag's indiscretions to his very doubtful friend . . . it seems to me that we should dismiss him, explaining that he has broken his side of the bargain and that from now on he need expect no assistance from us in any trouble he may find himself in the future."

Nor should he be allowed to work as an intelligence agent for anyone else: "We should impress upon Zigzag that we would take the strongest possible exception to any approach which he might feel inclined to make to the Americans or French or any other government." In Ryde's view, Chapman should not receive another penny: "I should be opposed to paying him any further money, for once we do this we lay ourselves open to further approaches . . . We can now say to Zigzag that he can expect no further assistance, either financial or legal, we have obtained for him from the police a clean sheet, and he has a large sum of money which he would never have obtained without assistance. He has now let us down badly."

Ryde advised against continuing the Zigzag traffic with Germany without Chapman himself, arguing that any attempt to impersonate his radio technique would pose a "considerable risk, because Zigzag has a distinctive style." The case should simply be shut down in a clean break, leaving the Germans to believe that Chapman had been caught: "As far as the Germans are concerned Zigzag is away contacting a courier. Should he never reappear on the air again the assumption will be that he has been arrested."

Faced with Ryde's damning dossier, the MI5 chiefs had little choice but to agree. The Admiralty, with reluctance, acquiesced, although Operation Squid was still under way. "My feeling," wrote Masterman, "is that his case should be closed now, that we should pay Zigzag nothing and that the Yard should be informed." Tar Robertson did not object: "We should close it now." On November 2, 1944, Chapman was presented with a copy of the Official Secrets Act. Unaware of what was coming, he signed it, thereby stating: "I understand that any disclosure by me, whether during or after the present war, of facts relating to the undertaking upon which I have been engaged . . . will be an offence punishable by imprisonment." Having gagged Chapman, MI5 then sacked him.

Ryde was authorized to dismiss Chapman, which he did, "as forcibly as possible," throwing him out of the Hill Street flat after a fierce lecture on the error of his ways and warning him that if he dared to reveal what he had done during the war, he would be prosecuted. Ryde was exultant and ungenerous in victory and washed MI5's hands of Chapman with a flourish, and a threat: "He must understand that he must now stand on his own feet, and should he make any approach we, the office, will consider whether he should not be interned or otherwise disposed of."

Chapman had repeatedly risked his life for the British secret services. He had provided invaluable intelligence for the Allied war effort. He had penetrated the upper echelons of the German secret service, and helped disrupt V-weapon attacks on central London. Even now, German intelligence officers were poring over documents, furnished by Zigzag, describing a nonexistent antisubmarine weapon. He had extracted some £7,000 from the Nazi exchequer—$430,000 at modern prices—and cost the British government almost nothing. But he was also a criminal, expendable, and quite the wrong sort of person, in the eyes of many, to be hailed as a hero. This was the man MI5 would now "dispose of" if he dared to bother them again.

The Zigzag case was closed, and on November 28, 1944, at the age of thirty, Chapman's career as a secret agent came to an abrupt and permanent end. That evening, over dinner at his club with fellow officers, Major Ryde reviewed the fall of Eddie Chapman with placid self-satisfaction, concluding that "Zigzag should be thankful we are not going to lock him up."

Tin Eye Stephens, however, saw Zigzag differently: Chapman was the worst of men, in whom war had brought out the best. Years later, Stephens wrote: "Fiction has not, and probably never will, produce an espionage story to rival in fascination and improbability the true story of Edward Chapman, whom only war could invest with virtue, and that only for its duration." In Germany, Stephan von Gröning waited in vain for a message from his agent and friend. When the Nazis retreated, he continued to listen and hope, and as Hitler's regime crumbled around him, he was listening still.

Chapman, by rights and inclination, might have been expected to react to his sacking with indignation. Another man might have felt the sting of rejection, the cold humiliation of the double cross. But, as always, Chapman zigged when another man would have zagged. In truth, MI5's ungrateful farewell had set him free at last. He was no longer in thrall to either the German or the British secret services. He had money and a medal from the former, and an informal pardon from the latter; no other secret agent could claim to have been rewarded in this way by *both* sides. MI5 had threatened dire reprisals if he revealed his story, but he knew that one day it would be told.

Chapman returned to what he knew best, for Britain at the end of the war was a criminal's cornucopia. Through his old networks, he came into contact with Billy Hill, a nightclub owner and underworld boss who styled himself the "King of Soho." Hill had spent the war setting up some profitable black market and protection rackets. He was a "hard character with considerable dash and more verve," in Chapman's view, and the ideal ally. Making money by drugging greyhounds was strictly a pastime. New moneymaking schemes beckoned. Chapman and Hill went into partnership.

Dismissal from his country's service also left Chapman free to pursue matters of the heart once more, for he had conceived yet another romantic quest. This time the focus was not Dagmar (who waited in Oslo); nor Freda (who continued to draw her stipend from MI5); nor his ex-wife, Vera; nor Anita, the Portuguese prostitute from George's Bar. Chapman was now determined to find Betty Farmer, the girl he had left behind at the Hotel de la Plage, nearly six years earlier. Perhaps she was dead; perhaps she was married, or had moved away. But Chapman knew that if he could find Betty, and she would let him, he could make amends.

Chapman contacted Paul Backwell and Allan Tooth, the two former policemen who had served as his minders, and asked for their help. He also recruited a private detective, Doughy Baker. The search began to obsess Chapman, driving out every other thought, and every other woman: "Uppermost in my mind was the desire to find Betty, my girl, whom I had last seen when I dived through a hotel window before my arrest." Backwell and Tooth traced Betty only as far as a hotel on the Isle of Man in 1943. Her family thought she was working in a factory somewhere near London. A friend said Betty had been walking out with a Spitfire pilot, who was shot down in the sea off Margate.

Chapman arranged a summit meeting to discuss the search for Betty Farmer. Over lunch at the fashionable Berkeley Hotel (Chapman was as profligate and generous as ever), the ex-policemen explained that searching for a single woman in the chaos of wartime Britain was no easy task, particularly without a photograph: "Is there anyone here who looks like her at all?" Chapman looked around the dining room, with its lunchtime clientele of debs and guardsmen, bankers and mobsters. He pointed to a slim woman with blond hair, seated at a corner table, her back to the room. "That girl," he said, "looks exactly like her from the back." At that moment, the woman turned around.

"Jesus!" exclaimed Chapman. "It *is* Betty. Excuse me, gentlemen."

Backwell and Tooth, discreet to the last, slipped away, as a waiter swept up the remains of a coffee cup that had dropped from Betty Farmer's astonished fingers when a man she had last seen in a Jersey courtroom tapped her on the shoulder. Chapman pulled up a chair.

"I shall go," he had told her in the distant days before the war. "But I shall always come back."

CHAPTER TWENTY-NINE

Aftermath

WITH THE END of the war, the Double Cross team was quietly disbanded. It would be decades before anyone outside the Most Secret circle knew it had existed. A few eventually emerged from the shadows of British intelligence to tell their stories and reap some glory, but most did not.

Tommy "Tar" Robertson gave up the spy game, and spent the rest of his life farming sheep in Worcestershire. The "real genius" of the double-cross operation was awarded the U.S. Legion of Merit by Harry Truman, the Royal Order of the Yugoslav Crown by King Peter in a bizarre ceremony at Claridge's, and an Order of the British Empire from Britain for work too secret to be described. John Masterman, muscle-bound by duty, considered Tar's early retirement to be "one of the greatest losses which MI5 ever suffered," but Robertson was entirely happy tending his sheep. He stopped wearing tartan trousers, but he continued to talk to strange characters in pubs. When Tar died in 1994, a small poem was offered as an epitaph to the spymaster who never lost the knack of listening.

> *Blessed are they with cheery smile*
> *Who stop to chat for a little while.*
> *Blessed are they who never say:*
> *"You've told me that story twice today."*

John Cecil Masterman, who liked lecturing more than listening, was knighted, feted, and awarded the OBE. He returned to Oxford, his clubs, his cricket, and his mystery novels. He became provost of Worcester College, and then vice chancellor of Oxford. In 1957, he published another detective novel, *The Case of the Four Friends,* featuring a character called Chapman, which discussed the nature of the criminal mind: "To work out the crime before it is committed, to foresee how it will be arranged, and then prevent it! That's a triumph indeed." He sat on industrial boards and accepted governorships at the major public schools, a stalwart member of the great and good. "Everything which is good in this curious world owes its origin to privileged persons," he maintained.

But in 1970, for the first time in his life, Masterman broke ranks with the ruling classes by publishing a book about the Double-Cross organization. His account had been written immediately after the war, strictly for internal MI5 reading, but he had secretly kept a copy for himself. The spy scandals of the 1960s had shattered the morale of the British intelligence community, and Masterman was determined to restore some of its confidence by relating this story of unalloyed success. Roger Hollis, the head of MI5, and Alec Douglas-Home, the prime minister, refused to authorize publication, so Masterman published *The Double-Cross System in the War, 1939–1945* in the United States, where the Official Secrets Act could not stifle it. Many establishment figures, including some of Masterman's former colleagues in MI5, were scandalized; John Marriott never spoke to him again. In 1972, the British government bowed, and the book was published, subject to the removal of a number of contentious passages. "How strange it was," wrote Masterman, "that I, who all my life, had been a supporter of the Establishment, should become, at eighty, a successful rebel."

Others followed suit: Ewen Montagu published his account of Operation Mincemeat, the successful deception plan that had convinced the Germans the Allies intended to invade the Balkans and Sardinia rather than Sicily. Montagu, by then judge advocate of the fleet, even played a cameo role in the 1956 film *The Man Who Never Was.*

Paul Backwell, Chapman's wartime minder, became a captain in the Intelligence Corps, and Allan Tooth remained a senior NCO in the Field Security Service.

Ronnie Reed accepted a job with MI5 after the war as senior technical adviser to the security service. Between 1951 and 1957, he headed the counterespionage section, responsible for investigating Soviet moles in Britain, including the Burgess, Maclean, and Philby cases. Reed officially retired in 1977, but was invited to stay on in MI5 as a senior adviser. He later wrote the definitive monograph on wartime radio work, which was published as an appendix to the official account of British Intelligence in the Second World War. Reed was much too self-effacing to put his name to it. He died in 1995, at the age of seventy-eight. The Iron Cross presented to Chapman by von Gröning for services to the Third Reich, and then passed on to Reed as a souvenir of their friendship, remains in the possession of the Reed family.

Victor, Lord Rothschild, won the George Medal for his wartime work with explosives, joined the Zoology Department at Cambridge University, and went on to become security adviser to Margaret Thatcher. His student membership in the Cambridge Apostles, and his links with the KGB spies Guy Burgess and Anthony Blunt, led to allegations that he was the "Fifth Man" in the Cambridge Spy Ring. He furiously denied the charges, and published an open letter to British newspapers in 1986 stating: "I am not, and never have been, a Soviet agent."

Michael Ryde, Chapman's last case officer, left MI5 soon after the war and rejoined the family firm of chartered surveyors. He soon drank himself out of a job, however, and began a sad descent into alcoholism. One marriage disintegrated, and he walked out of the next, leaving two young children. In the pub, to general disbelief, Ryde would boast of his role in the case of Eddie Chapman, a man he had despised.

Terence Young survived the Battle of Arnhem to become a highly successful filmmaker, and directed the first and second James Bond films, *Dr. No* and *From Russia with Love* (in which a Russian spy develops a plan to kill Bond and steal a coding machine). The persona of the world's most famous secret agent was probably based on Young himself, with some cast members remarking that "Sean Connery was simply doing a Terence Young impression."

Jasper Maskelyne, the conjurer, virtually vanished after the war, to his intense irritation. He received no decoration, no formal recognition for his deception schemes, and official accounts of the North African campaign barely mentioned him. The audiences for his magic shows grew smaller, and the venues steadily less glamorous. Embittered, he gave up magic, emigrated to Kenya, set up a successful driving school, took part in the campaign against the Mau Mau rebels, and died in 1973.

Reginald Kearon, captain of the *City of Lancaster*, went on to take command of five more merchant vessels in the course of the war. He was awarded the OBE for war service and the Lloyd's War Medal. The sea kept trying, and failing, to claim him: in 1948, unsinkable Reg Kearon went on a solo pleasure cruise in the Mediterranean and was later found "drifting on a wreck in Haifa Bay." He retired in 1954, the same year that the *City of Lancaster* (renamed *Lancastrian*) was broken up.

From 1945, Robin "Tin Eye" Stephens ran Bad Nenndorf, the Combined Services Detailed Interrogation Centre (CSDIC) near Hanover, a secret prison set up following the British occupation of northwestern Germany. This was the German version of Camp 020, where Tin Eye was charged with flushing the truth out of the numerous intelligence officers and spies picked up as the Allies pushed into Germany, including Himmler's assistant, Walter Schellenberg, and Ernst Kaltenbrunner, Heydrich's successor as head of the RSHA (a "giant of evil" in Stephens's view). Tin Eye was accused of using brutal methods to extract confessions, but he was acquitted of all charges, having damned his accusers as "degenerates, most of them diseased by VD [and] pathological liars."

Stephan von Gröning was arrested by American forces and held in a prison camp outside Bremen. Homeless, he had been staying with his sister Dorothea and her adopted Jewish daughter when the soldiers arrived. The Americans got lost escorting him to the prison, so the half-American von Gröning showed them the way, in perfect

English, with an upper-class accent. He was allowed to send one card a month to relatives. The man whose linen had always been ironed by servants found himself pleading for handkerchiefs and tooth-paste. He was released after six months and discovered, to his intense annoyance, that in order to obtain a ration book, and thus to eat, he had to get a job. Through family friends, he was found nominal employment at the Bremen Museum, but he rarely turned up for work.

The money may have all gone, but von Gröning lived on his name, "loyal to his own class" to the end. He married a much younger woman named Ingeborg, and though she worked, he did not. He would lie for long hours on the sofa, reading borrowed books. Von Gröning seldom spoke of the war. He believed Eddie Chapman had been captured, exposed as a spy, and executed. He kept a photograph of La Bretonnière in his wallet.

Walter Praetorius, alias Thomas, the Nazi who loved folk dancing, was arrested, transferred to Bad Nenndorf, and interrogated by Tin Eye Stephens. Stephens considered the camp inmates to be "invariably foul," but Praetorius impressed him, perhaps because his Anglomania chimed with Tin Eye's raw jingoism. Praetorius was released after several months of interrogation, with the verdict that he had "had a long and possibly creditable record of service as a permanent official of the German Secret Service." Praetorius settled in Goslar, West Germany, where he returned to teaching and dancing.

On May 5, 1945, troops of the 41st U.S. Cavalry liberated Mauthausen-Gusen concentration camp and found a scene from hell—human skeletons staggering through an abandoned factory of death. Among the emaciated ghosts was Anthony Faramus. He had lost a lung and seven ribs, his body had been racked by diphtheria, scarlet fever, gangrene, and dysentery. But somehow the frail Jersey boy who blushed so easily had survived. Back in Britain, he was treated in an RAF hospital, and then discharged with £16 in cash and a weekly allowance of £2. He arranged to meet up with Eddie Chapman through the journalist Frank Owens, who witnessed their "awkward" meeting.

"I thought you were dead," said Chapman.

"I thought so too, sometimes."

"How did you make out?"

"Not so good."

"I was always worried about how you got on."

"I often felt the same way about you, Eddie, and wondered whether you'd make the grade. That was certainly a tricky game you were playing."

There was an embarrassed silence.

"Where did you go?" asked Chapman.

"Many places so bad, Eddie, that I was sometimes even tempted to give your game away to the Jerries. Anyway, rather than do those swine a favor, I kept quiet."

There was another long pause before Chapman said: "You know, Tony, if it hadn't been for me you wouldn't have had to go through all that."

Faramus had never betrayed Chapman, and Chapman had maintained the confidence of the Germans, in part, he believed, to protect Faramus. They went to a nearby pub and got very drunk. "Millions died without being able to utter a single word," Chapman reflected to his friend. "We at least have lived to tell our stories."

Faramus wrote a harrowing memoir, and obtained work as a film extra. In a painfully ironic piece of casting, he played the part of a prisoner of war in the film *The Colditz Story*. The inhabitants of Colditz may have suffered, but never as he had done.

Faramus emigrated to Hollywood—and ended up as Cary Grant's butler.

•   •   •

Dagmar Lahlum waited in vain for Chapman to come back, while Norway carried out a grim accounting. Vidkun Quisling was arrested at his mansion, Gimli, tried for treason, and executed by a firing squad. Two members of the Norwegian resistance were tried for the murder of the Feltmans, but acquitted. Dagmar's neighbors back in Eidsvoll whispered behind her back, and called her a "German tart."

She heard them, but said nothing. She never told her neighbors or family that she had assisted the British secret services during the war. To get away from the "Mrs. Gossips," she took a job as an assistant nurse aboard the cruise ship *Stvanger Fjord,* which sailed between Oslo, New York, and Nova Scotia. She and Chapman had both learned to love the sea, and, like him, "she was always restless." She worked in a bookshop, then as a hairdresser, and finally as an accountant. Dagmar still wore the most fashionable clothes, and smoked Craven A cigarettes. She never remarried, never had children, and never lost her looks. In old age, she wore makeup and leopard-skin hats, and once her niece caught her dancing alone in front of the mirror. When Dagmar died of Parkinson's disease in 1999, her niece found a box of letters, carefully written out in English, on sheet after sheet of airmail paper. They were addressed to Eddie Chapman. None had ever been sent. Dagmar's niece burned them all.

Freda Stevenson, rightly, saw no point in waiting. She became a shorthand typist, and in 1949, she married a bank clerk five years her junior. Four years later, she had become a newsagent's clerk, divorced her second husband, and married a wealthy garage proprietor called Abercrombie. Though the security service was careful to destroy the agreement under which she was to be paid £5 a month until further notice and removed all references from the files, Freda may have continued to receive checks from the London Co-operative Society, the fruits of Chapman's deal with MI5, until the day she died. Like Faramus, Freda was a survivor.

At the Berkeley Hotel, Eddie Chapman and Betty Farmer talked for hours, and got married shortly thereafter. It was a happy, enduring marriage, even though Chapman's eye wandered more or less continuously for the next fifty years. He left often, but he always came back. A daughter, Suzanne, was born in October 1954.

Zigzag never did go straight. After the war, he returned to the demimonde of London's West End, where the wastrels welcomed him home. During the 1950s, he smuggled gold across the Mediterranean. After buying a share in Billy Hill's yacht, the *Flamingo,* a former minesweeper, Chapman and a like-minded crew sailed to

Morocco, where they became involved in a ludicrous plot to smuggle 850,000 packets of cigarettes and kidnap the deposed sultan. The plan collapsed when the villainous crew got into a dockside brawl, and they were expelled from Tangier, hotly pursued by a reporter from the *Sunday Chronicle*, whom they invited on board and then locked in his cabin. The *Flamingo* caught fire in the Toulon harbor, possibly for insurance purposes, giving rise to suspicions that Chapman's sabotage skills had not deserted him. Soon after, the Hill gang knocked off a post-office van, escaping with £250,000. During the 1960s, Eddie and Betty Chapman moved to Africa's Gold Coast. Chapman became involved in a complicated building contract. There was a corruption inquiry, but by then he had come home.

Tin Eye Stephens had wondered "what will happen when Chapman, embroiled again in crime, as he inevitably will be, stands up in court and pleads leniency on the grounds of highly secret wartime service?" He duly found out. Chapman would appear in court repeatedly over the next twenty years, but he never returned to prison. When he was charged with passing forged currency in 1948, he produced a character reference from an unnamed "senior officer of the War office" stating that he was "one of the bravest men who served in the last war." The referee was almost certainly Ronnie Reed. MI5 had not entirely welched on its debt. Again, in 1974, he was found not guilty of hitting a man on the head with a glass during a dance party at the Watersplash Hotel in the New Forest. The fight was over a young woman named Theresa Chin. Chapman told the court: "I was trained in unarmed combat for my wartime activities and I didn't need a glass to defend myself in a pub brawl. I could have killed him with my bare hands." When he was acquitted, he offered to buy the jury a drink.

Chapman still mixed with blackmailers, high rollers, and low thieves. He drove a Rolls-Royce (though he never passed a driving test) and wore fur-collared coats. The newspapers loved him— "Eddie Chapman, the gentleman crook." He was even, for a time, the "honorary crime correspondent" of the *Sunday Telegraph*, "whose readers he proceeded to warn against the attentions of people like him." In 1960, a reporter asked him if he missed the old days of crime. "I do a bit," he said wistfully. "I've no regrets. No conscience about anything I've done. I like to think I was an honest villain."

John Masterman once wrote: "Sometimes in life you feel that there is something which you *must* do, and in which you must trust your own judgment and not that of any other person. Some call it conscience and some plain obstinacy. Well, you can take your choice." War, briefly, brought out in Chapman an obstinate conscience. His vices were as extreme as his virtues, and to the end of his life, it was never clear whether he was on the side of the angels or the devils, whether he deceived the deceivers, or whether he had made a pact with his German spymaster. He died in 1997 of heart failure, at the age of eighty-three. He may have ascended heavenward; or perhaps he headed in the opposite direction. He is probably zigzagging still.

Chapman tried to publish an account of his wartime exploits, but like John Masterman he was blocked by MI5. He wrote a bowdlerized version of events that appeared in a French newspaper, *L'Etoile,* and then in the *News of the World* in 1953, but when Chapman strayed into official secrets, the government lawyers stepped in. He was fined £50, and an entire edition of the newspaper had to be pulped. A second attempt at publication was thwarted by D-Notice, the official government request to news editors not to publish for reasons of national security. Eventually, a ghosted and semifictionalized memoir, *The Eddie Chapman Story,* which described his time in Germany but not his MI5 work, appeared in 1954. "What is the truth about Eddie Chapman?" demanded the *News of the World.* "Why, if these astounding claims are true, was he not arrested and convicted as a traitor to his country?"

Finally, in 1966, Chapman was allowed to publish another version, *The Real Eddie Chapman Story,* which referred, without giving details, to his work for MI5. This provided the basis for a rather poor film, *Triple Cross,* directed by Terence Young and starring Christopher Plummer as Chapman. The film bore only a superficial relation to the truth, and Chapman was disappointed by it. He never received the recognition he thought he deserved; but then, Chapman could probably only have achieved *that* level of recognition by assassinating Hitler. Somehow, he became rather rich, and for a while owned a castle in Ireland and a spa in Hertfordshire, not far from the De Havilland Mosquito plant.

In 1974, in a London bar, Chapman bumped into Leo Kreusch, the toothless German prizefighter who had taught him to shoot at La Bretonnière. Leo told Chapman the real name of the man he had always known as Graumann, revealing that he had survived the war and that he was now living in Bremen. Chapman wrote von Gröning a letter, in which he recalled, with affection, the times they had spent together in Nantes, Paris, and Oslo. He inquired whether his old friend knew what had happened to the Norwegian sailing yawl purchased with his reward money, and whether he remembered Dagmar Lahlum. "I suppose she is married now," he reflected nostalgically. Chapman described his properties, enclosing a photograph of the ancient Irish castle he had acquired, and invited von Gröning to come and stay: "What delightful memories we could exchange . . . I remember how much you used to like castles."

This was not, perhaps, the most tactful approach, but Eddie could not know that von Gröning was no longer wealthy.

Suzanne Chapman was married in 1979 at Shenley Lodge, the thirty-two-room health spa owned by Eddie and Betty. Among the wedding guests that day was an elderly, shortsighted German gentleman who amused the children by reciting old-fashioned English nursery rhymes. When the party wound down, Eddie Chapman and Stephan von Gröning linked arms and wandered off together, deep in reminiscence. Betty was surprised and moved by the enduring bond between the spy and his spymaster: "They were like brothers." As the last wedding guests departed, laughter and singing could be heard drifting from the garden: the faint strains of "Lili Marlene."

Epilogue

A FEW WEEKS after the publication of Agent Zigzag in Britain, I received a telephone call from the German ambassador to London, Wolfgang Ischinger. "I have just finished your book," he said. "You describe how Eddie Chapman was flown across the Channel by the Luftwaffe and then parachuted into Britain. I thought you might be interested to know that the man who commanded that flight was my father. Both he and the pilot, Fritz Schlichting, are still very much alive."

Schlichting had been the tall, shy pilot with the iron cross at the controls of the Focke-Wulf reconnaissance plane in 1942, while Karl "Charlie" Ischinger was his commanding officer and navigator, described by Chapman as a "small, thickset young man of about 28, with steady blue eyes." Chapman himself had believed these men were dead: "The whole crew had been shot down and killed over England on their sixtieth sortie," he wrote.

The discovery that the pilot and navigator had not only outlived the war but survived still led to a meeting with Fritz Schlichting at his home in Detmold, Germany. At the age of eighty-four, charming and hospitable, the former pilot recalled that day as if he had stepped off the runway at Le Bourget last week, rather than a lifetime ago.

"We were the Luftwaffe Reconnaissance Squadron number 123 stationed in the Château du Buc, outside Versailles. We flew night flights over Britain, photographing the effects of bombing raids and helping to identify targets. It was dangerous work. I lost more than eighty comrades. The average number of flights before being shot down was about forty. I flew eighty-seven in all.

"One day my commanding officer, Major Gobin, told Charlie [Ischinger] and me that we had been chosen for a special mission. He told us to dress in civilian clothing and go to Paris. We met the English spy and his handlers in a restaurant for dinner; we knew him only as "Fritz," like me. Much later, I discovered his real name. He was delightful, excellent company. We all got on famously.

"We all met a few weeks later at Le Bourget airfield, and I showed him the plane. Chapman seemed quite calm, although he asked lots of questions. On the way over the Channel, we sang songs. There was a bad moment when Chapman was preparing to jump, and we realized that his parachute cord was not properly tied. If he had jumped like that, he would have fallen to his death. Charlie gave the signal, and Chapman opened the hatch. He had this huge pack on his back—heaven knows what was in it—and as he jumped it got wedged in the hole. He was struggling, but it wouldn't budge, so Charlie got out of his seat and gave him a big boot in the back.

"That was the last we saw of Chapman for about four months, but we heard that his mission had been successful. Everyone was very pleased with him. It never occurred to anyone that he might be working for the British. We met up with him again in Paris. It was a great reunion. Chapman handed Charlie and me two packages, containing a big box of chocolates and a pound of coffee that he had bought in Madrid on his way back. It was real coffee beans, not the fake stuff, so we were delighted.

"After the Chapman mission, as a reward, we were each presented with a special engraved silver goblet. I have always treasured it. Charlie is still my best friend. He is ninety-seven now, and his health is not good, but we still have get-togethers when we remember the extraordinary night we dropped the English spy into Britain."

The courtly Luftwaffe pilot is only one of several people to emerge from Chapman's past, adding fresh myths and memories, some affectionate, and some decidedly less so. An elderly, rather refined female voice came on the telephone at the *Times,* and without giving her name declared angrily: "He was an absolute shit, you know. The handsomest man I ever met. But a prize shit." Then she hung up. In Norway, another of Chapman's wronged women finally won recognition for her heroism. The Norwegian media picked up the Chapman story, and the national newspaper *Aftenposten* ran a front-page story with the headline "SHE DIED A GERMAN COLLABORATOR, BUT SHE WAS REALLY A BRITISH SPY." It emerged that Dagmar had been brought before a war crimes tribunal after the war, imprisoned for six months, and agreed to acknowledge her own guilt in lieu of a formal conviction. Reviled and ostracized by her countrymen, Dagmar had kept her promise to Chapman, and never revealed her wartime links with the British secret service.

John Williams, a friend of Chapman's, recalled the first time they met, when Shenley Lodge was being run as a country club with a bar and roulette table before its more respectable incarnation as a health resort. "I arrived at the impressive front entrance of Shenley only to hear the most fearsome of noises from the roof of the mansion. It was on this roof I met Eddie strapped into a Vickers machine gun firing at a sheet draped between two oak trees half a mile away!" Another acquaintance, the journalist Peter Kinsley, wrote a letter to the *Times* after Agent Zigzag was serialized in it. "Eddie would have loved the publicity. His old friends said he should have worn a T-shirt emblazoned 'I am a Spy for MI5.' The last time I met him he described how he had missed a fortune in ermine (to be used in coronation robes) during a furs robbery, because he thought it was rabbit. He also said he successfully convinced a German au pair girl that he was a post office telephone engineer, and robbed the wall safe. He was also once visited by an income tax inspector, and produced a doctor's certificate that he had a weak heart and could not be 'caused stress.' Ten minutes later, he drove, in a Rolls-Royce, past the inspector waiting in the rain at a bus stop, and gave him a little wave."

I also received a mournful letter from Brian Simpson, a collector of wartime medals who had lived near Shenley Lodge in the 1980s.

Simpson had heard of Chapman's adventures through a mutual friend, and asked if he could buy his Iron Cross. Sure enough, a few weeks later, Chapman duly produced the German medal; indeed, he produced two, saying that he had been given another one by Hitler himself. A deal was struck: Eddie Chapman took the money, and a delighted Simpson took the medals. Two decades later, on reading this book, the collector realized that he had been conned. Chapman, of course, had given his own Iron Cross to Ronnie Reed many years earlier. Those in Simpson's possession were replicas. "Your book came as quite a shock," wrote Simpson. "It now seems that Eddie had the last laugh. My wife was also offered a small jeweled dagger that Eddie said was given to him by Hermann Göring. She declined to take it." Chapman, needless to say, had never laid eyes on Göring.

One after another, Chapman's former associates, ex-lovers, and victims emerged from the past to add their stories—some true, some the legacy of Chapman's self-mythologizing. But then, to my astonishment, there reappeared the only person who really knew the truth about Eddie Chapman: Eddie Chapman himself.

John Dixon, an independent filmmaker, called me to say that he had six hours of footage of Chapman talking about his life, not one second of which had ever been broadcast. Dixon had shot the film in 1996, the year before Chapman died, with a view to making a documentary. That never happened. But he had kept the film safe, thinking that one day Chapman's story would be told. He now offered to show it to me.

Sitting in a small screening room in Soho, meeting Chapman for the first time from beyond the grave, was one of the strangest experiences of my life. Chapman was old and already ill when the film was made, but still vital. He still exuded a feral charm, as he lounged in an armchair, reminiscing, smoking, chuckling, winking, and flirting with the camera. He described parachuting into Britain, his relationship with von Gröning, the faked bombing of the De Havilland aircraft, and his life in Jersey, France, Lisbon, and Oslo. His criminal exploits were recalled with airy pride.

But there was a valedictory tone to his words: this was the last testament of a man talking to posterity, and setting the record straight—or, in some instances, bent. Because at the age of eighty-two, Chapman was still a shameless liar. In one passage, for example, he describes being taken to see Winston Churchill in 1943 and sharing a bottle of brandy with the prime minister while the latter sat in bed in his dressing gown. It is a splendid story. It is also completely untrue.

Chapman could never have imagined that MI5 would decide to release its records, and that the truth about his wartime service would one day be revealed. His own death appears imminent in John Dixon's footage, but there is Eddie Chapman still playing by his own rules: a grinning villain, spinning a yarn, looking you straight in the eye while he picks your pocket.

Ben Macintyre
March 2007

APPENDIX

This is an exact copy of the explanation of Chapman's code, contained in the MI5 archives (KV2 455) held at the British National Archives in Kew, London.

MULTIPLICATION CODE
Given to
An English Parachutist

This code is based on the word: "CONSTANTINOPLE" which is agreed upon before the agent's departure. Constantinople is then given its numerical position in the alphabet in the following manner and multiplied by the date on which the transmission takes place. In this case the 8th has been chosen.

C	O	N	S	T	A	N	T	I	N	O	P	L	E
2	9	6	12	13	1	7	14	4	8	10	11	5	3
													8

23	6	8	97	05	3	7	15	8	4	80	92	2	4

The next procedure:

Write out the alphabet in full, giving each letter its numerical position.

a	b	c	d	e	f	g	h	i	j	k	l	m	n	o	p	q	r	s	t	u	v	w	x	y	z
1	2	3	4	5	6	7	8	9	10	11	12	13	14	15	16	17	18	19	20	21	22	23	24	25	26

The result of the multiplication is then written out and the message to be transmitted—in this case:

'I HAVE ARRIVED AND IN GOOD HEALTH'

is written below.

It will be noticed that the first five letters are 'f's. This is the agreed sign between the agent and his German Control that he is operating of his own free will. Should he be forced to transmit, the omission of the five 'f's would immediately disclose to the German Control that he had been apprehended.

The Method of Coding:

Add 'f' (which is the 6th letter) to the 2 above it, making 8, and selecting the 8th letter in the alphabet—'h'—

In the second instance 'f' again (the 6th letter in the alphabet), added to 3, making 9 which is—'i'—

This method is continued throughout the message including the signature 'FRITZ'.

2	3	6	8	9	7	0	5	3	7	1	5	8	4	8	0	9	2	2	4
f	f	f	f	f	I	H	A	V	E	x	A	R	R	I	V	E	D	A	N
h	i	l	n	o	p	h	f	y	l	y	f	z	v	q	v	n	f	c	r
D	I	N	G	O	O	D	H	E	A	L	T	H	x	F	R	I	T	Z	x
f	l	t	o	x	v	d	m	h	h	m	y	p	b	n	r	r	v	b	b

The Groups of 5

are then read off horizontally instead of vertically as in other cases.

Thus:

HILNO PHFYL YFZVQ VNFCR FLTOX VDMHH MYPBN RRVBB

<u>Note</u>: It is always necessary to include the exact number of letters in the code before commencing the coded groups of five.

ACKNOWLEDGMENTS

DOZENS OF PEOPLE IN FIVE countries have generously contributed to the writing of this book, with research help, interviews, advice, and access to photographs, documents, and memories. In Britain, I am indebted to Betty Chapman; Tony Faramus; Howard Davies; Hugh Alexander at the National Archives; Mary Teviot for her splendid genealogical sleuthing; Professor M. R. D. Foot and Calder Walton for their invaluable historical expertise; Major A. J. Edwards and the late Colonel Tony Williams at the Military Intelligence Museum archive; Caroline Lamb at the Liddell Hart Centre for military archives; Dunia Garcia-Ontiveros at the National Maritime Museum; George Malcolmson, Royal Navy Submarine Museum; and David Capus, Metropolitan Police Service Records Management Branch. Andrea and Edward Ryde, Sophia and Charles Kitson, Margery Barrie, Carolyn Elton, Nicholas Reed, and Charles Chilton all helped me to build up a more complete picture of the various case officers. In Jersey, I am grateful to Steven Guy-Gibbens, governor of HM Prison La Moye, and Paul Matthews, deputy judicial greffier, for granting me access to closed prison, police, and judicial records; to Linda Romeril and Stuart Nicolle at the Jersey Historical Archives; and Jan Hadley and John Guegan of the *Jersey Evening Post*. In Norway, Alf Magnussen of *Aftenposten* was supremely helpful in tracking down memories of Dagmar through Bibbi Røset, Leife Myhre, and Harald Næss (who kindly allowed me to destroy part of his roof with a crowbar in the search for Chapman's concealed film). In the United States, Anne Cameron Berlin carried out useful preliminary research in the U.S. National Archives. In Germany, I am grateful to Peter Steinkamp for his work at the Bundesarchiv-Militärarchiv in Freiburg, and to Petra and Ingeborg von Gröning for their hospitality and help. I am also grateful to Georges and Caroline Paruit, the owners of La Bretonnière in Nantes.

For a secretive organization, MI5 has been a model of openness: not only providing access to hitherto classified files, but assisting in the search for additional material. To the other individuals who prefer not to be named: You know who you are, and how grateful I am.

Robert Thomson, Keith Blackmore, Anne Spackman, Daniel Finkelstein, and all my colleagues on the *Times* have been supportive and tolerant, and occasionally both. Michael Evans was typically generous with his expertise. Denise Reeves performed several miracles of picture research.

John Glusman has been, as always, a delight to work with.

Finally, my thanks and love to Kate Muir, as always, for her support, patience, and fine editorial judgment. This book is dedicated to her.

NOTES

Unless otherwise noted, all interrogations are of Chapman by the MI5 officer named.

Where three or more subsequent note entries refer to the same source, only the first and last entries from the main text are shown as prompts. Any comments not taken directly from the source material quoted are the author's own.

Chapter One. The Hotel de la Plage

3 **"with all the trimmings":** Interview with Leonard Maxie, former waiter at Hotel de la Plage, Jersey, July 2006.

3 **"in the film business":** Interview with Betty Chapman, Amersham, November 25, 2005.

3 **"I shall go":** Ibid.

3 **"How would you like to go":** Edward Chapman, *The Real Eddie Chapman Story* (London, 1966), p. 32. Hereafter cited as *Chapman*.

4 **"prince of the underworld":** Robin Stephens, January 7, 1942, KV2 457.

5 **"off the rails":** Interview with Betty Chapman, November 25, 2005.

6 **"jail-crop haircut":** *Chapman*, p. 27.

6 **"three days doing crowd work":** Laurie C. Marshall report, January 15, 1943; MI5 ref. 133B. This file, newly released by MI5, has been allocated to KV2 457. Hereafter, material in this file will be cited as KV2 457 (additional).

6 **"wire and whipcord body":** Frank Owens, foreword to ibid., p. 9.

6 **"I mixed with all types":** Ibid., p. 27.

6 **"behaving in a manner":** Police record, KV2 455.

7   **"with good looks":**   Owens, foreword, p. 9.

7   **"women on the fringes":**   R. "Tin Eye" Stephens, *Camp 020: MI5 and the Nazi Spies* (London, 2000), p. 218. Hereafter cited as *Camp 020.*

7   **"infected a girl of 18":**   Ibid.

7   **"best cracksmen":**   KV2 457.

7   **"cool, self-possessed":**   *Chapman,* p. 28.

7   **"shivering with fear":**   Interrogation by Ronald Reed, January 7, 1943, KV2 457.

8   **"He was able":**   Interview with Terence Young, January 22, 1943, KV2 458.

8   **"He is a crook":**   Ibid.

9   **"I don't go along":**   *Sunday Telegraph,* March 23, 1963.

9   **"went back to 'work' ":**   Paul Backwell report, KV2 456.

10   **"Be prepared for trouble":**   *Jersey Evening Post,* February 13, 1939.

Chapter Two. Jersey Gaol

14   **"done with deliberation":**   *Jersey Evening Post,* February 14, 1939.

14   **"dangerous criminal who had failed":**   Ibid.

14   **"dreary little cage":**   Anthony Charles Faramus, *The Faramus Story* (London, n.d.), p. 12. Hereafter cited as *Faramus.*

15   **the governor's personal batman:**   Minutes of the Jersey prison board, Jersey Historical Archive.

15   **"keep an eye on Chapman":**   Ibid.

15   **"At that moment":**   Warder Packer's evidence to Jersey prison board, Jersey Historical Archive.

16   **"Do you know":**   *Jersey Evening Post,* July 6, 1939.

16–18   **"interested in quarries"** to **"Your name is Chapman":**   Ibid.

18   **a free-for-all ensued:**   *Daily Express,* July 8, 1939.

18   **"This appeared to distress":**   *Jersey Evening Post,* July 6, 1939.

19   **"gross misconduct":**   Minutes of the Jersey prison board, Jersey Historical Archive.

19   **"You have never":**   Ibid.

Chapter Three. Island at War

22   **"Nationalism as a God":**   H. G. Wells, *Outline of History* (London, 1920), p. 209.

24   **"sort of dispossessed"**:   *Faramus,* p. 10.

25   **"Look, we've reason"**:   Interrogation, January 1, 1943, KV2 456.

25   **"If I could work a bluff"**:   Interrogation, December 17, 1942, KV2 455.

26   **"It all sounds fine talk"**:   *Chapman,* pp. 48–49.

26   **"His whole theme"**:   *Faramus,* p. 29.

26   **"tale of loathing"**:   Ibid., p. 30.

28   **"The British police"**:   Interrogation, December 17, 1942, KV2 455.

Chapter Four. Romainville

30   **"stank of drink"**:   *Faramus,* p. 39.

30   **"How would you"**:   Ibid., p. 36.

30   **"*Alles verboten*"**:   *The Trial of German Major War Criminals,* vol. 6 (London, 1946), p. 141.

30   **"Madame prisonniers"**:   *Faramus,* p. 40.

31   **"professional denouncer"**:   Interrogation by E. Goodacre, December 18, 1942, KV2 455.

32   **"It wasn't safe to talk"**:   Interrogation by E. Goodacre, December 17, 1942, KV2 455.

32   **"were real love affairs"**:   *Faramus,* p. 43.

33   **"the scholarly, staid"**:   Interrogation by Victor Rothschild, January 28, 1943, KV2 458.

33   **"What happened?"**:   *Faramus,* p. 48.

33   **"All right for you"**:   Ibid., p. 37.

34   **"Supposing you didn't feel like coming back"**:   *Faramus,* p. 49.

34   **"You'd have to trust"**:   Ibid.

35   **"They'll probably send you"**:   *Faramus,* p. 37.

35   **"simply a trained brute"**:   *Chapman,* p. 62.

35   **"a man of understanding"**:   Ibid., p. 62.

36   **"no use"**:   Interrogation by Robin Stephens, January 7, 1942, KV2 457.

36   **"In times of war"**:   Interrogation by Robin Stephens, December 17, 1942, KV2 455.

36   **"half-threat"**:   Ibid.

36   **"Supposing you slip up"**:   *Faramus,* p. 37.

37   **"Goodbye and good luck":**   Ibid., p. 49.

37   **"You are among friends":**   *Chapman,* p. 64.

38   **"Welcome to the Villa":**   Ibid., p. 66.

Chapter Five. Villa de la Bretonnière

40   **"one of the most important":**   Interrogation by Robin Stephens, December 17, 1942, KV2 455.

41   **"respectable business man":**   Ibid.

41   **"surprisingly soft":**   Ibid.

41   **"Look, you will see":**   Interrogation by Victor Rothschild, January 2, 1943, KV2 456.

41   **"absolutely first-class":**   T. A. Robertson (attributed), report of SOE training course, KV4 172.

41   **"by the time of the fall":**   John Curry, *The Security Service, 1908–1945: The Official History* (London, 1999), KV4 1–3.

44   **"There is a well-defined":**   Cited in Emily Jane Wilson, "The War in the Dark: The Security Service and the Abwehr, 1940–1944," Ph.D. diss., Cambridge University, 2003, p. 42.

44   **"typically Prussian neck":**   Ibid.

44   **"Suspect everyone":**   Evelyn Waugh, cited in ibid.

44   **"was left with the":**   Curry, *Security Service.*

46   **"Chiefly line of Clan":**   Letter by Walter Praetorius, 1979, on Thomas family website.

46   **"kind, gentle type":**   Walter Praetorius file, KV2 524.

47   **"rabid Nazi":**   Ibid.

47   **"superiority of the German":**   Ibid.

47   **"might be trained":**   ISOS intercept, February 2, 1942, KV2 456.

Chapter Six. Dr. Graumann

49   **"He just got hold":**   Interrogation, January 1, 1943, KV2 456.

50   **"pocket money":**   Ibid.

50   **"He liked life":**   Interrogation by Victor Rothschild, January 1, 1943, KV2 456.

51   **"Had a good trip?":**   Interrogation, January 1, 1943, KV2 456.

51   **"What do you want":**   Interrogation by Victor Rothschild, January 2, 1943, KV2 456.

51   **"take it out and light a cigarette":**   Interrogation by E. Goodacre, December 17, 1942, KV2 455.

51   **"Good God!":**   Interrogation by Robin Stephens, December 17, 1942, KV2 455.

51   **"Look here, if you":**   Ibid.

51   **"more or less reckless":**   Interrogation by Victor Rothschild, January 28, 1943, KV2 458.

52   **"Mary had a little lamb":**   Interrogation by Victor Rothschild, January 2, 1943, KV2 456.

52   **"These were things":**   Ibid.

52   **"terribly English accent":**   Interrogation by Robin Stephens, January 3, 1943, KV2 456.

52   **"very good private tutor":**   Interrogation by Ronald Reed, December 21, 1943, KV2 456.

52   **"I'll show you a photograph":**   Interrogation by Robin Stephens, January 3, 1943, KV2 456.

52   **"really good brandy":**   *Chapman,* p. 66.

54   **declared the experience "uncomfortable":**   Interview with Ingeborg von Gröning, Bremen, May 22, 2006.

54   **"He was delightful":**   Ibid.

54   **"illicit association":**   Gladys von Gröning, immigration file, HO 405/16169.

55   **"He could mix in":**   Interview with Ingeborg von Gröning, Bremen, March 22, 2006.

56   **"Home corner":**   *Chapman,* p. 73.

56   **"German spirit":**   Ibid., p. 71.

56   **"Heil Hitler":**   Ibid., p. 69.

56   **"the hopes of every man":**   Ibid., p. 72.

57   **uniforms "of every kind":**   Interrogation by Robin Stephens, December 17, 1942, KV2 455.

58   **"a fairly high bug":**   Interrogation by Robin Stephens, December 19, 1942, KV2 455.

58   **"one of our best men":**   Ibid.

58   **"like a gigolo":**   Report by Ronald Reed, January 1, 1943, KV2 457.

58   **"an old Gestapo man":**   Interrogation by E. Goodacre, December 17, 1942, KV2 455.

58 **"black senders":** Ibid.

59 **the code was "unbreakable":** Ronald Reed report, March 15, 1943, KV2 459.

59 **"my little mottoes":** Interrogation, January 1, 1943, KV2 456.

59 **"It is very cold":** ISOS intercept, October 20, 1942, KV2 460.

59 **"A man went":** Ibid., October 23, 1942.

60 **"What silly business":** Ibid., October 14, 1942.

60 **"I had everything":** Interrogation by Robin Stephens, December 17, 1942, KV2 455.

Chapter Seven. Codebreakers

61 **"Dear France":** ISOS intercept, October 13, 1942, KV2 460.

62 **"brilliant guesswork":** Peter Twinn, in F. H. Hinsley and Alan Stripp, eds., *Codebreakers: The Inside Story of Bletchley Park* (Oxford, 2001).

62 **"It's amazing how people smile":** Cited in Penelope Fitzgerald, *The Knox Brothers* (London, 2001), p. 98.

62 **"My Golden Eggs":** Cited in Emily Jane Wilson, "The War in the Dark: The Security Service and the Abwehr, 1940–1944," Ph.D. diss., Cambridge University, 2003.

64 **"By means of the double-cross":** J. C. Masterman, *The Double-Cross System in the War, 1939–1945* (London, 1972), p. 3.

64 **"Immensely personable":** Address by Christopher Harmer at memorial service for T. A. Robertson at Pershore Abbey, Worcestershire Liddell Hart Centre for Military Archives, London.

64 **"Tar was in no sense":** J. C. Masterman, *On the Chariot Wheel: An Autobiography* (Oxford, 1975), p. 219.

64 **"involved a great deal":** Harmer address.

65 **"Passion Pants":** Ibid.

65 **"almost obsessively anxious":** Masterman, *On the Chariot Wheel*, p. 108.

66 **"My predominant feeling":** Ibid., p. 114.

66 **"real genius":** Cited in Wilson, "War in the Dark," p. 105.

66 **At 58, St James's Street:** Masterman, *On the Chariot Wheel*, p. 377.

67 **"Some had to perish":** Masterman, *Double-Cross System*, p. 54.

67 **"certain persons who":** Ibid., p. 1.

67 **"see with the eyes":** Ibid., p. 22.

68　**"is prone to be vain":**　Ibid., p. 24.

68　**"principle of generosity":**　Ibid., p. 25.

68　**"of high intelligence":**　Masterman, *On the Chariot Wheel,* p. 219.

69　**"We were obsessed":**　Ibid.

69　**"Could any intelligence service":**　Ewen Montagu, *Beyond Top Secret Ultra* (London, 1977), p. 134.

70　**"now prepare sabotage material":**　Ronald Reed notes of ISOS intercepts, June 30, 1942, KV2 456.

70　**"any connection with the enemy":**　Ibid., July 28, 1942.

70　**only succeeded "in making corrupt characters":**　Ronald Reed report, August 20, 1941, KV2 455.

70　**"When he arrives":**　RSS report, September 19, 1941, KV2 455.

70　**"practically every day":**　Memo, KV2 455.

70　**"learned to recognise":**　Ibid.

70　**"Is my message decipherable?":**　Ronald Reed report, August 20, 1941, KV2 455.

Chapter Eight. The Mosquito

72　**"to shoot his way out":**　Ronald Reed report, February 8, 1942, KV2 458.

73　**"I was suffering more":**　Interrogation by Victor Rothschild, January 2, 1943, KV2 456.

73　**"made all the right":**　Interrogation by E. Goodacre, December 17, 1942, KV2 455.

73　**"Monsieur Ferdinand":**　Ibid.

73　**"a tremendous bloodbath":**　Interrogation by Major D. B. "Stimmy" Stimson, December 17, 1942, KV2 455.

73　**"very cleverly planned":**　Ibid.

74　**"courage and daring":**　KV2 457.

74　**"full-scale attack":**　Paul Backwell report, December 30, 1942, KV2 456.

74　**"terrific Blitz":**　Interrogation by Robin Stephens, December 17, 1942, KV2 455.

74　**"You can imagine":**　Ibid.

74　**"It is rather awkward":**　Interrogation by Victor Rothschild, January 2, 1943, KV2 456.

76   **"He insisted on exact proportions":**   Ibid.

77   **"like bloody monks":**   Interrogation, January 1, 1943, KV2 456.

77   **"There was a hell of a lot":**   Ibid.

77   **"undesirable emotional activity":**   ISOS intercept, October 2, 1942, KV2 460.

77   **"nihilistic" frame of mind:**   Paul Backwell notes, KV2 456.

78   **"Could something be done":**   Interrogation by E. Goodacre, December 18, 1942, KV2 455.

78   **"impossible":**   Ibid.

78   **"if he could return":**   Paul Backwell notes, KV2 456.

79   **"I don't suppose":**   Memo, KV2 456.

80   **"It makes me furious":**   See *A Short History of the DH98 Mosquito,* bbc.co.uk.

80   **"preliminary detailed":**   ISOS intercepts, October 12, 1942, KV2 460.

80   **"Things seem at last":**   Memo, September 24, 1942, KV2 456.

Chapter Nine. Under Unseen Eyes

81   **"terrific Chrysler":**   Interrogation by E. Goodacre, December 17, 1942, KV2 455.

81   **"the chief wanted":**   Interrogation by Robin Stephens, December 17, 1942, KV2 455.

82   **"Let Fritz go first"** to **"Each time I looked":**   Ibid.

82   **"Americans?":**   Interrogation by Victor Rothschild, January 2, 1943, KV2 456.

82   **"No, it's just two":**   Ibid.

82   **"Well, we would like":**   Ibid.

82   **"a big mission":**   Interrogation by Robin Stephens, December 17, 1942, KV2 455.

82   **"in all probability":**   Memo, KV2 456.

83   **"West End":**   Ibid.

83   **"You have remembered":**   Interrogation by Robin Stephens, January 3, 1943, KV2 456.

83   **"I am highly satisfied":**   Ibid.

83   **"exploding in all directions":**   Interrogation by Victor Rothschild, January 1, 1943, KV2 456.

83 **"in a rotary motion":** Interrogation by R. Short, December 18, 1943, KV2 455.

83 **"a faint greeny color":** Ibid.

84 **"like a mosaic":** Interrogation by Robin Stephens, January 3, 1943, KV2 456.

84 **"Look, don't think":** Interrogation by Victor Rothschild, January 2, 1943, KV2 456.

84–5 **"If you feel you're not"** to **"I don't think":** Ibid.

85 **"Fritz is spiritually":** ISOS intercepts, September 26, 1942, KV2 460.

85 **"Show Fritz photos":** Memo, KV2 456.

86 **"safer than anywhere else":** Ibid.

86 **"new operational objective":** Ronald Reed note, ISOS intercept, December 7, 1942, KV2 456.

86 **"made familiar in every detail":** ISOS intercepts, December 7, 1942, KV2 460.

87 most appeared **"apathetic":** Interrogation, January 1, 1943, KV2 456.

87 **"There were no scenes":** Interrogation by Robin Stephens, December 17, 1942, KV2 455.

87 **"Why should I send them":** *Chapman,* p. 103.

87 **"Rendez-vous with so-and-so":** Interrogation by E. Goodacre, December 18, 1942, KV2 455.

88 **"very small fry":** Ibid.

88 **"I think it was to see":** Interrogation by Robin Stephens, December 17, 1942, KV2 455.

Chapter Ten. The Drop

89 **"visibly relieved":** Ronald Reed note, ISOS intercept, December 10, 1942, KV2 456.

89 **"some place further inland":** Interrogation by E. Goodacre, December 17, 1942, KV2 455.

89 **"British red tape":** Eddie Chapman statement, December 18, 1942, KV2 455.

90 **"Young couple require":** Memo, KV2 455.

91 **"nuisance work":** Interrogation by Victor Rothschild, 2.1.43, KV2 456.

91 **"Take your time":** Interrogation by Robin Stephens, December 17, 1942, KV2 455.

91 **"Of course our agents":** Ibid.

91 **"Walter is ready to go":** Interrogation by Robin Stephens, January 7, 1942, KV2 457.

91 **"give as little information":** Interrogation by E. Goodacre, December 18, 1942, KV2 455.

92 **"a number of small acts":** Ibid.

92 **"various people who":** Interrogation by Robin Stephens, December 17, 1942, KV2 455.

92 **"Joli Albert":** Ibid.

92 **an extended "holiday":** Camp 020 report, July 11, 1944, KV2 459.

92 **"in the first or second row":** Ronald Reed report, January 1, 1943, KV2 456.

92 **"Don't you worry":** Interrogation by E. Goodacre, December 18, 1942, KV2 455.

93 **"it was hard to tell":** *Faramus*, p. 74.

93 **"It was hard to believe":** Ibid., p. 78.

93 **"If you do this":** Interrogation by Robin Stephens, December 17, 1942, KV2 455.

93 **"I have rather":** Ibid.

94 **"anything which could":** Interrogation by Victor Rothschild, January 2, 1943, KV2 456.

94 **"You don't mind":** Ibid.

95 **"if there was any trouble":** Interrogation by Robin Stephens, January 7, 1942, KV2 457.

95 **the only "home":** *Chapman*, p. 107.

95 **"genuine comradeship":** Ibid.

95 **"Reichsbank, Berlin":** Interrogation by Robin Stephens, January 7, 1942, KV2 457.

95 **"You have beautiful planes":** Interrogation by Robin Stephens, December 17, 1942, KV2 455.

96 **"of the larynx type":** Interrogation by D. B. Stimson, December 17, 1942, KV2 455.

96 **"evade attack":** Ibid.

96 **"We shall be waiting":** Interrogation by Robin Stephens, December 17, 1942, KV2 455.

96 **"Far from being nervous":** Interrogation by D. B. Stimson, December 17, 1942, KV2 455.

Chapter Eleven. Martha's Exciting Night

99 **"Keep a close watch":** Memo, KV2 455.

99 **"very soon be going":** Ronald Reed notes on ISOS intercepts, KV2 456.

99 **Agent X is probably:** Memo, KV2 455.

100 **"It may be of intelligence":** RSS memo, October 8, 1942, KV2 455.

100 **"too many possibilities":** Memo, KV2 455.

100–101 **"flying column"** to **"pretend to be looking":** Ibid.

101 **"fully fledged saboteur":** Memo, October 1, 1942, KV2 455.

101 **"We quite realise":** Memo, October 4, 1942, KV2 455.

102 **"Who is it?":** Police report, KV2 455.

103 **"Yes," the man said:** Ibid.

103 **"just arrived from France":** Report of Sergeant J. Vail, KV2 455.

104 **very polite:** Ibid.

104 **"George Clarke will do":** Report of Deputy Chief Constable Ely, KV2 455.

105 **"mentally and physically spent":** Robin Stephens report, December 17, 1942, KV2 455.

Chapter Twelve. Camp 020

106 **"A breaker is born":** *Camp 020,* p. 107.

106 **"Italy is a country":** Ibid., p. 306.

106 **"weeping and romantic":** *Camp 020,* p. 54.

106 **"shifty Polish Jews":** Ibid., p. 73.

107 **"unintelligent" Icelanders:** Ibid., p. 295.

107 **it had "lunatic cells ready":** Ibid., p. 40.

108 **"No chivalry":** Ibid., p. 19.

108 **"It is a question":** Ibid., p. 71.

108 **"Your name is Chapman":** Interrogation by Robin Stephens, December 17, 1942, KV2 455.

109 **"That was plain, unvarnished blackmail"**: Robin Stephens report, December 18, 1942, KV2 544.

109 **"with some bitterness"**: Ibid.

109 **"blow hot–blow cold"**: *Camp 020*, p. 109.

109 **"They treated you pretty well"**: See interrogation by Robin Stephens, December 17, 1942, KV2 455.

110 **"I don't know what"**: Cited in Ewen Montagu, *Beyond Top Secret Ultra* (London, 1977), p. 108.

110 **"No spy, however astute"**: *Camp 020*, p. 105.

110 **"Physically and mentally"**: Ibid., p. 58.

111 **"It is quite clear"**: Ronald Reed memo, December 21, 1942, KV2 456.

111 **"He is a hostage"**: Interrogation by E. Goodacre, December 18, 1942, KV2 455.

111 **"That was a private letter"**: Interrogation by Robin Stephens, December 17, 1942, KV2 455.

111 **"natural inexactitudes"**: Robin Stephens memo, KV2 455.

112 **"confessed to an experiment"**: *Camp 020*, p. 218.

112 **"Today there is no trace"**: Robin Stephens report, January 7, 1942, KV2 457.

112 **"one of the principal"**: Ronald Reed notes on ISOS intercepts, July 28, 1942, KV2 456.

113 **"On no occasion"**: T. A. Robertson memo, December 24, 1942, KV2 456.

113 **"today was the supposed start"**: Eddie Chapman statement, December 18, 1942, KV2 455.

113 **"It is important"**: Ibid.

113 **"Dr. Graumman especially"**: Ibid.

113 **"in sharper focus"**: Ronald Reed report, March 15, 1943, KV2 459.

114 **Mon Commandant**: Eddie Chapman to Robin Stephens, December 18, 1942, KV2 455.

115 **"If Chapman is to be believed"**: Robin Stephens report, January 7, 1942, KV2 457.

115 **"hatred for the Hun"**: Ibid.

115 **"As I figure it out"**: Robin Stephens report, December 18, 1942, KV2 455.

115　"**he will go sour**" to "**My opinion**":　Ibid.

115　"**In our opinion**":　Joint statement by interrogators, December 18, 1942, KV2 455.

116　"**We have chosen**":　T. A. Robertson memo, December 18, 1942, KV2 455.

Chapter Thirteen. 35 Crespigny Road

118　"**Ah, Mr. Reed**" to "**I'm going underground**":　Transcript of video-taped interview with Ronnie Reed, 1994, courtesy of Nicholas Reed.

118　"**humble genius**":　Interview with Charles Chilton, October 5, 2006.

119　"**lurid past**":　Ronald Reed memo, December 19, 1942, KV2 455.

119　"**he would have to work**":　Ibid.

119　"**Mon Commandant**":　Eddie Chapman to Robin Stephens, December 19, 1942, KV2 455.

120　"**rather weakly**":　Ronald Reed report, December 20, 1942, KV2 455.

120　FFFFF HAVE ARRIVED:　Ibid.

120　"**definitely Fritz**":　ISOS intercepts, September 20, 1942, KV2 460.

120　"**recognised his style**":　Ronald Reed notes on ISOS intercepts, KV2 456.

120　FFFFF GET MORRIS:　Ronald Reed notes, KV2 456, and ISOS intercepts, December 21, 1942, KV2 460.

120　THANKS FOR MESSAGE:　Ronald Reed notes, KV2 456.

121　"**Zigzag's powers of observation**":　Ronald Reed report, KV2 458.

121　"**the Germans had not a photograph**":　Memo, KV2 456.

121　"**gratuitous**" sharing of information:　Memo from John Masterman to T. A. Robertson, 17.12.42, KV2 455.

122　"**a very good means**":　Report, December 19, 1942, KV2 455.

122　"**It does seem rather extraordinary**":　T. A. Robertson memo, January 30, 1943, KV2 458.

122　"**something queer was taking place**":　Air Ministry report, January 7, 1943, KV2 458.

122　"**They pandered to his vanity**":　Robin Stephens report, January 7, 1942, KV2 457.

122　"**a dangerous criminal**":　T. A. Robertson briefing, December 21, 1942, KV2 456.

122–3　"**The success of this operation**" to "**stand his round**":　Ibid.

123 **"who had looked after him":** Note, KV2 456.

123 **"permanent companions":** Ibid.

123 **"Conversation was strained":** Paul Backwell notes, KV2 458.

124–5 **"settle in":** to **"a mine of information":** Ibid.

125 **"often speaks of various methods":** Paul Backwell notes, KV2 456.

125 **"what it was that made him":** Allan Tooth notes, KV2 456.

125 **"In Germany"** to **"I can only glean":** Ibid.

126 **"I think we should":** Ronald Reed memo, December 26, 1942, KV2 456.

126 **"Running a team":** J. C. Masterman, *The Double-Cross System in the War, 1939–1945* (London, 1972), p. 90.

127 **"I had, with my memories":** J. C. Masterman, *On the Chariot Wheel: An Autobiography* (Oxford, 1975), p. 212.

127 **"made defeat seem impossible":** Ibid.

127 **"the rabble of the universe":** Robin Stephens report, January 7, 1942, KV2 457.

127 **"most fascinating case":** Ibid.

127 **"What manner of man":** *Camp 020*, p. 105.

128 **PLEASE COME:** Ronald Reed report, KV2 456.

128 **"We should know":** Ronald Reed report, January 1, 1943, KV2 456.

129 **"Eddie had moods":** Paul Backwell notes, KV2 458.

129 **"a method not calculated":** Reed memo December 23, 1942, KV2 456.

129 **CALL AT 1000:** Reed report, February 10, 1942, KV2 458.

129 **"My God, I believe":** Reed report, December 28, 1942, KV2 456.

Chapter Fourteen. What a Way Out

130 **"He was non-judgmental":** Harmer, op. cit.

131 **"From the fact":** Ronald Reed report, December 28, 1942, KV2 456.

131 **"undoubtedly have done"** to **"They may forget":** Ibid.

131 **"Message of 14 letters":** ISOS intercepts, December 27, 1942, KV2 460.

131 **the mistake was merely "annoying":** Ronald Reed report, December 28, 1942, KV2 456.

132 **"Preparations should now":** Undated note, KV2 456.

132   **"silly joking messages":**   Laurie Marshall interrogation, December 24, 1942, KV2 456.

132   **"The men must be"** to **"a little sinister":**   Ibid.

133   **"We should do all":**   John Masterman memo, December 26, 1942, KV2 456.

133   **"the principle of verisimilitude":**   J. C. Masterman, *The Double-Cross System in the War, 1939–1945* (London, 1972), p. 19.

133   **"also conveyed an air":**   Frank Ruskell, cited in *A Short History of the DH98 Mosquito.*

134   **"He seemed more nervous":**   Paul Backwell report, KV2 456.

134   **"would completely ruin":**   Cover story narrative, KV2 459.

134   FFFFF WENT DOWN: Memo, KV2 456.

135   PLEASE SEND SPECIFIC: Ronald Reed report, KV2 458.

135   PLEASE GIVE NAME: Memo, KV2 456.

135   FFFFF LANDED TWO MILES: Ibid.

135   **"well known and accepted":**   Paul Backwell notes, KV2 458.

136   **"Eddie soon began"** to **"terribly restless":**   Ibid.

136   **"feelings of nihilism":**   Allan Tooth notes, KV2 456.

136   **"His inherent boisterousness":**   Ronald Reed report, KV2 459.

136   **"quite impossible to run him":**   Minutes of meeting, December 31, 1942, KV2 456.

136   **"cloistered life":**   T. A. Robertson report, January 11, 1943, KV2 457.

137   **"very pale":**   Allan Tooth notes, KV2 456.

137   **"reference to secret inks":**   Ibid.

137   **"I have another":**   Ronald Reed report, January 1, 1943, KV2 456.

138   **"I believe he has":**   Ibid.

Chapter Fifteen. Freda and Diane

139   **"He wants to provide":**   Paul Backwell report, KV2 456.

139   **this was "impossible":**   Ibid.

139   **"know of his existence":**   Laurie Marshall report, January 15, 1943, MI5 ref. 133B, KV2 457 (additional).

139   **"Personal matters":**   Paul Backwell report, KV2 456.

139   **"My sources of information":**   Handwritten note, accompanying Paul Backwell note of January 12, 1943, KV2 457 (additional).

139   **"He feels his present position"**:   Paul Backwell note, January 12, 1943, KV2 457 (additional).

140   **"The question of Freda"**:   Ibid.

140   **"if she bore any malice"**:   Ronald Reed report, March 15, 1943, KV2 459, document 254 B.

140   **"truculent and moody"** to **"feminine relaxation"**:   Ibid.

141   **"Luckily there was a pub"**:   Paul Backwell report, KV2 458.

141   **"just back from abroad"**:   Ibid.

142   **"There was one amazing thing"**:   Ibid.

142   **"cat-burglar"**:   Laurie Marshall report, January 7, 1943, KV2 457 (additional).

142   **"slightly drunk"**:   Allan Tooth notes, January 7, 1943, KV2 457 (additional).

142   **"some jocular remark"**:   Ibid.

143   **"The man apologised"**:   Paul Backwell report, KV2 458.

143   **"I suppose it is natural"**:   Ronald Reed report, January 7, 1943, KV2 457 (additional).

143   **"so far our inquiries"**:   Ronald Reed memo, January 13, 1943, KV2 457 (additional).

143   **"it was not in the interests"**:   Laurie Marshall report, January 15, 1943, MI5 ref. 133B, KV2 457 (additional).

144   **"talk to him"** to **"folly of expressing"**:   Laurie Marshall report, January 23, 1943, KV2 458.

145   **FFFFF DISGUSTED:**   Ronald Reed report, March 15, 1943, KV2 459, document 254 B.

145   **"not to reap"**:   Ibid.

145   **"new arrangements"**:   Ibid.

145   **"Kalium"**:   Interrogation by Victor Rothschild, January 2, 1943, KV2 456.

146   **"This kept Eddie busy"**:   Paul Backwell notes, KV2 458.

146   **"In this frame of mind"**:   Ronald Reed report, March 15, 1943, KV2 459, document 254 B.

146   **"tends to break down"**:   Laurie Marshall report, January 15, 1943, MI5 ref. 133B, KV2 457 (additional).

146–7   **"serious and intimate"** to **"Do you consider"**:   Ibid.

148 **"a most valuable character study":**   Ronald Reed handwritten note on ibid.

148 **"He would now join":**   Ronald Reed report, January 1, 1943, KV2 456.

148 **"part of the household":**   Paul Backwell notes, KV2 458.

149 **"quite content to limit"** to **"to get Freda up":**   Ibid.

149 **"Eddie, we're on the air"** to **"Oh no, not just fifteen minutes":**   Interview with Ronnie Reed, 1994, Nicholas Reed.

149 **"Freda must have got very used":**   Paul Backwell notes, KV2 458.

150 **"Although she knew":**   Ibid.

150 **"Since he has seen Freda":**   Allan Tooth notes, 26.1.43, KV2 458.

150 **"his capacity to live":**   Allan Tooth notes, KV2 456.

150 **"would fulfill his need":**   Ibid.

150 **"Previously, he had":**   Allan Tooth notes, January 26, 1943, KV2 458.

150 **"What a man!":**   Ronald Reed handwritten note on ibid.

150 **"It is extraordinary":**   Ronald Reed report, March 15, 1943, KV2 459, document 254 B.

151 **"this resolution provides":**   Ibid.

Chapter Sixteen. Abracadabra

153 **"look, from the air":**   Charles Fraser-Smith, *The Secret War of Charles Fraser-Smith* (London, 1981), p. 121.

153 **"danger that the Germans":**   John Masterman handwritten note on Ronald Reed memo, January 7, 1943, KV2 457.

154 **"vast hole":**   Fraser-Smith, *Secret War.*

154 **FFFFF WALTER READY:**   Ronald Reed report, March 15, 1943, KV2 459.

154 **"extremely difficult":**   John Masterman memo, January 27, 1943, KV2 458.

155 **"publish a small paragraph"** to **"not having taken place":**   Ibid.

155 **"meant him deliberately publishing":**   John Masterman memo, January 27, 1943, KV2 458.

155 **"the censors":**   Ibid.

156 **FFFFF ARRANGEMENTS:**   Ronald Reed report, KV2 458.

156 **"to see if high high altitude":**   Colonel Sir John Turner memo, KV2 458.

156   **"something had occurred":**   Ronald Reed memo, KV2 458.

156   **"inky blackness":**   Ronald Reed report, January 31, 1943, KV2 458.

157   **"in a state of great excitement"** to **"scene of destruction":**   Ibid

157   **"masterpiece":**   Fraser-Smith, *Secret War.*

157   **FFFFF WALTER BLOWN:**   Ronald Reed report, KV2 459, document 254 B.

157   **"champagne all round":**   Robin Stephens report, January 7, 1942, KV2 457.

157   **CONGRATULATIONS:**   Ronald Reed report, March 15, 1943, KV2 459, document 254 B.

158   **"The Security Service":**   T. A. Robertson memo, January 11, 1943, KV2 457.

159   **"to depart in a blaze of glory":**   Ronald Reed Report, March 15, 1943, KV2 459, document 254 B.

159   **had been "vague":**   Ibid.

159   **"to be immortalised":**   Ibid.

159   **"declined to encourage":**   J. C. Masterman, *The Double-Cross System in the War, 1939–1945* (London, 1972), p. 132.

159   **"Perhaps we missed an opportunity":**   Ibid.

159   **"frank and straightforward":**   Reed report, March 13, 1943, KV2 459.

160   **"a man whose stock-in-trade":**   Shanks report. January 6, 1943, KV2 457.

160   **"a spark of decency"** to **"whether a patriot or opportunist":**   Ibid.

160   **"a refined manner":**   Laurie Marshall report, January 15, 1943, MI5 ref. 133B, KV2 457 (additional).

160   **"His natural and instinctive speech":**   Ibid.

160   **"the bogus certainties of science":**   Malcolm Muggeridge, *Chronicles of Wasted Time,* vol. II (London, 1979), p. 222.

161   **"When one takes a fuse":**   Cited in Kenneth Rose, *Elusive Rothschild: The Life of Victor, Third Baron* (London, 2003), p. 67.

161   **"I think it's terrific":**   Interrogation by Victor Rothschild, January 2, 1943, KV2 456.

Chapter Seventeen. The Greater the Adventure

164   **"I consider you":**   T. A. Robertson report, February 2, 1943, KV2 458.

164   **"few, a very few":**   *Camp 020,* p. 176.

164   **"far too valuable":**   Ronald Reed note, KV2 456.

164   **"I am not at all keen":**   T. A. Robertson report, February 2, 1943, KV2 458.

165   **"people for whom"** to **"We are preparing":**   Ibid.

165   **"Always speak slowly":**   T. A. Robertson (attributed) report on SOE training course, KV4 172.

165   **"procuring *mental* breakdown":**   Ibid.

165   **"one with a brutal manner":**   Ibid.

166   **FFFFF PICK UP BY:**   Ronald Reed notes on ISOS intercepts, KV2 456.

166   **IMPOSSIBLE PICK YOU UP:**   Ronald Reed report, March 13, 1943, KV2 459.

166   **the "normal" way:**   Ibid.

166   **"The suggestion was absurd":**   Ronald Reed report, March 15, 1949, KV2 459, document 254 B.

166   **"any attempt to return":**   Ibid.

166   **"not over-anxious to pay him":**   Ronald Reed report, March 13, 1943, KV2 459.

166   **"not prepared to offer":**   T. A. Robertson memo, KV2 457.

166   **"unenviable and practically impossible":**   Ronald Reed report, March 13, 1943, KV2 459.

166   **"provided the man":**   Memo, KV2 457.

166   ***"Points I would like":***   Eddie Chapman note, n.d., KV2 458.

167   **"in a position to repay":**   Laurie Marshall report, February 2, 1943, KV2 456.

167   **"Zigzag is fully convinced":**   Ibid.

167   **"to get as much money":**   Ibid.

167   **"paying for his stay":**   Allan Tooth notes, KV2 456.

167   **"principle of generosity":**   J. C. Masterman, *The Double-Cross System in the War, 1939–1945* (London, 1972), p. 18.

168   **"the risk to his life":**   Laurie Marshall report, February 2, 1943, KV2 456.

168   **"If Zigzag successfully"** to **"substantial payment be made now":**   Ibid.

168   **"It was almost too good":**   Ronald Reed report, March 15, 1943, KV2 459, document 254 B.

168   **"going rather too smoothly":**   Ronald Reed memo, February 10, 1943, KV2 458.

169 **"After making such":**   Ronald Reed report, March 15, 1943, KV2 459, document 254 B.

169 ꜰꜰꜰꜰꜰ ᴅᴀɴɢᴇʀᴏᴜꜱ ᴛᴏ ᴄᴏɴᴛɪɴᴜᴇ: Ronald Reed memo, February 10, 1943, KV2 458.

169 **ignoring the awkwardness** to **"seen a chance":**   Ibid.

170 ɢᴇʟɪɢɴɪᴛᴇ ɪɴQᴜɪʀɪᴇꜱ: *Evening Standard,* February 12, 1943.

170 **"A man was questioned":**   Ibid.

170 **"185 names have been taken":**   *News Chronicle,* February 10, 1943.

170 ꜰꜰꜰꜰꜰ ᴊɪᴍᴍʏ ᴀʀʀᴇꜱᴛᴇᴅ: Ronald Reed memo, February 10, 1943, KV2 458.

170 **"No further transmissions":**   Ibid.

170 **"absolutely inexcusable":**   Ronald Reed report, March 15, 1943, KV2 459, document 254 B.

170 **"to live as man":**   Ronald Reed report, February 8, 1943, KV2 458.

171 **"Victor, do you mind":**   Interrogation by Victor Rothschild, January 28, 1943, KV2 458.

171 **"Freda returned home":**   Paul Backwell notes, KV2 458.

171 **tell his cover story "unhesitatingly":**   Ibid.

171 **"What shoes was Jimmy Hunt wearing?":**   Ronald Reed notes, February 10, 1943, KV2 458.

171 **"not shaken in any way":**   Ronald Reed memo, February 10, 1943, KV2 458.

171 **"Poor Freddy Sampson":**   Paul Backwell notes, KV2 458.

171 **"We can rely":**   Ronald Reed report, February 8, 1943, KV2 458.

172 **"Blue starfish":**   Ronald Reed report, March 15, 1943, KV2 459, document 254 B.

172 **"AA guns camouflaged":**   Ibid.

173 **"picked up the names":**   Robin Stephens notes, KV2 456.

173 **"There is no information":**   T. A. Robertson, January 11, 1943, KV2 457.

173 **"It is imperative":**   Ronald Reed memo, February 10, 1943, KV2 458.

173 **painting a "gloomy picture":**   Reed report, March 15, 1943, KV2 459, document 254 B.

173 **"a vast number of intercepts"** to **"that the code in use":**   Ibid.

174 **"instructions which, if he were captured":** T. A. Robertson note, KV2 457.

174 **"in spite of the fact":** Paul Backwell report, KV2 456.

174 **"deep-seated liking":** T. A. Robertson memo, January 11, 1943, KV2 457.

174 **"You may see lots":** Interrogation by Victor Rothschild, January 28, 1943, KV2 458.

174 **"Obviously if he were":** Ronald Reed report, March 13, 1943, KV2 459.

174 **"It all depends on":** Interrogation by Victor Rothschild, January 28, 1943, KV2 458.

175 **"You will see that":** Ronald Reed report, March 15, 1943, KV2 459, document 254 B.

175 **"genuinely inspired":** T. A. Robertson memo, January 11, 1943, KV2 457.

175 **"the excellent personal relations":** Ibid.

175 **"He will be greeted":** Ronald Reed report, February 8, 1943, KV2 458.

175–6 **"Zigzag is confident"** to **"might possibly enable him":** Ibid.

176 **"Except in special circumstances":** T. A. Robertson memo, January 11, 1943, KV2 457.

176 **The story of many a spy:** Robin Stephens report, January 7, 1942, KV2 457.

Chapter Eighteen. Stowaway Spy

179 **"a man who had a bad record":** Ronald Reed report, March 3, 1943, KV2 458.

179 **"From now on this man's life":** Ibid.

180 **"impressed me as being discreet":** Ibid.

180 **"lie low":** Ronald Reed memo, February 10, 1943, KV2 458.

180 **"complete set of forged":** Ronald Reed report, March 3, 1943, KV2 458.

180 **"vast and complicated":** Ronald Reed report, March 15, 1943, KV2 459, document 254 B.

181 **"This course":** Ronald Reed report, March 3, 1943, KV2 458.

181 **"ham chat":** Ronald Reed notes, KV2 458.

181 **"suspicious":** Ibid.

181 **"The 'laughing out' sign":** Ronald Reed report, March 15, 1943, KV2 459. Document 254 B.

182 **"We shall not have":** Ronald Reed notes, KV2 458.

182 **"Mrs. West thanks":** Ronald Reed report, March 15, 1943, KV2 459, document 254 B.

182 **"that if any other members":** Ibid.

182 **"It is Lew Leibich":** Ibid.

182 **"Goodbye for the present":** Handwritten note to Laurie Marshall, March 3, 1943, KV2 458.

183 **"did not know what they were doing":** Ronald Reed report, March 3, 1943, KV2 458.

183–4 **"in the approved style"** to **"which he had coveted":** Ibid.

184 **"Zigzag is himself":** Ronald Reed report, March 15, 1943, KV2 459. Document 254 B.

184 **"The case of Zigzag":** Ibid.

Chapter Nineteen. Joli Albert

185 **"fearing prying fingers":** Ronald Reed report, March 26, 1943, KV2 459.

185 **"bad lad":** Ibid.

185 **"Nervous expectancy":** *Chapman,* p. 137.

186 **"Anson was seasick":** Ronald Reed report, April 18, 1943, KV2 461.

186 **"no harm would be done":** Ronald Reed report, March 26, 1943, KV2 459.

186 **"a high-class burglar":** Major R. L. Brown report, April 26, 1943, KV2 461.

187 **"for pleasure":** Ibid.

187 **"Several members of the crew":** Ronald Reed report, March 26, 1943, KV2 459.

187 **"The gunlayer summed up":** Ibid.

187 **Happy go lucky,:** Major R. L. Brown report, April 26, 1943, KV2 461.

187 **"He said he did not like":** Extracts from ship's log, *City of Lancaster,* KV2 459.

187 **"sort of international clearing ground":** J. C. Masterman, *The Case of the Four Friends* (London, 1961), p. 19.

188 **"Pay no attention":** Major R. L. Brown report, April 26, 1943, KV2 461.

188 **"If I find this friend":** Ibid.

188 **"No names":** Ibid.

188 **"brûlé," or "burned":** Ronald Reed report, March 15, 1943, KV2 459, document 254 B.

188 **"*Joli Albert*":** Camp 020 report, July 11, 1944, KV2 459.

188 **"blank faces":** Robin Stephens report, June 29, 1944, KV2 459.

188 **the word "telephone":** Camp 020 report, July 11, 1944, KV2 459.

189 **"did not know anything":** Ibid.

189 **"forget the whole business":** Ibid.

190 **"mind his own business":** Extracts from ship's log, *City of Lancaster*, KV2 459.

190 **"any future offence":** Ibid.

190 **"He instructed me":** Reed report, March 26, 1943, KV2 459.

190 **"apologised for the inconvenience":** Camp 020 report, July 11, 1944, KV2 459.

190 **"connected with Johnny":** Robin Stephens report, June 6, 1944, KV2 459.

191 **"contravened the established policy":** ISOS intercept, May 27, 1945, KV2 459.

191 **"told the Germans":** Memo, March 23, 1943, KV2 459.

192 **"not to interrupt":** Report of meeting, March 22, 1943, KV2 459.

192 **"Whatever view we took":** Ibid.

192 **"acquainted with the relevant facts":** T. A. Robertson, in ibid.

192 **"brought back in irons":** Ibid.

192 **"It would be quite natural":** Ibid.

192 **"a small aperture":** Memo, n.d., KV2 459.

193 **"could not possibly be detected":** Ibid.

194 **"the Queensberry rules":** Extracts from ship's log, *City of Lancaster*, KV2 459.

194 **"Have you met a better man":** Ibid.

194 **"trying to get a special bomb":** Ronald Reed report, March 26, 1943, KV2 459.

194–6 **"he had put to them"** to **"in order to send up":**   Ibid.

196 **"Convinced Z playing straight":**   Telegram, KV2 459.

196 **"This is typical":**   Robin Stephens report, June 27, 1943, KV2 460.

196 **"with possibly fatal results":**   Ibid.

196 **"He thought that the value":**   Ibid.

196 **"politically complicated":**   Ronald Reed report, March 26, 1943, KV2 459.

196 **"It would be most unfortunate":**   Ibid.

197 **"I come from Ronnie":**   Victor Rothschild memo, March 28, 1943, KV2 461.

197 **"if possible intact":**   Ibid.

Chapter Twenty. Damp Squib

198 **"Are you Fritz?":**   Camp 020 report, July 11, 1943, KV2 459.

198 **"other articles difficult to obtain":**   Ibid.

199 **"in disgrace":**   Ibid.

199 **"old friend":**   Major Michael Ryde report, October 24, 1944, KV2 460.

199 **"about 50":**   Camp 020 report, July 11, 1944, KV2 459.

199 **"vague replies"** to **"his request for an advance":**   Ibid.

200 **"Timing is the essential factor":**   T. A. Robertson (attributed), report of SOE training course, KV4 172.

200 **I landed at about 2:30:**   Ronald Reed report, March 15, 1943, KV2 459, document 254 B.

204 **"The life of a secret agent":**   J. C. Masterman, *The Double-Cross System in the War, 1939–1945* (London, 1972), p. 32.

204 **"would bring him":**   Camp 020 report, 11.7.44, KV2 459.

204 **"reserve the more interesting details":**   Ibid.

205 **"I had two suitcases":**   *Chapman*, p. 158.

205 **"certainly raised his stock":**   Camp 020 report, July 11, 1944, KV2 459.

205 **"The Germans have shown":**   John Masterman memo, April 18, 1943, KV2 461.

205 **"There must either be an explosion":**   Ewen Montagu memo, April 18, 1943, KV2 461.

206 **"perfectly good merchant ship"**: Victor Rothschild memo, April 25, 1943, KV2 461.

206 **"as big a bang"**: Ibid.

206 **"A good decent bang"**: Ibid.

206 **"who will previously"**: Victor Rothschild, "Plan Damp Squib," KV2 461.

206 **"fall down and pretend"** to **"The story of the sabotage"**: Ibid.

206 **"sharp explosion"**: Letter, Colonel Leslie Wood to Victor Rothschild, KV2 461.

206 **"Herewith your three toys"**: Ibid.

206 **"binding up a notional"**: John Masterman, handwritten note attached to Rothschild, "Plan Damp Squib," KV2 461.

207 **"When the *City of Lancaster"*:** John Masterman memo, KV2 461.

207 **"as each piece of coal"**: Brown report, April 26, 1943, KV2 461.

207 **"who was very dirty"**: Ronald Reed report, April 26, 1943, KV2 461.

207 **"holding in his hand"**: Ibid.

207 **"swanking" manner:** Brown report, April 26, 1943, KV2 461.

207 **"beyond his station"**: Ibid.

207 **"The standard of the poetry"**: Ronald Reed report, April 26, 1943, KV2 461.

208 **"infernal machine"**: Ibid.

208 **"a spur to rumour-spreading"**: Rothschild, "Plan Damp Squib," KV2 461.

208 **"Approximately 50 people"**: Memo, April 26, 1943, KV2 461.

208 **"He has no objection"**: Ronald Reed report, April 26, 1943, KV2 461.

208 **"discussed Zigzag"**: Duff Cooper to Dick White, May 5, 1943, KV2 459.

208 **"if and when contact"**: Ibid.

208 **"comprehensive memoranda"**: Victor Rothschild memo, December 6, 1943, KV2 461.

208 **"I promised Mr Hoover"**: Ibid.

Chapter Twenty-one. The Ice Front

209 **"deeply affected"**: Interview with Ingeborg von Gröning, Bremen, May 22, 2006.

209   **"Thank God you are back":**   *Chapman,* p. 161.

209   **"the old man":**   Major Michael Ryde report, October 24, 1944,
       KV2 460.

210   **"enjoy a well-earned":**   Camp 020 report, July 11, 1944, KV2 459.

210   **"bachelor flat"** to **Chapman's "companion":**   Ibid.

211   **"pathetically grateful":**   *Chapman,* p. 164.

211   **"proud of his protégé":**   Camp 020 report, July 11, 1944, KV2 459.

211   **"best security":**   Major Michael Ryde report, October 24, 1944,
       KV2 460.

211   **"man who had 'made' him":**   Camp 020 report, July 11, 1944, KV2
       459.

211   **"Absolute personal integrity":**   J. C. Masterman, *The Double-Cross Sys-
       tem in the War, 1939–1945* (London, 1972), p. 187.

211   **"better for selfish reasons":**   Ibid., p. 72.

212   **"watchful" expression:**   Interview with Ingeborg von Gröning, Bre-
       men, May 22, 2006.

212   **"Stephan made up":**   Ibid.

212   **"as and when he":**   Camp 020 report, July 11, 1944, KV2 459.

212   **"If they will not":**   Olav Riste and Berit Nökleby, *Norway, 1940–45:
       The Resistance Movement* (Oslo, 2004), p. 51.

213   **"it was an uneasy feeling":**   *Chapman,* p. 171.

213   **"wall of hatred":**   Ibid.

213   **"appeared somewhat suspicious":**   Camp 020 report, July 11, 1944,
       KV2 459.

214   **"complete freedom":**   Robin Stephens report, June 29, 1944, KV2
       459.

214   **"not to work":**   Camp 020 report, July 11, 1944, KV2 459.

214   **"battle against the Reds":**   *Chapman,* p. 172.

214   **"hero complex":**   Ibid.

214   **Chapman's "companion":**   Camp 020 report, July 11, 1944, KV2 459.

215   **"the only successful sabotage":**   Victor Rothschild interview with
       Agent JIGGER (von Schoenich), Paris, November 8, 1944, KV2 460.

215   **"controlled by the British"** to **"one of those":**   Ibid.

215   **"beaming with pleasure":**   *Chapman,* p. 174.

215   **"good work in England":**   Camp 020 report, July 11, 1944, KV2 459.

216   **"in notes"** to **"draw on it when necessary":**   Ibid.

216   rose "solemnly": to "If I stay with this mob":   *Chapman*, p. 175.

216   "You are free":   Camp 020 report, July 11, 1944, KV2 459.

216–17   "Go yachting" to "to buy a boat":   Ibid.

218   "enhance his stock":   Camp 020 report, July 11, 1944, KV2 459.

218   "truly brave":   *Chapman*, p. 171.

218   *"Bitteschon":*   Ibid., p. 176.

218   "most attractive":   Ibid.

Chapter Twenty-two. The Girl at the Ritz

220   "She was young":   Interview with Bibbi Røset, Oslo, June 15, 2006.

220   "She wanted to improve":   Ibid.

220   "wanted adventure":   Ibid.

221   "beautiful and adorable":   Camp 020 report, July 11, 1944, KV2 459.

222   "Because she had nice clothes":   Interview with Bibbi Røset, Oslo, June 15, 2006.

222   "fancied slight":   Camp 020 report, July 11, 1944, KV2 459.

222   "anti-Quisling":   *Chapman*, p. 177.

222   "Nazi's tart":   Interview with Bibbi Røset, Oslo, June 15, 2006.

222   "hawk-like" gaze: *Chapman*, p. 178.

222   "some kind of psychologist":   Robin Stephens report, June 29, 1944, KV2 459.

222   "with a view to testing":   Camp 020 report, July 11, 1944, KV2 459.

222   "Where could you leave":   Ibid.

223   "I myself expect":   Ibid.

223   "uncomfortable moment":   Robin Stephens report, June 29, 1944, KV2 459.

223   "periodically asking awkward questions":   Ibid.

223   seemed more "benign":   *Chapman*, p. 179.

223   "You are not absolutely sincere":   Camp 020 report, July 11, 1944, KV2 459.

223   "I know I am not":   Ibid.

223   "The doctor was quite satisfied":   Ibid.

224   "I think you are a British spy":   *Chapman*, p. 180.

224   "Leave it to me":   Ibid.

225   "It is the work":   Camp 020 report, July 11, 1944, KV2 459.

225   "kept woman":   Ibid.

225   **"sufficient money"**:   Ibid.

225   **"pocketed the balance"**:   Major Michael Ryde report, October 24, 1944, KV2 460.

225   **"help himself"**:   Ibid.

226   **"It was a delightful spot"**:   *Chapman*, p. 196.

227   **"they were fair"**:   Interview with Leife Myhre, Oslo, June 16, 2006.

227   **"They were in extremely good physical condition"** to **"I am not working for them"**:   Ibid.

228   **"certain people"**:   Camp 020 report, July 11, 1944, KV2 459.

228   **"applied himself freely"** to **"disgusted with the whole affair"**:   Ibid.

228   **"It all depends"**:   Interrogation by Victor Rothschild, January 28, 1944, KV2 458.

229   **"under the influence"**:   Camp 020 report, July 11, 1944, KV2 459.

229   **"Nazi whore"**:   Interview with Bibbi Røset, Oslo, June 15, 2006.

230   **"he risked losing her"**:   Camp 020 report, July 11, 1944, KV2 459.

230–232   **"details of Chapman's work"**: to **"she intimated"**:   Ibid.

Chapter Twenty-three. Sabotage Consultant

233   **"new sabotage work"**:   Camp 020 report, July 11, 1944, KV2 459.

233–4   **"did not consider"** to **"there would be"**:   Ibid.

234   **"The only thing"**:   Winston Churchill, *Second World War,* vol II., p. 187

235   **"need coaching"** to **"extremely high"**:   Camp 020 report, July 11, 1944, KV2 459.

236   **"the address of an engineering depot"**:   Robin Stephens report, June 29, 1944, KV2 459.

236   **"continually stared at him"**:   Camp 020 report, July 11, 1944, KV2 459.

236   **"x-ray apparatus"**:   Ibid.

236   **"picked up by five seaplanes"**:   Robin Stephens report, June 29, 1944, KV2 459.

236   **"the use of a compass"**:   Camp 020 report, July 11, 1944, KV2 459.

236–7   **"Chapman was just the type"** to **"each wanting their part"**:   Ibid.

237   **"kind of honorary consultant"**:   J. C. Masterman, *The Double-Cross System in the War, 1939–1945* (London, 1972), p. 171.

237   **"more interested in"**:   *Camp 020,* p. 350.

238   **"touring Germany"**:   Camp 020 report, July 11, 1944, KV2 459.

238 **"useful background":**   Major Michael Ryde report, July 27, 1944, KV2 460.

239 **"Hitler is by no means in charge":**   Robin Stephens report, June 29, 1944, KV2 459.

239 **"It is entirely in the hands": to "aired his anti-Hitler views":**   Ibid.

239 **"knew he would one day":**   Camp 020 report, July 11, 1944, KV2 459.

239 **"keep her eyes and ears open":**   Ibid.

239 **"trust nobody":**   Ibid.

240 **"mind their own business":**   Interview with Bibbi Røset, Oslo, June 15, 2006.

240 **"Mrs. Gossips":**   Ibid.

240 **"double transposition":**   Camp 020 report, July 11, 1944, KV2 459.

240 **"Liverpool, Leeds or Birmingham":**   Ronald Reed memo, July 7, 1944, KV2 459.

241 **"If the message does not include":**   Ibid.

Chapter Twenty-four. Lunch at the Lutétia

242 **"provide a cover address":**   ISOS intercept, December 15, 1944, KV2 459.

242 **"whose appearance and activities":**   *Camp 020,* p. 298.

243 **"into the wastelands":**   Ibid.

243 **"guttural protestations":**   Ibid.

243 **"unsubtle retainers":**   Ibid., p. 299.

243 **"worried still":**   Ibid.

243 **"mysterious figure":**   J. C. Masterman, *The Double-Cross System in the War, 1939–1945* (London, 1972), p. 171.

243 **"an old friend":**   Ibid.

244 **"The whole city":**   Camp 020 report, July 11, 1944, KV2 459.

244 **"resignation and misery":**   Ibid.

244 **"locate our night fighters":**   Camp 020 report, July 11, 1944, KV2 459.

244–5 **"Cossors of Hammersmith" to "made no secret of":**   Ibid.

245 **"converting much of":**   Robin Stephens report, June 29, 1944, KV2 459.

245–6 **"If their weapons" to "Life under the Germans":**   Ibid.

246 **"owing to the danger":**   Camp 020 report, July 11, 1944, KV2 459.

246 **"if he landed in England" to "astute in posing":**   Ibid.

246 **"Is he working":**   *News of the World,* October 25, 1953.

246 **"How the hell":**   Ibid.

247 **"If and when I come":**   *Faramus,* p. 93.

247 **"approximately six months":**   Ibid., p. 100.

247 **"an extermination camp":**   Ibid., p. 136.

247 **"All the time":**   Ibid., p. 82.

247 **"to think furiously":**   Camp 020 report, July 11, 1944, KV2 459.

248 **"knowing" smile:**   *Chapman,* p. 241.

248 **"having a good time":**   Camp 020 report, July 11, 1944, KV2 459.

248 **"any uniform he liked":**   Robin Stephens report, June 29, 1944, KV2 459.

248 **"for the shelling of":**   Camp 020 report, July 11, 1944, KV2 459.

249 **"dimples":**   Robin Stephens report, June 29, 1944, KV2 459.

249 **"never leave":**   Ibid.

249 **"fall to bits":**   Cited in obituary of Erich Vermehren de Saventhem by Richard Bassett, *Independent,* May 3, 2005.

249 **"excess of brandy":**   *Chapman,* p. 237.

249 **"Terrible devastation will ensue":**   Camp 020 report, July 11, 1944, KV2 459.

250 **"slight," even nonchalant:**   Ibid.

250 **"few casualties":**   Ibid.

250 **"a flop":**   Report, July 13, 1944, KV2 460.

250 **"at Chapman's disposal":**   Camp 020 report, July 11, 1944, KV2 459.

251 **"harmless chatter":**   Ibid.

252 **"unreal":**   *News of the World,* November 1, 1953.

252 **"two bottles of cognac":**   Camp 020 report, July 11, 1944, KV2 459.

252 **"a profound effect":**   *News of the World,* November 1, 1953.

252 **"triumph":**   Ibid.

252 **"half-smile":**   *News of the World,* October 25, 1953.

252 **"The last glimpse":**   *Chapman,* p. 244.

Chapter Twenty-five. The Prodigal Crook

253 **"out of the direct light":**   *News of the World,* November 1, 1954.

254 **"Peeved":**   Camp 020 report, July 11, 1944, KV2 459.

254 **"Don't be silly":**   Ibid.

254 **"That's exactly what":**   *News of the World,* November 1, 1953.

255 **"It's Eddie":** Transcript of videotaped interview with Ronnie Reed, 1994, courtesy of Nicholas Reed.

255 **"whether operation possible":** ISOS intercept, June 10, 1944, KV2 459.

255 **"a wiry type":** Memo, September 25, 1944, KV2 460.

255 **"expansive in his conceit":** *Camp 020,* p. 224.

255 **"splendid time":** Memo, June 28, 1944, KV2 459.

255 **"The courageous and ruthless":** Robin Stephens in Camp 020 report, July 11, 1944, KV2 459.

255 **"tired beyond the point":** Camp 020 report, July 11, 1944, KV2 459.

255 **"moral degenerate":** *Camp 020,* p. 218.

255 **"The outstanding feature":** Robin Stephens in Camp 020 report, July 11, 1944, KV2 459.

256 **"greeted as a returned friend":** Helenus Milmo memo, June 29, 1944, KV2 459.

256 **"back safely":** Transcript of videotaped interview with Ronnie Reed, 1994, courtesy of Nicholas Reed.

256 **"purposely put ashore":** Camp 020 report, July 11, 1944, KV2 459.

256 **"mentally quite fit":** Dr. Harold Dearden, cited in Robin Stephens report, June 29, 1944, KV2 459.

256 **"All the evidence appears":** Ronald Reed memo, June 28, 1944, KV2 459.

257 **"it would be a first-rate check":** Robin Stephens in Camp 020 report, July 11, 1944, KV2 459.

257 **"I think this goes far":** Ibid.

257 **"The only safe place":** Memo, July 10, 1944, KV2 459.

257 **"a man whom they":** Ronald Reed memo, June 28, 1944, KV2 459.

257 **"escape":** Thaddeus Holt, *The Deceivers: Allied Military Deception in the Second World War* (London, 2004), p. 853.

257 **"money and a Leica":** Ronald Reed report, June 28, 1943, KV2 459.

258 **"Zigzag will be given":** Helenus Milmo memo, August 1, 1944, KV2 460.

258 **"Although no one thinks":** Helenus Milmo memo, June 28, 1944, KV2 459.

258 **"It must always be":** Memo, June 29, 1944, KV2 459.

258 **"a very able man":** Camp 020 Report, July 11, 1944, KV2 459.

258 **"a form of insurance"**:   Robin Stephens report, June 29, 1944, KV2 459.

258 **"Chapman is a difficult subject"**:   Camp 020 report, July 11, 1944, KV2 459.

259 **"quite convinced that"**:   Major Michael Ryde, memo of meeting, August 14, 1944, KV2 460.

259 **"Although we do not"**:   Helenus Milmo memo, June 28, 1944, KV2 459.

259 **"the inevitable girlfriend"**:   Camp 020 report, July 11, 1944, KV2 459.

259 **"blundered badly"**:   Robin Stephens report, June 29, 1944, KV2 459.

259 **"She is not a 'fast' girl"**:   Camp 020 report, July 11, 1944, KV2 459.

259–60 **"he would have"** to **"One of his objects"**:   Ibid.

260 **"There was some sort"**:   John Marriott memo, July 29, 1943, KV2 459.

260 **"Dagmar is in contact"**:   Camp 020 report, July 11, 1944, KV2 459.

260 **"I do not wish to be held"**:   Robin Stephens in Camp 020 report, July 11, 1944, KV2 459.

261 **"one of the most"**:   Robin Stephens report, June 29, 2004, KV2 459.

261 **HARD LANDING BUT ALL OK:**   Ibid.

Chapter Twenty-six. Doodlebugs

263 **"It was clear that"**:   J. C. Masterman, *The Double-Cross System in the War, 1939–1945* (London, 1972), p. 179.

263 **"If St Paul's was hit"**:   Ibid.

263 **"decide what measure"**:   Ibid.

263 **"learned to live"**:   Michael Howard, *Strategic Deception in the Second World War* (London, 1995), p. 178.

263–4 **"terrible responsibility"** to **"I am certain you"**:   Ibid.

264 **"his German masters"**:   Ronald Reed memo, June 28, 1944, KV2 459.

264 **"should report actual incidents"**:   Masterman, *Double-Cross System*, p. 181.

264 **"We could give correct"**:   Ibid.

264 **"reduce the average range"**:   Ibid.

265 **"It is essential"**:   Memo, KV2 460.

265 **"I am afraid we cannot"**:   Note from Air Ministry, August 29, 1944, KV2 460.

265 **"slight errors introduced"**:   J. A. Drew memo, July 11, 1944, KV2 459.

265 **"The outgoing traffic":** Major Michael Ryde report, July 26, 1944, KV2 460.

265 **"The Zigzag channel":** Major Michael Ryde to Robertson, 13.9.44, KV2 460.

266 **"held his place":** Masterman, *Double-Cross System,* p. 172.

266 **"I was as frightened":** J. C. Masterman, *On the Chariot Wheel: An Autobiography* (Oxford, 1975), p. 212.

266 **"secret equipment for":** Memo, KV2 460.

266 **"tapping out such messages":** Major Michael Ryde, memo of meeting, August 14, 1944, KV2 460.

266 **"If this state of affairs":** Ibid.

267 **"Take your pick!":** Transcript of videotaped interview with Ronnie Reed, 1994, courtesy of Nicholas Reed.

267 **"I do feel his exploits":** John Marriott memo, July 29, 1943, KV2 459.

267 **"I agree":** Ibid.

267 **"desired that no such":** Sir Alexander Maxwell memo, July 15, 1944, KV2 460.

267 **"No action should be taken":** D. I. Wilson note, with ibid.

267 **"comb out any German":** Major Michael Ryde, memo of meeting, August 14, 1944, KV2 460.

267 **"Any question of Zigzag's":** Ibid.

267 **"anxious to write to Freda":** Robin Stephens report, June 29, 1944, KV2 459.

267 **"very busy and would":** Ibid.

267 **"autobiography":** Major Michael Ryde memo, July 26, 1944, KV2 460.

268 **"impossible for him":** Major Michael Ryde memo, August 6, 1944, KV2 460.

268 **"while it was still fresh":** Major Michael Ryde memo, July 26, 1944, KV2 460.

268 **"his old criminal activities":** Ibid.

268 **"stimulate Zigzag's interest":** Major Michael Ryde, memo of meeting, August 14, 1944, KV2 460.

268 **"deceptive material about":** Memo, August 1, 1944, KV2 460.

268 **"in continual active operation":** Ibid.

268 **"steal a document":** Ibid.

268   **"the increasing number":**   Ewen Montagu, *Beyond Top Secret Ultra* (London, 1977), p. 114.

268   **"careless talk":**   Ibid.

269   **"While we should not":**   Ibid., p. 124.

269   **"After passing the":**   Ibid., p. 125.

269   **"all secret manufacture":**   Memo, August 1, 1944, KV2 460.

269   **"worth keeping sweet":**   Major Michael Ryde memo, August 6, 1944, KV2 460.

270   **"wonderful experience":**   Transcript of videotaped interview with Ronnie Reed, 1994, courtesy of Nicholas Reed.

Chapter Twenty-seven. Going to the Dogs

271   **"disagreeably surprised":**   Camp 020 report, July 11, 1944, KV2 459.

271   **"with some apprehension":**   Ibid.

271   **"I have spent a good":**   Major Michael Ryde report, August 24, 1944, KV2 460.

272   **"most discontented at":**   Major Michael Ryde memo, August 8, 1944, KV2 460.

272   **"He has been keeping":**   *Camp 020*, p. 225.

272   **"always in the company":**   Ibid.

272   **"The Zigzag case must":**   Major Michael Ryde, memo of meeting, August 14, 1944, KV2 460.

272   **"the way his case":**   T. A. Robertson memo, August 15, 1944, KV2 460.

272   **"did not seem":**   Ibid.

272   **"He is quite clearly":**   Ibid.

272   **"a suitable person":**   Memo, August 1, 1944, KV2 460.

273   **"the friends he hoped to employ":**   Ibid.

273   **"in a French letter":**   Ewen Montagu, *Beyond Top Secret Ultra* (London, 1977), p. 126.

273   **"After they had received":**   Ibid.

273   **Dear Fleming:**   Fake letter from A. B. Wood, KV2 460.

274   **"We never found out":**   Montagu, *Beyond Top Secret Ultra*, p. 126.

274   **"I do not myself":**   Major Michael Ryde to T. A. Robertson, September 13, 1944, KV2 460.

275   **"not quite reliable":**   ISOS intercept, September 25, 1944, KV2 460.

275 **"The messages sent"**: Major Michael Ryde to T. A. Robertson, September 13, 1944, KV2 460.

275 **"Zigzag is liable"**: Memo, 1.8.44, KV2 460.

275 **"It is unlikely that his"**: Ibid.

276 **"Zigzag himself is"**: Major Michael Ryde memo, August 6, 1944, KV2 460.

276 **"making quite large sums"**: Ibid.

276 **"To take advantage"**: Ibid.

276 **"served his purpose"**: T. A. Robertson memo, August 15, 1944, KV2 460.

276 **"done an extremely good"**: Ibid.

276 **"by giving him"**: Ibid.

276 **"if he could put up"**: Ryde memo, August 6, 1944, KV2 460.

276 **"waste of money"** to **"It is obvious that we"**: Ibid.

277 **"if we no longer require"**: Major Michael Ryde, memo of meeting, August 14, 1944, KV2 460.

277 **"I have seen Zigzag"**: Major Michael Ryde to T. A. Robertson, September 13, 1944, KV2 460.

277 **"I am able to curb these"**: Ibid.

277 **"The war may end"**: Major Michael Ryde report, August 24, 1944, KV2 460.

277 **"the necessity of closing"**: Major Michael Ryde, memo of meeting, August 28, 1944, KV2 460.

277 **"It is becoming increasingly"**: Major Michael Ryde to T. A. Robertson, September 13, 1944, KV2 460.

278 **"Try to get latest editions"**: ISOS intercept, September 4, 1944, KV2 460.

278 **"General report"**: Ibid.

278 **"radio controlled rocket"**: Robin Stephens report, June 29, 1944, KV2 459.

278 **"Continue giving data"**: ISOS intercept, September 4, 1944, KV2 460.

278 **"Heard many rumours"**: Message sent September 14, 1944, KV2 460.

279 **"War situation need not"**: ISOS intercept, August 28, 1944, KV2 460.

Chapter Twenty-eight. Case Dismissed

280   **SORRY YOUR BAD NEWS:**   Major Michael Ryde report, August 24, 1944, KV2 460.

280   **"has a post-war plan"** to **"get the Germans to lay":**   Ibid.

280   **"a collection of words":**   Ewen Montagu memo, August 29, 1944, KV2 460.

281   **"The Germans have told":**   Ibid.

281   **"German knowledge is":**   Ibid.

281   **"we should out of our":**   Major Michael Ryde memo, August 6, 1944, KV2 460.

281   **"I still maintain that we are":**   Major Michael Ryde, memo of meeting, August 14, 1944, KV2 460.

281   **"settlement of our indebtedness":**   Ibid.

281   **"dealt with fairly":**   Major Michael Ryde report, August 24, 1944, KV2 460.

282   **"at least £6,000":**   Major Michael Ryde to T. A. Robertson, September 13, 1944, KV2 460.

282   **"reliable sailor":**   Major Michael Ryde report, September 19, 1944, KV2 460.

282   **"Such promises are generally empty":**   Major Michael Ryde to Robertson, 13.9.44; KV2 460.

282   **"I think it would be":**   Major Michael Ryde report, September 19, 1944, KV2 460.

282   **"Zigzag has always":**   Major Michael Ryde report, October 24, 1944, KV2 460.

283–6   **"whether the Germans"** to **"As far as the Germans":**   Ibid.

286   **"My feeling":**   John Masterman, handwritten note on ibid.

286   **"We should close it now":**   Ibid.

286   **"I understand that":**   Signed copy of Official Secrets Act, November 2, 1944, KV2 461.

286   **"as forcibly as possible":**   Major Michael Ryde report, October 24, 1944, KV2 460.

287   **"He must understand":**   Ibid.

287   **"Zigzag should be thankful":**   Ibid.

287   **"Fiction has not":**   *Camp 020,* p. 217.

288   **"hard character":**   *Sunday Chronicle,* July 24, 1954.

288 **"Uppermost in my mind":** Eddie Chapman, *Free Agent: The Further Adventures of Eddie Chapman* (London, 1955), p. 11.

289 **"Is there anyone":** Interview with Betty Chapman, November 11, 2005.

289 **"That girl":** Chapman, *Free Agent*, p. 12.

289 **"Jesus!":** Ibid.

289 **"I shall go":** Interview with Betty Chapman, November 11, 2005.

Chapter Twenty-nine. Aftermath

290 **"real genius":** Cited in Emily Jane Wilson, "The War in the Dark: The Security Service and the Abwehr, 1940–1944," Ph.D. diss., Cambridge University, 2003.

290 **"one of the greatest":** J. C. Masterman, *On the Chariot Wheel: An Autobiography* (Oxford, 1975), p. 219.

290 **"Blessed are they":** Address by Christopher Harmer at memorial service for T. A. Robertson at Pershore Abbey.

291 **"To work out the crime":** J. C. Masterman, *The Case of the Four Friends* (London, 1961), p. 14.

291 **"Everything which is good":** Masterman, *On the Chariot Wheel,* p. 371.

291 **"How strange it was":** Ibid., p. 361.

292 **"I am not, and never":** *Daily Telegraph,* December 4, 1986.

293 **"Sean Connery was simply":** Lois Maxwell (Miss Moneypenny), cited on Wikipedia.

293 **"drifting on a wreck":** Lloyd's Register of Captains, National Maritime Museum.

293 **"giant of evil":** *Camp 020,* p. 22.

293 **"degenerates, most of them":** FO 371/70830 paper CG 2290/G, cited by Hoare in *Camp 020,* p. 8.

294 **"loyal to his own class":** Interview with Ingeborg von Gröning, Bremen, May 22, 2006.

294 **"invariably foul":** FO 371/70830 paper CG 2290/G.

294 **"had a long and possibly":** *Camp 020,* p. 72.

294 **"awkward" meeting:** *Faramus,* p. 177.

295 **"I thought you were dead":** Ibid.

295 **"Millions died":** Eddie Chapman's foreword to ibid., p. 7.

295 **"German tart":** Interview with Bibbi Røset, Oslo, June 15, 2006.

296   **"Mrs. Gossips":**   Ibid.

296   **"she was always restless":**   Ibid.

297   **"what will happen when":**   *Camp 020,* p. 226.

297   **"senior officer":**   *Evening Standard,* October 13, 1948.

297   **"one of the bravest men":**   Ibid.

297   **"I was trained":**   *Daily Telegraph,* October 10, 1974.

297   **"honorary crime correspondent":**   Obituary of Eddie Chapman, *Times* (London), December 12, 1997.

298   **"I do a bit":**   "The Sentimenal Screwsman," *Daily Express,* October 21, 1960.

298   **"Sometimes in life":**   Masterman, *On the Chariot Wheel,* p. 361.

298   **"What is the truth":**   "A Traitor or a Hero?" *News of the World,* January 10, 1954.

299   **A lot of water:**   Eddie Chapman to Stephan von Gröning, November 1, 194, courtesy of Ingeborg von Gröning.

299   **"They were like brothers":**   Interview with Betty Chapman, November 25, 2005.

SELECTED BIBLIOGRAPHY

Archives

National Archives, Kew

National Martime Museum, Greenwich

Bundesarchiv-Militärarchiv, Freiburg

National Archives, Washington, D.C.

British Library Newspaper Archive, Colindale, London

Jersey Historical Archives, St. Helier, Jersey

Jersey Newspaper Archives, St. Helier, Jersey

Jersey Judicial Archives, St. Helier, Jersey

Printed Sources

Andrew, C. Secret *Service: The Making of the British Intelligence Community*. London, 1985.

Bennett, R. *Behind the Battle: Intelligence in the War with Germany, 1939–45*. London, 1999.

Carter, M. *Anthony Blunt: His Lives*. London, 2001.

Chapman, Edward. *The Eddie Chapman Story*. Foreword by Frank Owens. London, 1954.

———. *Free Agent: The Further Adventures of Eddie Chapman*. London, 1955.

———. *The Real Eddie Chapman Story*. London, 1966.

Curry, John. *The Security Service, 1908–1945: The Official History*. London, 1999.

Farago, Ladislas. *The Game of the Foxes: The Untold Story of German Espionage in the United States and Great Britain During World War Two*. New York, 1972.

Faramus, Anthony Charles. *The Faramus Story*. London, n.d.

———. *Journey into Darkness: A True Story of Human Endurance*. London, 1990.

Foot, M. R. D. *SOE: The Special Operations Executive, 1940–1946.* London, 1999.

Harris, Tomás. *Garbo: The Spy Who Saved D-Day.* Introduction by Mark Seaman. London, 2004.

Haufler, Hervie. *The Spies Who Never Were: The True Stories of the Nazi Spies Who Were Actually Double Agents.* New York, 2006.

Hesketh, R. *Fortitude: The D-Day Deception Campaign.* London, 1999.

Hinsley, F. H. *British Intelligence in the Second World War: Its Influence on Strategy and Operations.* Vol 1. London, 1979.

Hinsley, F. H., and C. A. G. Simkins. *British Intelligence in the Second World War: Security and Counter-Intelligence.* Vol 4. London, 1990.

Holt, Thaddeus. *The Deceivers: Allied Military Deception in the Second World War.* London, 2004.

Howard, Michael. *Strategic Deception in the Second World War.* London, 1995.

Kahn, David. *Hitler's Spies: German Military Intelligence in World War II.* New York, 2000.

Knightley, Phillip. *The Second Oldest Profession.* London, 1986.

Liddell, G. *The Guy Liddell Diaries, 1939–1945.* Vols. 1 and 2. Edited by Nigel West. London, 2005.

Macksey, Kenneth. *The Searchers: Radio Intercept in Two World Wars.* London, 2003.

Masterman, J. C. *The Double-Cross System in the War, 1939–1945.* London, 1972.

———. *On the Chariot Wheel: An Autobiography.* Oxford, 1975.

Miller, Russell. *Codename Tricycle: The True Story of the Second World War's Most Extraordinary Double Agent.* London, 2005.

Montagu, Ewen. *Beyond Top Secret Ultra.* London, 1977.

———. *The Man Who Never Was.* Oxford, 1996.

Paine, Lauran. *The Abwehr: German Military Intelligence in World War II.* London, 1984.

Popov, Dusko. *Spy/Counterspy.* New York, 1974.

Rose, Kenneth. *Elusive Rothschild: The Life of Victor, Third Baron.* London, 2003.

Schenk, P. *Invasion of England, 1940: The Planning of Operation Sealion.* London, 1990.

Sebag-Montefiore, Hugh. *Enigma: The Battle for the Code.* London, 2000.

Stephens, R. "Tin Eye." *Camp 020: MI5 and the Nazi Spies*. Introduction by Oliver Hoare. London, 2000.

Stevenson, William. *A Man Called Intrepid: The Secret War of 1939–45*. London, 1976.

Waller, John H. *The Unseen War in Europe: Espionage and Conspiracy in the Second World War*. New York, 1996.

West, Nigel. *MI5: British Security Service Operations, 1909–45*. London, 1981.

Wilson, Emily Jane. "The War in the Dark: The Security Service and the Abwehr, 1940–1944." Ph.D. diss., Cambridge University, 2003.

Winterbotham, F. W. *The Ultra Secret*. London, 1974.

INDEX

ABOUT THE AUTHOR

Ben Macintyre is a columnist and associate editor at the *Times* of London. He has worked as the newspaper's correspondent in New York, Paris, and Washington, D.C. He now lives in London with his wife and three children. *Agent Zigzag* is his fifth book.